THE NEWER DEAL

THE NEWER DEAL

Social Work and Religion in Partnership

Ram A. Cnaan

with Robert J. Wineburg and Stephanie C. Boddie

COLUMBIA UNIVERSITY PRESS   NEW YORK

Columbia University Press

Publishers Since 1893

New York   Chichester, West Sussex

Copyright © 1999 Columbia University Press

All rights reserved

Library of Congress Cataloging-in-Publication Data

Cnaan, Ram A.

The newer deal : social work and religion in partnership / Ram A. Cnaan ;
with Robert J. Wineburg and Stephanie C. Boddie.

p. cm.   Includes bibliographical references and index.

ISBN 0–231–11624–1 (alk. paper). — ISBN 0–231–11625–x (pbk. : alk. paper)

1. Church charities—United States. 2. Social service—United States.

I. Wineburg, Robert J. II. Boddie, Stephanie C. III. Title.

HV530.C62 1999

361.7'5'0973—DC21   99–30601

Casebound editions of Columbia University Press books
are printed on permanent and durable acid-free paper.

Printed in the United States of America

c 10 9 8 7 6 5 4 3 2 1

p 10 9 8 7 6 5 4 3 2 1

Dedicated to my parents, Genia and Reuben,
who unfortunately can no longer appreciate it

CONTENTS

PREFACE

Times change. Especially our times. Within the last half of the twentieth century, we have seen the advent of the computer age, space exploration, and other technological breakthroughs. We have seen the world map reconfigure itself in the rise and fall of nations. We have seen dramatic advances in civil rights on a scale undreamed of by previous generations. Prosperity, peace, and progress made it seem as though we finally had all the answers.

As times changed, so did the thinking about social ills and poverty. Governments around the world began to invest in countless programs to combat these problems. Optimism ruled. The key to eradicating social needs had at last been found: continued investment by national governments in social services for their people. Social welfare became a right of citizens rather than an act of charity. It was a vision shared by the majority of the world's great democracies.

We, too, shared this vision. Like many of our generation, we believed the responsibility assumed by governments for the welfare of their citizens to be irrevocable. Because we believed, we wholeheartedly supported the expansion of government responsibility for social welfare, whether through a national health insurance program or initiatives to improve quality of life in the inner cities. Our convictions led each of us to choose social work as a vocation.

Our interest in and advocacy of social policies, however, have not met with universal approval from our colleagues. At times we have been labeled "softhearted liberals," even "Commies." We mention this because it is likely that some who hear that we have written a book on religion and social work will label us "religious fanatics." Nothing is farther from the truth. We are not religious zealots. Two of us were raised in secular homes, are not currently affiliated with any congregation, and have partners whose religious beliefs differ from our own. The third was raised in a religious home and is now affiliated with a Protestant denomination that is more socially conscious than the church of her childhood. Then the question becomes, If we are not religious zealots, why would we write a book like this?

We have written this book because, as critical thinkers and social observers, we see dramatic changes taking place in the social and political terrain of the United States. Social progress that to us and so many others seemed inevitable in the not-too-distant past has rapidly been losing ground under the stress of more volatile times and more voluble complaints. Loudest of these are the criticisms that the government is failing its responsibility to its citizens. The social work community finds such criticism to be justified, and we agree. We, too, would prefer a world in which the government would assume full responsibility for social services, but in the United States the reality is quite different.

In the United States, *devolution*—the central government's surrender of its responsibility for the welfare of citizens—has been gaining momentum since the 1970s. We see it in the cutbacks and the shift of responsibility for service delivery to local authorities and nonprofit organizations, and in the lack of national standards for the process. Devolution consisted of two complementary trends: privatization of service delivery and federalism, that is, decreased influence of the federal government and increased influence of state and local governments. *Devolution* now also connotes the end of entitlements. Under previous programs such as Aid to Families with Dependent Children (AFDC), families and their advocates could use the court system to challenge bureaucratic decisions regarding their right to care and service. Under the system of block grants and temporary assistance, which emphasizes service within a limited budget by local providers, appeals to the court system will have no effect.

Devolution of social welfare is a broad national process that originated with the Reagan administration to shift responsibility for the administration of funding of social and health services to state and local governments and nonprofit organizations (Smith 1996). Devolution, as we discuss in chapter 1, is the antithesis of the welfare state in which the central government assumes full responsibility for the social and health needs of individuals with low income. In the United States, the process of devolution has resulted in the replacement of federal allocations for social services by smaller block grants to states. The states, in turn, asked counties and cities to do more with less and to engage nonprofit organizations in the provision of services. This process culminated in 1996 welfare reform legislation, which we discuss in chapter 12. This legislation not only substantially reduced the responsibility of the federal government for social welfare but also heightened both the visibility and the role of the religious-based services providers as a viable replacement.

How do we account for devolution? One explanation can be found in our fast-changing society. The "job-for-life" tradition of America's past is giving way to frequent job changes, often the result of corporate downsizing. Unskilled workers are finding it more difficult to get work in today's high-tech environment, and more people are living at or below poverty level. Social Security Insurance for older Americans is no longer secure and is under constant political threat. Homelessness and AIDS are on the upswing, especially among women and children. Meanwhile, the nation's tax policies continue to favor the haves, while its social policies put the have-nots at even greater risk. The optimistic hope of yesterday has given way to today's grim reality of mounting social needs and decreased public commitment.

An important outcome of this trend to devolution, and one that the social work community has systematically ignored, is that the religious community is becoming a major provider of social services. Unfashionable and unpopular as this may be in social work circles, we believe it is essential that the role of religious-based organizations in welfare provision be addressed because of its significance for the directions that provision of social services will take in the years ahead. We are acutely aware that neither the religious community nor the social work community can be described as a unified, homogeneous community. Rather, each is widely diverse and composed of subgroups that are often out of touch and/or at odds with one another, particularly in the religious community. Nevertheless, for the purpose of clarity in this book, we have at times referred to one or the other of these communities as a whole. At other times, we have been more specific and identified the particular subgroup within the community that is under discussion.

Our purpose in this book is threefold. First, we want to demonstrate that the historical role of religious-based services provision in maintaining the local social services infrastructure is currently stronger than ever. To do so, we present findings from our research that illustrate the complexity and extent of the religious-based social service system. In chapter 5, we address theological tenets of various religions, including Christianity, Judaism, Islam, Buddhism, and Hinduism, that constitute the basic underpinnings of religious-based social services that have served so many in our nation for so long. Second, we review the social work/social welfare literature and curricula to determine the extent to which the role of the religious provision of social services has been addressed. We also identify issues of social policy and philosophy that have led to the current distancing of social work from the religious community. Finally, we present our rationale as to why more research and course content about the role of religious-based social service provision is essential to determining the most effective and efficient delivery of personal services in the coming century.

Overall, we call for a "newer deal," that is, a partnership between social work and religion that allows each to preserve its values and preferences yet jointly focuses on helping those in need across America. This "limited partnership" is one that can work at all levels—for example, a neighborhood partnership between a religious congregation and a secular social service agency or a national partnership between the National Association of Social Workers and the National Coalition of Churches.

ACKNOWLEDGMENTS

As the author, I have chosen to use the editorial "we" in grateful acknowledgment of the important contributions of my colleagues. Robert J. Wineburg, who contributed most of the material in chapters 1 and 10, collaborated with me in the development of several of the themes in this book. Stephanie C. Boddie, who contributed to chapters 2 and 11, was responsible for bringing the chapters together into a cohesive whole. I am indebted to them for their unflagging dedication and commitment to this project.

The responsibility for the thesis presented in this book rests solely with me. My arguments represent a synthesis of my many years of research on the role of religious-based organizations in the provision of social services.

The concept for this book began with research grants from the Lilly Endowment to study the role of the religious community in the welfare system toward the end of the twentieth century and to disseminate the findings. I am most grateful to the Lilly Endowment and to many others who have assisted me along the way. Peter Dobkin Hall, of the Yale Program on Non-Profit Organizations, enabled me to present some of my initial findings at Yale University. He also introduced me to many scholars and practitioners in the nonprofit field who provided me with new perspectives on the topic. I am grateful to David Mason, of Mason Enterprises, Corpus Christi, Texas, and Mark Stern, of the University of Pennsylvania, who provided helpful suggestions on earlier drafts of this book as well as encouragement in tackling such a controversial and unpopular issue. In this regard, I am also in debt to the editor of *Social Service Review*, who rejected a manuscript by Robert Wineburg and me dealing with this topic. Had that work been accepted, I might not have persisted in the effort and written this book.

Seven colleagues who reviewed earlier versions of the manuscript made many cogent comments and suggestions that helped me to improve the quality of the final product. The remaining errors are, of course, still mine, but they are fewer, thanks to that detailed and constructive critique. These colleagues, each an expert in the field, are John Dilulio, from Princeton University's Woodrow Wilson School; Catherine Faver, from the University of Tennessee School of Social Work; Margaret Harris, from the London School of Economics Centre on Voluntary Organizations; Peter Dobkin Hall, from the Yale University Divinity School; Frank M. Loewenberg, from the Bar Ilan University School of Social Work (Israel); John Messer, of the Susquehanna Institute; and Edward Newman, from the Temple University School of Social Administration. I also wish to acknowledge Eileen Lynch, who has provided superb editorial assistance.

I am particularly indebted to Diane Cohen and Robert Jaeger, codirectors of Partners for Sacred Places, a national nonprofit, nonsectarian organization founded in 1989 to help Americans embrace, care for, and make good use of older and historic religious properties that continue to play an important role in the lives of their communities. In appreciation of their support, which enabled me to carry out my pilot study on this topic, I am donating all royalties from this book to Partners for Sacred Places so that they may continue to support the social as well as the structural needs of America's congregations.

Gaynor Yancey, who was a doctoral student at the University of Pennsylvania School of Social Work, is responsible for educating me and introducing me to this important area of study. She served as a research director for the study of congregations supported by Partners for Sacred Places. She noted the gap between social work and religion long before I did and encouraged me to undertake this study.

Last, but definitely not least, Femida Handy was a great emotional and personal support for me in the weeks and months when I toiled over the writing task. Her patience and encouragement are greatly appreciated. Her questions and interest stimulated me to think and read further and resulted in a richer manuscript than I could have produced otherwise.

To all of the above, I am grateful. To my former teacher, mentor, and friend, the late Roy Lubove of the University of Pittsburgh School of Social Work, I owe a special debt of gratitude. It was Dr. Lubove who taught me to go beyond the conventional and search out the truth. It was he who taught us to look with new eyes at what others considered obvious. And it was he who would caution again and again: "Social policy, despite the simplemindedness of its formulators, is a very complex and ever-changing issue." I offer this book in this spirit.

THE NEWER DEAL

CHAPTER 1

THE CHALLENGE OF DEVOLUTION AND THE PROMISE OF RELIGIOUS-BASED SOCIAL SERVICES: AN INTRODUCTION

The past is consumed in the present and the present is living only because it brings forth the future.
— James Joyce, *A Portrait of the Artist as a Young Man*

BACKGROUND

As Joyce noted, the past, present, and future are all intertwined. Unless we understand the effect of the past on the present, the future may indeed seem uncertain. How do we begin to understand the past when even history, according to Henry Glassie (1982), is a cultural construct? The fact is that people organize, interpret, and revise reality on their own terms. We have seen different perceptions of "what really happened" played out in the O. J. Simpson trial, for example, where the verdict split America along color lines. While most African Americans believed in Simpson's innocence, most Caucasians thought he was guilty, even though the "reality" is beyond the knowledge of any of us. The Vietnam War is another event that polarized the American public, as people judged that war based on their own perceptions of whether America should be involved in it. We have also seen this happen in the case of political leaders: Joseph Stalin once was considered a national hero and is now depicted as a villain. Even in academe, scholars must continue to reinterpret past events with respect to new knowledge and perspectives. To this noblest of all tasks—the pursuit of truth—we must bring an open mind.

When it comes to social work and its history, a variation on an old cliché is pertinent: If the field does not know where it has been, how will it know where it is going? We question whether social work understands, or wants to understand, its history in terms of the profound influence that religion has had on its development. We will show that there is a widespread oversight regarding the role that religious organizations and congregations played in the provision of social services. Social work may have had to separate from its religious roots to gain legitimacy as a profession. Yet social work scholars and educators have given little attention either to the extraordinary role of religion in the provision of social services or to its considerable influence on social services development. We believe this omission is misguided and that the role of the organized religious community (as defined in chapter 2) in social service provision merits serious critical review. The discussion of religious organizations as social service providers has all but disappeared from our academic discourse. Such organizations are essential to the functioning of the larger social service delivery system. They also are the key to understanding how services may devolve locally, especially in the wake of shrinking public budgets and demands on the private sector to deliver more services. This process may already be under way:

> The secular United Way funds the following sectarian services in local communities nationwide: 717 religious Family Service Agencies such as Catholic Family Services, Lutheran Family Services and Jewish Family Services in communities around the country receive United Way allocations for "non-religious" service provision; 1,273 Salvation Army agencies with community-based secular programs are allocated funds and the funds comprise 14% of their budgets. It should be pointed out that the Salvation Army is a church. A combined 1,902 YMCAs and YWCAs receive United Way funding, and the funds comprise 6 percent and 14 percent of their budgets, respectively.   (United Way 1996)

But this is not so much a new trend as a renewed one. The history of the United Way started with Community Chests and United Foundations, which as early as the late 1950s supported these same religious organizations.

The role of religious-based social service provision has been consistently downplayed or ignored in social work literature except in religiously affiliated schools of social work or religious-based social work journals. Harris (1995:33), for example, noted that "little attention has been paid to the welfare contribution of religious congregations." Garland (1992:4) characterized social work's ambivalence toward religion as follows:

> Social workers have viewed churches as any one or a mixture of the following: Significant community resources, dangerous organizations which foster dysfunctional coping in clients, powerful reactionary groups calling for perpetuation of a status quo that oppresses and marginalizes certain groups, voices for constructive societal action to change the status quo, an institution so irrelevant to the work of the social work profession that its role in

clients' lives is ignored, a profoundly significant source of informal social support and existential hope in the lives of client[s].

The separation of social work from its religious roots not only jeopardizes its moral foundation and public support but also makes it difficult for the profession to chart its future course—one that will undoubtedly find strong connections between secular and religious-based social services at many levels. Post-1980 social policy is focusing on service development at the local level, where agencies, both public and private, sectarian and secular, are using the resources of religious organizations. This, in turn, is forcing social work to reconnect with its religious roots.

We acknowledge that religious institutions may and do conflict and clash with social work values and principles on issues ranging from abortion and birth control to the status of women and gays and lesbians in society. We also acknowledge that some religious groups and organizations were, are, and will be among the leading conservative forces in society. Nevertheless, there is no unified religious front regarding social issues. There were and continue to be numerous religious groups and organizations at the forefront of social care. Just to name Mother Teresa and liberation theology or Jewish Family and Children's Services or the Salvation Army brings to mind concern and care that have a religious basis. This side of religion is often neglected and ignored. It is this side of religion that can collaborate with social workers in providing local social services if the profession is willing to take the required steps in developing a newer social deal, one of limited but effective partnership between the religious community and the social work community. Acknowledging the diversity in the religious community and recognizing the prosocial forces within it will enhance our understanding of welfare provision in the United States as well as pave the road for a more comprehensive set of services for people in need. But what is actually happening in the community these days, as towns and cities struggle to provide social services that were once the responsibility of the federal government?

THE NEW ACTORS

No social change happens overnight, and the split between social work and religion is no different. Two major historical events are most often linked to the secularization of social work. The first was the quest for scientific methods of philanthropy, which was prominent in the Progressive Era and gave rise to the secular nature of the Charity Organization Societies (COS). The second was the passage of the Social Security Act of 1935. The Social Security Act was the result of Great Depression and the New Deal era and symbolized federal responsibility for the care of all people in need. While the United States did not develop a full-scale welfare state, as many other advanced democracies did, it nevertheless developed more public social and welfare services, which offered a guaranteed level of care and culminated in the War on Poverty of the 1960s. Throughout this era, local responsibility became less important and federal and state programs were prominent; thus local organizations such as religious congregations were no longer considered relevant and they received scant attention. What we observe since 1980 is the reverse trend—a newer deal. A continuing trend of dismantling federal and state responsibility for the welfare of people and shifting this responsibility to the local level. Under this new reality, local actors—especially religious-based ones—regained prominence and importance and should be the focus of attention.

Of importance to social work today is an understanding of why and how religious-based social service providers have taken center stage to become the new actors highlighted by the media and politicians alike. Understanding what has happened is not always easy. It is noteworthy to observe how policy makers view the role of religion in social service provision since 1980.

Sometimes the line between politics and accurate data becomes blurred when the discussion turns to religion and social service provision. For example, Senator Dan Coates (R-Ind.) likes to tell the story of the Gospel Mission, a drug-treatment center for homeless men not far from the nation's capital. Under the leadership of John Woods, the mission successfully rehabilitates two-thirds of its clients. Just three blocks away is a government-operated shelter with similar goals. Although the government-operated shelter spends twenty times more per person, it boasts only a 10 percent success rate. Senator Coates has an explanation for the disparity: "The Gospel Mission succeeds because it provides more than a meal, more than a drug treatment. It is in the business of spreading the grace of God" (Frame 1995:65). Most social scientists will argue that these high rates of success are not the result of superior programming. It is more likely that the Gospel Mission picks and chooses its clients, or the clients self-select, therefore increasing the chance for success. The government shelter, on the other hand, does not have this luxury. Comparing the success of a program that in some way selects its clients to one that has to serve any client in need might make for good politics but not necessarily for good social science or social work. In addition, the study data come from different sources (as no one study compared both religious and public programs); therefore the definitions of success are not likely to be the same, and such a variation would contribute to the disparity in reported outcomes.

Senator John Ashcroft (R-Mo.), a pivotal figure in the design of the new welfare reform, proposed the charitable-choice initiative, which helped pave the way for religious communities to team up with providers of social services. Approved in September 1995 as part of the Senate's welfare reform bill and incorporated as section 104 of the Personal Responsibility and Work Opportunity Reconciliation Act of 1996, the charitable-choice initiative prohibits discrimination against a social service organization "on the basis that the organization has a religious character." This means that faith-based charities can contract with all levels of government, or receive funds in the form of vouchers or certificates, without having to change or suppress their religious identity. (This topic will be further discussed in chapter 12.)

The legislation also specifies that religious charities receiving government funds may require employees to "adhere to [their] religious tenets and teachings" and to submit to organizational rules regarding the use of drugs or alcohol. Participating religious organizations would not be required to remove "religious art, icons, scripture, or other symbols." Ashcroft's bill is now so commonplace in the "religious social service realm" that it is merely called "section 104" formally referred to as the "Charitable Choice Provision" part of the Personal Responsibility and Work Opportunity Reconciliation Act of 1996. As a concession to those who feared a religious requirement for service, the measure also prohibits religious-based service organizations from discriminating against beneficiaries of their services "on the basis of religion, a religious belief, or refusal to actively participate in a religious practice." It specifies that no funds "provided directly to institutions or organizations to provide services . . . shall be expended for sectarian worship or instruction" (Frame 1995:65).

Senators Coates and Ashcroft have not been the only politicians to recognize the religious community's provision of services. President Bill Clinton, on the campaign stump speaking to the National Baptist Convention, U.S.A., which represents 33,000 primarily black Baptist churches, urged the nation's churches to take the sting out of the tough new welfare bill by hiring people off the public payrolls (Associated Press 1996). Newt Gingrich, impressed by the volunteer spirit of Habitat for Humanity, a Christian home-building operation, supported legislation introduced by Representative Rick Lazio (R-N.Y.), for a $50 million federal grant for Habitat and other organizations that build homes for the poor (Merline 1995). Republican Governor Kirk Fordice of Mississippi proposed a program called Faith and Family (Edwards 1995), which encouraged each of the state's 5,500 churches and synagogues to adopt at least one of the state's 55,000 welfare families. While the state would continue its financial support for families receiving AFDC congregations would provide practical and spiritual support through such an effort.

Another Southern governor, Jim Hunt (D-N.C.), called on the religious community to "pitch in and make this happen" in a speech at Highland United Methodist Church in Raleigh (*Greensboro News and Record* 1996b). He was referring to the Work First Program, which is North Carolina's welfare reform program. Coordination by welfare reformers with the religious bodies is essential if reformers are to succeed in helping people retain their jobs and develop careers. Volunteers from faith communities will now be working alongside paid social service professionals in new local partnerships between the religious organizations and the state. In Charlotte, North Carolina, for example, congregational leaders and social service staff have been meeting since October 1996 to plan ways of helping people most affected by welfare reform in a project called A Faith Community United.

Planning for change is not exclusive to Charlotte. In San Diego, California, Ruby Shamsky, a social worker at the department of social services and chairperson of the Department of Social Services Congregational Mobilization Team, and the Reverend Booker T. Crenshaw, co-chairperson of the team, sent a letter in January 1997 to pastors and church members that welcomed congregations to join a partnership whose goal is to "create a service delivery system . . . which meet[s] the needs of the community in a manner which promotes self-sufficiency and the development of healthy families and individuals." The San Diego community has developed a nonprofit corporation called All Congregations Together (ACT), in which volunteers from congregations working at the department of social services refer people in crisis to places in the community for help with emergency food, shelter, transportation, and other basic necessities.

Other states and communities have been preparing for the changes as well. Witness the example of three other partnerships—the Community-Directed Assistance Program in Maryland, the Family Mentoring Program in Hampton, Virginia, and the new Family Support Program in Fairfax County, Virginia—that have been set up between public social services and the faith community to help people make a smooth transition from welfare to work (Sherman 1997b).

These views are not singularly Republican or Southern Democrat but are shared by President Clinton and former HUD secretary Henry Cisneros, as well as Senator Joseph Lieberman (D-Conn.).

NEW FORCES AT WORK

To understand the process by which the religious community has now taken center stage in national, state, and local policy and program development circles, it is important to trace out two seemingly independent strands in the development of policy since the Reagan era. The first is the increased focus of public discourse of the Reagan era on the good works of the religious community and the demonization of government programs in the rhetoric that shaped policy making and development. The second is the increased involvement of religious organizations in social and community services provision, which was correlated with the decrease in federal welfare spending.

On April 14, 1982, the *Washington Post*'s Herbert Denton reported a speech by President Reagan in an article titled "Reagan Urges More Church Aid for Needy." President Reagan told a group of more than a hundred religious leaders that "churches and voluntary groups should accept more responsibility for the needy rather than leaving it to the bureaucracy." He then proceeded to put a new spin on the parable of the Good Samaritan. In doing so, he created a new metaphor for the causes of poverty and instantly undercut the liberal view of poverty as the result of failures in large systems like government, the marketplace, or schools. Reagan reinforced the conservative viewpoint that personal character flaws and government-operated social programs were to blame for poverty:

> The story of the Good Samaritan has always illustrated to me what God's challenge really is. He crossed the road, knelt down, bound up the wounds of the beaten traveler, the pilgrim, and carried him to the nearest town. He didn't go running into town and look for a caseworker to tell him that there was a fellow out there that needed help. He took it upon himself
> (Denton 1982; Reagan Home Page 1997).

President Reagan had created a public devil—"the government bureaucrat"—by pitting the godless, uncaring, bureaucratic caseworker against the Good Samaritan. It is important to recognize here that policies and the programs they engender reflect the values of those who shape the policy. Government policies and programs ought to reflect public attitudes and beliefs. Charismatic and popular leaders, however, are masters of attitude-shaping and agenda-setting. They initiate and influence public opinion and attitudes and then craft the policies relevant to the newly formed attitudes. By introducing an issue into the public discourse and presenting it as truth, one can easily manipulate the social agenda of the time (Cnaan and Bergman 1990; Stern 1984). One can easily see how Ross Perot, a presidential candidate in 1991, forced onto our national agenda a debate on the national debt, an issue that no one had considered relevant before he championed it through his infomercials and political candidacy.

Summoning local congregations and religious charities to deliver more of the nation's social services in the 1980s, especially against a backdrop of political rhetoric that depicted public social programs and public servants as instruments of the devil, paved the way for easy budget cutting in the Reagan era. This strand in policy development was reinforced by the Bush metaphors and social policies whose essence was encapsulated in President George Bush's famous "Thousand Points of Light" campaign speech that simultaneously called for decreased governmental spending and increased local voluntary support for social welfare efforts. A March 8, 1990, request for new program proposals (*Federal Register* 1990, 8555) stated the Reagan-Bush view clearly: "Human service needs are best defined through institutions and organizations at the local level."

As academe was not participating in the public discourse, the media began to present its own version of what was happening during that time. It was a story, we believe, that virtually ignored how the policies of the era catapulted mainline religious congregations and charities into increasing provision of services, both on their premises and in support of community agencies, by providing volunteers, money, and use of their facilities. The media's story shaped the consciousness of the public to the point that policy makers designed welfare reform—the most dramatic social policy shift since the New Deal—with the idea that the religious organizations would, could, and should solve problems locally. In other words, the media sparked a call for *a newer deal*, one that would deal with problems left unsolved under the new welfare reform.

The increasing influence of extreme Christian groups in the United States on religious-based social service delivery needs to be highlighted. Two televangelists who garnered much media attention during the 1980s and 1990s were Jerry Falwell and Pat Robertson. They were instrumental in softening the environment for conservative Christianity's increasingly visible presence in politics in the early 1980s and its role as moral architect of welfare reform in the mid-1990s. The Reverend Jerry Falwell, leader of the Moral Majority and pastor of Liberty Road Baptist Church in Lynchburg, Virginia, rose to dominate the print and electronic media. He was close to the Reagan administration in the 1980s and helped shape its social agenda (Willis 1990). Falwell is especially important and interesting because he was publicly and privately supporting Republican politicians early in the Reagan years. In turn, politicians of all stripes increasingly supported the Christian Coalition.

This PAC (political action committee) was the religious and political force that grabbed Falwell's baton in the 1990s. Falwell and Robertson had a spirit similar to that of evangelist Dwight Moody, who, a century earlier, saw himself as a lifeboat in a world of wrecked vessels. There is one major difference. To Moody, any organized effort to improve society was a distraction from saving souls (Marty 1980). To Falwell and Robertson, influencing government was the means to cleanse an immoral public and return government to its Christian roots. Their homilies were played over and over until they became part of the public discourse and ultimately undergirded the formation of the current public welfare policy. They attacked both the lack of individual responsibility on the part of welfare recipients and a public bureaucracy staffed by secular social workers who did the devil's work.

This thinking peaked in Marvin Olasky's book *The Tragedy of American Compassion* (1992), which shaped much of the recent discussion and trends in welfare reform policy and the corresponding social service development. Olasky, a professor of journalism at the University of Texas at Austin, was raised a Jew but found God in an extremely conservative Protestant church. In the book, Olasky calls for a return to a pre-twentieth-century golden age of service design and delivery, a time when compassionate, pious people helped one another through their religious communities and organizations and eschewed any kind of charity that would create dependence. In Olasky's view, those were the days when charity was not the devilish dole of large and impersonal welfare bureaucracies, as we know it today. Furthermore, Olasky believes that unless personal transformation is triggered by religious salvation, any means of public assistance is a mere waste. While Olasky's book is viewed by many as a revisionist history, it was preceded by a decade of public moralizing in the print and electronic media by the forces of the Christian Right that helped stiffen views of the poor and the welfare bureaucracy. Eventually the tide of public opinion began to turn. Poverty now became a matter of moral flaw, aided and abetted by a bureaucratic system that created dependency. It was time to redraw the lines of social responsibility, which, according to the Christian Right, started and ended at the congregation's door. Only good and caring local neighbors can assess and provide humane and, hopefully, religious-transformative assistance that will encourage personal responsibility, pride, and social rehabilitation. The political solution to the moral flaw in the individual, quite obviously, would be to return people to the institution that handles moral problems—the religious congregation. The only problem with such an analysis, as we will demonstrate later, is that the overwhelming majority of the religious community was already deeply involved in service provision in the 1990s. But the public discourse has already begun shifting in one clear direction: Welfare will be saved by religious people and organizations, i.e., the religious community.

The reality of ending welfare as we know it is a complicated rationale for ending the welfare state and returning to a situation in which religious institutions play a central role in the delivery of social services. The rationale goes something like this: Large-scale government programs that serve anybody and everybody are too large and too bureaucratic to inspire those in need to help themselves. The major flaw in large-scale government programs, besides huge costs, is that they, unlike the programs of their religious counterparts, do not treat people as whole human beings. As President Reagan said in his Good Samaritan speech in 1982, no government caseworker can ever repair a broken spirit. Olasky, and politicians inspired by his work, would like to see public programs phased out over time and private, especially religious, charity revived (Shapiro and Wright 1996).

DEVOLUTION AND RELIGION FROM THE 1980S TO THE MID-1990S

The second independent strand in policy development is the hardly documented changing tide with respect to religious involvement in social services. The research that has become available sporadically shows that local communities were responding to the Reagan cuts in the 1980s and that an evolving infrastructure of religiously based social services was in fact responding to the changes.

What is often underreported and rarely discussed is that faith-based social service providers were already active in the welfare arena before the Reagan/ Bush administrations. In fact, the census reported in 1981 that 47 percent of private social service expenditures were associated with religiously affiliated agencies (U.S. Bureau of the Census, 1981). The difference is that before 1980 fewer services were provided by private agencies. As a result of devolution, a larger share of the services were shifted to private agencies and many faith-based providers were already prepared to undertake the tasks (U.S. Bureau of the Census 1981, 238).

Despite the lack of a comprehensive analysis as to why the religious community has taken on such importance in the policy debate, a good starting point for examination of this development would be in the research world of the early and mid-1980s. This body of work demonstrated that local service systems were, in fact, retooling because of the Reagan cuts. Religious congregations were important to the redesign efforts, and their community service activities were increasing. Much of the research on local responses to federal budget cuts was well documented (Magill 1986; Nathan and Doolittle and Associates 1987; Salamon, Altschuler, and De Vita 1985). However, this research did not include the role of religious-based social service providers. The most interesting development in this funding shift was the reemergence and emergence of local religious institutions in providing for needy members of their communities (McDonald 1984; Salamon and Teitelbaum 1984; Wineburg and Wineburg 1986; Hodgkinson, Weitzman, and Kirsch 1988; O'Neill 1989). The first three works cited did allude to the Reagan budget cuts as a factor in increased religious response at the community level.

Throughout the 1980s, social work scholar Ellen Netting noted the many interconnections between the religious community and the social service community, a historical legacy that has never really vanished but that, as we will argue later, has been neglected in social work historical analysis. For example, Netting illustrated similarities, differences, and ambiguities between social work and clerical roles in sectarian agencies (Netting 1982a). She also outlined the changing funding patterns of church-related agencies, informing the unsuspecting public that government support of religiously affiliated agencies had grown steadily from the 1950s to 1980 as agencies became increasingly enmeshed in the web of local services (Netting 1982b). Sectarian agencies like the Salvation Army, Catholic Social Services, Jewish Family and Children's Services, and various Protestant welfare agencies have been integral parts of the social service system in virtually all major communities across the country and have often relied heavily on government support. In the face of the changing funding and services environment, sectarian agencies balanced religious and secular concerns in the face of constant change (Netting 1984). Sosin's (1985) study showed that agencies under religious auspices provided for clients' material needs better than secular organizations did. These sectarian agencies, already strategically positioned in community systems of service, naturally expanded their roles as government funds decreased.

The first national study to explore the role of expanded religious involvement was conducted by Salamon and Teitelbaum (1984). They found that religious congregations had increased their activities in providing direct services; they expanded their efforts in helping other service providers and increased their financial support of religiously affiliated funding federations.

McDonald (1984) found that many congregations awarded grants to nontra-ditional or untested social programs. Case studies of increased congregation-al involvement focused on specific services, such as crisis intervention, welfare advocacy, and services to the elderly (Doll 1984; Negstad and Arnholt 1986; Wineburg and Wineburg 1986). Evidence mounted during the early and mid-1980s showing that private-sector involvement from the religious quar-ters was taking shape. But research during that period did not strongly tie the increased activities of congregations to the operations of the broader service, and little was said about the implications of the changes for social work the-ory and practice.

The research of Hodgkinson, Weitzman, and Kirsch (1988) was the first to shed light on the philanthropic efforts of the nation's religious congregations. Their work made enormous progress in outlining the national scope of con-gregational voluntary action in the United States and in mapping out avenues for further investigation, but no social work scholars or practitioners used this research to propel the field forward in expanding its role in the changing social service environment. Their study found that:

Individuals gave about $41.4 billion to 294,000 congregations of all denom-inations in 1986. Of that amount, $19.1 billion, or 46 percent, was used by the churches and synagogues for nonreligious programs, including sub-stantial donations to other organizations.

Of the $8.4 billion given to other organizations, $5.5 billion went to denom-inational charities and organizations; $1.9 billion went to other charita-ble organizations; and $1 billion was given in direct assistance to individuals.

Members of congregations donated $13.1 billion worth of volunteer time, about half of which went to nonreligious programs. Twelve percent, or $756 million, went to human service activities.

About 87 percent of congregations surveyed had one or more programs in human services and welfare, including 80 percent in family counseling and 68 percent in health programs.

Over 90 percent of religious groups reported that their facilities were avail-able to groups within the congregation. Six of 10 said their facilities were available to groups in the community.

Sixty percent of the congregations reported that they provided in-kind sup-port like food, clothing, and housing to human service programs oper-ated by outside groups. As such, they formed working alliances with other service providers in the community (Hodgkinson, Weitzman, and Kirsch 1988).

Those results showed impressive involvement of religious congregations in providing social services and meeting the material needs of people. The findings also raised many questions about what an increased congregational involvement at the time would mean for the operation of human service systems in communities across the United States. Some of the major recommendations for further study suggested by this research included matters directly concerning social work, such as the importance of determining which community programs congregations operated directly or participated in through denominational agencies; understanding the connections between the volunteer work of members of congregations and support of organizations in the community; determining the relationship between congregations and denominational organizations like Lutheran Children and Family Service or Catholic Charities. It was thought—and we believe correctly so—that a better understanding of those issues would make it easier to determine the implications of increased congregational involvement in current domestic social policy and trends in service development that were likely to emerge from it. These areas are of concern to those who do community service planning, as they directly relate to quantity and use of resources to help those in need. We will focus on these concerns in later chapters.

Two studies emerged in the early 1990s that demonstrated the depth of congregational involvement in social service provision. The one cited most often in the literature is the follow-up to the 1988 study (Hodgkinson, Weitzman, and Kirsch 1988) cited above. It was the Independent Sector's second national study: *From Belief to Commitment: The Community Service Activities and Finances of Religious Congregations in the United States* (Hodgkinson et al. 1993). This work demonstrated to a greater extent than did the 1988 study the indisputable involvement of religious congregations in providing social services. While this study suffers from numerous methodological and conceptual limitations, its key findings were repeatedly supported by other studies. In a 1994 study of the riots following the not-guilty verdict in the Rodney King trial in Los Angeles, researchers at the University of Southern California, in a larger discussion of the religious response to the riots that followed the verdict, reflected a sense of disbelief at the number of congregations involved in social service delivery. They characterized the religious social service infrastructure in Los Angeles as follows:

The vastness of the social service infrastructure that has been created by the city's religious institutions rarely becomes visible. . . . The religious social service infrastructure has become vast, because the needs of the city have been vast, and because California's publicly supported infrastructure has been cut back in the face of the state's tax revolt and of its long lasting recession.   (Orr et al. 1994:3).

These researchers went on to discuss how religious congregations in Los Angeles had set up nonprofit corporations to tap into public, corporate, and foundation support in order to deliver social services from congregational facilities:

> Religious leaders are very clear that their use of non-profit corporations (which accept public funds) requires that their human service activities be guardedly secular both in design and execution. But most are aware that they are working in a gray area. The board of many of these non-profit corporations are made up of clergy and persons associated with the churches in the areas served. Church sites are used to distribute services.
>
> (Orr et al. 1994:20).

In the 1992–1995 study of public and private agencies in Greensboro, North Carolina, Wineburg, Ahmed, and Sills (1997) found a substantial increase in the use of congregational resources during the Reagan and Bush years. Forty-two percent of the local public and private agencies that used congregational volunteers and another 42 percent that used congregational facilities started doing so during the period 1982 to 1992, a time frame that reflects the beginning of the Reagan budget cuts taking hold and the end of the Bush presidency. Wineburg also found that 69 percent of the agencies that reported receiving money from the religious sources started doing so during that same time period. Even the local public health agency in this study reported receiving de facto grants from congregations that were paying for prenatal care for teen mothers. The local department of social services started an Adopt a Social Worker program, in which local congregations were asked to help social workers provide more than the bare essentials for some of their clients (Wineburg 1996).

RHETORIC AND FACTS ABOUT RELIGIOUS-BASED SOCIAL SERVICES DELIVERY

There is a major difference between the political climate of the Reagan-Bush era and that of today. There is now a conscious effort to target religious institutions specifically as the local organizations most suited to take the service baton from government. It is somewhat perplexing that the talk from Washington and some of the nation's statehouses seems to ignore the fact that over the last seventy-five years congregations and religious charities have already expanded their involvement in social service. These political actors who are pushing for greater involvement by religious providers of services are unaware that this same community has become a much more vital player in the design, delivery, and financing of local services than since the days of the New Deal. It is noteworthy that neither scholars of the nonprofit sector nor those of religion have paid much attention to this important development (Cnaan 1994; Cormode 1994; Smith 1983).

Two independent forces are at work. One is that since the 1980s mainline congregations and religious organizations have been stepping in locally and meeting new social and community demands, and doing so with little fanfare. They have become an integral and necessary part of the local service system's resource base and partners in the design and delivery of services. Their impressive role is even further highlighted by the public sector's withdrawal from its obligation to provide welfare. The other force is that the growing rhetoric, public influence, and political gains of the religious right in the 1990s have created an atmosphere in which politicians have become increasingly comfortable in making the religious community a focal point in a new social policy.

Currently, there has been a clear shift from a time when government wanted individual agencies in the broader nonprofit sector merely to be one indiscernible bright spot to the present situation in which politicians are expecting the religious community to be the ark in the storm. Furthermore, the religious community's importance may well continue to grow because it holds by far the majority of private charitable resources in an increasingly shrinking pool of such commodities. These resources include: (1) a mission to help the poor, (2) a semi-organized pool of volunteers, (3) space to use for programs, (4) the potential for raising and distributing discretionary funds to designated causes, (5) space for forums and community discussions, (6) the potential for political influence, (7) presence in neighborhoods across America, and (8) moral clout. In an era of public retrenchment, the religious community holds an important asset for the health of both local citizens and society as a whole. In the world of practical politics of social service development at the community level, those who contribute "the gold" help make the rules. As the religious groups contribute more locally, they may want to shape the policy agenda in partnership with local departments of social services. As noted above, such partnerships are already forming in many localities.

CLARIFYING THE ROLE OF THE RELIGIOUS COMMUNITY IN SOCIAL SERVICES PROVISION

Several interesting issues need clarification. Very little systematic research has been conducted either to explain what congregational social service means to local service systems or to clarify what the Reagan-era cuts meant to local communities. During the Reagan-Bush era, Catholic Charities (Britt, August 28, 1995, personal communication) alone saw a 700 percent increase in volunteers. According to the 1993 study by the Independent Sector, the umbrella research and information organization for U.S. nonprofits, members of the nation's religious congregations provided 125 million hours a month in volunteer services to local nonreligious health, welfare, and educational organizations (Hodgkinson et al. 1993). Many social workers are hardworking and devoutly religious people who see their direct practice and community work as expressions of their faith. Their numbers are many more than one might expect, given that the public discourse has presented these good souls as demons. We know that when the people they serve cannot make ends meet, social workers enlist their religious congregations to help alleviate the real pain that they see daily (Wineburg 1996). They are, in many instances, the Good Samaritans who bind the wounds of kids who go to school hungry, cradle moms who have been beaten bloody by their husbands, and serve the old people who have nothing and nobody. They do battle with county commissioners who fund jail construction at the drop of some contractor's hat but disguise themselves as parsimonious bookkeepers when it comes to funding a child protection worker.

Social workers, individually and institutionally, need to advocate a newer deal—a coherent public policy that brings together what practice, wisdom, and emerging research have taught us: that the religious-based social service system can be nothing less than an important partner in a complex system of services at the local level.

THE BROADER PERSPECTIVE

An important question remains for those of us interested in the country's welfare program: Does the religious community have the capacity to take on the government's constitutional responsibility of providing for the general welfare? To answer that question appropriately, we will examine in later chapters three assumptions that have steered the public discussion of religion's involvement in provision of services: (1) The religious community has the capacity and the capability to shift from a role as an important, but comparatively minor, service provider to a role as a major social service provider that not only dispenses services but also generates resources for service provision. (2) The religious community wants to expand its service role. (3) The religious community ought to become the major provider because, being local and voluntary, it will automatically provide better services than the public sector. With regard to these three questions, we wonder, What is the position of social work?

Does the religious community have the capacity and capability to keep expanding? In later chapters we will provide more detailed examples of the extent to which religious organizations and congregations are already involved in provision of services. We argue that as the welfare state continues its redevelopment, we can expect the religious community to play a greater role in community affairs. Nevertheless, there is no way that the religious community can play more than a stepped-up utility role in supporting the public and nonprofit agencies in their communities. Our social problems are far too intricate and expansive and our public and private nonprofit system of services, including the current system of services offered by religious congregations, is too structured and vast to expect a major redesign that would make religious-based social service organizations the main providers of our country's social services. The nation's 250,000 to 350,000 churches, synagogues, and mosques would each have to put up $225,000 to make up for the proposed social service cuts (Shapiro and Wright 1996). Raising those kinds of funds would be extremely difficult on the congregational level; for example, consider that Father Fred Kammer, president of Catholic Charities USA, estimated the average congregational budget to be $100,000 (Shapiro and Wright 1996).

In light of this, religious-based organizations should be considered a valuable community resource in a pool of caring public and nonprofit organizations—not the sole source of salvation. Many congregations will become more active in local service design and delivery. Nevertheless, when one stops to think that the primary function of religious congregations is to provide a gathering place for communal worship, the extent to which such organizations expend their energy and spirit to help their own members, offer their facilities to the community, support community agencies, and reach out with money and services nationally and internationally is truly amazing. If you want to give blood, attend an AA meeting, or start a Scout troop, chances are good that you will wind up at a local congregation's facility.

Fifty years hence, when social welfare historians compare the system of the 1990s to that of the 2040s, they will observe dramatic differences. The local system of social services will be more responsible and more involved in solving, managing, and preventing problems than it is today. To function in those capacities, the system itself needs to be reconceptualized. Instead of the traditional public, private nonprofit, for-profit, and religiously based services vernacular, we will need a new language and a new way of understanding the relationships, something along the lines of *a newer deal: a limited partnership of care*. Just as no one can imagine a car going anywhere without its wheels, even though the engine is its most important part, no one in the future will be able to imagine a *limited partnership of care* solving, managing, or preventing problems without assistance or direct involvement from the religious community, even though that entity is not its engine. Furthermore, the notion of eligibility will be detached from entitlements, and there will be no national, or even state, standards. In each local community, a *limited partnership of care* will be the norm, and each will have a distinct character based on the specific needs, services, resources, and religious groups available.

Does the religious community want to increase its service efforts? We can say with assurance that we know of no major religious-based services provider pleading to take over more of the nation's social services. Thirty-seven percent of the budgets of religious charities already come from public support. If these charities doubled their size, they, too, would become large, unwieldy bureaucracies. The calls for increased services from the religious organizations and the romanticizing of their capabilities are coming from the political arena, the religious right, and conservative think tanks. Quite a few congregations and religious groups, in fact, oppose taking any role in social service provision and especially public-supported programs.

Only 220 of Mississippi's 5,500 congregations signed on for Governor Fordice's Faith and Family program, and only 622 of the 55,000 families have been adopted by those religious congregations (Sherman 1997a). Yet if we take the long view and see this as the early stages of a welfare reform system that relies increasingly on the religious community to help those who are no longer entitled to any assistance, then Governor Fordice's program will have created a venue for Mississippi's religious social service infrastructure to expand exponentially. This approach would be Mississippi's application of the Reagan-Bush ideology that seeks to transform welfare from a federal system to a state structure with a local voluntary delivery system. From the perch of Mississippi's statehouse, it seems to make good sense to gradually change to a statewide web of 5,500 community-based voluntary organizations already in place whose purpose is to help those in need. Nothing is more in tune with the times than eliminating mass-produced welfare services that perpetuate rather than solve problems and replacing them with smaller and more-efficient programs run by caring and humane religious organizations.

But, from our perch, it seems to make much better sense that before launching a program like Faith and Family, every prospective congregation be asked whether it wants to participate, assessed as to its capability of doing what is asked, reviewed for the type of practical support it can offer, and queried as to whether a religious membership in general or in a particular denomination was required to be eligible for support. Social work can play a critical role in shaping community policy by asking these kinds of important questions. Such an assessment would give a far clearer picture of whether congregations want to participate and of what resources participating congregations can and cannot offer.

Will the religious community offer better services than the public sector? If politicians reduce the fiscal outlay for public-sector services and try to meet the current demands with only religious resources, then the religious community will have to expand its services exponentially and contribute more volunteers, space, and money, which they may or, most likely, may not have. The religious community has neither the capability nor the capacity to do that. The irony here is that when government pressures voluntary organizations, either subtly or directly, to do something beyond their missions, they become no longer voluntary organizations. In an interview with Major Tom Jones, national director of development and community relations for the Salvation Army, we were told that there is more demand in this thriving economy than the Salvation Army can meet. For the first time in the history of the Salvation Army, some local corps are running deficits. If the 132-year-old Salvation Army, with its extensive network of services and programs, many of which are collaborative efforts with public agencies, cannot meet needs, how are we going to enlist newcomers to the field and build an effective service system without creating a coordination, fund-raising, volunteer recruitment, and evaluation infrastructure at the local level? Yet by all indications, more religious organizations are expected to enter the welfare arena and other areas to increase their involvement.

Governments continue to cut their programs and are laying the groundwork for far better programming through civic responsibility and collaboration with congregations and other voluntary organizations in mapping strategies to solve some complicated problems. The support that religious-based organizations can lend to local social services is attractive because they are small, less bureaucratic than government agencies, and better prepared to solve problems and meet needs immediately. Their effectiveness results in part from the voluntary nature of their efforts. Cutting programs that force people to seek help from religious organizations and thereby compel those organizations to develop services is not the optimum way to create the type of local system that is everyone's ideal: a system that is humane, caring, responsive, and cost-effective.

If we are ever to solve, manage, or prevent the problems that localities are increasingly called on to handle, then we will need to understand all the players involved, build a language, and establish a set of values that form the foundation of the local system of care. We should not believe for a minute that the religious community can handle our social ills outside a well-planned, well-executed, and well-maintained public, private, nonprofit, and civic partnership. While religious-based organizations have become central to the operation of local human service networks, commanding 34 percent of all volunteer labor and 10 percent of all wages and salaries in the nonprofit sector (Hall 1990:38), the assumption that they could eventually take over the nation's huge social welfare apparatus is nothing short of fantasy.

So what is going on? The religious community as a whole is playing and will continue to play an increasing role in the social service arena in the decades to come. It will not do so on its own, and it will be further supported by public funds. This body, from local congregations to national charities, will assume an increased and more central role in a field once dominated by social work, and social work can and should adapt itself to the arrival of this old-new partner. As we will demonstrate, social work will have to adopt a new approach, one that accepts the religious community's role and is willing to enter into coalitions and working arrangements with the only other pro-poor force in our society. This book thus serves as a wake-up call for social work to rediscover its past and harness it for a better future.

PURPOSE

In this book we want to demonstrate that in the coming century, social work and the religious community can best serve those in need by working together. Further, we want to make the academic social work community aware that the trend toward local religiously affiliated services provision is real and that it has been growing more rapidly since the Reagan era. Welfare provision by religious congregations and sectarian agencies increased enormously during the 1980s and 1990s (Hodgkinson et al. 1993). The continued success of these entities in serving people in need in the coming years is going to depend increasingly on a full and mutual alliance between the religious community and social work. With more social problems, fewer federal services, and the country in no mood for a tax hike at any level of government, it will fall to the local communities to make up the differences in provision of services.

Where can communities turn for help? One answer is that they will be turning to a range of religious organizations—from national charities to store-front congregations—to help those in need. Many religious groups have a mission to help the poor, a pool of volunteers, discretionary money, and space for programming. Leaders of the secular service system therefore will need to forge alliances with religious organizations if they want to meet human need in the near future—no matter how difficult such partnerships seem in the abstract. This will require some ideological compromises and bold leadership. Rather than focus on the process of such necessary collaboration, we will use this venue to review the role of religious-based social services as past, present, and future allies with social work.

It is our contention that, with a few notable exceptions, social work for various reasons (which we detail in chapter 4) is avoiding the topic of religion. This is a great and costly omission in the teaching, studying, and practicing of social work, a profession that champions care for the needy and has its roots in religious traditions of charity and social justice. If we can contribute to bridging this rift, our aim will be achieved.

STRUCTURE OF THE BOOK

Part 1 of our study begins with an analysis of what we mean by *religious-based social services*. Chapter 2 is devoted to the various forms of the religious community and provides examples that are relevant to delivery of social services. Chapter 3 reviews the literature on the relationships between social work and religious-based social services. Our review suggests that social work has given little attention to the role of the religious community in providing social services. To determine why this is so, we examine in chapter 4 several factors that have divided social work and religious social services and discuss policy concerns related to religion and social welfare. We conclude this part by explaining why assumptions about the rift between the social work and religious communities exists despite the fact that both communities are actively committed to helping those in need.

In part 2 we focus on the past and present role of the religious community in the field of social service provision. In chapter 5 we present the theological teaching and emphasis on helping the needy. We show that helping the needy is a primary theological expectation in each of the major religions. In chapter 6 we highlight the religious roots of the American service system and document numerous cases and examples of services by religious-based organizations that have become the core of social services. In chapter 7 we review the literature on religion and the quality of life of individuals. We show that findings are mixed and that while religion has some benefits in some areas of life, it can, in various situations, be harmful. In chapter 8 we review current social service provision by religious organizations. Again, we use only a sample of cases and findings, as space does not allow a more exhaustive documentation of religious-based social services. In chapter 9 we pay special attention not only to direct services provision but also to religious-based contribution in social change. We focus exclusively on empowerment through organized religion. Finally, we review the network of social services in two geographical locations: chapter 10 discusses findings from a small town (Greensboro, North Carolina) and chapter 11 discusses findings from a large city (Philadelphia). In combination, the chapters in part 2 provide an impressive picture of the role of the religious community in social service delivery, one that cannot and should not be ignored.

Part 3 consists of concluding observations and comments. In chapter 12, we continue with some of the themes raised in this chapter. We present evidence of current political and cultural acceptance of the involvement of the religious community in social service provision. These recent and emerging trends suggest an even larger role for religious-based service providers in the future and further substantiate our argument that provision of service would be much more effective if social work and the religious community would acknowledge each other and work together. It is clear from the evidence, some of which has already been presented in this opening chapter, that the religious community is expected to be an important player in the social welfare arena in the coming decades. Finally, in chapter 13 we suggest reasons and the means by which social work and religious organizations can collaborate to help those in need. It is our hope that this book will be a first step in initiating a professional dialogue between social work and the religious community that will ultimately lead to mutual cooperation in alleviating human misery.

PART I

THE AMBIVALENT COEXISTENCE OF SOCIAL WORK AND RELIGIOUS-BASED SOCIAL SERVICES

CHAPTER 2

WHAT DO WE MEAN BY "RELIGIOUS-BASED
SOCIAL SERVICES"?

In presenting our arguments, we have defined the terms *social welfare* and *religious-based social services* as follows: all the means that societies have historically used to bring about well-being. While *welfare* and *social services* are not equal concepts and should be used differentially, we use them interchangeably in this book to denote all services that aim at improving the quality of life of people. We use these terms in the broadest sense, in that they encompass efforts of individuals and families, institutional efforts of religion, collective efforts of nonprofit organizations, and efforts of the state. These efforts can be separate or can work in concert with one another. We believe, as we will demonstrate in chapter 5, that religious values such as helping one's neighbor undergird most service efforts, be they public or private.

When the term *religious* is attached to any organization that is not fully geared to carry out faith commands and practices, it becomes elusive. Whether the soup kitchen is run by the public sector or by a religious congregation the food will be the same and may often be provided by volunteers. Can we define as religious an organization that uses a religious congregation's property just because it is housed in a sacred place? Can we define an organization that began as a social ministry of a church and ultimately became independent as a religious organization? The line is blurred, and we intend to make clear what types of organizations will be included in this book as religious-based social service organizations.

We use the term *religiousness* here in a manner similar to the usage of Netting, Thibault, and Ellor (1990). They noted that "religiousness is defined as a relationship to or membership in an organized faith community that institutionalizes a system of religious beliefs, attitudes, and practices" (p. 16). Wilson

(1974) defined faith-based service agencies as purposive organizations that draw staff, volunteers, and board members from a certain religious group and are based upon a particular religious ideology that is reflected in the agency's mission and operations. For our purpose, the important element is a formal contact with an organized community or organization. Our focus is on membership in a religious collective. This focus excludes the feelings of connectedness to a higher being, also known as spirituality, as the latter does not imply membership in any religious collective. It is the religious collective that can garner resources and channel them to provide social services that have a religious base. We note, however, that shared religious values provide the core impetus for individuals to form organizations that assist those in need as a means of practicing their faith.

The uniqueness of religious-based social services as opposed to secular services is not always clear. Some have become an arm of the government and disassociated from their religious origins. In their ideal form, religious-based organizations consider seriously two authorities: one organizational and one divine. They are less likely to change their mission and mode of action than are secular agencies. Their mission is not a board creation but a reflection of a higher authority and faith. Service is often the devotional activity. That is, the service is not done solely for helping others, but is a means of practicing the faith to its fullest. Further, the theology of the group takes precedence over secular requirements and regulations. Some such organizations will waive support if it entails compromising theological principles. In practice, we find great variation in the extent to which religious practices and expressions are incorporated in various social service organizations.

The level of religious impact on the social service agency can vary widely. At one end of the spectrum are organizations like the Salvation Army. Well known for its social involvement, which ranges from homeless shelters to thrift shops, the Salvation Army is in fact a network of local churches. The mission of these churches, which is highly religious, states: "The Salvation Army, an international movement, is an evangelical part of the Christian Church. Its message is based on the Bible. Its ministry is motivated by the love of God. Its mission is to preach the gospel of Jesus Christ and to meet human needs in His name without discrimination." At the other end of the spectrum are organizations that originally were affiliated with a religion but currently have little or no affiliation with any religious groups. An example of this type of religious organization is the Young Men's Christian Association, popularly known as the YMCA. As the name implies, the YMCA began as a religious group whose aims were similar to that of today's Promise Keepers. Over time, the YMCA has become similar to secular community centers that offer social and recreational services. In this book, we refer to all types of such organizations, but we focus primarily on those that overtly express their religious origin and affiliation.

In our definition, *religious-based* (or faith-based) *social services* are not determined by the level of religious commitment and attachment, but rather by the size and geographical coverage provided by the religious-based social service organization. Hence, our definition includes six types of religious service organizations: (1) local congregations, (2) interfaith agencies and ecumenical coalitions, (3) citywide or regionwide sectarian agencies, (4) national projects and organizations under religious auspices, (5) paradenominational advocacy and relief organizations, and (6) religiously affiliated international organizations. In this chapter we describe these six types and present an example of social welfare services provided by each. In subsequent chapters, we use examples and data from all six types of religious service organizations to document the nature and scope of the religious community's involvement in social services delivery.

We have chosen to use a typology that is based on the geographical locus of service and, by default, the organizational complexity. However, other important typologies exist that can also be relevant. One such typology focuses on the degree of relatedness to the religious parent body, described by a continuum that ranges from total dependence to full independence. It is important to note that historically, organizations have moved from one point on this continuum to another. Another typology focuses on control over funds. In congregational programs, the continuum ranges from full clerical authority to lay control. In other organizations, the control over funds can move between the parent religious body and a secular board of trustees. Finally, one typology focuses on the target population. Here again we can observe two trends: one is service to members of the religious group versus service to the community at large; the other is a service whose primary purpose is missionary vis-à-vis a service whose primary purpose is to help people in need, even if they are theologically and socially undeserving.

While these typologies are helpful and worth further discussion, the typology based on locus of service is preferable for our purpose. Like many typologies, ours is one of conceptual convenience. Upon close scrutiny one can identify a few religious-based social services that could be placed in more than one category. For example, we categorize Habitat for Humanity as a national organization, even though it is active internationally and its local chapters may initiate projects of their own. The reason for our decision is that its primary impact is as a national organization that has a central administration. In this respect, it differs from Pioneer Clubs, which also has local branches but no national headquarters and hence is a paradenominational organization.

LOCAL CONGREGATIONS

Congregations are groups of persons who voluntarily band together for religious purposes and who share an identity with one another. These groups of people usually own a property where they periodically meet and observe a theological doctrine that to some extent guides their governance and worship practices (Garland 1997). Religious congregations in the United States are among the most diverse social organizations imaginable. There are close to 350,000 congregations, affiliated with more than 200 denominations and religions. Many of these congregations carry out numerous social programs to improve the quality of life of their communities. The terms applied to these efforts include *social ministry, social outreach, congregation's mission stance,* and *social action*. Programs, underwritten by the congregation, are often the means by which the members express their faith. Programs offered by congregations range from the small and informal (church-based services) to incorporated organizations with their own boards and tax-exempt status (Jeavons and Cnaan 1997). Examples of such programs include food pantries, provision of space for AA meetings, clothing closets, volunteer visitors, day care for children or the elderly, free transportation, soup kitchens, in-home assistance and/or support for agency efforts with volunteers or money.

It is often suggested that evangelical and conservative congregations are less interested in providing social services and more concerned with saving souls and converting others. For example, Roozen, McKinney, and Carroll (1984) asserted that the social activity of the evangelical congregations was "not for the purpose of social reform or change, but to share the message of salvation with those outside the fellowship" (p. 36). Yet recent empirical evidence suggests that provision of social and community services is a perceived norm among American congregations that is rooted in the theological teaching of most religions and based on the shared and normative experience of most congregations and congregants (Cnaan 1997; Mock 1992; Ward et al. 1994). In this respect, Mock (1992) noted that "within the identity of virtually every congregation or parish lies the justification and impetus for community involvement—possibly even for advocating the rights of disadvantaged groups" (p. 28).

Los Angeles's First African Methodist Episcopal Church (FAME) is an example of a congregation that has taken leadership in tackling problems of unemployment, homelessness, AIDS, and drug addiction in its community (Billingsley 1992; Gite 1993). Its mission statement reads: "First A.M.E. Church, Los Angeles, exists to improve the spiritual, social, educational, physical, and economic lives of all those embraced in the earthly Kingdom of God." FAME is the oldest black congregation in Los Angeles. It has a membership of 9,500 people. Following in the A.M.E. tradition and its own mission of community services, FAME has developed community programs in business development, housing, clothing, feeding the homeless, and education awareness on issues such as AIDS, health care, and child care.

FAME's commitment to improve the spiritual, social, educational, and economic lives of the people in its community has evolved into the establishment of the following 501(c)(3) corporations: First African Methodist Episcopal Church of Los Angeles, Cecil L. Murray Educational Center, FAME Operation of AIDS Prevention and Education Corporation, FAME Assistance Corporation, FAME Housing Corporation, and FAME Good Shepherd Housing Development Corporation. Each of the six corporations serves a unique purpose and function in the community. First A.M.E. itself offers premarital, job stress, family, and crisis counseling, provides referrals to mental health professionals, and runs a member-owned savings-and-loan credit union. The Cecil L. Murray Educational Center, founded in 1994, serves children in pre-kindergarten to fourth grade. The FAME Assistance Corporation addresses a broad range of social needs through food and shelter programs, tobacco control programs, relief programs, L.A. Renaissance programs, and twenty-seven youth programs. The FAME Operation of AIDS Prevention and Education Corporation trains teens to implement educational programs on AIDS/HIV prevention. Future plans include establishing an AIDS hospice.

Since 1985, FAME has provided affordable housing through property owned by the church. The FAME Housing Corporation currently manages 182 housing units for low-income individuals and families and operates a child care center that serves seventy-six children. FAME Good Shepherd Housing Development Corporation manages forty Section 8 housing units for physically challenged individuals. The tobacco control program, which operates under contract with the Los Angeles County Tobacco Control program, reaches the community with antismoking messages. FAME Renaissance, founded in 1992, develops programs to create business and economic opportunities for the minority community. The FAME entrepreneurial training program has provided instruction on principles of business to more than 850 students. The

FAME Water Conservation Program, through funding by the Department of Water and Power, provides water-conservation devices (toilets and shower-heads). This program represents savings of more than a hundred million gallons of water per year, entrepreneurial opportunities for minority plumbers, and employment for individuals who have served time in a federal penitentiary. The FAME Immediate Needs Transportation Program serves more than 50,000 seniors, students, and physically challenged individuals per month. This program also provides employment for twenty people and entrepreneurial opportunities for the taxi industry.

The FAME Job Creation and Employment Program has provided more than two thousand full-time, part-time, summer, and holiday positions for youth and some adults. Employment opportunities have been created through collaboration with the Century Business College and corporate employers such as Disneyland, Disney Hotel, Disney Store, Vidal Sassoon Foundation, Bank of America, and PepsiCo. The FAME Micro-Loan Program has provided fifty-two loans in a one-year period to minority-owned businesses with funds from private industry. FAME Renaissance also provides technical assistance and training through the FAME Business Resource Center.

FAME is a unique and most successful church. Its two senior clergy are dynamic professionals who are actively involved in all levels of the church organization. They have generated funds from businesses and public agencies, hired paid staff (mostly from the neighborhood), recruited hundreds of volunteers, and most important, served low-income residents in Southeast Los Angeles. The majority of people who benefit from the church's impressive social ministry are not members of the congregation, and the impact of this church is way above and beyond its congregants and its immediate location. Fewer than one hundred congregations nationwide can boast of such a magnitude of social services. Yet, as we will document in chapters 10 and 11, most congregations are, to a lesser degree, involved in serving the social needs of individuals and families in their community.

Another interesting example is a Philadelphia mosque called the United Muslim Movement (UMM). The United Muslim Movement was founded in 1993 by Muhammad Luqman Abdul-Haqq (best known as renowned recording artist Kenneth Gamble), along with other practicing orthodox Muslims. Luqman united his faith as a servant of Allah and his commitment to rebuilding communities ravaged by crime, drugs, poverty, and unemployment. His vision in establishing the United Muslim Movement was to unite Muslims with other groups and individuals in a common effort to better our society. Under the commandment to "Enjoin what is Good and forbid what is Evil," the United Muslim Movement has become an active and respected part of community life in Philadelphia. This has not been an easy task, as Islam is a religion that has been viewed with cynicism.

UMM offers formal and informal programs that include counseling, scouting, recreational programs for children and teens, family night, financial assistance, clothing closet, and food distribution. The UMM staff also responds to at least one family in crisis per day. Of the total budget, 25 percent is allocated to assisting families with urgent needs and 40 percent to social programs and outreach. UMM has also shown initiative in establishing a cooperative relationship with the police district and providing community crime watch and other security services for community events. This effort has helped restore hope to a neighborhood known as a "vacant community," with high rates of unemployment, substance abuse, poverty, illiteracy, gang and teen violence, and crime. The United Muslim Movement is renewing family life by attracting men and teenagers to the mosque as a family and by providing young people with alternatives to "street life" activities. UMM outreach has been a welcome response to the crisis and decay in this Philadelphia neighborhood.

The focus of the United Muslim Movement is spiritual, social, and economic. While also working toward restoring prosperity in Philadelphia, UMM recognizes that this goal will be achieved only by combining efforts with other groups to revitalize communities. To this end, UMM established Universal Community Homes (UCH), a nonprofit community development corporation that brings Muslims together with community, government, foundations, private business, banks, and other funding sources. To date, UCH has gained support from such organizations as the Office of Housing and Community Development, the Pennsylvania Housing Finance Agency, Commerce Bank, the Local Initiative Support Collaborative, Housing and Urban Development, the Mayor's Office of Community Service, the Commerce Department of Philadelphia, the Philadelphia International Record, the William Penn Foundation, the Delaware Valley Community Reinvestment Fund, and the Private Industry Council. With such a wide base of support from both public and private partners, UCH has launched several projects to rehabilitate abandoned homes and develop affordable housing. These include a partnership with Penrose Properties in the construction of thirty-three low-to-moderate-income rental units; Youth Build to develop properties for home ownership as well as provide training and educational programs for teens who have dropped out of high school; and home repair service for seniors and handicapped residents.

UMM recognizes that job creation and business development are critical to community revitalization. To that end, UCH currently has the following projects under development: a mini-market and deli, a (micro-business) African-American cultural market, day care facility, retail mall, and a "self-improvement" training center. UCH will act as recruiter and trainer to ensure that community residents have an opportunity to benefit from the jobs and new businesses created in their neighborhood.

INTERFAITH AGENCIES AND ECUMENICAL COALITIONS

The second type of religious service organization includes such interfaith agencies as ecumenical coalitions (Johnson and Dubberly 1992). In these coalitions, organizations, local congregations from different religions, and denominations join together for purposes of community solidarity, social action, and/or providing large-scale services that are beyond the scope of a single congregation. In some cases the coalition is based on one religion (such as all Christian denominations of a certain area or a local evangelical alliance). In others, the coalition may include congregations of all religions.

One example of a religious coalition is the Fresno (California) Leadership Foundation and Evangelicals for Social Action (ESA), also in Fresno. These two groups, which work in concert, are clearly motivated by their religion. They promote citywide group prayer for the quality of life of Fresno residents. But these organizations also provide an impressive array of social services. In cooperation with the local police, Fresno city schools, businesses, and apartment-complex owners, they are working to improve the quality of life, one neighborhood at a time. The police department pays for one full-time policewoman who works at ESA, and the city pays the salaries of two chaplains who work under the housing department. In the more than twenty participating Fresno neighborhoods, the police have reported a 7 percent decrease in crime, fewer calls for police service, and fewer arrests as a result of the cooperative efforts and increased resources of neighborhood churches, schools, and residents (Galvon 1996).

The one-neighborhood-at-a-time approach used by this coalition is working. In 1996 twenty churches joined with neighborhoods in a partnership called Care Fresno. They have focused on twenty-one elementary schools and thirty-four apartment complexes. In neighborhoods served by the program, crime has been reduced, and 911 calls have decreased by as much as 70 percent. School performance has also improved. For example, in the Pinedale Elementary School, reading proficiency increased by 17 percent, a record improvement in the Clovis Unified School District. Another school was removed from the list of State Schools at Risk after volunteers assisted students in improving reading and basic skills. In addition, truancy rates dropped approximately 12 percent in one year. Members of the coalition deliberately chose elementary schools as a point of entry to a neighborhood because they recognized that people in the community are willing to work with them for change when the program is school-oriented and not church-based. Yet the religious message is loud and clear. Pastors from all churches joined this truly interracial coalition, expanding it from a sometimes typical model of white workers serving African-American and Hispanic neighborhood residents. To date the coalition has targeted twenty-nine communities within the Fresno area, and it plans to expand its outreach (Spees 1996).

The Fresno Leadership Foundation, also a part of Evangelicals for Social Action, evolved from an organization called No Name Fellowship, which originated as an ecumenical Christian coalition founded by Bufe Karraker, pastor of Northwest Church in Fresno. Hearing about the L.A. riots after the Rodney King trial, Karraker realized that Fresno also was at risk and that the churches needed to take the lead in improving the quality of life in their communities. He convened a group of religious leaders as the No Name Fellowship, which later gave rise to other religious-based organizations involved in the community.

What is happening in Fresno is a striking example of community organization and mobilization of services under religious auspices, and it is being replicated all across the country. Similar examples, such as Tying Nashville Together (TNT), are discussed in later chapters.

CITYWIDE AND REGIONWIDE SECTARIAN AGENCIES

The third type of religious services organization and the one most often identified with religious-based social services delivery is the city- and region-wide sectarian agency. Sectarian agencies can be further differentiated based on their governance, affiliation with a religious body, and funding sources. For example, agencies such as the Salvation Army are church organizations that provide social programs and receive government contracts and funding. Catholic Charities, Lutheran Children and Family Service, and Episcopal Adoption Agencies are religious-based organizations that maintain affiliation with the originating religious body while developing services and programs that are provided primarily by professional staff and significantly funded by government revenue. Their boards of trustees consist of clergy or lay leaders from the relevant denomination. They were established by members of the religious order and receive some financial support from the religious parent body, either directly from an area-wide headquarters (such as a diocese) or through local congregational fund-raising (Netting 1982b). Jewish Family and Children's Services, in many cities, is essentially a secular organization that maintains a Jewish identity and commitment to the Jewish community, both secular and religious. The organization is often partially or fully funded by the local Jewish Federation.

Sectarian agencies often employ social workers as service providers and managers and serve as placement sites for social work students. The organization of many sectarian agencies is similar to that of secular social service agencies because, as recipients of public funds, they are required to employ qualified professionals and cannot discriminate on the basis of gender, race, religion, disability, or sexual orientation.

One such example is the Lutheran Mission Society of Maryland (LMS), a statewide, nonprofit, evangelical Christian agency. LMS was founded in 1905 by nine Lutheran congregations in response to the increasing needs of immigrants in the Baltimore area. Congregational development, community relations, and volunteer activities also began during the early years of the organization. From 1905 to 1998, LMS has expanded from a small ministry providing emergency and community services to a multisite organization providing services that include pastoral visitation, Christian lifestyle education, community outreach, church planting, and community relations. LMS is distinguished by its mission to provide compassionate Christian services that address the spiritual, emotional, and physical needs of individuals and families served.

The development of the Compassion Centers during the 1970s created a setting in which holistic services could be provided by professional and community volunteers. The services of LMS, once provided in institutional settings, are now largely provided through the six Compassion Centers located in Fell's Point, South Baltimore, Essex, Annapolis, Cambridge, and Havre de Grace, Maryland. The six LMS Compassion Centers provide the space and services that extend to those in need the compassion that "suffers with" and acts out of the love of Jesus. Each center, designed with ministry, service, and volunteer activities areas welcomes both those seeking to be served and those seeking to serve others. The Compassion Centers are best known as one-stop day centers where one can find assistance with food and clothing, Christian counseling, health care services, chapel services, fellowship, and volunteer activities. More than three hundred people come to the Compassion Centers each day seeking answers to their problems. During 1996–1997, LMS served 109,000 visitors, distributed 194,000 pounds of food and 78,500 pieces of clothing, and provided 2,400 counseling sessions, 2,450 health care sessions, and 30 eye exams and new eyeglasses.

The Lutheran Mission Society also offers services to women and children through the Compassion Homes in Baltimore and Annapolis. Begun in 1988, this program's primary mission was to provide shelter, parenting and employ-ment training, and Christian education for young mothers with babies. Since its inception, the program has provided assistance to women who are leaving a lifestyle of prostitution or substance abuse, women who are being released from prison, and women who are homeless. Through this program, many women have gained the support and knowledge to care for their children and to rebuild family relationships—and have discovered a relationship with God in the process. The Compassion Homes program continues to expand to address the needs of older women with children, as well as grandmothers with children, who find themselves homeless and without the employment and financial skills necessary to maintain a household.

Community relations and educational services are a vital part of LMS community outreach. LMS assists congregations in assessing and developing services to address community needs. The outreach to communities through congregations is based on these words of Jesus: "By this all will know that you are My disciples, if you have love for one another" (John 13:35). Christian serv-ice and Christian education are the foundation of all activities provided by LMS. Counseling for people struggling with substance abuse, AIDS, loneli-ness, or other issues is addressed within the context of relationships and with the expectation of accountability for one's actions.

Central to the operation of the LMS programs is the volunteer ministry, which provides opportunities to join with others in serving and witnessing their faith. For example, the volunteer ministry of LMS offers the services of doctors and nurses who perform health checks and eye exams, lawyers who provide estate planning, and accountants who provide financial planning. During 1996–1997, 1,187 LMS volunteers provided 37,686 volunteer hours at a value of $436,404. Of the total number of volunteers, 183 were Compassion Centers volunteers who provided 27,662 hours of service and 168 were profes-sionals who provided 3,364 volunteer hours. The remaining 836 volunteers served on special projects and community ministry or provided office sup-port, for a total of 6,660 hours. With only one part-time or full-time paid staff person at each center, it is the volunteers from the community and supporting congregations who keep the Compassion Centers in operation.

The Lutheran Mission Society of Maryland is recognized as a "healing force" in the community. LMS is often called upon by both public and private agencies to consult in program development for the populations with the greatest needs. Dr. Richard Alms, CEO of the Lutheran Mission Society, believes that the Society is successful because it has put its ministry first and is not dependent on government funds that would change the Christian character of the organization.

NATIONAL PROJECTS AND ORGANIZATIONS UNDER RELIGIOUS AUSPICES

The fourth type of religious service organization is the national organization under religious auspices. These organizations, which have multiple affiliates or chapters throughout the nation and even the world, have become a major force in provision of services to communities. Yet it is not commonly recognized that they had their beginnings in religious service organizations. In this model, a central headquarters coordinates and monitors the activities of the local branches and dictates the parameters within which they can function. While the services are provided locally, often at the neighborhood level, the national headquarters represents all chapters. The main examples are Habitat for Humanity, the YMCA, and the YWCA.

Habitat for Humanity is an international nonprofit organization dedicated to building homes with and for deserving low-income families. It was founded in 1976 in Americus, Georgia, by Millard and Linda Fuller. In 1965, after leaving a successful business in Montgomery, Alabama, to begin a new life of Christian service, the Fullers visited Koinonia Farm, a small interracial Christian farming community founded in 1942 by farmer and biblical scholar Clarence Jordan. In the discipleship setting of Koinonia, Jordan and the Fullers developed the concept of "partnership housing" in which those in need of adequate shelter would work side by side with volunteers to build simple, decent houses.

The houses, financed by a revolving Fund for Humanity, would be built with no profit added and no interest. Money for the Fund for Humanity would come from donations, the new homeowners' mortgage payments, and no-interest loans provided by supporters. These monies would then be used to build more houses. In 1968, Koinonia laid out forty-two half-acre house sites, with four acres reserved as a community park and recreational area. Capital was donated from around the country to start the work. And the basic working model for Habitat for Humanity was under way.

Habitat has an open-door policy: all who desire to be a part of this work are welcome, regardless of race, color, or creed. One of Habitat's official purposes is "to enable an expanding number of persons from all walks of life to participate in this ministry." The work of Habitat for Humanity is driven by a few key theological concepts: the necessity of putting faith into action, the "economics of Jesus," and the theology of the hammer. Its "faith-into-action" ministry is based on the conviction that Christian discipleship necessarily involves acting in ways that manifest the love of Jesus Christ. Justification for this ministry is found in the Bible: "Our love must not be just words; it must be true love which shows itself in action" (John 3:18).

The unique perspective of Habitat comes from "the economics of Jesus," namely, the view that when people act in response to human need, giving what they have without seeking anything in return, God multiplies the effects of their small efforts and great things are accomplished. As an example, Habitat cites the story of Jesus feeding thousands of people with a few loaves and fish (Mark 8:1–9). Habitat's "no profit, no interest" policy is based on Exodus 22:25: "If you lend money to any of my people who are poor, do not act like a moneylender and require him to pay interest." According to the economics of Jesus, when human need, not profit, is the motive for action, God magnifies the results of human endeavors. The "theology of the hammer" refers to the work of Habitat as a partnership founded on common ground that bridges theological differences. Habitat founder and president Millard Fuller has explained it this way: "We may disagree on all sorts of other things—baptism, communion, what night to have prayer meeting, and how the preacher should dress—but we can agree on the imperative of the gospel to serve others in the name of the Lord. We can agree on the idea of building homes with God's people in need, and in doing so using biblical economics: no profit and no interest" (Habitat for Humanity 1997; Vuyst 1989).

The principle of Habitat for Humanity is relatively simple. Families purchase homes from Habitat after construction and after contributing several hundred hours of their own "sweat equity." Volunteers representing congregations, labor, and business organizations provide most of the labor for the project. Funding comes from contributions by congregations, foundations, businesses, and individuals. Habitat forms partnerships with local churches, large and small businesses, civic groups, individuals, and other nonprofit organizations committed to helping those in need.

Potential homeowners are selected by a local family selection committee, which must comply with federal antidiscrimination laws. Selections are based on three principles: (1) the family's need for adequate shelter, (2) the family's ability to pay, and (3) the family's willingness to provide "sweat equity." Sweat equity is an important concept in the philosophy of Habitat for Humanity. Accordingly, those selected to become homeowners, although they are poor, invest hundreds of hours of their own labor into building their Habitat house and the houses of others. Sweat equity reduces the monetary cost of the house, increases the personal stake of the family members in their house, and fosters the development of partnerships with other people in the community. The amount and type of sweat equity required of each partner family varies from affiliate to affiliate. On average, each family contributes three hundred to five hundred hours.

Currently, a three-bedroom Habitat house in the United States costs the homeowner an average of $38,000. Prices differ slightly depending on location and the costs of land, professional labor, and materials. In developing nations, a Habitat house costs between $500 and $5,000, depending on design, materials, and location. Habitat houses are affordable for low-income families because there is no profit included in the sale price and no interest charged on the mortgage. The average length of a Habitat mortgage in the United States is twenty years. Internationally, mortgage length varies from seven to thirty years. The program's success is well documented and is confirmed by the fact that Habitat has built more than 60,000 houses around the world, providing more than 300,000 people with safe, decent, affordable shelter. There are now more than 1,300 active affiliates located in all fifty states and the District of Columbia. There also are more than 250 international affiliates coordinating some 800 building projects in fifty-seven other countries around the world.

In 1984 former President Jimmy Carter and his wife, Rosalyn, launched the Jimmy Carter Work Project, under the aegis of Habitat for Humanity. Joined by dozens of volunteers, the Carters began work on renovating a six-story, nineteen-unit apartment building in New York City and returned the following year to help complete the work. In 1997 the Carters spearheaded the "Hammering the Hill" project, which, in a single week, provided some four dozen needy families with new housing. Building houses is just one aspect of the Jimmy Carter Work Project. The other is raising public awareness of the critical need for affordable housing everywhere, and the plan is working. Within a year, the Jimmy Carter Work Project was the catalyst for the construction of another one hundred new homes, involving thirty-one Habitat for Humanity affiliates in Kentucky and Tennessee and other states. Another sixty homes were constructed through a unique partnership with the Federation of Appalachian Housing Enterprises. The Jimmy Carter Work Project also focuses on environmental awareness—assuring that both the construction process and the homes being built are energy- and resource-efficient. This involves building the homes to meet Model Energy Code standards; minimizing material and food service waste during the construction phase; and recovering waste materials through reuse, recycling, and composting.

The Young Men's Christian Associations (YMCAs) are charitable nonprofit 501(c)(3) organizations. The YMCA was founded in London, England, in 1844 by George Williams and a few coworkers. They established the YMCA to help young men like themselves find God by gathering together to pray and study the Bible as an alternative to vice. The first YMCA in the United States was begun in Boston in 1851 with the work of Thomas Sullivan, a retired sea captain. This program quickly expanded from serving men and boys to include services to women, girls, and families.

Today, each YMCA operates independently and locally. The 964 member YMCAs, their 2,197 associations, and 1,233 branches make up the nation's largest nonprofit community services organization: the National Council of Young Men's Christian Associations of the United States of America. Statistics for 1996 show an increase of 29 associations and 26 branches over the previous year. The YMCA provides technical support, consultation, archival, program development, and resource services to local YMCAs. YMCAs are located in neighborhoods in all fifty states. The YMCA of the USA also oversees Jerusalem Operations, a YMCA branch in Israel that is managed by local citizens. In 1996 YMCA served approximately 14.8 million men, women, and children. The YMCAs in America are also a part of the World Alliance of YMCAs, an organization of independent YMCAs from more than 130 countries. They serve people of all religions, races, ethnic groups, socioeconomic status, ages, and abilities, regardless of their ability to pay. Their mission is to put Christian principles into practice through programs that build healthy spirits, minds, and bodies. YMCAs carry out their mission by providing tools and resources to nurture children, strengthen families and communities, and foster the values of caring, honesty, respect, and responsibility. YMCAs meet the needs of individuals, families, and communities through activities such as teen clubs, substance abuse prevention, family nights, vocational counseling, job training, child care, camping, exercise classes, and domestic abuse programs.

In 1996 the combined operating budget for YMCAs totaled $2.3 billion. The YMCA of the USA received $52 million in funding from the following sources: program and services fees (16%), membership dues (57%), charitable contributions (10%), investments and royalties (9%), and grants (8%). The member associations received funding from the following sources: membership dues (30.8%), program fees (17.2%), child care fees (17.7%), residence revenue (2.4%), resident camp income (5.2%), food service and sales (1.2%), government contracts (8.3%), investment income (2.0%), general contributions (3.1%), contributed volunteer services (0.8%), special events (1.0%), legacies and bequests (0.6%), associated organizations (0.3%), annual campaign (3.2%), foundation grants (1.0%), United Way (3.6%), and miscellaneous income (1.3%). YMCAs also received contributions for capital improvements that totaled $190 million in 1996. The portion of contributed income received by YMCAs is 20 percent of their total income. YMCA facilities are run by 56,357 volunteers serving on boards and committees, 413,033 program volunteers, countless other volunteers, and 10,959 paid staff.

YMCAs maintain a significant presence in their communities through their services and collaborative efforts with government agencies, schools, colleges and universities, hospitals, public housing, parks and recreation, youth agencies, neighborhood associations, and churches. Nationwide, 431 YMCAs collaborate with 796 churches, 1,350 elementary schools, 916 high schools, 500 colleges and universities, 836 parks and recreation departments, 701 hospitals, 393 juvenile courts, and 295 low-income public housing developments to serve their communities. YMCAs also collaborate with religious-based organizations such as Habitat for Humanity. In Phoenix, Arizona, for example, the Valley of the Sun YMCA is working with Habitat for Humanity to build 196 homes in South Phoenix. The twelve Valley of the Sun YMCAs offer scholarships for recreation, child care, and other health and social services. The YMCAs are also sponsoring the construction of the homes: providing volunteers to assist in building the homes and sharing with Habitat their expertise on fund-raising, working with volunteers, and setting up endowment programs.

YMCAs recognize the challenges ahead with welfare reform and have stepped in with solutions. In Boston, the Dorchester branch is helping welfare recipients gain the necessary skills, education, and self-confidence to reenter the job market. In Illinois, the Paris Community YMCA has provided eight unpaid positions to help families that need to keep their welfare benefits. Of the eight unpaid workers, two have been permanently hired. The YMCA in Fort Worth is collaborating with the public housing community to provide child care for parents returning to work. In Sarasota, Florida, the YMCA Children, Youth, Family Services, Inc., works in partnership with the state to administer child care subsidies to welfare recipients and to refer parents to certified child care providers. This YMCA not only assists in making child care more affordable and accessible but also provides curriculum specialist visits to child care centers to ensure that children receive quality care. These are a few of the ways that YMCAs are helping families to make the transition to work and to help the state to implement services at the community level.

PARADENOMINATIONAL ADVOCACY AND RELIEF ORGANIZATIONS

The fifth type of religious service organization is the paradenominational advocacy and relief organization. Such organizations serve or advocate for people in need and are concerned with improving educational opportunities for people. What is unique here is that although the organizations are not officially affiliated with any religion or denomination, they are based on religious principles and have strong theological undertones in their mission statements. Their goal is to improve the social condition by applying religious principles to a secular world. Often a group of concerned citizens who are members of a particular denomination or religion may form an organization for the purpose of helping others. Although not formerly affiliated with any congregation, denomination, or other form of organized religion, these organizations freely acknowledge that their activities are influenced by denominational or religious doctrines, but in a way that makes them independent of any religious body. Their members prefer not to be affiliated with any specific denomination so that their activities will attract a wider range of support and clients.

Examples of such national organizations, some of which have local branches, include Bread for the World, founded by the Lutheran Church to foster education and research on hunger, and Pax Christi USA, a Catholic peace education and activist organization. Some organizations may have local branches (Coleman 1996).

A subtype is the local paradenominational service organization. An example is Hope House in Nampa, Idaho, a residential facility for fifty-one abandoned and severely abused children. The twelve full-time staff members work without pay as an expression of their religious beliefs (Shapiro and Wright 1996). In this case, the people who established the residential facility based on their religious ideology came into conflict with the authorities not because of payment for services but rather because it was uncertain whether or not they have the credentials and qualifications to provide the services they are offering.

Friends in Service Here (FISH) is another example of a special-purpose religious organization. FISH, which operates in more than eight hundred locations, provides services to the needy in the community without regard to their religious affiliations or beliefs. These services include transportation for the handicapped, elderly, and sick; companionship for shut-ins; lawn care and home repairs for those who can no longer care for their property; and meals. The raison d'être of this organization is Christian care and compassion. FISH has no central headquarters and no paid staff; the local chapters are the organization. As such, FISH represents a special-purpose religious-based organization that helps thousands of people in need nationwide but is not affiliated with any specific denomination (Wuthnow 1988).

Another interesting example for our purpose is Pioneer Clubs. The focus of this agency is religious education for Christian children. Originally founded in 1939 as Pioneer Girls, the organization began to include boys' clubs in 1981 and the name was changed to Pioneer Clubs. These clubs are church-sponsored weekly programs and Bible-study clubs for children of age two to grade 12.

The purpose of Pioneer Clubs is to help children (1) put Christ in every phase of their life; (2) form healthy relationships that foster a sense of belonging and community responsibility; and (3) develop a positive self-concept. To achieve this purpose, Pioneer Clubs emphasizes Christian values, family life, cooperation, participative learning, and self-improvement. Much like the Boy Scouts and Girl Scouts, these clubs also provide activities in the arts, camping, sports, and hobbies.

Pioneer Clubs serves more than 4,000 churches and 160,000 children annually throughout the United States and Canada, representing a significant service to many families and communities. Pioneer Clubs also operates twenty-six Camp Cherith camps in the United States and Canada. The camp program incorporates skill-building and outdoor activities with Bible studies and other Bible-related recreational activities.

A more controversial paradenominational organization is Promise Keepers, a multidenominational Christian organization founded by University of Colorado football coach Bill McCartney in 1990 and headquartered in Denver (Ross and Cokorinos 1997). Discouraged by the negative behavior and values of his national championship players in particular and American men in general, McCartney established Promise Keepers as a way of "building great men to build great people who will love the great savior and fulfill the Great Commission." The stated mission of Promise Keepers is to reclaim male responsibility and reestablish male leadership in a nation beset by the ills of poverty, illegitimacy, drug abuse, juvenile delinquency, and disease, all because American men have forsaken Christian values. Currently, the organization has annual revenues of $87 million and 360 paid staff members. That Promise Keepers has struck a responsive chord is evident from the October 4, 1997, Stand in the Gap rally, which attracted more than a million men to the Capitol Mall in Washington, D.C.

The Promise Keepers' philosophy is at odds with many social work values. The membership, for example, is extremely conservative regarding homosexuality, abortion, and obscenity laws. McCartney has denounced homosexuality as "an abomination of almighty God." In 1992 he defended his involvement with Colorado for Family Values, which was supporting the anti-gay rights amendment. He has also called gays "stark-raving mad" and undeserving of the same legal rights as "people who reproduce" (Howard 1994). Promise Keepers has no formal policy regarding abortion, but its leaders have gone on record against abortion and have participated in pro-life rallies.

Promise Keepers strongly disavows racism, but the organization is less egalitarian concerning women. *Time* magazine reported in October 1997 that, although women married to promise keepers can be assured of devoted, supportive, and nonviolent spouses, they are not equal. According to the Promise Keepers philosophy, women should start their own ministries, pray for the financial health of the group, and "spiritually prepare" the home for the return of their husbands. To date, only a few such women's ministries have been established. These ministries promote the idea that women must not be a discouragement or a hindrance to the work God wanted to do in their husbands' lives, but rather should step back and leave their husbands in control (Stodghill 1997). It is no surprise that the National Organization for Women has passed a resolution declaring Promise Keepers "the greatest danger to women's rights."

RELIGIOUSLY AFFILIATED INTERNATIONAL ORGANIZATIONS

Religiously affiliated international organizations that focus on helping people in other countries are directly related to or influenced by a certain denomination or religion. Many such organizations originated in the missionary movement, whose aim was to convert people in undeveloped countries to Christianity. While missionary work acquired a questionable reputation in many countries in previous centuries, the emphasis of today's religiously affiliated international organizations is to bring relief and aid to underserved peoples of the world's poorest nations. In many countries in which these organizations are active, they are defined as and operate as nongovernmental organizations (NGOs); in other countries they take the form of missionary agencies. It is often assumed that religious-based international NGOs have greater clout that enables them to serve people who otherwise may not be served, such as the "untouchables" in India. Some such groups collect donations from the public at large, while others restrict their collection to members of the faith.

Examples of religiously affiliated international organizations and their service include the Catholic Relief Committee (Caritas); the International Friends Service Committee, which provided assistance in the Rwandan and Somalian famines; and the Joint Distribution Committee, which supports Jews in Ethiopia and Eastern Europe.

The American-Jewish Joint Distribution Committee (AJJDC or "the Joint") has been the overseas arm of the American Jewish community since 1914. Its activities range from rescuing Jews from danger and helping Jews in need to reconstructing and strengthening Jewish community life in Israel and throughout the Diaspora. The AJJDC, supported through funds raised nationally in the United States, has helped Jews and Jewish communities in more than seventy countries. The AJJDC, for example, aided Jews in Ethiopia during the time of national famine and insurgency, assisted them in immigrating to Israel, and at the request of the Government of Israel, provided monthly assistance and medical care for the 2,800 Felas Mora while their eligibility for Aliyah (immigration to Israel) was decided. When the Ethiopian Jews arrived in Israel, the AJJDC provided them with material assistance and guidance during their assimilation period.

The AJJDC established Israel's first nursing homes for older people. Since 1969 the organization, through its arm ESHEL (Association of Services for the Elderly), has built thirteen homes for the aged, with a total of 1,775 beds; assisted other agencies in establishing an additional seventy-nine homes; provided hundreds of additional beds for new immigrants in existing homes; and established the first home for the aged serving the Israeli Arab population in the town of Daburiya. In an attempt to help elderly people avoid institutionalization, ESHEL has helped initiate, plan, and develop twenty-five sheltered housing projects for the independent elderly (some 1,600 units) in partnership with government and public agencies. These efforts include adapting housing units for low-income disabled elderly, renovating and adapting public apartments to serve as sheltered housing, and developing a support/protection system for the elderly in government-supported sheltered housing. These AJJDC initiatives represent 85 percent of government-assisted housing developments and 25 percent of all sheltered housing in Israel. The AJJDC was also among the agencies providing services to war victims in the former Yugoslavia.

Of special interest is the work of the AJJDC in the countries that composed the former Soviet Union. Their populations include an estimated 450,000 elderly Jews. At least half of these are on meager pensions. They lack sufficient funds for food and medication and no longer have the safety net that municipal social services in these countries once provided for those in need. To assist them, the AJJDC helped establish and continues to support 139 welfare societies in 127 locales throughout the former Soviet Union. The model for AJJDC's social service programs is that of the Jewish *hessed* (welfare organization). The *hessed* embodies the Jewish tenet "All Jews are responsible for one another." The first *hessed* was established in St. Petersburg in 1994. There are currently twenty-eight Hassadim groups in the former Soviet Union. These organizations provide services that meet the most basic needs of the Jewish population, namely, food distribution and hot meals, home care, medical equipment and consultations, and social care. Hessed Avraham in St. Petersburg has become a practice center for students of social work and an important source of expertise for other Hassadim in smaller towns.

The Hassadim sponsor social clubs in communal buildings and activities for small neighborhood groups in the homes of elderly Jews who act as hosts. These Bayit Cham (Warm Home) home-based day care centers reduce the feelings of isolation among the elderly and allow them to reconnect to their heritage. The Warm Home program is expanded for the festivals in the Bayit Patuach (Open Home) program. The celebrations are led by volunteers trained by the Institute for Communal and Welfare Workers. On Rosh Hashana, 7,000 participants gathered in forty apartments in forty cities. At Chanukah, more than 9,000 participants gathered in 650 apartments in forty-nine cities. The Hassadim and welfare centers care for a caseload of some 70,000 elderly throughout the former Soviet Union. In a recent three-year period, the AJJDC distributed more than 65,000 food packages and provided heating materials in regions hit hard by winter cold. AJJDC currently supports twenty-four soup kitchens throughout the region and annually provides home care to more than 15,000 needy elderly Jews.

To address the acute shortage of qualified welfare workers, the AJJDC established the Institute for Communal and Welfare Workers. The institute has become the leading center for social services training in the former Soviet Union. Its mission is to train Jewish professionals, paraprofessionals, and volunteers to implement welfare services based on Jewish values. To date, more than two thousand workers have participated in the institute's activities, and more than one thousand welfare workers have been trained. To strengthen local resources, the Institute has opened branches in Dnepropetrovsk and Kiev.

Religious-based social service organizations, regardless of the type, set their own agenda and march to their own drummer when it comes to their social ministries. Their members act voluntarily and out of conviction, not because of any secular mandate. Their mission traditionally has been to target populations in need, organize services to meet a multitude of needs, and help eliminate social problems, while providing both the human and the financial resources necessary for provision of services. The motives behind their service are as diverse as the many faiths they represent. For some, the social ministry is a way to actualize their faith or follow in the faith tradition of their parents or culture. For others, it is a means of observing the Golden Rule by joining others to help those most in need. And for yet others, it is a way to proselytize and save souls.

These religious-based social service organizations are diverse in structure, ranging from small and informal local groups to large and bureaucratic national groups. This same diversity extends to their theological and political philosophies, which range from the conservatism of fundamentalism to the radicalism of liberation theology. While these religious-affiliated social service organizations likely influence social policy indirectly, their very diversity, as we noted in chapter 1, prevents them from being an organized, unified influence on the making of social policy. Nevertheless, they make an immense contribution to the public good, even though the social work community refuses to acknowledge it. As a whole, these religious-affiliated organizations represent a resource for the social work community that could and should be tapped for partnership. In a meaner society that has increasingly shed its public responsibility to aid those in dire need, such a partnership could be both lifeline and safety net.

In the next chapter we make the case that social work as a profession, represented by its research, education (Council on Social Work Education), and practice (National Association of Social Workers), deliberately or by omission, neglects the role played by the religious community in the provision of social services. We contend that religion is a topic that social work has, as a rule, ignored or presented negatively. There are two exceptions to this rule. One has to do with the history of the profession, i.e., the origin of social care in religious-based concern for the stranger, a concern that dates back hundreds of years. The other has to do with the issue of spirituality, which social work defines as a state of mind divorced from the realm of organized religion.

CHAPTER 3

RELIGIOUS-BASED SOCIAL SERVICES PROVISION IN SOCIAL WORK LITERATURE AND EDUCATION

Many social workers, regardless of their personal religious affiliations, do not think that their religion has any particular relevance for everyday professional practice. Just as they are committed to the principle of separation of church and state in government, so have they accepted the principle of separating the sacred and the profane in their own lives.
—Frank M. Loewenberg, *Religion and Social Work Practice in Contemporary American Society*

In the previous chapters we have taken the position that social work and human service organizations have, for the most part, ignored the religious community, which is increasingly becoming a central actor in the social service arena. Such a position must be substantiated. In this chapter we apply five empirical methods of assessing the coverage of religious issues by social work institutions and social service agencies. We then review the century-old rift between leading social work organizations and religious practices, communities, and social services, a rift that has become more pronounced since the passage of the Social Security Act in 1935.

The five methods we used were (1) abstracts of papers presented at annual meetings of key social work conferences; (2) articles abstracted in the Wilson Indexes of the social sciences index and in Social Work Abstracts; (3) textbooks used in social work education; (4) course outlines used in schools of social work; and (5) the National Association of Social Workers yearbooks and encyclopedias of social work. In the following sections, we report on the methods used and the specific findings. In addition, we reviewed the literature regarding practice issues that pertain to collaboration with, or working under the auspices of, religious-based social service agencies.

It can be reported at the outset that all five methods and the evidence from the field of practice produced strikingly similar results: little or no mention of religious-based social services. In general, social work education and research disassociate themselves from religion and its contribution to the profession from as early as the days of the Charity Organization Societies (COS) in the late nineteenth century to the Social Security Act of 1935. The written material on social work and religion is limited to a few religious-based journals, religiously affiliated schools of social work, and religious-based social service organizations. A tacit separation exists that allows religion to function on the margin of the social work profession, yet precludes religion's being formally acknowledged or becoming a legitimate partner in the quest to improve the life conditions of those in need. We also found evidence that we are not alone in our views and that social work is not the only profession to ignore religion. In this chapter we cite others who have observed the ever-growing rift between social work and the religious community and show that this rift is not limited solely to social work.

PAPERS PRESENTED AT ACADEMIC CONFERENCES

We analyzed abstracts of all papers presented at five Annual Program Meetings (APM) of the Council on Social Work Education (1990–1994) for content on religion. We chose conference papers because they are indicative of trends in research and what researchers in the field see as the relevant issues of the day. We selected the APM because it is the only forum in which social work professors meet to share their research findings. It is also the setting of choice for social work faculty to present new theoretical developments or teaching initiatives. Our analysis was facilitated by the fact that the conference organizers list the papers by topical areas, one of which is religion and spirituality.

Of the 1,500 papers presented at the APM, only 30 (2%) dealt with religion and service delivery. Most of these had to do with the history of service provision, such as the development of the religiously inspired Charity Organization Societies, while others described ways in which a spiritual focus might help in the therapeutic settings. Sectarian-based or denominational services received little attention. Even the small History Affinity Group, which is part of the APM, did not cover religious issues. Only two papers dealt with the contemporary concerns of religious-based social services. This is quixotic because throughout the 1980s, it was the religious community that bolstered the efforts of agencies cut from federal support (Wineburg 1993). The three largest networks of religious social services—Catholic Charities, Jewish Family and Children's Services, and the Salvation Army—not only expanded during this period but also began to hire BSWs and MSWs as a matter of course. Similarly, the Southern Baptist Convention inaugurated a policy requiring that those appointed to direct their more than six hundred outreach missions have an M.S.W. degree. In fact, Catholic Charities and Jewish Family and Children's Services nationwide have employed mostly qualified MSWs since the middle of the century.

In the two years preceding the publication of this book—1997 and 1998—little changed. The 1997 Annual Program Meeting of the Council on Social Work Education listed five papers in the religion and spirituality category. Four dealt specifically with spirituality, and the only paper that dealt with religion was our presentation of the ideas that led to the writing of this book. In the 1998 Annual Program Meeting of the Council on Social Work Education, six papers were listed under religion and spirituality. Four dealt specifically with spirituality, and one dealt with the burning of black churches. Again, the only paper that dealt specifically with religion was our presentation. It should be noted, however, that in the 1984 annual meeting of the Council on Social Work Education, a session (symposium) was devoted to the topic "Religion and Values in Social Work."

Lack of attention to religious issues by the social work community is no recent trend. This was made very clear in Frank J. Bruno's book *Trends in Social Work as Reflected in the Proceedings of the National Conference of Social Work, 1874–1946*, published in 1948. Bruno's conclusion for that lengthy period echos our findings: "As it happens, the one social institution with which the objective of social work is in closest agreement is the church, and yet the give-and-take between the two has been less significant than between the other professions and social work" (p. 282).

JOURNAL ARTICLES

Like academic conferences, journal articles are a means by which academicians communicate new information to one another. Generally, quality presentations at academic conferences find their way into refereed journals. We were therefore interested in determining how many articles in social work journals were related to religion. We used two sources: the Wilson Indexes for the social sciences index and Social Work Abstracts.

We searched abstracts in these two sources to locate articles that contained both the terms *social work* and *religion* in the title, abstract, or keywords. In the Wilson Indexes, from late 1983 to December 1996, there were 5,787 articles with the term *social work* and 22,228 articles with the term *religion*. For this fourteen-year period, we identified only 22 articles (.0038%) that contained both terms.

Since the number of relevant articles was so small, we reviewed all twenty-two articles. One article appeared twice, and another was written by an English scholar and published in England (Harris 1995). The remaining twenty articles were by Americans. Three articles had appeared in the *Humanist*, and one article in each of the following nonsocial work publications: *U.S. News and World Report*, the *New Republic*, *America*, and the *Futurist*. None of these is a social work journal. This limited the number of articles listing "social work" and "religion" and published in American social work journals between 1983 and 1996 to thirteen. Of these thirteen articles, five dealt with services to the elderly and three were concerned with issues of sexuality.

We applied the same method to Social Work Abstracts. This database, designed specifically for social workers, lists more than 35,000 sources for the period of January 1977 to March 1997. In it, we identified 220 sources (.0063%), mostly articles, that contained the term *religion*. In many of these articles, however, that term referred to spirituality, not to organized religion or religious-based social service. When we excluded (a) articles/dissertations/publications that did not address religion; (b) articles published in a journal from another discipline, such as sociology, psychology, criminology, or in a religious journal, such as *Social Thought*, *Social Work and Christianity*, or *Journal for the Scientific Study of Religion*; and (c) those published outside the United States, the number of pertinent sources decreased to 38 (.001%).

Our content analysis of the 220 sources in Social Work Abstracts for the years 1977–1997 revealed an interesting finding. As noted above, many of these sources discuss issues of spirituality but not issues of religious services. This distinction merits an elaboration. As Siporin (1985) noted, spirituality refers to "the individual psyche, consciousness and unconsciousness, that is also called the human soul. It is in terms of the spiritual dimension that a person strives for transcendental values, meaning, experience, and development" (p. 210). Spencer (1961) defined the term *spiritual* as "those aspects of individual feelings, aspirations, and needs which are concerned with man's effort to find a purpose and meaning in life experiences, and which may occur without the individual's being related to an organized church body or his making use of a systematized body of beliefs and practices" (p. 162). The focus on spirituality in these articles perpetuates the notion of religion as a tool that the professional uses to meet the needs of clients for whom religion is an important issue (see, for example, Kilpatrick and Holland 1990). In this respect, religion through spirituality is associated with the client's pathology and is used as a means to access the client and help him or her function better. While this is a constructive and helpful method of intervention, it views religion mostly in terms of the individual client's psyche and as gratuitous. This approach regards religious beliefs as belonging to the client alone (the helper is supposedly free of such "irrational" beliefs) and as available to the benevolent helper as a lever to get to the client rather than as a means of sharing and bridging with clients. Religious beliefs are used as an entry point, to be dismissed later. In essence, it views religious beliefs paternalistically. According to Kilpatrick and Holland (1990), "faith is a person's way of making sense of life. It is a dynamic system of images, commitment to values that guide one's life" (p. 126). This view detaches spirituality from religion and overlooks the role of the congregation, the religious communities, and religious-based organizations. Furthermore, neither spirituality nor participation in organized religion is viewed in most social work articles as a source of strength that enables people in need to weather the crisis and continue as constructive members of society. One notable exception to this use of spirituality in social work practice exists in Ronald Bullis's (1996) book *Spirituality in Social Work Practice*; Bullis, however, is the minister of the First Presbyterian Church in Hopewell, Virginia.

There are a few journals geared toward social work and religion in which social workers routinely publish—for example, *Journal of Jewish Communal Services*, *Social Thought*, and *Social Work and Christianity*. The problem with these journals is twofold. First, articles from them are seldom included in Social Work Abstracts. Second, they allocate articles with religious content to a niche frequented only by those already interested in religious issues.

Siporin (1985), on the other hand, noted: "Religion is one means and context for the expression and satisfaction of these spiritual aspects, striving, and needs" (p. 211). As used in the context of religious-based services, this approach equates organized religion with the helper, not with the one being helped, and acknowledges the role of organized religion as a major contributor and provider in the field of human services delivery. In other words, organized religion makes possible communities of believers who seek to express their faith by assisting others and is to be distinguished from one's individual spirituality. In many ways, becoming a member of a religious-based service organization is akin to the process of becoming a social worker; namely, one's values and interests culminate in service that has established norms and practices. Thus, two paths can lead to social service. One is by way of a professional organization, the other by way of a community of faith.

A close review of Social Work Abstracts failed to identify a single source that dealt with the religious-based social service organization as a service provider and/or a partner for social work. Nor was there any mention of religious-based social services that complement the services provided by the state, foundations, residents' associations, and academic disciplines.

Even the tiny niche allowed religion in social work literature is somewhat deprecated. For example, an important article by Jim Nakhaima and Barbara Dicks (1995) focused on family counselors who, with family consent, use a religious consultant in the therapeutic process. This is an important and novel approach in current social work practice, which complements the treatment of religious families seeking help from secular "open-minded" professionals. Yet, it keeps the religious factor marginalized. Nakhaima and Dicks noted: "In social workers' provision of services to families, the impact of religion is often overlooked" (p. 360). Many articles contain a similar slant: religious issues as a therapeutic means to assist needy clients. An example is the paper "The Role of Social Workers' Religious Beliefs in Helping Family Members Forgive," by Frederick A. DiBlasio (1993). In an interesting study, DiBlasio found that religious and nonreligious social workers were very similar in their attitudes. Both groups scored the same on four major attitudinal constructs. The only exception was their attitude toward forgiveness. To make his findings publishable, DiBlasio framed the results around the role of social workers in helping clients forgive. What we found from our review was that published articles focused on religion only as a means used by secular practitioners to help religious clients. What is missing from the literature is any mention of the ways in which religious organizations and beliefs serve clients.

We are not the first to carry out such a review only to wind up disappointed. M. Vincentia Joseph, in 1987, noted: "The social work literature barely touches these areas [spirituality] and does not present in a systematic fashion personal development in relation to belief in God" (p. 16). Furthermore, Joseph noted that "the major social work journals contained only a few articles on religion, which may reflect an ambivalence around religion or its isolation in practice to religious settings." Joseph found only five articles dealing with the provision of religious-based social services, and most were published before 1980. Our review of the literature, some ten years after that by Joseph and aided by new information technology, revealed very similar findings and conclusions.

Notable social work scholars such as Hoff (1990) and Vitillo (1986), published in the area of social work direct practice and religion, have suggested how Christian (Catholic) theology can guide social work from direct services to social action and through community education and community development. Sherwood (1997) examined the compatibility between social work values and religious beliefs, a topic also discussed by Loewenberg (1988). Ed Canda (1988) compared Christian, existentialist, Jewish, shamanist, and Zen Buddhist perspectives on social work practice. Van Hook (1997) suggested incorporating religious issues into assessment and highlighted the importance of social workers' being aware of their religiosity. Finally, Catherine Faver (1986) suggested expanding social work research to incorporate all types of inquiry including the importance of religion.

No matter how one counts these articles, it is obvious that social work faculty have neglected the issue of religion. While there may be articles dealing with a specific religion, such as the Jewish approach to parental care or the Christian approach to abortion, the role of the religious community as a whole in social service provision has clearly been ignored in social work articles.

TEXTBOOKS

In our third method, we compiled a list of the twenty textbooks most often used in courses of social policy and social welfare history and philosophy. We then analyzed their content. Textbooks are important because they influence the students' perception and understanding of the profession. What is read, discussed, and taught in class becomes part of the professional socialization. If a topic is presented as important, then the future professional will consider it to be important. Conversely, topics given little or no attention will be considered unimportant by students.

At the Annual Program Meetings (APM) of the Council on Social Work Education, faculty members are asked to post their course outlines so that they might be available to colleagues from other schools. We reviewed the 1993 and 1994 listed course outlines in social welfare policy and/or introduction to social work and identified the books required. We limited our analysis to the twenty most frequently used books, although the total list was significantly longer. Our purpose was to determine whether these books included any religious-oriented topics.

Our analysis revealed that, with few exceptions, the texts made no mention of any congregational or sectarian aspect of social work with the exception of the obligatory nod to Charity Organization Societies (COS). Any textual references to religious-based social services ended with the Great Depression and the Social Security Act of 1935. It should be noted that most texts mentioned the religious origin of the Charity Organization Societies and that some others referred to other historical religious roots in social work. The main emphasis in the texts, however, was on issues of state and federal legislation, and the religious heritage of the profession received only a vague mention. These findings concur with Martin Marty's (1980) observation that "most of the time the literature of the profession [social work] genially and serenely ignores religion" (p. 465).

A few books, such as those by Magnuson (1977), Morris (1986), and Loewenberg (1900), did emphasize sectarian social services, but they did not make the top-twenty list. With the exception of Morris's book, the others specifically emphasized the social work–religion nexus and would therefore not be used in most secular schools of social work. However, some recent texts do include larger sections on religion, albeit mostly spirituality. For example, Cynthia Crosson-Tower's (1998) text *Exploring Child Welfare: A Practice Perspective* contains sections on religion and spirituality in several chapters. Popple and Leighninger's text (1996) *Social Work, Social Welfare, and American Society* and Johnson, Schwartz, and Tate's (1997) text *Social Welfare: A Response to Human Needs* both contain sections on congregations and social work. The pattern found in the analyses of the textbooks was strikingly similar to those found in the analyses of conference papers and abstracts.

COURSE OUTLINES

Our fourth method involved content analysis of fifty social welfare course outlines posted at the 1993 and 1994 APM meetings. Our aim was to determine whether any of the courses focused in full or in part on religious-based social services or religion in general. Again, we noted a similar trend. Only five course outlines (10%) mentioned religiously affiliated social service provision, and that was in the context of either the history of the profession or the threats to social work from the extreme religious right. A notable exception was religiously affiliated schools of social work that offer courses in issues such as church social work.

Our review of course outlines indicated that religious issues are generally ignored in secular schools. These findings are consistent with those of Martin Marty (1980), who noted: "Schools of social work rarely include curricular references to the religious roots or implications of the profession or to the manifestly religious contexts of most of the beneficiaries of social welfare activities" (p. 465). Given that the overwhelming majority of schools of social work are under the auspices of secular universities (state or private universities with no religious or denominational affiliation), it may safely be assumed that religious topics are not covered in social work education.

The long-standing debate over religious content in social work education was highlighted in 1994 when the *Journal of Social Work Education* published two articles debating the question "Should social work education address religious issues?" The positive argument was presented by Katherine Amato-von Hemert; the negative, by James Clark. The essence of their debate is discussed later in this chapter, but it is important to note here that our course outline review clearly indicates that religion is a marginal topic in social work education.

This rift between social work education and religion is not limited to courses dealing with policy and history of the profession. Religious content is minimal even in courses of human behavior and the social environment. For example, Ronald K. Bullis and Marcia P. Harrigan (1992) noted that, in social work education, "historically, religion and sexuality have been presented as isolated dimensions of human behavior" (p. 304). Having reviewed the position of various religions and denominations on sexuality, they asserted that "understanding, if not appreciation, of such diverse religious and theological policies can assist in both assessment and intervention" (p. 304). Similarly, M. Vincentia Joseph (1988) stated: "Religious and spiritual factors that significantly affect other life-cycle concerns of individuals are rarely discussed in social work literature" (p. 443). Interestingly, in 1961, Spencer had already asserted that educators were wary of any presentation of religion in social work curriculum as being unnecessary and illogical. This was not Spencer's opinion, but rather her impression of social work education and practice in the early 1960s. While few would use such harsh terms as *unnecessary* or *illogical*, most would agree that educators are skeptical about using religion in social work curriculum.

REVIEW OF YEARBOOKS AND THE ENCYCLOPEDIAS OF SOCIAL WORK

This section reviews the relationship between religious social services and social work in all editions of the *Social Work Yearbook* and the *Encyclopedia of Social Work*. These volumes document the contrasting views and approaches that religious-based social service organizations and social work have maintained in their efforts to help those in need.

In most of the issues of the *Encyclopedia of Social Work*, the origins of social work were attributed to the settlement movement or to the Charity Organization Societies. The omission of the religious roots of social work in the early editions of the encyclopedia fails to recognize the legitimacy and importance of the provision of social services under religious auspices. Instead, social services provided by religious-based organizations are delineated according to religious groups: Catholic, Jewish, Mormon, and Protestant. Each group is presented with unique values, understanding of the nature of man, and reason for helping. For example, social service for the Catholic is expressed as charity to an individual, recognizing his supreme worth and people's brotherhood in Christ. In the Jewish tradition charity is stated as a human obligation to care for one's community. Likewise, the Mormon rationale is presented as the belief that the church bears responsibility for both physical and spiritual needs. The Protestant motive for providing social services is based on love for God and one's neighbor.

In later editions of the *Encyclopedia of Social Work*, religious organizations are classified as one group. From the 1965 edition to the 1968 edition and onward, social services provided by religious-based organizations are referred to as religious sponsorship. In the 1971, 1977, and 1987 editions, social work in religious-based social services is classified as sectarian agencies. In 1997, with more activity and interest in social work by religious organizations, the nineteenth edition and supplement give more attention to the work of religious organizations: Church Social Work, Christian Social Work, Jewish Communal Services, and Spirituality.

The *Encyclopedia of Social Work* documents the quest of religious-based social services to remain relevant and distinct as social work emerged as a legitimate profession. Several religious-based organizations sought affiliations and memberships in social work organizations like the Mormon Church's National Women's Relief Society, Jewish social service agencies, and Catholic social service agencies (Goldsmith 1933; Lund 1929; O'Grady 1937). Years later, Protestant organizations became more active in partnering through annual meetings with the National Conference of Social Workers (Boyd 1949). These volumes provide an account of the shift in the social service provision of religious-based organizations as they moved from services provided to their members to services offered to the public, from general relief services to specialized services for children, families, or the disabled, from religious-based contributions to some government funding, from faith-based practice to theory and skill-based approaches.

The 1997 edition of the *Encyclopedia of Social Work* and its expansion on religious content may be an indication of a new trend. Yet, it goes back only to what was incorporated in the earlier editions of the *Encyclopedia of Social Work*, without recognition of the changing times and the religious origin of social work.

DIRECT PRACTICE OBSERVATIONS

Little is known about either the use of religious-based services by practitioners or the use of social service agencies by religious leaders. An interesting work in this area is a dissertation by Lucy Steinitz (1980). She found that the links between religious groups and social service agencies were few, infrequent, and informal. Social service directors reported that religious groups and organizations were not an important aspect of their work and planning. As a result, the two camps most concerned with helping the elderly operated independently of each other and may have invested in similar services without benefiting from each other's means and experience.

Goldberg (1996), an experienced therapist who has worked with many religious clients and religious organizations, asked: "How does one listen and respond to religious material in a therapy?" (p. 125) and provided her own answer: "There is a facile answer which is that, of course, we listen as we do to any other kind of content, but I am proposing that in actual fact this is easier said than done" (p. 125). Goldberg points out what others know to be the case: most social workers feel embarrassed when religious topics are raised in the context of the helping relationship, especially if the social worker does not share the client's beliefs. Yet, as Kilpatrick and Holland (1990) noted, many clients would prefer to be assisted in an environment where their religious beliefs were acknowledged and discussed as part of the helping process.

Carlton Cornett (1992), in a *Social Work* op-ed piece, noted that social work should broaden its perspective to include spiritual aspects in the helping process. The op-ed article was not about working with religious organizations, but about merely acknowledging religious issues and incorporating them into practice. Cornett summarized the social work position regarding clients' religion as follows:

> Mental health practitioners have an almost instinctive negative reaction to the introduction of the word "spirituality" into clinical discussions. In some cases this reaction seems to represent a distaste for something that is not quantifiable or totally observable. In other cases it appears to spring from a fear of imposing a specific perspective (for instance, conservative Protestant theology) on clients through the therapeutic dialogue. In yet other cases this reaction appears to represent a spiritual perspective in itself: that of the organization of the universe around the rational, problem-solving ego of the individual. (p. 101)

More than forty years earlier, Sue Spencer (1957), director of the University of Tennessee School of Social Work, had already posed the question regarding social work practice and religion when she wrote:

> If these spiritual needs and impulses are so real a part of life for such a large number of people, and if the use of a religious faith has actual or potential value for so many people, one may well ask why social workers are hesitant to recognize and to meet the need in this area of human welfare, and why they are much more comfortable in the areas of physical, mental, and emotional need. (p. 520)

And almost a hundred years ago, the tension between social work as a scientific profession and religion had already been documented. In 1907, Mangold noted: "It has sometimes been observed that the relations between the churches and efficiently controlled charitable societies are not altogether friendly" (p. 524).

One attempt to link social work and religion took place on March 5, 1998, during a symposium sponsored by the National Association of Social Workers at Washington's National Cathedral. More than one hundred social workers and religious leaders were attracted to this "Partners in Compassion" event. The participants stressed the theme we highlight in this book: social work and religious organizations share compassion for the poor and needy and hence should collaborate to increase the volume and efficiency of service.

BIAS IN THE LITERATURE

Indicative of the bias of omission in the literature toward religious-based social services provision is the following example. In many texts and course outlines, Jane Addams and the Chicago settlement houses were hailed as pioneers for developing the innovative settlement house model. For Addams and many other reformers, however, Christianity was a religion of social action and faith that demanded service to the poor (Garland 1994). According to Jane Addams, Christian humanitarianism was taking place "without leaders who write or philosophize without much speaking, but with a bent to express in social service and in terms of action the spirit of Christ. Certain it is that spiritual force is found in the settlement movement, and it is also true that this force must be evoked and must be called into play before the success of any settlement is assured" (Addams 1910:124 as quoted in Garland 1994:81). Review of the texts showed no mention of any other settlement houses and only minimal reference to Addams's view on Christianity and service. This omission gives the impression that religion had little to do with the settlement movement in general and with Addams in particular.

What is omitted from most social welfare and social work history textbooks is that the settlement house concept was originally developed in England by a clergyman, Samuel Barnett, and imported to the United States by yet another clergyman. Barnett first conceived the idea after seeing the work being done by St. Jude's Parish in London's East End. Barnett, who was a liberal thinker and a Fabian, nevertheless considered the founding of settlement houses to be a religious act in service of society (Bruce 1966). Chambers (1963) noted that many settlement house leaders possessed strong Christian conviction. Chambers also cited the example of Owen Lovejoy, who while giving the presidential address at the 1920 National Conference of Social Workers "bore witness to his faith." Regardless of formal religious commitment, he said, "the social worker and the social reformer were in the line of the devoted, the communion of those who did good works. Concern for the youth of the nation must take precedence over all else, for it was through an uplifting and liberated youth that the kingdom of God on earth be won."

The same texts and course outlines also fail to mention that, at the same time as Jane Addams's settlement house movement was developing, "the Salvation Army launched a program of slum work in which teams of two 'slum sisters' lived in depressed areas year-round" (Tice 1992:66). It is also of interest that, in "Army homes," they never spoke of "fallen women" but always of "sisters"; never "cases" but always "our girls" or "sisters who have stumbled" (Magnuson 1977:86). We discuss this contrasting approach to service in greater detail in a later section. In brief, the religious community held that healing began with spiritual change. For social work, it began with personal and social change, an approach that was more amenable to "scientific understanding" than was spiritual change. In fact, about 40 percent (167 of 400 registered ones) of all settlement houses were identified as religious (Davis 1984). Davis also reported a survey conducted by William Dwight Porter Bliss in 1905 among employees of settlement houses. In this survey 88 percent of the 339 workers polled were active church or synagogue members, and nearly all of them stated that religion had been a dominant influence in their lives.

The attempt to color the settlement house movement as secular started almost as early as the settlement houses themselves. In an interesting contrast, *The Annals of the American Academy of Political and Social Sciences* published in 1907 two accounts of this movement, one secular and one sectarian. Secular forces within the movement were represented by Mary Kingsbury Simkhovich, head resident of Greenwich House in New York. She claimed that "the common creed of the settlement which constitutes its motive power is its faith in democracy as a political system and its serious attempt to realize democracy in social and industrial life" (p. 493). Sectarian forces within the movement were represented by Thomas S. Evans, head resident of University Christian Settlement in Philadelphia. He asserted that "our position is that morality is the basis of settlement work and all social work, that religion is the basis of morality, that Christianity is the final religion, and that constant conscious fellowship with the living Lord Jesus Is the sum total of Christianity and of life" (p. 485). Clearly the contention between secular and sacred forces within social service is a century old, and each side paints reality based on its needs and ideology.

In Chicago there were two famous settlement houses. One, Hull House, was viewed as secular while the other, the Chicago Commons, was known as religious. The latter was established in 1894 by Reverend Graham Taylor, who was the first professor of Christian sociology at Chicago Theological Seminary. In this house, seminary students lived with local residents as a means of serving them as well as studying to become congregational clergy who would work within the community (Popple and Leighninger 1996).

Much of what we know today as social services in America had its origins in religious organizations. Even as social work began to emerge as a profession in the 1920s and 1930s, there were attempts to link social work with the work of religious congregations. For example, in 1920, Monsignor John A. Ryan (1983) pointed out that professional social work and religion shared compatible philosophies of social service and suggested that these two providers of social services needed to understand each other better, reconcile, and accept their differences. Similarly, in 1930, F. Ernest Johnson published *Social Work of the Churches: A Handbook of Information*, in which he noted growing public interest in the "social implications of the Gospel" and the conviction that Christian conversion should reflect in a "Christian way of life" (p. 9). This growing social concern was evident in conferences between social workers and ministers, interest in teaching casework at seminaries, opposition to war, and a long list of common interests and areas of operation. He also noted: "The development of social case work bears testimony to the fact that permanent changes in individual life and character are not brought about merely by manipulating the environment" (p. 9). Johnson cited Mary Richmond's book *What Is Social Case Work?* as contributing to the understanding of personality and motivations as well as the application of religion and the spiritual.

Some extreme religious leaders of the day, however, saw social work as an enemy. William A. "Billy" Sunday, for example, attacked the professionalization of help because he believed that it put evangelism at risk. He criticized Christian attempts to provide scientific and organized methods of helping. He argued that they had taken up sociology and settlement work but were not winning souls to Christ (McLoughlin 1976). Johnson's approach, however, was more typical of religious people in the 1930s than was that of Billy Sunday.

Johnson further noted that in some circles religion had become a scientific discipline (e.g., the psychology of religion), which opened up opportunities for collaborative research, experimentation, and application of knowledge between religion and social work. According to Johnson, acceptance of the scientific view "dethroned religious and ethical authority" in favor of materialistic and individualistic pursuits, but such acceptance "has been accompanied by popular confusion over values and standards and general questioning of formerly revered authority" (p. 13). Acceptance of the scientific view was also believed to be associated with increased lawlessness. Hence, it was important for religion and social work to work together.

Johnson continued: "As the moral problem arises out of the widespread disregard of the law, there is general agreement that the principal task confronting the church is moral education" (p. 22). In his view, changing moral standards and social trends raised the following social concerns and responsibilities for the church: (1) opposition to war; (2) systematic preparation for marriage; (3) sex education in cooperation with the social hygiene movement; (4) care for the increasing number of immigrants; (5) adjustment of migrants from farms to cities; (6) rehabilitation of the home as a dominant religious, moral, and social factor; (7) socialization of socially disinherited racial and national groups; (8) improvement of the quality of entertainment (decreased emphasis on sensory experience); (9) recognition of the moral effects of discriminatory laws; (10) strengthening the moral conscience of citizens through education; (11) raising the status of women in the churches and capitalizing on their leadership capabilities; (12) understanding of the moral implications of idleness resulting from "technological unemployment" (p. 26); (13) understanding of the moral relationship between work and leisure; and (14) recognition of the status of the worker with respect to the organized industry.

Johnson raised other issues that are still debated and still pertinent to both social service and religious communities. He noted that the institutional church was less readily accepted in social services provision because of the availability of secular services in the community and the diminished interest in religious education and church activities. Nevertheless, as church architecture shifted from the cathedral to the "skyscraper" church or church-apartment building, opportunities grew for income-producing property and/or programs. During the 1920s, most churches were large; many had classrooms, a social room, clubrooms, assembly hall, dining hall, kitchen, and gymnasium. Most churches also employed a director of religious education, a part-time director of youth work, and frequently a social worker. "The tendency at this time was to study the use of rooms and equipment for social and educational purposes" (p. 37). The fact that most prosperous city churches were regarded as capitalistic, and therefore an impediment to urban Christianity, caused Johnson to call for an intensive examination of the effectiveness of religious and social tasks in city churches. He asked: "What is the actual result of the educational, social, and worship activities of the church? What is the sound theory of the church's relation to community life and welfare, political and economic relationships, and to what extent is it being applied?" (p. 41).

We have discussed Johnson's work to demonstrate that social work, in the early stages of its professional evolution, did have relationships with the religious community. Although social work had become secular and moved away from its religious heritage, the religious community had accepted this development and sought linkages between the two. As we have already shown, this is no longer the case. Something happened over the past sixty years that has created and sustained the rift between religion and social work. In chapter 4, we outline several key reasons for this development and provide evidence that we are not the only ones who have observed this parting of the ways.

In the mid-1950s the National Council of Churches published a three-volume report examining service provision by its member denominations. Like Johnson's work in the 1930s, these three volumes detailed a long history of religious involvement in welfare. In the first volume, Bachmann (1955) outlined the historical development of social concerns among Protestant denominations. In the second volume, Clayton and Nishi (1955) provided a detailed picture of religious-based social services provision. They reported that many religious social services are isolated and operate without cooperation or support from any other agency. They noted that 2,783 health and welfare programs operate within Protestant churches. In the third volume, Bachmann (1956) reported findings from a national conference on the roles and functions of churches in social welfare provision. Again, like Johnson's pioneer work, these three volumes represent an attempt by religious organizations to systematize their welfare work.

PARTING OF THE WAYS

Regina G. Kunzel (1993), in her book *Fallen Women, Problem Girls: Unmarried Mothers and the Professionalization of Social Work, 1890–1945*, has identified an important aspect of the origin of the rift between social work and religious-based social services:

> Although by the 1920s evangelical women could boast a national network of more than 200 maternity homes, they increasingly had to compete for the authority to define unmarried motherhood, and eventually, and most painfully, to control the homes they founded. As social workers sought to establish themselves as professionals, they claimed "illegitimacy" to be within their realm of expertise and eventually demanded places of central importance in homes for unmarried mothers. In order to distance themselves from evangelical reform and to dissociate their own work from the

earlier style benevolence so heavily informed by "feminine" values, they described work with unmarried mothers in a very different light. "Success," one caseworker wrote in 1921, "is achieved in inverse ratio to the degree of emotion involved." Trading the explicitly gendered language of evangelical reform for the ostensibly gender-neutral, objective, rational, and scientific language of professionalism, social work articulated the reform outlook of a new generation of women. Maternity homes—which were once shelters dedicated to the redemption and reclamation of "fallen women"—were now redefined by social workers as places of scientific treatment. Rather than unfortunate "sisters" to be "saved," unmarried mothers became "problem girls" to be "treated." (p. 2)

As Kunzel has noted, the parting of the ways between social work and religion occurred because social work took the path of professionalization, and religious social services took the path of less-formal, more faith-based services. And because these paths have diverged, social work has failed to recognize the legitimacy and importance of religious-based social services in the nation's current social service system. As we will show later, the scope and range of these services is truly extraordinary.

Lester Salamon (1995) voiced a similar sentiment when he wrote:

For most of the fifty years prior to 1980 the nonprofit sector [of which religion is more than half] essentially disappeared from public discourse in the United States as attention focused instead on the dramatic growth of the state. To read analysis of American social policy during that period, one could easily conclude that the nonpublic sector had ceased to exist sometime during the New Deal era of the 1930s, when federal involvement in social welfare began to grow. Both those on the political left and the political right seemed to join in this conspiracy of silence: the former out of concern that acknowledging the continued presence of a vital voluntary sector might weaken the case for an expanded governmental role, and the latter out of fear that the continued presence of a sizable nonprofit sector might throw into question longstanding conservative claims about the threat the expanded state activity supposedly posed for such private groups.

This glaring oversight is not altogether surprising, given the ethos regarding the separation of church and state in the United States. Nevertheless, we believe that the church-state argument may carry more weight in academic circles than it does in the community that benefits from the work of the religious community. Interestingly, Reinhold Niebuhr, one of the most noted theologians of the twentieth century, asserted that the separation of social work and religion is, to a large extent, a Protestant way of doing business. In his book *The Contribution of Religion to Social Work*, Niebuhr (1932) asserted that Protestantism places heavy emphasis on lay activity and leadership in the social world as opposed to the clerical work in the church. Thus, the responsibility for social services was delegated to the nonreligious arm of the church and from there to the secular organizations of society. Even in Niebuhr's time, three of every four social workers were practicing under secular auspices.

Another clue to the process of separation between the two communities can be found in the social work literature from the early 1950s. One example is the book *The Philosophy of Social Work*, by Herbert Bisno, published in 1952 and no longer in use. In this book, which had a strong bearing on the development of social work as a profession, Bisno cited several key principles in social work, such as self-determination and client-oriented intervention, which emphasize flexible service according to each client's needs. Bisno also made it clear that the antithesis of this philosophy was Catholic—and by extension, all religious-based, social work—because it adhered to fixed absolutes and failed to reflect a "relativistic-scientific perspective." In Bisno's words:

> The church . . . has continued to hold firmly to the existence of certain fixed unchanging moral principles, and this, in the nature of things, she must continue to do. The possession of these principles must have a far-reaching effect on the endeavors of Catholic social workers; for in the Catholic scheme of things such principles not only determine the pattern of our individual lives; they determine to a large extent our relationships with others, the social program at which we aim and the objectives we endeavor to place before those in whose behalf we work.   (p. 92)

Bisno further noted that Catholic social workers must oppose on moral grounds clients' requests for abortion, contraception, divorce, and gay and lesbian relationships. Bisno therefore called for a separation of the new profession from its religious roots.

In 1952, the same year in which *The Philosophy of Social Work* was published, the American Association of Schools of Social Work (now the CSWE) adopted the *Curriculum Policy Statement*. This curriculum statement made no reference to spirituality or religion, since its drafters assumed that the humanistic emphasis of social work spanned all human needs and required areas of knowledge. The statement reflected the prevailing opinion of the day, namely that presentation of religious issues and subjects is unnecessary and illogical for most schools of social work and in the training of future social workers for careers in sectarian agencies (Spencer 1957; 1961).

We are not the only ones within the profession calling upon social work to open its doors to religious issues. In 1994, for example, when the *Journal of Social Work Education* posed the question "Should social work education address religious issues?" Katherine Amato-von Hemert answered in the affirmative. She asserted that the exclusion of religion from the social work profession has reduced the effectiveness of social work practice and poses an ethical challenge. She further contended that ignoring the issue of religion causes social work practitioners to forget their "whole self" and act in a stilted manner. Her position was that not only should social work collaborate with religious-based organizations, but also the religious values and beliefs of social workers and their clients should be incorporated into practice and into the training of future social workers. James Clark took the opposite side in the debate. He argued that neglect of religious issues is not an ethical compromise and that religious issues should be raised by the profession only when they are relevant. He further asserted: "Social work must resist reactionary efforts to redefine complex social problems as the result of moral and spiritual failure, of specific individuals or the nation as a whole" (p. 11). Clark's position suggests much more than is actually stated. While he contends—and we agree—that victims of society should not be defined as moral failures, he also defines working with religious-based social services as archaic and reactionary. In this latter respect, Clark represents the majority of social workers who, as we noted in chapter 1, see only one side of the religious community—that of the Moral Majority and the extreme conservatives—and fail to see such impressive service providers as Catholic Charities.

A similar sentiment to that of Amato von-Hemert was voiced by Max Siporin (1986). He said that religious values can help renew the value systems of both social work and the law to make them more effective. However, Siporin's article was published not under social work auspices but in *Social Thought*, a Catholic journal. In 1989, the same journal carried an article by Edward Ryle claiming that post–Vatican II changes in the Catholic church have invalidated Bisno's criticism and that there is no longer any ideological tension between social work and Catholic social services. Nevertheless, the rift between social work and religious-based social services still persists.

In 1990, Netting, Thibault, and Ellor called for the inclusion of organized religion in social work education on the basis that organized religion is an important force in community change, in working with social and health services, and in policy development and implementation. They pointed out: Even when the unit of analysis is a church-related social service agency, it is helpful for the social worker to understand the agency's theological foundations, its formal structural relationship to the parent religious body, and its potential for either attracting clients or frightening them away" (p. 15). Consequently, they proposed that macro practice courses, those dealing with planning, administration, policy, and so forth, include content about organized religion. This approach, though unique, would nonetheless limit the teaching of organized religion to the few social work students who choose macro practice (less than 10%) and make it only one of many topics to be covered in the courses. Another call for the inclusion of religious content in social work education came from Michael J. Sheridan and Katherine Amato-von Hemert (1999), who studied 208 students from two schools of social work. They found that although students favored learning about religion and spirituality and endorsed incorporating religion and spirituality in practice with clients, they also reported little exposure to content on religion and spirituality in their educational programs. From a more sectarian perspective, Cnaan, Goodfriend, and Newman (1996) called for the inclusion of Jewish content in social work education as a means to help social workers better care for Jewish clients and work more effectively with Jewish organizations.

What is most ironic is that most social workers are quite sympathetic to religious issues. In a survey of practitioners conducted by M. Vincentia Joseph (1988), most respondents (more than 80%) reported that they believed it was important to focus attention on religion in social work practice, yet more than 50 percent said they rarely or never dealt with religious issues in their practice.

One scholar who currently calls for organized religion to work with social work on solving social problems is Paula Allen-Meares (1989). In noting the problem of adolescent sexuality and teenage parents among the African-American community, she stated: "I propose that the black church should assume a leadership role by developing educational programs that address sexual development from childhood through adolescence" (p. 140). Allen-Meares proposed that church youth programs should teach youth "responsible decision-making and interpersonal skills by using realistic role playing and situations that they will encounter in life" (p. 141). She used three arguments to justify her position on recruiting churches to solve a social work problem. One is that more than half of the members of America's black community have strong ties to the church. Another is that pastors are also community and educational leaders. Finally, the church is the social institution in which both parents and children participate. While Allen-Meares's position is more forward-looking than that of most social work academicians, it should be noted that the profession tends to view cooperation with the black church more positively than cooperation with any other segment of the religious community. The reason is that the black church works to assure the rights of an ethnic minority, a position that social work advocates.

Finally, it is worth noting that Cesar Chavez, highly regarded by social work activists for his work on behalf of migrant farmworkers, called for churches to join the laborers' struggle. Although Chavez did not agree with every aspect of their theology, he realized the power and influence of the church: "We ask for the church's presence with us, beside us, Christ among us. We ask for the church to sacrifice with the people for social change, for justice, and for love of neighbor. We don't ask for words; we ask for deeds. We do not ask for paternalism; we ask for servanthood" (as quoted in Hessel 1992:145).

As such, Chavez was calling for a limited partnership between the laborers and the church, the same type of alliance that we are advocating between the social work and religious communities. He stressed that he did not expect to agree with the church on everything but he did expect the church to support laborers' struggles and he expected that the church and social workers would collaborate to benefit both. Such a limited partnership is a model for social work to pursue.

In this chapter we reviewed the literature and reported on several empirical investigations to assess the degree to which religion is central in social work education and practice. Our findings suggest that, by and large, religious issues and religious-based social services have been ignored. The role of religion in the social work literature ended with the formation of the COS and the enactment of the Social Security Act in 1935. Most references to religion are restricted to issues of spirituality, and even these are often limited to the spiritual needs of the clients. As such, spirituality is portrayed not as a human phenomenon common to both clients and social workers equally but as something exhibited by clients only. Through acknowledging spirituality, the social worker can better align with the client. Most references on religious values and religious social services have been restricted to religious-based journals, schools of social work, and social service agencies and are seldom, if ever, found in mainstream social work.

Netting, Thibault, and Ellor (1990) suggested that competing dogmas are frustrating to social workers. Given that many social workers and their clients have experienced personally and/or professionally the effects of religious passivity or fanaticism (for example, the historic failure of America's churches to speak out against slavery and the killing of physicians who work in abortion clinics), it is not surprising that the profession finds it easier to ignore organized religion than to admit its role as a caring social services provider. Yet we should not ignore the impact of organized religion in the field of social service delivery or the possibility of future cooperation between social work and religion, despite past differences.

Why is the incorporation of religious issues into social work education and research so crucial to social service professionals? As evidence, consider the World Value Survey conducted from 1990 to 1993. It found that more people in the United States (82%) defined themselves as religious than do those in any other county (*Economist* 1995). In a 1993 CNN/*USA Today*/Gallup poll, 71 percent of Americans reported membership in a church or synagogue, and 41 percent reported attendance at a church or synagogue in the seven days before to the poll (McAneny and Saad 1993). Kilpatrick and Holland (1990) noted that "ministers are more often sought out for guidance in resolving personal problems than are social workers" (p. 129).

Given that most Americans define themselves as religious and as members of a religious congregation, and that a substantial number attend religious services regularly, it is astonishing that the academic literature continues to ignore the way Americans act on their religious beliefs by providing religious-based social services. Even more astonishing is the failure of the literature to address the unavoidable implications of devolution policies that call for increased ties between religious and secular service provision. This dearth of scholarship deprives social work educators, scholars, and practitioners alike of the opportunity to consider important facts and trends that are critical to the present and future of the profession. This has a bearing on effective service delivery in the long term. We therefore argue that social work must pay more attention to its own roots, which are firmly grounded in religious traditions. In this respect, we fully agree with the following statement by Martin Marty (1980): "Now professional social work and religious service agencies tend to work apart from each other out of lack of interest or, in some cases, even out of hostility. The separation between the functions of these two branches of social work is, however, artificial" (p. 463).

CHAPTER 4

REASONS FOR THE RIFT BETWEEN SOCIAL WORK
AND RELIGIOUS-BASED SOCIAL SERVICES

In chapter 3, we made the case that social work and human services organizations have long ignored religious-based social services provision, despite its important role in the American social service system. Now we will highlight several of the many reasons why social work and secular human service organizations have traditionally distanced themselves from faith-based social service organizations and why social work seldom acknowledges in its research, education, and professional discourse the role of the religious community in providing social services. These reasons often overlap, and when considered together, they explain why religious-based social service is an almost taboo topic in social work circles. This is regrettable because it denies social work scholars and practitioners the opportunity to examine this domain for alternative solutions to pressing problems in service design and delivery. It is our hope that by acknowledging factors that have contributed to the rift between social work and religious-based social services, we will be able to reverse the trend, make this important nexus a fertile ground for the newer deal era, and foster scholarship, education, and practice in a limited and well-considered social service partnership between social work and the religious community.

Over time, social work has gradually divorced itself from its religious roots, and the religious community has distanced itself from social work; hence, at the end of the twentieth century the two communities are at loggerheads. Social service managers are suspicious of clerical involvement, while staff of faith-based social services are equally wary of secular human services organizations. Identifying the factors that have contributed to the current tension and distrust between the social work community and the religious community will not be enough to repair the rift, but it is an important step toward that end.

In this chapter we identify and discuss eleven key factors that explain why social work and social services have disassociated themselves from the religious community:

1. Belief that professional knowledge and technology will eradicate social ills and minimize dependency without reliance on religion
2. Secularization theory, which assumes the decline of religion in modern, urbanized, and well-educated societies
3. Quest of social work for a professional status
4. Need of an empirical approach to social work research
5. Conflicting value bases of social work and the religious community
6. Eligibility/right for service
7. Criteria for service—need versus church membership
8. Conflicting views of client—sinner versus partner in change
9. Obtaining massive financial support for social services
10. Separation of church and state under the First Amendment
11. "Europe envy": the social security thesis

The relevance of each of these factors to the rift between social work and religious-based social services is discussed in the following sections.

BELIEF THAT PROFESSIONAL KNOWLEDGE AND TECHNOLOGY WILL ERADICATE POVERTY AND NEED

Social work and religion differ considerably in their views on how to eradicate need and social problems in our society. For social work, the answer lies in scientific knowledge rather than in the "do-gooder" and "well-intentioned citizen" approaches. The scientific approach to social work is predicated on the theory that technology, long equated with improved quality of life, will one day eradicate poverty and minimize dependency and need. While today such a claim sounds naive and irresponsible, this was the claim of social work pioneers and scientific charity advocates at the beginning of the twentieth century and the cause for the call to strip churches and religious groups of the role of providing relief and social care (Mangold 1907). Mangold quoted an eminent, though unidentified source who claimed that "to a considerable extent churches pursue antiquated, short-sighted policy, giving relief from sentimental motives without personal knowledge of its effects upon those who receive it." (p. 529). Moreover, the rise of rationality in science and education in modern times has definitely undermined religious epistemology (Glock 1973). To a large extent, social work's claim to societal resources has been as a profession with the knowledge to solve social problems and eradicate poverty and need.

The religious approach to social work is much less optimistic. Some religious-based services operate under the assumption that there will always be those who are less fortunate. While it is hoped that some effective means of assistance can be found, the primary impetus for service is to do good and help the person or family in need rather than to eradicate poverty altogether. The religious perspective can be summed up in the biblical saying "For the poor shall never cease out of the land: therefore I command thee, saying, Thou shalt open thine hand wide unto thy brother, to thy poor, and to thy needy, in the land" (Deut. 15:11). This pessimistic outlook offers taxpayers and donors little return for their money, because funds are used not for improvement, rehabilitation, or prevention but to sustain the needy, who will always be with us. Thus, while the current religious approach to social service provision may be more realistic, it is less popular and more difficult to defend and market to public funders. When the two communities cross paths, these fundamental differences surface, and each side views the other as unrealistic and detrimental to the chance to help those in need.

SECULARIZATION THEORY AND ITS IMPACT ON SOCIAL WORK

The secularization theory accounts, in part, for the neglect of the religious community in the social services literature. This theory, most clearly articulated by Peter Berger (1969), holds that religion in modern societies, especially in America, will continue to weaken and society will become secular. The secularization theory also holds that cities are inimical to religion and that with urbanization the impact and followers of religions will diminish (Lewis 1994). Proponents of this theory believe that religion is a marginal force in modern society and need not be included in our policy, social services, and research agenda. The manifestation of this theory in practice is predicated on the belief that a person's religious involvement reflects unresolved child-parent conflicts and is detrimental. Hence, a client's religious beliefs should be viewed as a means to meet him or her where they are and also as a springboard for resolving the unresolved conflict, but not as a positive force in the client's life. The theory of secularization has gained acceptance, and other fields of study have begun to realize its impact on their analytic perspective. For example, Kathleen Neils Conzen (1966) noted the following about urban history:

> Few of the numerous programmatic essays in the field (including my own) make any effort to address issues of urban religion; urban history syntheses are similarly taciturn. Religion conventionally intrudes in the American urban history narrative at only a few points: as an instrument for the social control of the new urban proletariat in the antebellum reform and Social Gospel movements. . . . Thus, church-going parishioners are generally ignored by studies of working class formation. . . . In effect, American urban history has accepted an implicit secularization thesis without really examining its assumptions or implication.   (pp. 109–110)

Conzen further acknowledged that "churches have served as community centers, neighborhood definers, marriage markets, recreational sponsors, and labor exchanges. Religiously sponsored schooling, health care, social services, and insurance have preceded and supplemented public provision" (p. 113). In the face of all this, urban history still tends to ignore these roles and the political impact of congregational and denominational groupings. Cormode (1992) reported that in the first twenty years of the *Journal of Urban History*, only one article and two review essays have focused on religion.

Conzen and Cormode are not alone in acknowledging the tendency to ignore the role of churches in the community. Richard Turner (1997) noted that in most English departments of secular universities the topic of religion is considered too sensitive and is hence avoided. Although religion offers an important angle for criminologists, Ellis (1996) and Stack and Kanavy (1983) reported that the vast majority of texts in criminology avoid any discussion of religion. Similarly, it was only recently that religion was declared as a nonpathological diagnosis in psychiatry.

Stephen L. Carter (1993) raised the question of why it is that we cannot take religion seriously as a force in our lives that can be used in our daily discourse and yet preserved outside of government. Why is it that we give secular explanations to every phenomenon even if the event is religious in nature? Carter noted that many of the decisions people make in life are guided by religious conviction rather than by secular values. He argued that many decisions are not rationally based, and without an appreciation of the person's religious beliefs these decisions appear to be inconsistent. Yet in public we attribute secular meaning to such decisions. Carter further noted that the media and the public tend to undermine and even ridicule religious motivation and beliefs. As such, religious perspective, because of the secularization/Enlightenment is viewed as the inferior perspective.

Martin E. Marty (1980), a distinguished theologian at the University of Chicago Divinity School, noted: "Secularization has many meanings, but at least it includes the notion that religion in both ideological and institutional senses has little part in informing the world of social work" (p. 465). Social science researchers generally assume that religion plays a marginal role in urban centers, where level of education is high and modernity is most advanced. According to Warner (1993), this theory holds true in most European countries, but not in the United States, where religion and modernization are walking hand in hand. A greater percentage of Americans today are reporting belief in God and attendance at religious services than at any time in our history (Finke and Stark 1992). Yet many scholars, still under the influence of secularization theory, continue to dismiss religious institutions and activities as irrelevant. Religion in America today, contrary to the secularization theory, is stronger than in the past. As Warner stated: "The early decades of American independence were times of eclectic spiritual ferment but thinly distributed church membership" (p. 1050). If the secularization theory is correct in predicting that society will become secular, then scholars and leaders in social work would be justified in ignoring the role of religion in the life of communities; yet every statistic that is being published in the field shows that this is not the case.

SOCIAL WORK'S QUEST FOR PROFESSIONAL STATUS

In a quest for professional identity and legitimacy, social work detached itself from its religious roots. Since Abraham Flexner's famous address of 1915, scholars like Lubove (1965) and Wenocur and Reisch (1989) have shown that social work, for several reasons, has been seeking recognition as a profession. Professions, such as medicine and law, have power over society derived from their expertise and their legal control over certain activities. Professions can prevent unqualified individuals from practicing or even calling themselves professionals. For example, only those with a medical degree can prescribe medications and refer to themselves as physicians. A person might be able to heal others more effectively than any M.D., yet the title and control over medication is legally conferred only on approved members of the medical profession. Similar claim to expertise and social power is given to lawyers as part of the legal profession. Social work aspires to be recognized as a profession whose members are highly regarded socially for their expertise and qualified to charge for services without competition from those outside the field.

In 1972, Nina Toren defined social work as a semi-profession: a group of professionals who have formed national associations and lobby for their unique status and contribution but lack a distinct body of knowledge and expertise. Social work has not given up the hope of becoming a full-fledged profession. Sue Spencer (1957) observed that, even in the 1920s and 1930s, there was "the further withdrawal of the social work profession from its previously close partnership with the church in order to establish more clearly its own identity as a profession" (p. 521). Almost fifty years ago, Spencer voiced the hope that social work had reached a level of maturity that would enable it to acknowledge its limitations and to join with others in the community, including the religious community. She saw these linkages as a way by which social work could broaden its knowledge base and expand its resources for providing service to those in need.

The recent passage of licensure bills in many states and the inclusion of social work among professions eligible for third-party payments have helped move social work closer to full professional status (Cherry, Rothman, and Skolnik 1989; Randall and Thyer 1994). If social work is to attain a status similar to that of medicine or law—namely, that its practitioners will be recognized as skilled experts in their field and authorized to charge for services not practiced by others—then it must be based on tested and approved knowledge. Furthermore, social work cannot be or even be perceived to be associated with empirically groundless, faith-based philosophies. Just as modern medicine is based on empirical testing and not on religious faith, so social work must be secular and empirical in its perspectives. Social work can acknowledge clients' spiritual needs while recognizing that spirituality is troublesome to define and difficult to document. Even with an acknowledgment of spirituality, the role played by religious-based organizations as social service providers is still often ignored. Social work and human service organizations, however, continue to distance themselves from any religious connection as they move toward a professional maturity based on scientific theory and empirical knowledge. Nevertheless, it is interesting to note that, as a mature profession, medicine has integrated "alternative" practices and moved toward a "holistic" approach. Social work may follow a similar path and integrate the mind, body, and spiritual connection into its practice theory. This new integration may be followed by recognition and collaboration with faith-based social service organizations.

SOCIAL WORK AND THE ACADEMIC MILIEU

Social work has long sought status as an academic discipline. Because of the relatively recent emergence of the scientific paradigm in helping people cope with life's hardships, it has been an uphill battle. Previously, theology had been the founding discipline of almost all European universities and the source of academic development until the end of the eighteenth century. When scientists began to base their research on empirical principles and to dispute theological dogma, they found themselves in competition with theological institutions. Frank Turner (1974) noted in his book *Between Science and Religion: The Reaction to Scientific Naturalism in Late Victorian England* that science as we know it today had to struggle against the authority of religion to demonstrate its validity and social superiority and thus the right to be publicly funded. It is only in the past hundred years that the natural sciences, the study of the natural world and its phenomena, have become a dominant force in academia vis-à-vis the command of public support.

If such is the case for the natural sciences, how long must a new social science wait for admittance to academic circles? Although the first schools of social work (at Columbia University and the University of Pennsylvania) were founded nearly a century ago, their formative years were spent outside academic institutions. These and other schools were originally established as training institutions and funded by social service agencies that needed qualified social workers. Within universities, social work has been recognized as an academic discipline for fewer than sixty years, a very short time in which to gain full academic acceptance and recognition. In fact, most schools of social work in the United States were founded after World War II. In many European countries, however, schools of social work are not admitted into universities but are viewed as post-high school vocational institutions.

Since schools of social work are relative newcomers on campuses and are professionally based, they are at a disadvantage in the competition with well-established academic disciplines such as sociology, psychology, and other social sciences, not to mention the natural sciences. If social work faculty are to gain academic credibility, then they will have to prove that they are as competent as their colleagues from other disciplines and cooperate in preserving the academic vantage point in the public sphere. Universities do not want to be embarrassed by "spiritually guided" research. This means that social work faculty, and in turn education and practice, will have to adopt an epistemological and empirical approach to their research and abandon the theological approach. Research papers that conclude that the success or failure of a program was attributable to God's will or to a certain theological belief will not pass muster with either professional journals or tenure committees. Furthermore, academic culture is not supportive of religious issues as key themes in social inquiry. This is true for most religious-based universities, and schools of social work in these institutions are expected to adhere to the same standards. The empirical approach to social work research and education gained even greater impetus when the Council on Social Work Education assumed the responsibility for the accreditation of schools of social work. The council, a nonreligious body, developed a complex set of guidelines for accreditation, none of which mentions religion. Thus, if social work faculty are to gain academic status, they must eschew theological approaches to research because the results cannot be verified or empirically tested.

CONFLICTING VALUE BASES OF SOCIAL WORK AND THE RELIGIOUS COMMUNITY

Social work and the religious community are concerned with helping the needy, yet they are at odds with each other on several issues. It should be noted here that the value-based division between social work and the religious community is not as clear-cut as this chapter might seem to indicate. There are many liberal congregations and denominations, for example, whose advocacy for women's rights, racial equality, and gay rights mirrors that of ultraliberal social workers. Similarly, there are very orthodox social workers whose values reflect those of the religious right and differ from many of the stated values of the National Association of Social Workers. Nevertheless, in order to understand major trends and social processes, we have chosen to focus on the broad picture and obvious points of dissension. Thus, in discussing value bases of religion, we will be referring to those held by the more-traditional conservative/evangelical denominations. In discussing the value bases of social work, we will be referring to those officially stated in the Code of Ethics and the Council on Social Work Education guidelines for accreditation.

Social work is fundamentally grounded in respect for the client and the client's freedom of choice and self-determination—values that can be described as humanistic whether derived from secular or religious beliefs. Furthermore, social work and religion believe in the individual's ability to "grow" and change. However, social workers practice these values without reference to finding God or, in the case of Christians, finding Jesus and spiritual transformation. In practicing such values, social workers are tolerant of many whom society and religion might label as social outcasts. For example, social work approves of and calls for preferential treatment for gays and lesbians, while most religious groups consider homosexuality to be morally wrong. While social work considers homosexuality a biosocial development, the traditional religious community considers it an immoral choice. Furthermore, based on strict interpretation of scripture, traditional religious groups accept only one form of family life: two adults of different sexes with or without children. The only exception is if one parent has died. Most fundamentalist religious groups accept single-parent families only as an alternative to abortion, which they equate with murder, whereas social work supports the right of women over their bodies. Many religious groups consider any deviation from the traditional family to be blasphemy. To the religious community, not only do gays and lesbians engage in immoral sex but they also threaten the religious meaning of family life. To social work, gays and lesbians are a minority, oppressed by a dominant, homophobic society and in need of support, approval, and protection. The Code of Ethics issued by the National Association of Social Workers states clearly in section 4.02 (discrimination):

> Social workers should not practice, condone, or collaborate with any form of discrimination on the basis of race, ethnicity, national origin, color, sex, sexual orientation, age, marital status, political belief, religion, or mental or physical disability.　　　　(pp. 22–23)

The Code then directs social workers to pro-action, stating that:

> Social workers should act to prevent and eliminate domination of, exploitation of, and discrimination against any person, group, or class on the basis of race, ethnicity, national origin, color, sex, sexual orientation, age, marital status, political belief, religion, or mental or physical disability.　　　(p. 27)

Another instance of conflicting values between the religious community and social work is the abortion issue. Most religions, especially conservative denominations and evangelical groups, oppose abortion and view it as murder of the unborn and a direct violation of God's command "Thou shall not kill." Social work, on the other hand, sees women as in sole command of their bodies and advocates choice. In the social battlefield over abortion, social work and the religious right are two of the most visible and hostile antagonists. Social workers, who often staff family planning clinics, view the pro-life camp as religious fanatics, while the religious right sees the pro-choice camp as enemies of the unborn and of God's law.

The Council on Social Work Education mandates that the curriculum include course content on gay/lesbian and women's issues as well as on ethnic minorities. The Code of Ethics adopted by the National Association of Social Workers emphasizes these same issues. Teaching the Code of Ethics and enforcing it through regional disciplinary committees is viewed as a successful method of socializing new practitioners and guiding the focus of scholarly work (Trolander 1997). It is somewhat ironic that social work educators include gays, lesbians, minorities, criminals, abusers, the elderly, and women as issues to be studied, yet give little or no attention to religious individuals and organizations. Yet the *Handbook of Accreditation Standards and Procedures* (Council on Social Work Education 1996) specifically includes religion in the following passage regarding diversity:

> Each program is required to include content about population groups that are particularly relevant to the program's mission. These include, but are not limited to, groups distinguished by race, ethnicity, culture, class, gender, sexual orientation, religion, physical or mental disability, age, and national origin.   (*Standards* M6.6, p. 140)

This seems to indicate that religion is equal in importance to other issues that social work education advocates for and actively supports. However, the language and preferences become clearer in standard M6.8, which discusses populations at risk:

> Programs of social work education must present theoretical and practice content about patterns, dynamics, and consequences of discrimination, economic deprivation, and oppression. The curriculum must provide content about people of color, women, and gay and lesbian persons. Such content must emphasize the impact of discrimination, economic deprivation, and oppression upon these groups.   (p. 140)

This is a clear demand for educational focus on these three groups as victims of an oppressive society. Other issues listed above may be taught but are not required. As Trolander (1997) noted, the Council on Social Work Education set itself apart from many other groups and organizations in actively--and successfully--promoting theory and practice about minorities, women, and homosexuals at a time when affirmative action policies in the United States were met with resistance or backlash.

There are other value-based differences between social work and religious groups that are of lesser magnitude. One concerns the right of clients to service; another, the right to religion-free service. Social work holds that the right to service is predicated on one's dignity as a human being. The NASW (1996) *Code of Ethics* states that "social workers' primary responsibility is to promote the well-being of clients. In general, clients' interests are primary" (p. 7). Services, accordingly, should be given to all. They should not be reserved for those who meet certain criteria, such as membership in a particular religion, and the level of service should not be based on whether the client is "accepting salvation." In contrast to this view, Marvin Olasky (1996) called for welfare to be provided to those who find God and are willing to transform from within. Fundamentalist groups view efforts to improve the quality of life of individuals as futile distractions from the task of winning souls. Clearly, social work takes the opposite stance on this issue.

But even liberal faith-based social services often provide care and help individuals and families in a setting where religious symbols are in evidence. A cross or a Star of David on the wall, along with grace or prayer, is not uncommon in religious-based social services. Social work, on the other hand, states that care should be provided in a religion-free environment and that religious symbols should be removed. The religious community sees itself as serving God and saving souls, while social work sees itself as advocating for the client regardless of his or her religion. In the next section, we elaborate on the values that have helped shape these two philosophies of care and service.

ELIGIBILITY AND RIGHT TO SERVICE

A factor in the rift between social work and religious-based social services concerns motivation to assist those in need. Social work, to a larger extent, acts on the premise that people have a right to assistance and that the assistance should be limited to the area of need. The professional relationship between a client and a service provider serves a distinct function within the guidelines of the agency. These relationships, with few exceptions, are time-limited and center on the problem that the client wishes to solve or that society mandates the professional to address. When the goal is achieved, or deemed impossible to meet, the relationship ends. Professional relationships are limited to the area of need and do not extend to personal or abusive spheres. For example, sex, personal loans, and social outings are forbidden, as is any political or ideological indoctrination on the part of the social worker.

These social work principles are stressed in academic training and advocated by the state ethics committees of the National Association of Social Workers.

Many religious-based social services, especially citywide services that receive governmental support—such as Catholic Charities or Jewish Family and Children's Services, employ professional social service workers who practice according to the principles outlined above. The case, however, may be different with religious-based social services provided locally, and with services provided by groups that are more evangelical or conservative. One reason is that religious-based assistance is commonly viewed as more interested in saving the souls of the needy than in solving their problems. For example, churches once provided missions and hot meals as a means of helping clients find their way back to God. Even in modern times, it is argued that some congregations use welfare activities to attract new members and involve more congregants in church work (Milofsky 1997; Warner 1993). Social workers, on the other hand, maintain a relationship between the service provider and the client only as long as the client has a need to solve an agreed-upon problem. Thus, key social work organizations view religious-based social services as restrictive and manipulative rather than as operating in the best interests of clients. Conversely, some religious-based providers see secular social services as restrictive, because they do not deal with the whole person and focus only on the individual's pathology rather than on potential strengths and spiritual resources. Furthermore, some clients of secular social services feel that in order to be eligible for service they need to placate the agency's policies and procedures.

CRITERIA FOR SERVICE

Despite any large-scale study to the contrary, it is generally assumed that religious-affiliated social services give preference to members of their own faith within the local community and are only marginally concerned with others. This view is based on two assumptions. First, many congregations in the United States were originally formed by people of similar ethnic origin and status. Members of these congregations often set up mutual benefit services to help the group prosper in a pluralistic society (Tenenbaum 1993; Warner 1993). Second, funding for many religious-based social services usually comes from members' contributions. The appeal for members to support Lutheran Youth Services, for example, is that there are Lutheran children in need. Support for members of other denominations is often not the goal per se of religious-based social services. There are two exceptions. One is the provision of services supported by the public sector, which mandates services to all. The other is the provision of services for the purpose of converting others. In the latter case, services are generally not provided to those who are unwilling or uninterested in being "saved." However, it should again be noted that the provision of social services for the sake of salvation is seldom practiced today (Wuthnow 1994). Accordingly, minority groups and newcomers are often neglected in cities where one religious denomination is more visible and powerful than others. Yet, as we will show in later chapters, religious groups, in fact, engage in social ministries to practice their faith and hence serve minorities and newcomers.

Social work and secular human service organizations, on the other hand, view themselves as the champion of disadvantaged populations irrespective of their denomination, ethnic background, or country of origin. Social workers actively advocate for eligibility based on human dignity alone. The driving principle of social work is to actualize human capacity regardless of whether the person is a member of any identified and approved group. Even in the debates over limiting or cutting services to legal and illegal immigrants, social workers argue that all people living in this country deserve health, social, and educational services. While many religious groups advocated in favor of retaining services for immigrants, some of those most opposed to retaining services to immigrants represented themselves as speaking for and on behalf of the religious community. Our own research projects, discussed in chapters 10 and 11, demonstrate that inclusion of all community residents is the practice in almost all religious-based social service provision. Since the scope of our studies is necessarily limited, however, more research needs to be done on this matter. In sum, it is evident that the public perceives services offered under religious auspices to be exclusive, whereas those provided by the government or secular human service organizations are perceived to be inclusive and open to all.

THE PERSON IN NEED: FALLING FROM GRACE OR A NEEDY CLIENT?

A factor in the rift between social work and the religious community is that their views of and approaches to individuals in need are widely different. Social work uses a partnership approach: the person is viewed as a client/consumer/partner who is valued and assisted to achieve his or her goals. The

NASW (1996) Code of Ethics stated as principle that "social workers understand that relationships between and among people are an important vehicle for change. Social workers engage people as partners in the helping process" (p. 6). This approach has its origins in psychiatric and psychological theories. The person in need is respected regardless of his or her beliefs and deeds. Furthermore, the reason for being in need is not necessarily the fault of the person in need of assistance. Often, people are the victims of social circumstances beyond their control, and they are unable to cope with these circumstances on their own. Thus, social work does not blame the person in need or see a moral pathology in the situation that led to the need. For example, social work would not view a person as having "weak character" or "succumbing to vice." A key helping principle is that the person is always approved but his or her actions may be disapproved. A child molester, for example, is accepted as a human being and assisted in full, but his acts are clearly not accepted or approved. In the social work model, the helper is not superior to the client but works with the client to determine what kind of help the client needs. Unfortunately, the failure of some social service professionals to adhere to this principle has led to the public image of social workers as tyrants who control the lives of their clients. Many debates surround the issue of client power and self-determination in the helping process (Hasenfeld 1987), but it is imperative to remember that the official position and accepted practice in social work is to acknowledge the client's power and will to change. It is the client who determines the goals of care and who must do the work required for the desired change.

In the classical religious approach, the individual in need is viewed as someone who has fallen from grace and needs to get on the right path to God. It is believed that there is a reason why the person is in need. If someone is unemployed, for example, it is not the result of economic conditions but rather the consequence of a personal fault. If the etiology of human misery and suffering lies in sin and not in psychological or environmental conditions, then salvation, rather than professional social work intervention, is needed. According to the evangelical approach, people in need have fallen from grace and lost God's favor. Under such assumptions, self-determination, as expressed in the rejection of God, is unacceptable and a sufficient reason to halt service provision. The appropriate role of the helper, which can be applied to all people in need, is to help sinners return to God. If they cannot find a path to God, then there is no point in assisting them, as they will always be dependent and resistant to change (Olasky 1996). Our studies indicate that this is not the case in actual practice, but in theory, many religions see the person as responsible for his/her lot in life. Offers of assistance therefore are linked to moral and spiritual uplift. This principle is in opposition to that of social work, which requires that the client determine the nature of the help received. The NASW (1996) Code of Ethics states that "social workers respect and promote the right of clients to self-determination and assist clients in their efforts to identify and clarify their goals" (p. 7).

FINANCIAL SUPPORT FOR WELFARE SERVICES: WHERE CAN SOCIAL WORK OBTAIN RESOURCES?

A highly pragmatic factor in the rift between social work and the religious community relates to funding for social services. Since the 1930s, federal, state, and local governments have become the major funding source for social service provision. With the passing of the Social Security Act of 1935, the federal government, and later state and local governments, assumed greater responsibility for social services. Social Security alone expanded from a federally administered old-age insurance program to a social insurance and transfer payment program that included the poor elderly, the handicapped, mothers with dependent children, and also provides medical insurance for all these groups. This expansion meant that a large percentage of the social wealth was being earmarked for those in need regardless of their religion or religious behavior. Further expansions of public welfare included services for people with mental illness and developmental disabilities and for those addicted to drugs and alcohol. Social service budgets of states, counties, and cities increased dramatically in the years 1935–1980. Although the United States has not become a welfare state, as have many Western European countries, the government has become the major player and the single most important funder in the social welfare field. Thus, in order to obtain sufficient public funds, social work and social service agencies had to distinguish themselves from religious auspices. This quest for resources exacerbated the rift between the two.

Secular social service organizations chose to align with government rather than religion for two reasons. The first has to do with the interpretation and application of the First Amendment. It is generally agreed that state/church separation means that any program funded by the government is to be carried out in a neutral environment devoid of religious symbols or influence. Thus, if services were to be provided under religious auspices, agencies had to demonstrate the nonreligious character of the services being provided (Esbeck 1996; Monsma 1996). This made the two communities unlikely partners. This issue of the separation of state and church, essential to an understanding of the rift between social work and the religious community, is discussed in the next section.

The second reason for social work's alignment with government in the provision of social services is that the government was and still is the major player in public welfare, providing mandated services or contracting them out to private agencies. In contracting out, the government requires private agencies to show proof that they are trying to serve all applicants regardless of religious beliefs or other characteristics (Salamon 1992). Over the past fifty years, the volume of welfare services financed and/or delivered solely under religious auspices has diminished. One reason is that government support constitutes approximately 37 percent of the budgets of religious charities (Shapiro and Wright 1996). To be eligible for those public funds, denominational social services must agree to exclude any religious element from their services and be supervised accordingly. Clearly, it is easier for the government to finance a large-scale social service delivery. Despite the altruistic motivation and valiant efforts of nonprofit organizations, including religious groups, it is unlikely that they will ever come close to doing what the government does in social service. Steinberg (1996), in a review of empirical studies, found that for every dollar of public funds cut, only between one and 10 percent is replaced by private money. Even the most optimistic scenario predicts less than 40 percent replacement. This means that the public sector is a more reliable partner for a profession interested in providing personal social services for the larger community. It is therefore understandable that, when faced with the choice between relatively poor religious auspices or value-neutral public support, social work opted to depend on the latter for continuation of service.

SEPARATION OF STATE AND CHURCH

Related to the issue of funding is the principle of separation of state and church as articulated in the First Amendment. As an example of this separation, religious symbols and prayers are forbidden in public schools and in government offices. This was not always the case in the United States, nor is it common in the rest of the world. In many European countries, including such key welfare states as Sweden, the state supports and protects the church. Salary for clergy and maintenance of religious properties come from general taxes or from a publicly collected church-designated tax. In Germany and Sweden, for example, the state collects a church tax that is distributed among various religious groups (Monsma and Soper 1997). This practice is referred to as the "establishment." In this case, one religion or denomination (or a select few, as in Germany) is designated as the state religion and is publicly supported. Other recognized religious groups receive less public support. In the United States, the process of "disestablishment" took place in the late eighteenth to the mid-nineteenth centuries. When the American colonies came into being, most had an "established" religion, such as the English Puritans in New England, the Dutch Reformists in New Amsterdam, the Anglicans in Virginia, and the Quakers in Pennsylvania. However, a movement to disestablish churches emerged along with the quest for independence and gathered momentum in the decades that followed. For example, in 1776, the Virginia legislature repealed most of the legal privileges granted to the Anglican Church and suspended the collection of taxes for the Anglican Church (Issac, 1982; Levy 1994). In 1833 Massachusetts became the last of the original states to disestablish its church. As a result of disestablishment, the United States has neither a state religion nor collection/allocation of public money to support any religion. Money for maintaining religious services and practices, clergy salaries, and building repair and maintenance is solicited from members of the religious groups and is not mixed with public funds. Moreover, government may not assist religious groups in the practice of their faith, as the Supreme Court has ruled this to be a violation of the Constitution (Warner 1993).

As Hammack (1995) noted, the First Amendment caused Americans to seek new and different modes of church-state relationships. This was difficult in a society without one dominant denomination as an unquestioned influence in public life. The multiplicity of religions and denominations fostered division and suspicion among groups; hence various groups mistrusted one another's motives for providing social services. Each doubted that the other would treat needy people from other faiths equally. Some suspected that a church or a denomination would use social service programs as a means to attract members of other faiths. Consequently, there was a call to establish sectarian services to care for one's own congregants and avoid losing members (Oates 1995). The social services provided by religious groups in the United States are of great magnitude and scope. The United States is the only modern country in which religious groups have no role in the state system and must function independently, especially when it comes to provision of public welfare. Thus, social work, whose values are incompatible with those of most organized religions, operates as much as possible within and under the civil law and advocates a secular nondenominational basis for eligibility. Given the above, social work elected to ally itself with the state rather than with the religious community.

"EUROPE ENVY": THE SOCIAL SECURITY THESIS

A final factor in the rift between social work and the religious community might well be called Europe envy. This is also known as the social security thesis, namely, that social work scholars who advocate for social services are influenced by models of European welfare states that may not be applicable to the American culture. In most Western European countries, provision of social services is legally mandated and considered to be a right of citizens. Not only are social security services guaranteed and protected but also services to populations in need are legislated—such as day care centers for adults or infants, vocational training, marital counseling, and youth programs. Under the European model, recipients of social services are seen as members of society and not as powerless individuals in need.

The most significant social service legislation in the United States was the 1935 Social Security Act. Although the government has expanded both benefits and coverage under Social Security, it has enacted little legislation of similar nature. Most social programs in the United States are line-budget items whose continued existence depends on yearly funding and the decision of those drafting the budget. What places social services in an even more precarious position is that clients are viewed as welfare cases and their continued eligibility for service is uncertain. When social welfare scholars look at Europe, they see social services guaranteed by law; when they look at the United States, they see social services neither protected nor assured. The end result is that European-style social legislation is deemed superior to American-style nonprofit and religious-based services. Many books on the evolution of social welfare in America agree with the European view that true success is achieved when the government guarantees the service to everyone who needs it and a citizen can go to court to demand service as his or her legally guaranteed entitlement. As a result, research and literature focus on federal programs rather than on locally based programs in which religious-based services are paramount.

Religious-based social services, on the other hand, are limited in scope, do not guarantee services even to current clients, and cannot be challenged legally. Furthermore, most evangelical-based social services prefer to withhold service from those who are unwilling to seek salvation, viewing their services not as a client's right but as a means of saving the client's soul. It is understandable, then, why social work advocates for national health insurance, better public education, and assured support for those in need would attempt to secure those services through the law and nonreligious institutions. What social work leaders and scholars have failed to take into account is that the social service system in the United States, more than in any other country, is predicated on voluntary services, many of which are religious-based. This blind spot is evident in the social work literature. Michael Katz (1983), for example, in writing about the "war on welfare," has argued that public programs have always been more important and more supportive in guaranteeing social welfare than private relief or voluntary efforts. He stated: "Voluntarism never was and never will be an adequate answer to the problem of dependence" (pp. xiii, 291), and he further asserts that even in the nineteenth century, more people were helped by public relief than by private charities, which relied heavily on public finds. Katz concluded that real support for poor and needy people can come only from the government.

In this chapter we have reviewed eleven factors that have contributed alone and in conjunction with each other to the rift between the social service community and the religious community. Some of these reasons are of long standing and are well known; others are more recent and less commonly discussed; still others are of historical consequence only. Yet, taken as a whole, they have widened the rift between social work and the religious community. It is important to keep in mind that we have portrayed those two communities in broad strokes, which makes them seem much more uniform than they are and contrasts them as if there were no middle ground. It is evident that in actuality there is a middle ground. Many religious groups are very liberal, and many social workers are very conservative and disagree with the principles stated in the Code of Ethics. Our goal was to present a clear view of key differences, some of which can be found only among staunch supporters of each community.

It is not our intention to blame or find fault with either social work or the religious community. We describe the reasons for the break so that a process of healing and rebridging might begin. Our goal in this book as a whole is to demonstrate that the welfare system that the United States has known since 1935 has ended and that a newer and less kind—deal is about to go into effect. This newer deal calls for a new partnership between social work and religious-based social services. However, it is also our obligation to show that the religious community is theologically, historically, and practically interested and invested in social service provision. We will begin with the theological issue in the next chapter by demonstrating that the major religions are enjoined by their theologies to help others. The major religions practiced in the United States carry out this mandate by calling on their followers to assist the needy. These theological tenets, we believe, are highly compatible with social work ethics and with the aim and function of social services.

PART 2

PROVISION OF RELIGIOUS-BASED SOCIAL SERVICES: THEOLOGICAL UNDERPINNINGS, HISTORICAL TRENDS, AND CURRENT FINDINGS

CHAPTER 5

THEOLOGICAL TEACHING AND EMPHASIS ON HELPING THE NEEDY

Alan Keith-Lucas (1972) reminded us that the desire to help those in need is not an instinctive act but a norm acquired through socialization and observation. All major religions have developed a theology, a corresponding set of rules, and mechanisms to help others (Queen 1996). It is not our aim to judge whether religious teachings were meant to help the needy or to facilitate social order and cohesion among their followers. Nor are we claiming that these teachings have always been followed by members of these faith communities. We also wish to point out how the major religions have interpreted their original texts and how their missions have changed over the centuries, and to say that current interpretations may not necessarily adhere to their original intention and meaning. With these caveats in mind, we wish to emphasize three points regarding theological teachings on helping the needy. First, the teachings of major religions emphasize mutual responsibility, the need to assist strangers in need, and most important, the legitimate claim of the weak and needy upon the community. Second, the major religions have advocated social care and compassion for the needy regardless of location and economic conditions. Third, religious teachings, even when they are not put into practice, are still part of the socialization process of younger generations into the faith tradition and serve as instructions for desired behaviors. If we assume that religion has a powerful and lasting effect on people's attitudes and behaviors, then religious teaching may contribute to a more civil and caring society.

In this chapter we review five major religions that over the thousands of years of their existence have affected individuals and cultures alike: Judaism, Christianity, Islam, Buddhism and Hinduism. It is our intention to show that the teachings of these religions regarding the poor and the needy are compatible with the principles of care and values held by social work.

JUDAISM

The Jewish tradition distinguishes between values and rules that define relationships with the Deity and those that define individual and communal relationships with others. It is the latter tradition that has given rise to the concepts of *tzedakah* and *hessed*, which have to do with justice or charity and deeds of love and kindness, even mercy.

The principle of justice required that everyone be judged on the same basis. This was a novel principle given that in many societies one's social status and wealth determined justice. Judges and other officials were not to receive gifts, "for gifts blind the eyes of even the wise and honest men, and cause them to give wrong decisions" (Deut. 16:19). This command—especially helpful for the poor, who, unlike the wealthy, could not afford expensive bribes—required judges to apply the law impartially. This concept was extended in the Hebrew Bible to social responsibility. In the words of the prophet Isaiah:

> The kind of fasting I want is this: Remove the chains of oppression and the yoke of injustice, and let the oppressed go free. Share your food with the hungry and open your homes to the homeless poor. Give clothes to those who have nothing to wear, and do not refuse to help your own relative.
>
> (Isa. 58:6–7)

The Hebrew Bible, or Old Testament, is filled with references to helping slaves, captives, orphans, widows, and the poor. These principles were translated into real-life practices, as seen in Leviticus:

> When you reap the harvest of your land, you shall not reap all the way to the edges of your field, or gather the gleanings of your harvest. You shall not pick your vineyard bare, or gather the fallen fruit of your vineyard; you shall leave them for the poor and the stranger: I the Lord am your God.
>
> (Lev. 19:9–10)

Although commands that made the crops a legal property of the poor were not always followed, they demonstrate a clear theological intention to assist the poor and needy. Another example is found in Deuteronomy 24:21–23, where it is stated that once the crops had been picked, the farmer should not go back a second time but should leave the remaining fruit or wheat for the needy. The text reads as follows:

> When you gather your crops and fail to bring in some of the grain that you have cut, do not go back for it: it is to be left for the foreigners, orphans, and widows. . . . When you have gathered your grapes once, do not go back over the vines a second time; the grapes that are left are for the foreigners, orphans, and widows. Never forget that you were slaves in Egypt; that is why I have given you this command.

In Judaism, the linking of social responsibility with the era of Hebrew slavery in Egypt is not coincidental. According to Jewish thought, just as God answered the Hebrews' cries for help during their oppression in Egypt, God expects the Hebrews to answer the cries of others in need. The fact that individuals and groups can be in need at times does not make them lesser people, and those who possess the means are obliged to hear their call just as God heard the call of the Hebrews enslaved in Egypt.

Other Jewish texts also emphasized helping others. In the Babylonian Talmud, for example, Rabbi Assi said: "Charity [*tzedakah*] is equivalent to all the other religious precepts combined" (Baba Batra 9a). In an important medieval Jewish text, the Mishneh Torah, Maimonides refers to eight levels of charity, based on various Talmudic sources and centuries-old practices. The lowest is giving with a scowl; the highest is helping a poor person become self-sufficient and doing it anonymously.

In biblical times, as cities grew larger and a class system began to evolve, society saw for the first time the exploitation of the poor. The prophet Amos is best known for the social justice message of his prophecies. As the Israeli society of his day prospered, Amos was struck by the indolence and selfishness of the parasitic rich on the one hand and the misery and exploitation of the poor on the other. He adamantly argued that such exploitation was contrary to God's wishes and that God would severely punish those who exploited others. According to Amos, if Israel was to survive, then the poor and the weak must be afforded justice, because this is what God wanted. Amos's words are still powerful and are often used in arguments for social justice. For example, in Amos 2:6, the prophet said: "Thus saith the Lord: For three transgressions of Israel, Yea, for four, I will not reverse the punishment thereof; because they sold the righteous for silver, and the needy for a pair of shoes." In other words, God would forgive Israel all its sins except social injustice. Another call for social justice appears in Amos 4:1:

Hear this word, ye cows of Bashan, that are in the mountain of Samaria, that oppress the poor, that crush the needy, that say unto their lords: 'Bring, that we may feast.' The Lord God had sworn by his holiness: Lo, surely the days shall come upon you, That ye shall be taken away with hooks, And your residue with fish-hooks.

Amos, however, was not the only prophet speaking out against social injustice. Ezekiel, who lived much later, told his contemporaries:

He has not wronged anyone; he has not seized a pledge or taken anything by robbery; he has given his bread to the hungry and clothed the naked; he has refrained from oppressing the poor; he has not exacted or accrued interest; he has obeyed My rules and followed My laws--he shall not die for the inequity of his father, but shall live.   (Ezek. 18:16–17)

This was a powerful statement. Previously, the Hebrews had been warned that God would revenge "the iniquity of the fathers upon the children unto the third and fourth generation" (Exodus 20:5). Now Ezekiel, in the name of God, offers people a way out: be charitable and just and God will end his wrath against future generations.

Even our current concept of family responsibility, mistakenly attributed to the English Poor Laws, has its origins in the commandment "Honor your father and your mother. . . ." (Exod. 19:3). This succinct treatment of filial responsibility and respect was later expanded in the Jewish tradition to include responsibility for relatives, particularly elderly parents (Blidstein 1975). The Babylonian Talmud was even more specific in explaining that the child should manifest both fear (respect) and honor in the following manner:

Our Rabbis taught, what is fear [respect] and what is honor? Fear means that he [the child] must neither stand in his [the parent's] place nor sit in his place nor contradict his words. Honor means that he must give him food and drink and cover [clothe] him and lead him in and out.
                    (Babylonian Talmud, Kiddushin, 31b)

Another Talmudic source says that walking in the way of God is helping the needy and showing charity and compassion for others.

Said Rabbi Hama bar Hanina: "What is the meaning of the phrase, 'After the Lord thy God ye shall walk'?" (Deut. 13:5). Is it possible for a man to walk after the divine presence? Has it not been said, 'The Lord thy God is

devouring fire?' Rather walk after the attributes of the Holy One, blessed be
He. As He clothes the naked, you clothe the naked. As He visited the sick,
you visit the sick, as He comforted mourners, so you comfort mourners.

(Sotha 14a)

These principles were also carried out in everyday life. Jewish tradition and
texts agreed that the child (usually the son, as married daughters owed their
loyalties to their new families) was obliged to care for parents, even if they
were physically or emotionally disabled. Parents were expected to provide for
their own care if they were financially able to do so. If not, the community
religious leadership could compel their children to contribute to their care. In
this respect, the ruling of Rabbi Yitzhak Al-Fassi, who lived between 1013 and
1103 in Spain and North Africa, is most revealing:

> The Rabbis ruled for Rabbi Jeremiah, some say for the son of Rabbi Jeremi-
> ah, in favor of those who hold at the expense of the father. [Yet] when the
> son profits and the father has not, we compel the son and we collect from
> him charity and we give to the father.

What is important here is not only that the child must pay for the care of his
or her parents in certain circumstances but also that the community has the
legal and moral power to enforce this obligation. The term *charity* as used
here does not mean a voluntary act, as it does today. Under Jewish tradition of
the time, communal leaders had the power to levy taxes in order to support
religious and social services. Thus, charity was tantamount to a tax or fine
collected by the communal bursar and transferred to the needy parent with
the full sanction of a religious law (Schnall 1995).

Tithing (*ma-aser*) and leaving grain and seeds in corners of the field (*pe-a*)
at the time of harvesting were commonly practiced as a means of supporting
the clergy and the poor. *Pe-a*, for example, was one of many harvesting rules
that guaranteed that some food would be left for the poor. Another practice of
long standing in many Jewish communities was caring for the needs of travelers (Loewenberg 1995). As in modern eligibility rules, however, those who
could help themselves were to do so:

> A poor man that is journeying from place to place should be given not less
> than one loaf worth of *pondion* [made from wheat], one *sela* [money], and
> four *seahs* [food]. If he spends the night he should be given what is needed
> to support him for the night. If he stays over the Sabbath he should be given

food enough for three meals. If a man has food enough for two meals he
may not take out from the [collective].   (Pe'a 8:7)

The Jewish tradition clearly favors self-reliance and community responsibility—issues that are of high currency today, as is evident in the new welfare
reform law of 1996. This tradition also holds that partnership is superior to
mere charitable relief:

May blessing come upon the one who provides relief. Better is the one who
makes loans. But the one who provides a share for the poor and holds a
stake in their success transcends them both.

                                                (Avot de Rabbi Natan, ch. 41)

In the Jewish tradition, the responsibility to help begins with one's neighbors, as is evident in the following note taken from the Mishneh Torah by
Maimonides: "The poor of your town, the poor of other towns: the poor of
your town take precedent" (Hilchot Matanot Ani'im, ch. 7, Halacha 13). In this
respect, the Talmud also dictates: "All Israel is responsible for one another." In
other words, mutual support and responsibility are to be honored and practiced because they strengthen the community as a whole and increase the likelihood that those in need will be helped. The Talmud also gives a rationale for
helping non-Jews: "For the sake of peace, the gentile poor should be supported as we support the poor of Israel." (B. Gittin, 61a)

When Jews came to the United States, most banks refused them loans or
lines of credit. Yet many Jewish immigrants had great economic success. A key
reason was the financial credit offered by some 509 loan societies and 2,367
mutual benefit societies (Feingold 1992; Tenenbaum 1993). These organizations offered small and short-term loans, which enabled Jewish immigrants to
finance small businesses or to purchase houses. The loans resembled what are
now known as micro-lending and micro-enterprises. The most famous example is the Hebrew Free Loan Society in New York. During its thirty years of
operation, the society loaned a total of $15 million to some 400,000 borrow-
ers. Because these small loans were returned in full with few exceptions, capital was always readily available. This financial arrangement was based on the
biblical teaching that states:

If you lend money to my people, to the poor among you, do not act toward
them as a creditor; exact no interest from them. . . . If you take your neighbor's garment in pledge, you must return it to him before the sun sets; it is

his only clothing, the sole covering for his skin. In what else shall he sleep? Therefore, if he cries out to Me, I will pay heed, for I am compassionate.

(Exod. 22:24–26)

One interesting issue is the Judaic attitude toward slavery. The Hebrew Bible was written at a time when slavery was common, yet it is contemptuous of those who willingly became slaves or did not seek freedom when it was available. Furthermore, those who wished to change their status from temporary slave to permanent slave were humiliated by having their ears pierced. In the same spirit, runaway slaves were not to be returned to their masters nor abused:

You shall not turn over to his master a slave who seeks refuge with you from his master. He shall live with you in any place he may choose among the settlements in your midst, wherever he pleases, you must not ill-treat him.

(Deut. 32:16–17)

CHRISTIANITY

Christianity's mandate to help others is illustrated in the parable of the Good Samaritan. In brief, the parable tells of a man traveling to Jericho who was attacked by thieves, stripped, robbed, wounded, and left for dead. A nobleman, a priest, and a Samaritan passed by, but only the Samaritan stopped to help. Jesus then said that he who showed mercy was the true neighbor and commanded his followers to do likewise. Wuthnow (1991) has found that most Christians who are engaged in helping others know this parable. The New Testament, like the Old Testament, has many references to helping the less fortunate. The passage from the Gospel of Matthew (25:31–46) is often cited as a direct command to feed the hungry, clothe the needy, help the stranger, and save the prisoner. The penalty for disobedience is "everlasting punishment."

An indication of how Christianity originally viewed charity can be found in the following statement:

Jesus said, "Beware of the scribes, who like to walk around in long robes, and to be greeted with respect at the marketplaces, and to have the best seats in the synagogues and places of honor at banquets! They devour widows' houses and for the sake of appearance say long prayers. They will receive the greater condemnation." He sat down opposite the treasury and watched the crowd putting money into the treasury [of the Temple]. Many rich people put in large sums. A poor widow came and put in two small copper coins, which are worth a penny. Then he called his disciples and said to them, "Truly I tell you, this poor widow has put in more than all those who are contributing to the treasury. For all of them have contributed out of their abundance; but she in her poverty has put in everything she had, all she had to live on."   (Mark 12:38–44)

This story, while indicative of the tradition of helping the poor that was practiced at the time, focuses attention on the giver. It says that although the wealthy may give large sums, those who sacrifice the little that they have to help others are truly the greatest givers.

In another text, Jesus tells his disciples that those who fed him when he was hungry and clothed him when he was naked will be rewarded on judgment day. When challenged by his disciples to reveal when anyone saw him hungry or naked, he responded: "When you did it to one of these [the poor and dispossessed of his time], the least of my brothers, you did it to me" (Matt. 25:31–46). Here the Christian text explicitly informs the reader that identification with Jesus involves the obligation to care for the poor.

The life of Jesus can be viewed as a ministry to the poor. In Luke 4:18–19, it is said that Jesus told the people of Nazareth:

The spirit of the Lord is upon me; because he has anointed me to preach good news to the poor. He has sent me to proclaim release to the captives and recovering of sight to the blind, to set at liberty those who are oppressed, to proclaim the acceptable year of the Lord.

Now, can there be a mission more committed to social justice and service than this? Throughout his life, Jesus was in constant conflict with the ruling elite of his day and sought to help the poor. Although he accepted well-to-do people in his camp, he made it clear that their spiritual needs were in no way superior to those of poor people. Furthermore, he saw virtue in the suffering of the oppressed and wanted to relieve their miseries not only in the next world, as in the "meek shall inherit the land," but also, and maybe even more so, in this life. It is not surprising that Jesus told Matthew that he will separate the nations by those who fed the poor, clothed the naked, and visited the prisoner. This is a clear call for followers to adhere to social justice. Hence, all Christians are called upon to model their lives after Jesus, to embrace his concern for the poor and oppressed, and to give to others who are in need.

Available research indicates that early Christian churches practiced what they preached. Ste. Croix (1981:434) noted: "The Christian churches do seem to have gone far beyond the ordinary pagan standard . . . the Church, unlike pagan associations and individuals, certainly spent very large sums on charity—perhaps a quarter of the income of its endowments." Similarly, Troeltsch (1992:80) asserted: "In the early centuries, it [charity] was directed inward toward creating a haven of mutual aid within the pagan environment. Later on, in times of great distress and misery which affected the masses of people, the Church lifted the burden from the State onto its shoulders, often creating its own centers of social service and charity." Even in medieval times, churches acted as "patrimony of the poor" under bishops' supervision. Wealthy members gave to the church, which, in turn, gave to the poor (Mollat 1986). In the first millennium, monasteries were removed from the public and concentrated on sustaining the welfare of their members. It did not take long for this to change. In the past millennium monasteries also became active in helping those in need (Queen 1996).

The Benedictines in the sixth century demanded a community care approach to service. Rule 4 of the Benedictine Order required the monks to aid the poor, clothe the naked, visit the sick, bury the dead, help the troubled, comfort the afflicted, and not forswear charity. Rule 31 required them to be particularly attentive to the needs of the sick, children, strangers, and the poor. They usually built their monasteries close to towns so that their members would have easy access to those in need.

In the thirteenth century, the Franciscans and Dominicans committed themselves to living in poverty like Jesus and the early apostles. Making their living by begging, they wandered the countryside, preaching to all who would listen. The monks were in constant contact with the poor and the despised. Both orders believed in the importance of all people and sought equal justice for everyone. Their work helped set the standard for social service in medieval Europe and led to the formation of hospices and hospitals. Thomas Aquinas, a Dominican monk of this period and one of the church's greatest theologians, wrote about charity (*caritas*) and beneficence in Question 32. He characterized charity as a disposition toward God on the part of the individual and the virtue that makes all other virtues possible. Charity, as the act of human friendship toward God, also requires love of others. Beneficence, according to Aquinas, is an act performed out of charity. He distinguished between corporal works (such as visiting the sick or clothing the naked) and spiritual works (such as counseling the doubtful and instructing the ignorant).

In 1520 Martin Luther proposed that the German authorities take responsibility for the poor and establish a "common chest" for receiving regular contributions for relief of the needy. This was a move that made Luther very popular among taxpayers and set the tone for hundreds of years of Protestant poor relief. Luther observed that few poor people were helped by the monastic system, and hence he concluded that caring for the poor is above and beyond the means of local churches. Helping the poor was a major problem, to be shared by all citizens. Luther argued that a collaboration between state and church would solve the problem. In 1525 the plan was approved and implemented. The "common chest" was innovative, as it served as the basis for taxes collected for income redistribution and a collaboration between state and church in domestic affairs.

In the seventeenth century, the work of Saint Vincent de Paul in France was a major landmark in Christian social service delivery. Vincent de Paul was no social reformer and saw no wrong in the social order of his time. In fact, he accomplished his monumental social service efforts by enlisting the financial support of the aristocracy. Some two hundred years later, Thomas Chalmers (see chapter 3) who pioneered the Charity Organization Societies would use the same approach. In 1623, de Paul founded the Congregation of the Missions, a Catholic order of priests (Lazarites), for the purpose of evangelizing and helping the rural poor. He encouraged the establishment of confraternities of charities in rural, and later city, churches. These confraternities gave church members, especially women, opportunities to fulfill their obligations to those in need by contributing money and goods and participating in organized care for the poor. De Paul's society is unique in that it was the first in the history of the Roman Catholic Church to enlist both the resources and the voluntary labor of lay church members in caring for the sick and the poor.

In 1633, during the Counter-Reformation, Saint Vincent de Paul together with Saint Louise de Marillac founded the Daughters of Charity, a unique order of uncloistered nuns who visited, bathed, fed, advised, and nursed poor people in their homes as well as in institutions such as hospitals and orphanages (Von Matt and Cognet 1960). Vincent de Paul not only preached love of the poor, he enlisted all the available resources of his time for them. The example he set of combining the church's religious mission with social ministry continues in the many social welfare organizations across the world that still bear his name.

Charity schools were the first social movements to change the nature of education. For centuries, the skills of writing and reading were reserved for the very rich and for members of the church hierarchy. Command of these skills or, more important, the lack thereof, determined one's social position.

In 1698, the Society for the Promotion of Christian Knowledge urged parish churches in England to establish schools to teach poor children to read the Bible and catechism. While the intent was to make the urban poor more moral, it also succeeded in making them more literate. Funding for the schools came from donations from business owners and rich people, and the priests conducted classes in the parish church. By 1715, some 25,000 children in London and throughout England were attending charity schools. These children were also trained to enter a trade. As such, the crusade to increase religious education resulted in an educated workforce that for many years was the backbone of civil and public structures of the British empire (Jones 1938). Even more impressive is the fact that charity schools were the first to lay the foundation for free public education, which would later become a right for all children in the Western democracies.

One concept used often in Christian teaching is agape. Agape, or agape love, is valuing, respecting, being willing to assist, and being committed to the well-being of another person who is in need. Agape love originated from the understanding of the nature of God as merciful and unconditional care provider (Keith-Lucas 1989).

A Christian denomination that is often ignored in the social work literature is the Russian Orthodox Church. In pre-Bolshevist Russia, Russian Orthodoxy was the dominant religion. This church, which originated in Byzantine Christianity, promoted the philosophy that poverty is a fact of life and not a vice. Accordingly, the poor are God's creatures who are the victims of circumstances and the tools of transcendental will. Class and wealth and inequality were seen as God's will. In Russia, the poor and feeble, the insane, and others in great need were called *oubogiye*, that is, those belonging to God or God's creatures. They were not looked down upon, but rather were considered as blessed by and belonging to God and blissfully pious (Dinello 1997; 1998). Consequently, the norm was to sympathize, help, and at times even glorify the needy rather than despise them and pressure them to work. They were considered "guilty though guiltless" victims who could not threaten the order of things (Lindenmeyr 1996).

In the sixteenth century, the Domsotroi, a Russian collection of Christian rules of behavior, was devised. This religious code of behavior required almsgiving and caring for the needy and travelers, including providing them with food and shelter.

Brian Kluth (1997), president of the Christian Fellowship Association, explained the difference between philanthropy and Christian stewardship in the following manner:

Christian stewardship is all about God. God provides resources to people; these people see themselves as managers (not owners) of God's resources. They choose to give a portion of those resources back to God; they give to ministries that advance the work of God, and they recognize that God will ultimately acknowledge the giving they did in life in the life to come.

(p. 4)

As we will show in the chapters to follow, this concept of Christian steward-ship has resulted in a large and continual stream of religious-originated and religious-oriented donations.

Hessel (1982) contended that correct Christian interpretation of the Bible requires, in addition to direct care for the needy, "service (*diakonia*) [that] has the objective of liberating persons and groups from miserable situations" (p. 147). Hessel thus concludes that Christians should be active in services that empower people. He justifies empowerment theologically by stating: "The bottom-up approach empowers people to form 'a community of the sinned-against' who struggle against policies and institutions that are in the grasp of dehumanizing principalities and powers" (p. 157).

There is a well-accepted notion that evangelists are not engaged in social care and that liberal Christians are much more involved in social care. Evan-gelicals are said to be more concerned with saving souls than with helping those in need. John Orr and his colleagues suggested that liberal and middle-of-the-road congregations tend to be more concerned with political efforts, whereas conservative religious communities tend to be more concerned with spiritual transformation, one person at a time (Orr et al. 1994). This notion, although somewhat correct, needs clarification. First, it is the fundamental-ists, not the evangelicals, who are disinterested in social service provision. Fundamentalist Protestants believe that personal growth, which comes from spiritual salvation, is the only solution to human poverty and need. Second, and more important, evangelicals and fundamentalists differ widely in their interpretations of the millennium, or Second Coming of Christ, as prophesied in the Bible. Pre-millennialist theology, which characterizes the fundamental-ists, argues that the Second Coming of Christ will take place only after the world is in total crisis. Only then will Christ return, and only then will he establish the millennium, a thousand years of righteousness and justice. Accordingly, fundamentalists believe that Christians who try to help the needy and make the world a better place are only delaying the coming of Christ. Post-millennialists, on the other hand, believe that good deeds of Christians in this world will bring about the desired millennium. This approach is in line with the Social Gospel movement and the emphasis of some evangelicals on social ministry.

In the late nineteenth and early twentieth centuries, the United States witnessed a unique nondenominational movement known as the Social Gospel. Jacob Dorn (1993) commented that the American Social Gospel was a Christian response to the massive urbanization, alienation, widening class gaps, and rapid rise of socialism and of the Socialist Party of America in particular. Dorn showed how the leading theologians of the times—Frances Greenwood Peabody, Washington Gladden, and Walter Rauschenbusch—embraced social concerns and criticism of the capitalist system in their writings. Most notable was Rauschenbusch, a German Baptist whose theology has been highly influential throughout the twentieth century. Even Dr. Martin Luther King Jr. was said to have been influenced by Rauschenbusch's attempts to bridge socialism and Christianity. As editor and contributor to a publication titled *Christian Socialist*, Rauschenbusch argued that the church and its members had a responsibility to promote social justice. He asserted that, of all social institutions, only business was not already "Christianized." In his 1907 book, *Christianity and the Social Crisis*, Rauschenbusch endorsed socialistic ideas. He believed that the true call of Christianity is not merely to prepare individuals for the kingdom of God to come, but to cultivate a just and harmonious society that reflects the spirit of Jesus and the prophets. He was endorsing not revolution but the evolution of a more just society, grounded in public morality. In his view, Jesus was a Hebrew prophet who came to prepare human beings for the righteous social order, which included caring for the needy. He also noted that Jesus and all the other prophets had sided with the poor and oppressed and condemned the rich who exploited them. In this respect, Rauschenbusch laid the groundwork for liberation theology, which will be discussed in chapter 9.

The new Catechism of the Catholic Church (1994) states: "Charity is the greatest social commandment" (1889). The Catechism also states that equity is a divine command: "The decisive point of the social question is that goods created by God for everyone should in fact reach everyone in accordance with justice and with the help of charity" (2459). More specifically the Catechism contends that it is the role of the state "to make accessible to each what is needed to lead a truly human life: food, clothing, health, work, education and culture, suitable information, the right to establish a family, and so on" (1908).

One recent development regarding Christian teaching and social services came from Canada. In October 1997, the Right Reverend Bill Phipps, moderator (head) of the United Church of Canada, the largest Protestant denomination in Canada, publicly declared that Jesus was not divine, but merely a very good man. He said: "Jesus would never claim to be God. . . . As a good Jew, Jesus would be appalled to think he was God." Reverend Phipps argues that the church has spent too much time focusing on the afterlife and not enough on working with the poor and the oppressed. He adds that, in any case, the business of Christianity was with the poor and disadvantaged and not theological musings. Phipps believes that faith is no longer a key part of our social sphere and that public policy decisions, such as cutting welfare, are missing a moral core. He is reported to state to his congregations that "the way of Jesus has everything to do with the Kyoto summit on global warming, on dealing with child hunger, on helping the homeless" (Dreidger 1997:47).

It should be emphasized that Phipps's claim surprised (and outraged) many in the church and attracted wide attention from the media. Even so, the dissension focused solely on the moderator's position about Jesus, not on social activism as a way to exhibit a Christian way of life. The former moderator of the United Church of Canada agreed with Reverend Phipps, saying that this is the current teaching in theological schools. It should be noted that the United Church itself, formed in 1925 as a result of the union of most Canadian Methodists (historically in the forefront of the Social Gospel movement in Canada), a majority of Canadian Presbyterians, and most of the much smaller group of Congregationalists, has usually downplayed theology in favor of an activist temper (McCarthy and Andersen 1997). This is a denomination that, after a bitter dispute, decided in 1968 to ordain gay men and women. It is the same denomination that, some ten years ago, chose to omit any references to God as "He" in its liturgy and revised its hymnal accordingly.

In sum, for Christians around the world, care for the poor is both theological teaching and mandate. In later chapters we will see how this theological expectation has manifested itself, historically and currently, in the United States.

ISLAM

Islam, like Judaism and Christianity, places a high value on charitable acts and giving. The Qur'an emphasizes the importance of *zakat*, which literally means "to thrive or to be wholesome." In practice, *zakat* is a contribution or tax on property that is earmarked for the poor, the needy, those in captivity, debtors, travelers in need, and those who serve Islam (Zayas 1960). The Qur'an also calls for the practice of *sadaqah*, which is a voluntary giving to those in need.

As in Judaism and Christianity, charity and social responsibility in Islam are moral obligations rooted in the belief that the world belongs to God and not to people. As such, giving is a statement about one's belief in God.

El Azayem and Hedayat-Diba (1994) noted that giving alms to the needy is one of the five pillars of the Islamic faith and that the Qur'an states that divine punishment and reward are determined by the extent to which the faithful fulfill these five principles. The other principles include: belief in one God and in Muhammad as his prophet, the saying of prayers five times daily, fasting during the month of Ramadan, and a pilgrimage to Mecca.

The call for alms appears in the Qur'an more than a hundred times, and true believers know that they cannot be fully Muslim and approved by God unless they heed his call. This expectation of almsgiving is made clear in the following paragraph:

> Righteousness does not consist in whether you face towards the East or the West. The righteous man is he who believes in God and the Last day, in the angels and the Book of the Prophets; who though he loves it dearly, gives away his wealth to kinsfolk, to orphans, to the destitute, to the traveler in need and to beggars, and for the redemption of captives; who attends to his prayers and renders the alms levy; who is true to his promises and steadfast in trial and adversity and in times of war. Such are the true believers; such are the God-fearing. (The Cow 2:177).

As to the question of how much one is expected to give to these charitable causes, the answer is quite clear: "One-fifth of your spoils shall belong to God, the Apostle, the Apostle's kinsfolk, the orphans, the destitute, and those that travel the road" (The Spoils 8:41).

In Islam, almsgiving is also a means to compensate for the inability to perform religious rites. For example, someone too weak to fast during Ramadan can postpone the fast. Of those unable to fast at any time, it is said: "For those of you who cannot endure it [the fast] there is a ransom: the feeding of a poor man" (The Cow 2:184). Similarly, if one has broken an oath, the penalty is feeding the poor: "The penalty for a broken oath is the feeding of ten needy men with such food as you normally offer to your own people; or the clothing of ten needy men; or the freeing of one slave" (The Table 5:89). Incidentally, the poor who cannot follow these expensive practices must fast for three days as the penalty for breaking an oath.

Similar to the distinctions made by the Jewish scholar Maimonides regarding the eight levels of charity, noted earlier in this chapter, the Qur'an also distinguishes between types of giving. The highest type of giver is one who gives willingly and who treats the person in need with dignity and respect. Giving with scorn and disdain, according to Islamic theology, is equal to not giving. The following excerpt from the Qur'an demonstrates distinction:

> Those that give their wealth for the cause of God and do not follow their almsgiving with taunts and insults shall be rewarded by their Lord; they shall have nothing to fear or regret. A kind word with forgiveness is better than charity with insult. God is self-sufficient and indulgent. Believers, do not mar your almsgiving with taunts and mischief-making, like those who spend their wealth for the sake of ostentation and believe neither in God nor in the Last Day. Such men are like a rock covered with earth: a shower falls upon it and leaves it hard and bare. They shall gain nothing from their works. But those that give away their wealth from a desire to please God and to reassure their own souls are like a garden on a hill-side: if a shower falls upon it, it yields up twice its normal produce; and if no rain falls, it is watered by the dew. God takes cognizance of all your actions.
>
> (The Cow 2:262–65)

Later on, believers are told that giving in public (where pride is high and praises are certain to come) is inferior to giving in private (where the generous act is not publicly celebrated). The believer is also instructed to treat people of lower social status with respect when they come to eat: "It shall be no offense to the blind, the lame, and the sick, to eat at your table" (Light 24:56).

Care for the family is an important aspect of Islam. Sura 4, for example, is totally devoted to family rules and expectations. It also provides clear instructions on how to handle family matters such as marital problems. Islam, like other monotheistic religions, calls for respect and care for the elderly. The Qur'an states: "Thy Lord hath decreed that ye worship none but Him, and that ye be kind to parents. Whether one or both of them attain old age in their life, say not to them a word of contempt, nor repeal them, but address them in terms of honor" (Sura 17:23). The joint mention of parental respect with the first principle of Islam (one God) shows the immense importance that the Qur'an places on this teaching.

In sum, the tenets of these three great monotheistic religious traditions—Judaism, Christianity, and Islam—have helped shape both the social values and the institutions that are the foundation of modern social services provision in the secular and religious arenas. Provision of services to the poor, orphans and widows, sick and disabled, prisoners and captives, travelers, and neighbors in times of calamity was both emphasized and fostered in the early

Jewish, Christian, and Muslim traditions (Loewenberg 1995; Hinson 1988), and this spirit of faith-based service remains strong among the modern-day followers of these faith traditions.

In the following section, we discuss two nonmonotheistic religions and assess their focus on helping others as a religious tenet.

BUDDHISM AND HINDUISM

We recognize that the placing of these two great southeast Asia religions in one section provides each with too little space in which to examine its rich charitable tradition. We resort to this approach only because their followers represent a very small portion of American society.

Gautama Buddha established the foundations for Buddhism about 500 B.C. He predicated Buddhism on sympathy to poor people and the virtue of poverty. Many Buddhists undertook to become—rather than support—beggars, as begging was considered breeding ground for many virtues such as modesty and appreciation of simplicity. This made possible a life of contemplation, which was considered the only justification of human existence. Others, who did not choose the life of a beggar, were expected never to pass a beggar without giving alms and never to refuse a request for supporting a philanthropic cause (Conze 1959).

In Buddhism, the one who practices charity and compassion is born to a state that moves him or her closer to Nirvana. It is believed that positive acts radiate positive karma, and in the same way negative acts radiate negative karma. Thus, all life is interdependent and reciprocity is a central influence in the Buddhist tradition. There remains, however, the deterministic belief that only a few will succeed in life, and the poor provide an opportunity for others to give in order to improve their karma. Kings in China were encouraged to care for the poor and address persistent social problems as a means to enhance their karma.

In Buddhism the individual's own welfare is linked to the welfare of others. Hence all people are viewed as equal. Buddhism rejects the categories and class restrictions that are imposed by society and seeks to assist all in their quest for enlightenment. For example, during the third century B.C., King Akosa of India practiced this principle and rejected the oppression of the caste system. Instead, he chose to offer a humanitarian system that provided women's welfare, criminal welfare, rural development, and free medical care. For King Akosa the welfare of the people was a priority, and he used taxes to care for the poor. Influenced by his Buddhist religion, King Akosa established the greatest welfare state of his day (Ghafur and Mannon 1968). In Japan, Buddhist temples were the first to provide a refuge for battered Japanese women (Suksamran 1977).

Voluntary giving is expected and viewed as a natural reflection of the quest for self-enlightenment as well as the desire to assist others in their quest. In some temple-centered Buddhist communities, a significant amount of an individual's wages is transferred to the temple. Suksamran (1977) reported that as much as 55 percent of an individual's total income can be contributed to temples in Thailand. In Cambodian peasant societies, resources contributed to the "monk sector" are used to provide social services such as health care and education (Ebihara 1966).

Snelling (1991) noted that the role of giving in Buddhism defines what it means to be a Buddhist. Gloria Goodwin Raheja (1988) recounted a story about Jaisal, a great Indian king, and Jagdev Panwer, a lesser king. It is said that Jaisal's wife told her husband that Jagdev Panwer was known as the greatest giver of *dan* (charity). Jaisal responded that he would give ten times more than Jagdev Panwer. Jagdev Panwer went home and asked his wife what he could give to remain the greatest giver, and she scolded him for trying to compete with a king as rich as Jaisal. Jagdev Panwer responded that he must compete, as the heritage of his kingdom dictated: "We can never be defeated; in place of wealth or pomp, we can give our lives." Jagdev Panwer then gave his head as a *dan*, the only thing that Jaisal could not give ten times over. The great king Jaisal had to admit defeat and acknowledged that "a greater *dan* than that could never be given." When Jagdev Panwer's head was returned to his wife, she reconnected it to his body and asked that he live. Her request was granted, and all people chanted: "Victory to Jagdev Panwer, the greatest giver of *dan*."

While this story could be viewed as calling for meaningless sacrifice, it can also be viewed as calling for ordinary people, not only kings, to try to outdo one another in acts of compassion and charity. For any religion to promote charity to such an extent is quite impressive. Compare this story about the greatest giver, who after giving all he could, was rewarded with his life and public acceptance, with the story of modern capitalism, which sees little wrong in the exploitation of others. The latter is the opposite of the Buddhist tradition, which holds that the better person is the one who gives the most.

The concept of nonviolence (*ashima*) has been central to most of India's religious and philosophical traditions since the Vedic period (1500–900 B.C.) and is clearly demonstrated in the classical Hindu text of the Upanishads.

Chekki (1993) noted that the Hindu, Buddhist, Jain, and Devotional religions, philosophies, and social reform movements have all valued nonviolence. Philosophers, writers, and religious leaders of all these traditions have continued to develop the concept of nonviolence from the eighteenth century B.C. to the present day. The most well-known example is Mahatma Ghandi, who advocated nonviolence as a national ethic and succeeded in liberating India from British domination by means of nonviolent disobedience. Ghandi argued that religion and nonviolence must be lived as well as preached. Although this approach of tolerance and respect to others is not uniquely Hindu, it is an important part of this tradition.

The Upanishads of Hinduism also make clear references to almsgiving and support of people in need. We are told that "the eighty verses [of the hymn] are alike food with reference to the gods as well as with references to men. For all those beings breathe and live by means of food indeed. By food (given in alms, etc.) he conquers this world, by food (given in sacrifice) he conquers the other" (Aitareya-Aranyaka, 2 Aranyaka, 1 Adhyaya, 2 Khanda:13). Like the monotheistic religions, the Hindu writing of the Upanishads makes it clear that the one who is generous to others will benefit while others will suffer. The following is one such example:

> Let him never turn away [a stranger] from his house, that is the rule. Therefore a man should by all means acquire much food, for [good] people say [to the stranger]: "There is food ready for him." If he gives food amply, food is given to him amply. If he gives food fairly, food is given to him fairly. If he gives food meanly, food is given to him meanly.
>
> (Taittiriyaka, Upanishad, 3 Valli, 10 Anuvaka:1)

These few references to Buddhist and Hindu texts and traditions are meant only to demonstrate that even nonmonotheistic religions call for support of the poor and the needy. In fact, all religions acknowledge that for a society to survive, members (believers) must assist those in need. With the increase of migration from Southeast Asia to the United States, the importance of Buddhist and Hindu tradition on social service delivery and on public social policy will most likely grow to reflect these rich traditions.

The Hindu religious community is most identified with the inequalities of the caste system, a belief in reincarnation, and a belief that poverty is inevitable. The Hindu faith tradition teaches social harmony and social order that is best reflected in collective responsibility among families, clans, and castes. Although the Hindu views being poor as a personal condition and the result of karma, the community remains responsible to care for the poor. Individual responsibility to perform actions that will gain merit in the next life and responsibility for the collective has created the motivation for giving to those in need. Gift giving not only became a religious ritual and means to distribute wealth among members of a clan but also a means to gain status for the donor and recipient of the gift. *Dana*, the act of giving, and *daks'ina*, gifts displaying purity and respect, were made to priests as sacrificial gifts or exchanges and redistribution of wealth among clan members. In the early Vedic (1700–1600 B.C.) period, *dana* was a protection and right for the disadvantaged and a means to address social problems. *Dana* later became the duty of all clan and tribe members to ensure the well-being of others as a means to accumulate merit and improve one's karma.

In addition to giving, education has also contributed to the social welfare of the poor. The Hindu shastra categorized charity as *arthadan, abhoydan*, and *vidyadan*. The practice of *vidyadan* allowed a student to study at the home of a guru without the payment of tuition (Ghafur and Mannon 1968). Although Kautilya (cited in Ghafur and Mannon 1968) wrote: "In the happiness of his subjects lies the happiness of the king; in their welfare," and again, "The king shall maintain the orphan, the aged, the infirm, the afflicted and the helpless," only a few rulers were known for this kind of generous charity. At the end of every five years Harsha distributed the surplus of his wealth as a service of divine merit (Ghafur and Mannon 1968).

This chapter has illustrated that the major faith traditions have theological and historical backgrounds that are strongly in favor of social justice and helping the poor. We have shown that these religions call upon their followers to help the needy, assist their neighbors, and even aid strangers. Our intent is not to show that religious people are better citizens and are more concerned with issues of equality and social services provision than nonreligious people, but to demonstrate that religious tenets, regardless of faith tradition, are prosocial, if only in the sense that they foster a just and supportive community of believers. These tenets are taught to children and adults in official religious classes and through reading of religious texts. We are not claiming that such teaching directly influences behavior. Without such tenets that are very much in line with the key principles of social work, however, less social care and concern would have been present in our social discourse.

We are well aware that there is often a wide discrepancy between what religion says ought to be done and what members of a religion actually do. In this respect, we quote Huston Smith (1958):

The full story of religion is not rose-colored. It is not all insight and inspiration. It is often crude; charity and wisdom are often rare, and the net
expressions bizarre when not revolting. A balanced view of man's religions
would record its perversions as well as its glories. It would include human
sacrifice and scapegoating, fanaticism and persecution, the Christian Crusades and the holy wars of Islam. It would include witch hunts in Massachusetts, monkey trials in Tennessee, and snake worship in the Ozarks—the
list has no end.   (p. 4)

The list of atrocities and harms attributed to the religious community can
indeed go on and on. But, as Smith suggested, we need a balanced view. While
acknowledging that the religious community has been a force for positive
change, empowerment, and above all, support for the needy, it must also be
acknowledged that it has been a force for regression and control. It is important that we recognize both the good and the evil that has been done in the
name of religion. This knowledge, however, should not stand in the way of a
collaboration between social work and the religious community's prosocial
forces. Such a collaboration could be enormously effective in carrying out the
social work mandate to help the needy and those who are discriminated
against in society.

CHAPTER 6
RELIGIOUS ROOTS OF AMERICA'S SOCIAL
SERVICES SYSTEM

The link between social services and health care and religion in America can be traced back to early days of the nation. Rosenberg (1987) noted that, in the eighteenth century, "American communities had grown proud of their hospitals; ethnic and religious groups saw their institutions as symbols of community identity and respectability" (p. 9). The influence of religion on American democratic institutions was noted by Alexis de Tocqueville, a French political philosopher who wrote in 1835: "Religion, which never intervenes directly in the government of American society, should therefore be considered as the first of their political institutions, for although it did not give them the taste for liberty, it singularly facilitates their use thereof" (Tocqueville 1969:292). Similarly, Leiby (1978) wrote: "Religious ideas were the most important intellectual influence on American welfare institutions in the nineteenth century" (p. 2). In her 1969 book *Perspectives in Public Welfare*, Blanche D. Coll stated that religious involvement in municipal social services is a legacy from English colonial rule. In prerevolutionary Virginia, for example, many Anglican clergy also served as municipal Poor Law officials, who had responsibility for the old, the sick, the deserted, and the illegitimate children of their communities. To understand the significant role that religion has played in forming our current social services system, it is necessary to consider America's historic religious tradition from its earliest days (1620) to modern times (1935).

One factor that had significant influence on the earliest beginnings of the American social system was colonization and the tension it brings between Old World and new practices. In the seventeenth century, those who fled religious and political persecution in Europe also left behind a tradition of the state as a social regulator and provider for those in need. They wanted the personal freedom that the New World offered, yet initially they still clung to many Old World traditions, especially that of the Elizabethan Poor Laws for helping those in need. But all that was to change as these first colonists began to blaze a new path in social welfare. Instead of relying on the state, they relied increasingly on voluntary help grounded in their own religious beliefs and in the power of their communities—expressed most effectively through the religious congregations of the New World.

In this chapter we examine the historical argument for the claim that the roots of America's social services system lay in America's religious community.

THE COLONIAL ERA (1620–1775)

Contrary to popular assumption, the colonial church of the seventeenth and eighteenth centuries played only a minor role in social services provision, although it was an important social institution in all of the colonies. Most civic leaders of the day were church members, and the best-educated and most-respected people in the community were usually the local pastors. The American church of colonial times, however, was not a benevolent institution per se. Most colonies had their own established religions, and the civil authority was empowered to punish those who persisted in false beliefs. This society of true believers, which tightly tied civil order to common doctrine, began to focus more on the welfare of people in the community only with the separation of church and state, a slow process that began with the passage of the First Amendment, which barred Congress from making any law "respecting an establishment of religion." The process became complete in 1833, when Massachusetts forswore Congregationalism as the state church. In fact, it took the combined efforts of Thomas Jefferson and James Madison to disestablish the church in Virginia during the same era that the new nation was born.

The institutional or state church in colonial America had immense power and influence. These churches were supported by taxes imposed on believers and unbelievers alike, willing or unwilling. Other forms of religions were strongly discouraged or even sanctioned. Clergymen were accountable only to their ecclesiastical superiors. In colonial days, membership in the established church was often a formal prerequisite for holding public office, serving on a jury, or sharing in the distribution of common and undivided lands. People of other denominations or religions were viewed as lesser citizens and often refused residency. Moreover, the formation of dissenting congregations was often forbidden or strongly discouraged, and the advocacy of unorthodox views punished. Even in those colonies—Rhode Island, Maryland, and Pennsylvania—founded on a belief in religious tolerance, no question was more complex or more persistently vexing than that of the status of the church in relation to civil government. As such, the American church of the period followed the European tradition and did not seek a new path.

The power of the institutional church was immense in the early colonial period and focused almost exclusively on matters of theology and belief, such as Puritanism. Puritanism was not a fixed body of beliefs, however, but a general doctrinal tendency about which leading ministers and laymen differed on major points of detail. Historian Peter Dobkin Hall reported that institutional crises related to the church authority came early, beginning with the Antinomian controversy of 1636, in which some of the Massachusetts colony's most prosperous and outspoken inhabitants challenged the authority of the ministry to dictate doctrine to congregations. The Antinomians were prosecuted and exiled. One of their leaders, Roger Williams, fled to Rhode Island, where he established a colony founded on liberty of conscience, whose government eschewed the power of the state to interfere in religious matters. Surprisingly, even in this state a state church was established. In this respect the sources of information and examples regarding the nexus between organized religion and welfare provision that are listed below represent some exceptions that only later, after disestablishment, became the norm.

Some key limitations of the establishment system should be mentioned here. While clergy salaries are financially secured and legally preferred under the wings of the state, the clergy are not compelled to make special efforts to recruit new members, revive their preaching, or manifest a dynamic leadership style. This being the case, clergy are not accountable to their congregants but are the local representatives of the state and its church. Furthermore, religious leaders are discouraged from speaking or acting against the state and its politicians, else they will lose monetary support. In the establishment system, clergy are also discouraged from developing social ministries, as such efforts are difficult to organize and unnecessary to establish the credibility and importance of the church in the community. In fact, in most European countries the state supports one or a few religions (churches), and the level of congregational involvement in local social welfare programs is minimal, for churches rely on the political power and social will of the state to act in behalf of those in need (see, for example, Chandler 1997).

Most communities in the colonial era were small in size, with usually less than a thousand inhabitants, and their means were quite limited. Thus, they were able to support only a small number of people, all of whom had to be deserving poor approved by the community. One religious leader, Cotton Mather, distinguished among the poor in his famous *Essays to Do Good* (1710), stating: "If there be any idle persons among [your neighbors], I beseech you, cure them of their idleness. Don't nourish 'em and harden 'em in that, but find employment for them" (cited in O'Connell 1983:46). This religious and economic tradition of differentiating the worthy and unworthy poor entered mainstream American thinking on welfare and even today is believed and practiced.

In seventeenth-century America, care for the poor followed the English tradition in that it was legally and socially based on the Elizabethan Poor Laws. These statutes called for low geographical mobility, care by relatives prior to communal responsibility, less eligibility criteria, and appointment of official overseers of the poor. In most New England towns church officials seldom served as municipal Poor Law officials, whereas in Virginia, Anglican church officials often served in this capacity (Coll 1969). Yet, even in Virginia, Anglican officials acted on behalf of the local authority and not on behalf of the church. Peter Dobkin Hall noted that in 1610 Sir Thomas Gates, "Knight and Lieutenant General," set forth "Articles, Laws, and Orders, Diune, Politique, and Martial for the Colony in Virginia." Notably absent from the articles is any notion of voluntary activity: Everything is dictated from and by the government, including religious obligations. Charity as a personal or Christian expression goes unmentioned.

With the exception of Virginia, churches in prerevolutionary America, like those in Europe, were seldom involved in the daily provision of social services to people in need. As most accounts from this era clearly demonstrate, responsibility for the provision of welfare was municipal, and towns disagreed on whether responsibility for the care of the poor should be based on place of birth or place of residency. By the end of the colonial era, religious involvement in care for those in need was to take a new turn, namely, the formation of new nonprofit corporations, for the provision of social services.

Denominational attempts to develop services in the colonial era had a significant impact. During the early 1700s, Philadelphia Quakers included help for the poor on the agenda of their monthly meetings, and the members discussed what and how much to give, usually in the form of food, clothing, shelter, and coal. In 1713 the Quakers also established the Friends Almshouse to provide relief to the poor (Compton 1980). In 1724 the Episcopalians established the Boston Episcopal Society to provide help to members in need (Axinn and Levin 1992). As early as 1729 in New Orleans, the Ursuline Sisters established the first home for children (including an orphanage) and their mothers who were the victims of the Indian massacres. Religious-based social services providers encouraged acts of charity and hence supported the practice of outdoor relief. For example, during the severe winter of 1761–1762, the Quakers distributed fuel stamps that could be redeemed for wood. According to Day (1997), it was during the colonial era that partnerships between the public overseers and churches began to be established. Churches, for example, were asked to take up collections to be used for support of public dependents. Other examples of mutual responsibility were soon to become the rule rather than the exception.

Universalists, Unitarians, and many other religious groups of the day believed that all able-bodied persons should be responsible for the needs of their own families. In chapter 1, we noted the influence of this sociotheological orientation in today's conservative ideology. Community support was available only for the deserving poor: those who could not help themselves but were deemed worthy of assistance were supported by the community. In most instances, the town officials were responsible for provision of support. It must be remembered, however, that in most colonies, civic officials and church leaders were often one and the same. Furthermore, the impact of the values of established religion was very strong when it came to deciding whether an individual was deserving of help.

FROM INDEPENDENCE TO THE INDUSTRIAL AGE (1776–1896)

An important figure in American welfare development was Mathew Carey (1760–1839). Carey, a Dublin news printer, had settled in Philadelphia, where he started a newspaper with the help of the Marquis de Lafayette. Carey was deeply interested in economic development issues, particularly the impact of industrialization on urban populations. Though concerned with religious and moral issues, as a political economist he concentrated his attention on the causes of poverty and the role of voluntary organizations in its amelioration. In 1792 he organized one of the first immigrant mutual aid organizations, the Hibernian Society for the Relief of Immigrants from Ireland, and helped found the nation's first Sunday School Society. Carey's arguments regarding welfare for people in need were based on economics rather than charity.

For Carey, helping the poor was a means of empowering them. In turn, this economic empowerment benefited the wider society. Similarly, voluntary philanthropy on the part of the wealthy was not only morally praiseworthy, it decreased the likelihood of enforced taxation. Carey also argued that voluntary organizations were more efficient and effective than government in meeting the needs of the poor—the same argument used today by neoconservatives and supporters of small government. In sum, he considered benevolence to be a social investment that yields both economic and moral returns. And finally, Carey was among the first to recognize that American women were assuming a central role in philanthropy and voluntary associations during the 1830s. He recognized that religious and civic welfare and advocacy organizations provided a legitimate avenue for women to leave home and engage in an educating mission. Although Carey's work and writing influenced both secular and religious social involvement, he viewed his work as originating from a moral and religious background that shaped his perception and advocacy (Baltzell 1958; Carey 1942).

In 1826 Joseph Tuckerman, a Unitarian clergyman from Boston, initiated "ministry-at-large" in response to the devastating economic depression of 1819. He proposed that the church should help needy families, regardless of their religious affiliations—a revolutionary idea at the time. Tuckerman at first was interested mostly in the spiritual needs of the poor, but seeing their desperate poverty, he became engrossed in such issues as housing conditions, wages, public education, delinquency, and public relief. He responded by organizing a company of visitors to the poor in 1832 and an interdenominational union of ministers to provide mutual help and consultation in 1833. These initiatives paved the way for the formation in 1834 of the Association of Delegates from the Benevolent Societies of Boston, with Tuckerman as its leader (Watson 1922).

Tuckerman had been a protégé of the influential William Ellery Channing, who categorically assumed that poverty was the fault of the individual and that the only remedy for poverty was spiritual salvation. After working with the poor, however, Tuckerman—and later Channing—realized that destitution was attributable more to social than to spiritual conditions and that poor people, even though saved, could do very little to uplift themselves socially and economically. Tuckerman anticipated today's social wage by suggesting that salary levels should provide enough for a respectable living. He also noted that the income of many working women was below subsistence level.

Hopkins (1940) referred to Tuckerman's ministry-at-large as the first serious attempt by a religious group to deal with the social and moral problems of the underclass in any large city in North America. At the same time that Tuckerman was active in Boston, the New York Mission and Tract Society was ministering to the poor and the imprisoned as well as to new immigrants. The society also provided temporary assistance to poor families and helped the unemployed find jobs.

Leonard Bacon summarized the concept of religious-based service in a sermon titled "The Christian Doctrine of Stewardship in Respect to Property," which he presented at the Young Men's Benevolent Society in New Haven in 1832. In this sermon, which was later published and widely circulated, he said that people must actively seek out ways to do what God expects of them. Such actions must extend to all aspects of life and link voluntary service and personal philanthropy as a means of doing God's will. Bacon's thinking on the role of religion and voluntary organizations in social welfare ran counter to that of the Jeffersonian and Jacksonian camps. Yet for many of his day, it was Bacon who best answered the moral question "Lord, what wilt thou have me do?" And the answer he gave was "the BUSINESS OF DOING GOOD" [sic]. Thus, Bacon's directive sparked the rise of church-affiliated civic associations that sought to spread the Word of the Lord and do good for others. In many ways, Bacon laid the moral ground for religious-based philanthropy that reflected the donor's religious beliefs.

Voluntary societies, another form of benevolent activity, came into being in the eighteenth and nineteenth centuries. These organizations, often born of religious awakenings in England and America, were independent bodies formed for particular social, missionary, or benevolent endeavors. For example, efforts to respond to the needs of those with disabilities resulted in the establishment of agencies such as the Hartford Asylum for the Education and Instruction of the Deaf and Dumb, under the leadership of the Reverend Thomas Gallaudet, and the Hartford Retreat for the Insane, founded in 1822–1824 (Ahlstrom 1972).

Conrad Wright (1992) noted that New Englanders, convinced of the efficacy of organized philanthropy, formed organizations for the relief of the poor, the care of orphans, the conversion of Indians, the spread of the Gospel, the comfort of the imprisoned, and other worthy causes. These new organizations of the early Republic made a profound impression upon American society in two ways. First, they served as models for the benevolent crusades of the antebellum years. Second, they established the modern eleemosynary corporation in America, the forerunner of twentieth-century philanthropic organizations. Religious involvement in health and welfare was the norm in all parts of the American city. For example, in Chicago, the churches were in the forefront of those who provided care to people in need. During the 1849 cholera epidemic, it was reported that Chicago's poorhouse was so badly overcrowded that orphan children were turned away. This caused such an uproar that the local

Protestant churches joined together to build the first orphan asylum in Chicago (McCarthy 1982).

Oates (1995) noted that in 1797 Philadelphia Catholic parishioners met to organize an orphanage for children whose parents had died following an outbreak of yellow fever. By 1806 they had established the Roman Catholic Society of St. Joseph for the Maintenance and Education of Orphans to support the St. Joseph Orphan Asylum and hired a matron as manager. In New York, in the mid-1830s, Bishop John Dubios ordered that all church collections on Christmas Day go to the care of orphans. In 1838 he allocated all collections on Easter Sunday to that purpose as well. These collections were the forerunner of the Campaign for Human Development, which annually distributes some $50 million to community-based social services that address poverty and empowerment. Early Catholic welfare work was not limited to forming institutions. For example, in 1836 the women of St. Peter's Parish in Cincinnati formed the Martha and Mary Society. Each member paid $1.50 a year, and each month they "elected a committee of eight people to identify the destitute, give them spiritual as well as temporal relief, and report their situation to the membership the following month" (Oates 1995:8). In fact, social service was so central to Catholicism in America that many nineteenth-century Catholic orders were first founded in order to operate a particular school, orphanage, or hospital (Misner 1988).

In 1835 the Young Catholic's Friend Society was formed in Boston's Cathedral Parish. Its goal was to teach and give in-kind help to poor neighborhood children. It should be noted that all of the above took place at a time when Catholics made up less than 4 percent of the American population. Jay Dolan (1992) reported that in 1896 the Holy Family Parish of Chicago's West Side had at least twenty-five spiritual, recreational, educational, and charitable societies, with a combined membership of more than ten thousand.

In 1817 the New York Society for the Prevention of Pauperism was formed. Between 1818 and 1824 this society published annual reports that traced the origins of pauperism. Ironically, among the causes of poverty, the last one of a list of ten was the numerous charitable institutions of the city. In the 1840s, Robert M. Hartley, through the Evangelical New York Tract Society, established the New York Association for the Improvement of the Condition of the Poor (AICP), a pioneer welfare program that he led for more than thirty years. In addition to his work in the AICP, Hartley was also a leading figure in the City Temperance Society. AICP was a nonsectarian regional organization, predicated on the services of "friendly visitors," all of whom were men. It should be noted that there were already thirty to forty sectarian charitable societies in New York, but during the economic turbulence of the 1840s, the resources of many of these charitable societies had been depleted. AICP's major contribution to the history of welfare was that it allocated service by dividing the city into 278 small sections and appointing friendly visitors to be in charge of each section, whereas services had previously been provided on the basis of nationality and/or type of need citywide. Before AICP granted material assistance, a friendly visitor would meet with the family and try to assess whether an agency could best meet the family's needs or AICP should provide in-kind support in the form of coal, food, or clothing; AICP, on principle, did not provide cash support. The friendly visitors also attempted to improve housing conditions, resolve health problems, and enhance child welfare. In fact, it was AICP's campaign that brought the first State Legislative Commission to investigate the tenement problem in New York. In addition, AICP advocated actively for compulsory education and the appointment of truancy officers because it saw free public education as the key to social and spiritual uplifting. In 1847 the association required every client to abstain from alcohol, send young children to school, and apprentice older children (Watson 1922). In 1852 AICP built a public washing-and-bathing institution and a year later enacted legislation to provide care and instruction for idle truant children.

The case of the First Baptist Church in Philadelphia illustrates the development of welfare under congregational auspices. In 1839 women in the congregation formed the Evangelical Sewing Society to sew for the poor. In 1873 the same congregation established the Baptist Orphanage, later known as Baptist Children's Services. A few years later, the congregation established the Philadelphia Home for Incurables. The facility is still in operation as an advanced-care center for people with severe disabilities and mobility problems. Today it is known as Inglis House (Thompson 1989). Another Baptist congregation in Philadelphia active at the time was the Baptist Temple, headed by Russell H. Conwell. Along with an impressive array of social services, in 1884 Conwell established a night school for working people so that those from a lower economic status could have an opportunity to advance their social and occupational standing in society. Conwell's night school was to become Temple University, one of the largest universities in Philadelphia. Conwell and his congregants also founded Samaritan Hospital with its auxiliary dispensaries and visiting-nurse services (Abell 1943).

Just as social services were rooted in religious tradition, so were social reform and advocacy. The following two examples demonstrate this point. Margaret Prior, the first missionary employed by the New York Female Moral

Reform Society, in 1837, helped prostitutes secure more acceptable employment. She also wrote extensively to dispel the stereotypes of prostitutes as evil temptresses, showing instead how they were the victims of a cycle of poverty and abuse (Gifford 1981). Susan Brownell Anthony, another nineteenth-century woman involved in social reform, was also an advocate for women's rights. Contrary to prevailing notions, she held that men were drunkards and women were the abused. She even suggested that wives should avoid having sex or children with husbands who were alcoholic—a subject that many felt a single woman should not discuss (Riegel 1980).

The 1870s saw the rise of regional and national conferences devoted to welfare. In 1872 the first meeting of charities representatives and correction people from three Midwestern states (Michigan, Wisconsin, and Illinois) took place at Sherman House. This was the modest beginning of the National Conference of Charities and Corrections. Two years later, in New York, a conference, held under the auspices of the American Social Sciences Association, was chaired by F. R. Sanborn of Massachusetts, William P. Letchworth of New York, and H. H. Giles of Wisconsin. The proceedings of that meeting indicate that key issues were care for the insane, residency rules and practices, and building a questionnaire to study juvenile delinquency. What is of interest for our purposes in this book is that almost two-thirds of the participants were church officials.

In 1876 John W. Kramer, assistant pastor at St. Mary's Church in New York City, published his *Manual for Visitors of the Poor*. In this fifty-six-page book, Kramer provided advice on how church visitors should conduct themselves during a visit, as well as procedures for keeping case records, rules of assistance, and issues of morality. This publication is important because it indicated that church visitors were so numerous that there was a need for a training manual. Surprisingly, many of Kramer's suggestions are still valid today.

Another key figure in the mid-nineteenth-century social services arena was Charles Loring Brace. Brace studied for the ministry and worked as a missionary with prisoners on Blackwell's Island just outside New York City. He left this ministry in 1853 to establish the Children's Aid Society, and he remained its executive officer for almost forty years. One of Brace's solutions for the city's growing social problems was to find foster families for at-risk children among Christian farmers in the West. Another was to teach religion to New York's many street children and, if possible, provide them with some form of education. The society also employed twelve doctors and four nurses, who provided care for sick children. The Children's Aid Society is still active today in many child welfare projects, though the practice of farming children out ceased to exist more than a century ago (Bremner 1972).

An 1851 book by Stephen Colwell, *New Themes for the Protestant Clergy*, was influential in redirecting the attention of churches to those in need. In this book Colwell criticized Protestant leaders for bickering about theology among themselves while neglecting the masses that need salvation. He urged churches and pastors to extend Christian charity to all people, including the poor, unskilled workers, the unchurched, and criminals. Such actions, Colwell argued, would be powerful demonstrations of God's love and would help people to open their hearts to God.

THE SOCIAL GOSPEL MOVEMENT

The Social Gospel movement was another powerful influence in the social services arena of the day. The term *social gospel* was first used in 1886 by Iowa Congregationalist minister Charles O. Brown in response to Henry George's *Progress and Poverty* (Dayton 1976). The idea was to introduce the Christian spirit and heritage into the social order. The Social Gospel movement represented an attempt to respond to serious social problems of the times such as slums, labor unrest, urban blight, and exploitation of the poor. It was also a reaction to the evolving social Darwinist approach, which called upon the wealthy to guide the poor. Proponents of the Social Gospel believed that the material blessings of the few would, with proper stewardship, "trickle down" to the impoverished many. Implicit in the Social Gospel approach was the belief that poverty might be a result of, if not the punishment for, sin (Leonard 1976).

In response to the Social Gospel movement, thousands of individual Christians and churches became actively involved in the resolution of social problems ranging from helping a neighbor to challenging the social order. The Christian response was similar to the work of Walter Rauschenbusch alongside the Socialist Party. Hopkins (1940) noted that the Social Gospel spawned a variety of social action initiatives such as "workingmen's clubs." These religious-based clubs practiced cooperative buying, and some owned their own libraries and meeting places similar to the co-op movement of the 1960s, which was—if anything—antireligious. Social Gospel participants were also involved in helping the poor, improving education, combating prostitution, opposing alcohol abuse, and helping immigrants assimilate into American society. The power of the Social Gospel was in its wide reach and the fact that a social theology managed to move so many people into being involved in social services provision and social change.

The Christian Women's Temperance Union (CWTU) represents an early advocacy effort of Christian women in America (Axinn and Levin 1992). This national organization summoned women to protest the damaging effects of alcohol on the family and to contain the manufacture and sale of alcoholic beverages. This organization formed in 1874 and quickly grew in influence and numbers, exceeding 200,000 members.

One group that was highly influential in the Social Gospel movement was the Salvation Army. In 1890 General Booth published *In Darkest England*, in which he called for members of the Salvation Army to reach out to the poorest people in society. He argued that the moral improvement of the poor was dependent upon the amelioration of their material conditions and well-being. The overt presence of the Army's religious and social soldiers made its campaign visible and popularized the responsibility of religious people to help others in need. The saying "No place was forsaken for the Army, no man or woman sunk so low as to be excluded from God's bounty" best represents this denomination's social perspective. Because all are God's creatures, the Salvation Army made no distinction between the worthy and the unworthy poor.

CHARITY ORGANIZATION SOCIETY

Only at the end of the nineteenth century did religious-based social services in America begin to give way to secular forms of help. Reverend Samuel H. Gurteen paved the way by establishing the Buffalo Charity Organization Society (COS) in 1877. New Haven (1878) and Philadelphia (1978) were the first to follow (Gurteen 1881). Gurteen based his society on the organizations of the same name in London and Glasgow (Leiby 1984), which in turn were based on the Reverend Thomas Chalmers's philosophy of parish responsibility to its neediest people, as well as other on European models (Buzelle 1892; Schweinitz 1943). The British model's principle was a simple one: members of the congregation, together with the wealthy members of the community, were obliged to meet the needs of the poor. Church deacons visited the poor, counseled them, and supervised their use of charitable alms. Under Gurteen's leadership the COS movement substituted "friendly visitors" for deacons, a major feature of what was to become the new benevolent gospel and a continuation of the tradition started in AICP. The COSs continued to change the face of American services. Through their efforts, social services eventually left their community/religious base for one that was citywide, temporal, and professional (Magnuson 1977; Tice 1992), and the delivery of social services became less arbitrary and more systematic. Gurteen's work laid the foundation for scientific charity, and his claim to fame was that the work of the Buffalo COS saved the city $50,000 annually. In Gurteen's words, "The Organization plan keeps taxation down to the lowest possible figure, and this without any unkindness to the poor; since in every case where either a person is cut off from receiving official aid, or is prevented from applying to it, work is invariably produced by the Society in order to make up for the degrading official dole which has been withheld or withdrawn" (1881:7).

George Mangold (1907) noted that the first COS in Buffalo adopted the Glasgow model of Chalmers, which used local churches and their deacons. The use of churches became problematic because churches were often given responsibility for districts in which many residents were not of their faith. Thus, the churches' friendly visitors did not visit as frequently as required; reports to COS headquarters were sporadic, and the churches were often unwilling to help. When the local COS worked directly with the friendly visitors, the results improved, so the COS gave up working through local churches. While delivery of social services through the churches had worked in London and in Glasgow, it did not work for America's COSs because of the nation's religious and ethnic pluralism. This movement of service delivery away from the churches presaged an even greater change that was to occur in the twentieth century: the secularization of social welfare, which occurred partly because of the contributions of Mary Richmond and the philosophy of the Charity Organization Societies (COSs). Lubove (1965) noted that "Charity Organization was the creation of middle-class Protestant Americans, denouncing rigid sectarianism in charitable affairs, but inspired by an evangelical sense of mission" (p. 16).

Although Mary Richmond is credited with the secularization of social work, that was not her intention. Like others in the COS movement, she saw her work in the wider society as a reflection of her religious convictions. Coughlin (1965) cited Richmond as follows: "The church furnishes us with the motive for all our work . . . and sends us forward . . . in a campaign that involves wider issues" (p. 22). Regrettably, the history of social work has paid scant attention to the religious background and motivation that imbued the work of Mary Richmond and many other social work pioneers.

The settlement house movement, as previously noted in chapter 3, also has deep religious roots. Samuel Barnett, a clergyman, originated the settlement house concept while serving in St. Jude's Parish in east London (Bruce 1966). Many religious groups formed settlement houses. Among them were the Salvation Army, the Methodist Church, and the Presbyterian Church. Even Jane Addams, who is most identified with the settlement house movement, was religiously motivated. Hull House, Addams's famous site in Chicago, had Bible groups as one of its primary educational activities. Yet most social work texts fail to mention the religious origin of the movement and the fact that many settlement houses were organized and staffed by religious groups.

EARLY TWENTIETH CENTURY

F. Ernest Johnson (1930) enumerated the elements of church work that were socially oriented and not faith-required and that overlapped with the newly evolving profession of social work. These included: (1) social evangelism; (2) miscellaneous services, such as employment services and hospital visitation; (3) cooperation/joint action with other agencies (e.g., provision of probation workers or hospital workers for those with religious affiliation or those who requested Christian care); (4) church advocacy for moral and social issues by supporting legislation and urging members to vote (e.g., prohibition law); (5) development of social attitudes on industrial relations, international issues, and race relations; (6) social education (training for volunteer service, industrial and racial situations, social hygiene) and research such as study of crime in Pittsburgh or social conditions in Baltimore; (7) social services experiments (e.g., coffee clubs as a social substitute for saloons, scholarships to provide juvenile delinquents with shelter, schooling, and employment placement); and (8) cooperation with agencies (e.g., Minneapolis Church Federation, 1928 conference for ministers and social workers). Johnson acknowledged that some religious organizations had not sought the aid of community organizations because "it would not be worth the resulting complications, public scrutiny necessary for endorsement, or compromise in their service" (p. 101). He concluded that "the role of religion as a vital factor in the social rehabilitation of failures and misfits has been increasingly recognized in recent years" (p. 101).

One of the most interesting facets of Johnson's work was his overview of social services provided by denominations and religious groups as early as 1930. These services were actually very similar to today's social work. Examples cited by Johnson give additional insights into the history of social care under religious auspices. The following paragraphs contain a selected list of examples that he cited.

Services by Denominations

The Northern Baptist Convention, through the American Baptist Publication Society, provided social services, temperance, social recreation, family welfare, industrial cooperation, and goodwill in the community. Similarly, the Social Relations Department of the Congregational Society and the Commission of Social Relations of the National Council of the Congregational Churches provided social services focused on investigations and social discovery, preparation of educational materials, and fostering of an atmosphere compatible with the ideals of social education. The Society of St. Vincent de Paul, a Catholic organization, assisted poor families in their homes, visited hospitals and prisons, and conducted child-placement programs.

Services by Federated Church Agencies

Quite a few commissions were established by interfaith groups. For example, the Commission on the Church and Social Services provided information on industrial relations, ethical issues of public importance, and resources for social emergencies. The Commission on International Justice and Goodwill focused on issues of world peace, disarmament, and arbitration. The Commission on the Church and Race issued informational and educational literature on race relations. The Committee on Goodwill Between Jews and Christians focused on promoting appreciation and respect between these groups.

Services by Other Religious Agencies

The Young Men's Christian Association (YMCA) provided services through various departments. The Industrial Department, for example, provided men employed in shops, factories, and trades with lodging as well as recreational, educational, and social opportunities; the Town and Country Department, the sole service provider in many rural and small towns, used schools, churches, and community houses to provide camps, conventions, leadership training institutes, thrift campaigns, boys' conferences, "keep fit " campaigns, and countywide enterprises. And finally, the Colored Department assisted colored men from the South in their social and economic adjustment to large cities by providing meals, physical accommodations, employment services, summer camps, entertainment, and gymnasium classes.

The Young Women's Christian Association (YWCA) provided a program of social work in conjunction with other social agencies, as well as programs of social education for social responsibility. The YWCA also participated in local councils of social welfare, state conferences of social work, and the National Conference of Social Workers. Social work activities included food service, housing, recreation, health education, vocational guidance, supplementary education, personality development through groups, and assistance with adjustments to work, home, and social situations. Social education activities focused on educating the community about issues of concern to women, such as interracial issues, citizenship education, economic education, and international issues.

Other examples of religious response to community problems in Indianapolis can be found in a newspaper published by the Polis Center (1996), which reprints reports from the city archives. Three of these reports were highlighted in a section titled "Religious Community Responds to Hardship." A 1902 report described the founding of St. Vincent Hospital: "Responding to a request from Roman Catholic Bishop Chartard to come and help the poor, sick, and injured, in 1881 four Daughters of Charity of St. Vincent de Paul arrived in Indianapolis. . . . During its first eight years, the hospital treated more than 1,000 patients. This order is still very active and in 1986 the sisters opened the St. Vincent School of Nursing" (Polis Center 1996:2). Another report from 1902 highlights an award given to a local rabbi by his congregation "for his many contributions to the poor and unfortunate of the city. . . . Rabbi Messing has worked hand-in-hand with clergy of other religions. . . . He and the Catholic bishop and the Presbyterian minister used to sit on their respective front porches with a list and they would go down the lists to see who needed personal help, who needed coal, and make out a list and go over it" (Polis Center 1996:2). In the third report, from 1934, Reverend William L. Clark of the Second Presbyterian Church discussed his church's response to the Great Depression: "In 1932 it [the church] gave 72 quarts of milk a day to undernourished children and distributed 2,500 garments, plus coal, to over 200 families. Many other Indianapolis churches and synagogues are responding similarly to the needs around the city" (Polis Center 1996:2). The same publication noted that in 1944 Flanner House, the well-known social services agency founded in 1911 by the Christian Women's Board of Missions (Christian Church–Disciples of Christ), was planning to add new services, including a health center, employment services, a day nursery for children of working mothers, and counseling, as well as self-help economic projects such as a cannery, a work camp, and a furniture and home-building program.

Religious congregations since the beginning of the twentieth century have provided space and support for many civic activities that have benefited the community as a whole. Warner and Lunt (1941), in their study of Newburyport (titled Yankee City in their study), found that liberal Protestants maintained extensive associational ties and were characterized by their sponsorship of community organizations, such as YMCA, Boy Scouts, and Campfire Girls, which served the whole community rather than their own members. For example, the Second Church of Yankee City sponsored a Boy Scout troop that drew a large portion of its members from other churches and religions. The church membership was predominantly Yankee, but the Boy Scout troop was commonly known as the "League of Nations because of the great number and variety of ethnics among its members" (p. 317).

With increased interest in social work and psychiatric knowledge, theological institutions of higher education were requesting training in these areas and especially in social work (Boyd 1949). By 1948 the Catholic Church, for example, had six accredited social work programs at the following institutions: Loyola University (1914), Fordham University (1919), St. Louis University (1923), Boston College (1936), Our Lady of the Lake University of San Antonio (1942), and Catholic University (1947) (McDonnell 1949). By 1954 other, non-Catholic theological schools were offering social work, schools such as Yeshiva University and Brandeis University, which originally catered to the needs of Jewish social services agencies (Johnson and Villaume 1957). The Institute of Social and Religious Research, founded in 1921, brought methods of social science to bear on such issues as the Christian church in its social setting, administration of religious agencies, sociological studies, foreign missions, religious character and education, and race relations (Johnson 1930). While more workers from religious organizations sought the skills and training of social workers, it has not been a widespread practice that social workers seek to know more about church work (Tippy 1939).

In 1957 Johnson and Villaume reported findings of a National Council of Churches survey of 70 percent of its Protestant membership. It was estimated that 4,000 agencies, some church-based, some denominational, and some local coalitions, served 17 million people each year. These agencies were also estimated to employ 37,500 nurses, 26,000 physicians, and 14,400 social workers.

INTERNATIONAL LINKS

Social services and social welfare efforts not only developed within a religious framework in the United States but also were carried out internationally. American missionaries traveled to all parts of the world, bringing the "word of God," health care, and social services long before the well-known international relief organization UNICEF was even conceived. In Canton, China, for example, the country's first mental health hospital was founded in 1898 by John Kerr, an American physician and Presbyterian missionary (Tucker 1983).

Midgley (1981) noted that religious groups opened schools of social work in developing countries. Among them are the school of social work founded by the YMCA at the University of New Delhi (India), a school of social work founded by a group of Jesuit priests in Zimbabwe, and the many schools of social work in Central America that are housed and supported by Catholic universities. Similarly, the Paul Bawerwald School of Social Work at Hebrew University in Jerusalem, Israel, was founded through the support of the New York–based American-Jewish Joint Distribution Committee. The Bawerwald School, the first school of social work in Israel, was followed by four additional schools that were established by the state education system. In 1974, through a partnership of the American-Jewish Joint Distribution Committee and the Israeli government, the JDC-Brookdale Institute of Gerontology and Human Development, a national center for applied research on human development and social policy in Israel, was established.

Churches and denominations around the world were among the first to demonstrate against apartheid and to boycott companies that dealt with South Africa. While apartheid is considered to be a racist policy of segregation and economic and political oppression, for years many corporations continued to do business with the government of South Africa despite its apartheid policies. Pratt (1997) noted that a coalition of denominations in Canada formed the Taskforce on the Churches and Corporate Responsibility. This group was the first and most vocal and effective in pressuring corporations to cut economic ties with South Africa that would perpetuate apartheid. As in Canada, churches in the United States protested against corporate investment in South Africa as well as the provision of military arms and technology by the U.S. government.

We have discussed these international initiatives of religious-based services to illustrate that the involvement of the religious community extends from the neighborhood to the world. Many denominations have sent both their people and their funds worldwide to help those in need. While some may argue that the missionary efforts of evangelical denominations, especially in the Third World, have been extensions of American nationalism, we nevertheless contend that the religious community has helped people all over the world to improve their quality of life, benefit from advanced medical care, and gain access to educational skills.

A CRITIQUE AND A RESPONSE

Paul S. Boyer (1978) in his book *Urban Masses and Moral Order in America, 1820–1920* noted that the growth of the city in the nineteenth century alarmed the Protestant elite of the time. Their response was to encourage and finance American evangelicals to uplift the morality of the urban dwellers. These evangelical groups first used revivalism. They then formed voluntary moral and religious societies for the purpose of printing Bibles, tracts, and inspirational books; founding domestic missions; and starting Sunday schools. When these measures failed to make the new urban centers more orderly and less vicious, new organizations emerged to take their place. "Three of these—the Association for Improving the Condition of the Poor, the Children's Aid Society, and the Young Men's Christian Association—were particularly important new departures" (p. 65). These relief organizations eventually became central components in the social services systems of all American cities. Boyer further explained:

> Relief societies with strong moral-reform overtones had sprung up in several cities as early as the 1790's, and the years surrounding the Panic of 1819 saw the emergence in Baltimore, Philadelphia, and New York of merchant-led "antipauperism" societies whose purpose was less material relief than greater social control of the destitute. Dividing their cities into districts, these societies proposed to hire agents who would not only aid the legitimately needy but also gather detailed information on the prostitution, gambling, intemperance, profligacy, and economic irresponsibility that were presumed to underlie most poverty . . . [so that] in the long run [they would] reduce the relief roles, cut the almshouse population, and diminish the number of beggars, including the "downright and detestable imposters" thought to be infesting the depressed coastal cities.   (p. 87)

Boyer, in essence, has suggested that American Protestantism used these and other services "to develop institutional modes that would enable it to exert moral influence, if not ecclesiastical authority, over the increasingly non-Protestant urban masses" (p. 121). Similar sentiments were expressed by Carroll Smith-Rosenberg (1971) in her book *Religion and the Rise of the American City*. Three issues should be raised in this respect. First, whatever the motives and origins of these organizations, they did serve as the first organized American response to need. These are also the same organizations that later gave rise to many other welfare-oriented organizations under the auspices of religious bodies. Second, in reading Boyer's criticism of the intentions of these "antipauperism" societies, one should remember that current state welfare agencies, in fact, are held to the same expectations. Furthermore, the public today is similarly hostile to dependency. Finally, Boyer goes on to suggest that in the beginning of the twentieth century, the Protestant elite realized that moral reform and urban control would not come through religious organizations, and so they actively distanced themselves from such endeavors. Boyer failed to report the development of these church and denominational social efforts after 1900. Did they give up social ministry in the face of the growth of the more secular COSs and parks and recreation movements? The answer, as we will show in the next chapter, is that the religious groups continued to serve their immediate communities.

It is our contention that as the welfare state and public social responsibility in the United States began to take shape after the advent of COSs in the late nineteenth century and especially from the impetus of the New Deal onward, secular services began to crowd out religious ones. The international sphere provided a venue for expanded service delivery by the religious community.

We still hold that public services are the best mechanism to meet massive human needs. We nevertheless do recognize that the United States has been a society long suspicious of public authorities and since its settlement by European settlers in 1620 has strongly preferred informal local arrangements to state-mandated services. This is not to say that the public and/or secular sectors were not involved in the provision of social services earlier than the COSs. In Pennsylvania, for example, two years after the signing of the Declaration of Independence, the Commonwealth's General Assembly reenacted a 1771 law that called for a local tax levy for the relief of the poor, as did other colonies. In other words, the public sector and secular nonprofit organizations have been engaged in welfare and in the provision of social services since the very early days of the nation.

What is unique about the United States when compared with most other Western democracies is the impressive involvement of the religious community in welfare and social services. This is not only advocacy involvement but also an involvement in actual provision of social services. Given this strong history that helped shape the welfare terrain and our culture, it is not surprising that religious-based social services organizations are called upon to be involved in social services provision toward the end of the second millennium. In the next chapter we demonstrate that this historical trend did not end at the beginning of the twentieth century. It was weakened for a while, but it is now experiencing a significant revival that should be highlighted and adequately acknowledged by policy makers, scholars, and practitioners alike.

CHAPTER 7

RELIGION AND THE QUALITY OF LIFE
OF INDIVIDUALS

C. S. Lewis, a British author and Oxford don best known for his literary works, witty satires, and classic children's books such as *The Lion, the Witch, and the Wardrobe,* was also a highly respected theologian and a popular public speaker on moral issues during the 1940s and 1950s. The current generation may also remember him from *Shadowlands,* a play and later a 1993 movie that told of how his life was shaken by his meeting American poet Joyce Grisham.

The title reflected Lewis's belief that life on earth is a shadow life; real life awaits in heaven. The tragic illness and death of the woman he loved, however, left Lewis inconsolable. He found no comfort in the advice he had so often given others, and he began to doubt his own religious beliefs. Over time, Lewis accepted his devastating loss by re-embracing God and the concept of an afterlife in which the meaning of all that happened in this life would be explained and loved ones would be reunited.

Lewis believed and advised many others that a belief in God and in a divine order that is beyond us is the key to overcoming stress and adversity. In no way is Lewis or the author of *Shadowlands* unique in this perspective. They echo what many people believe about religion. In essence, their message is that there is a purpose to suffering that is beyond our human understanding and that we must be willing to submit to God's will. Some psychologists theorize that religious belief protects people from taking adversity personally and blaming themselves when things happen. In principle and in the popular media this concept, healthy locus of control, is well rooted. The question is, How real is it? Are there empirical data that have found religious people to be less depressed than nonreligious people? Do we know whether religious people cope with disaster better than nonreligious people? Can we generalize from this to assume that religion and religious groups induce prosocial behavior?

There is a strong sentiment, even among Americans who are not practicing members of a religion, that belief in God and things of the spirit is positive. The role of religion in American society, however, continues to be debated. Moberg (1984) noted that "religious leaders commonly assume that among the effects of their work are both character education, which prevents people from becoming social deviants, and personal development which supports mental health" (p. 446). Yet many will argue that organized religion is to blame for many evils, such as wars, support of dictatorships, oppression—particularly sexism, and accumulation of wealth at the expense of the public good. Those at odds with organized religion argue that throughout history church leaders have collaborated with the ruling parties and helped to perpetuate undemocratic social order and exploitation.

Van-Dartel (1995) reminded us of the war in Bosnia and Croatia in which Muslims and Serbian Orthodox Church members killed one another and committed unspeakable atrocities in the name of religion. In 1994 Pope John Paul II visited Croatia, but his plans to visit Belgrade and Bosnia-Herzegovina had to be canceled when factions of the Serbian Orthodox Church, which held the Vatican partially responsible for the breakup of Yugoslavia, threatened violence. By drawing on its medieval religious history, the Serbian Orthodox Church has legitimated political and military struggles to prevent secession; hence religion was the key element in escalating the conflict. David Little (1995), who studied the formation of ethnic identities and nationalism in Sri Lanka, Sudan, and Tibet, concluded that religion significantly influences both the formation of nationalism and expressions of tolerance or intolerance. He further noted that certain parties use religion to further their own political and economic ends. In this respect, Wilson (1986) noted that religion, in and of itself a source of peace, has frequently been used as moral justification for violent conflict. He asserted that among small groups, religion is a means for peace but among large-scale communities, such as a state, religion can be used to manipulate emotions against a rival.

Karl Marx's famous dictum that religion is the opiate of the masses best exemplifies people's fear and distrust of organized religion. The most extreme example of this antipathy may be the book *God Hates Religion: How the Gospels Condemn False Religious Practice*, written by a Canadian minister of the Church of Christ (Levan 1995). Levan's thesis, as the provocative title implies, is that churches, denominations, and other forms of organized religion are anachronistic and should give way to modern practices of religion.

He asserts that organized religion as it is today is so appalling that even God would find it distasteful. Nevertheless, before a final verdict is rendered, the pros of organized religion and spirituality should be considered. Despite the many atrocities that have taken place in its name, religion has proved beneficial to many of its members and, by extension, to society as a whole.

In this chapter we review a wide range of articles, books, and reports that deal with the impact of participation in organized religion on the quality of life of individuals. Our aim is to determine whether active participation in organized religion, such as frequent church attendance and church membership, enhances an individual's quality of life. In other words, are practicing members of a religion at reduced risk of suicide, depression, substance abuse, deviance, and criminal behavior? It should be noted that these gains, if proved, are limited to members of the religious groups. Findings that may indicate an association between participation in organized religion and improved quality of life should be viewed with caution, as they may not be related to organized religion per se, but rather it may be that organized religion tends to attract people who are less prone to antisocial and unhealthy behaviors. Hence, religious practices have little to do with their prosocial behaviors. This is also known as the arousal theory and will be further discussed in this chapter.

Joseph (1987) noted that "religion has a remarkable capacity to provide a sense of *identity* and *rootedness* for both the person and the group. Through its corporate belief system and community of faith, a deep sense of affiliation can develop. This is particularly significant for many who feel alienated at this time of social and cultural transition" (p. 17). In other words, faith and spirituality are the individual set of beliefs and values that one holds regarding God and the world, while religion is the external expression of these personal beliefs. Religion is essentially a social institution with a cohesive system of behaviors, worship, and creed that people willingly share with others who have similar beliefs. It is through this organizing of people with similar beliefs that religious groups and organizations are formed. The benefits to religious individuals may come both from their personal faith and from the actual practice of belonging to a group, whether it be a congregation, a study group, a cult, or an informal gathering for revival and change.

In the United States, membership in a religion or denomination is a matter of personal choice or preference (Roof and McKinney 1987). Contrary to the situation in most countries in the world, religion in America at the present time is an expression of moral choice, identity, and conscience. In most countries, the choice usually is whether or not to belong to the church of one's parents. Most Europeans have chosen not to belong. In the United States, on the other hand, the choice usually is to which of the many faiths to belong. Most Americans belong to a church, though not necessarily the one of their parents. According to Roof and McKinney, "Today choice means more than simply having an option among religious alternatives; it involves religion as an option itself and opportunity to draw selectively off a variety of traditions in the pursuit of the self" (p. 40). For example, in the Roman Catholic Church today, many newly ordained priests are not young men who come to the seminary directly from high school in accord with parental expectations but mature men who have given up other careers in order to become priests (Niebuhr 1997). The point here is that in America, personal value and identity shape the individual's faith expression.

Unlike Europe, the United States has a plethora of religions and denominations. The choice of one's religion is based more on personal conviction, moral and behavioral concerns, and sense of comfort than on family history. In most European countries, the family plays a much larger role in determining one's religious identity, and converting from one religion or denomination to another is rare and dramatic. In the United States, the family plays a lesser role in determining an individual's religious identity, and changing religious/denominational membership is much more common (Warner 1993; Wuthnow 1988). Roof and McKinney (1987) note that "less and less bound to an inherited faith, an individual is in a position of 'shopping around' in a consumer market of religious alternatives and can 'pick and choose' among aspects of belief and tradition" (p. 67). The freedom to choose enables prospective members to go through a selection process that involves value clarification and understanding and prioritizing one's behavior, identity, and ideal worldview. As such, organized religion in America may provide individuals with many strengths and advantages. The following review of the literature will explore the effect of religious beliefs and religious participation on quality of life.

Two methodological notes are required at this stage. First, many of the studies that we cite distinguished between adults and adolescents, and we have made the same distinction. Second, as findings in the social sciences are sometimes contradictory, we have presented both positive and negative results in the interest of a more balanced perspective. What is quite disappointing is that some of these contradictions can be attributed to the ideological perspective of the authors. By and large, secular researchers reported little association between participation in organized religion and members' quality of life, while religiously affiliated researchers found the opposite.

SUICIDE AND RELIGION

The hypothesis proposed by the noted French sociologist Emile Durkheim (1897 [1951]) in his book *Suicide*, namely, that members of cohesive and inter-active collectives experience lower rates of suicide, is widely accepted by social scientists. It would therefore follow that religions, which traditionally form congregations of interacting individuals, would be instrumental in providing members with support in times of crisis and thus would deter self-destructive impulses. Durkheim suggested that a major function of communities in general, and of religious groups in particular, is to articulate values of restraint and to implement organizational systems that force members to conform to group norms and limit their individualistic inclinations. In fact, all major religions prohibit an individual from taking his or her own life. For example, the Qur'an says: "Do not kill (or destroy) yourselves: for verily God hath been to you most merciful" (Sura 41:35). Although Durkheim's work compared Catholic and Protestant societies, his thesis is readily generalized to any cohesive religious community (Stark and Bainbridge 1980).

Pescosolido (1990) suggested that the low rate of suicide among religious people is actually the outcome of the network aspect of religious affiliation, namely, that a social support system in which members provide support to each other helps alleviate an individual's pain and suffering. Alternatively, Bainbridge (1989) suggested that strong religious beliefs, especially belief in afterlife rewards, enhance the individual's ability to endure and cope with earthly travails such as death, unemployment, illness, divorce, and so forth. If this is true, then it is likely that those who actively participate in a religious community, with the exception of extreme cults such as Heaven's Gate, are less likely to consider or attempt suicide. Conversely, if it is true that depression has a biological basis, then participation in an organized religion will have only limited effect on suicide. Consideration must also be given to the fact that participation in a religious group often implies a high level of conformity to religious values and group norms and lower tolerance to deviance. People in crisis may be pressured by their religious communities to maintain their usual behavior and attitudes, and such pressure may in fact exacerbate suicidal ideation and practice.

Joubert (1994) found that in the United States and other countries church attendance is the variable most closely associated with suicide. He found a strong correlation ($r = -.57, p < .01$) between a nation's level of religious participation (measured as the percentage of persons defining themselves as having no religion or as agnostics) and tendency toward higher suicide rates. In a twenty-five-nation study that controlled for level of development and gender equality, Stack (1983a) found the greater the religious commitment, the lower the suicide rate. This relationship was, however, much stronger among females, who are often more religiously committed than males. He also found that the greater the level of economic development, the greater the rate of suicide. Lester (1991) found that participation in religion decreases the rate of suicide for both adolescents and adults.

Stack and Wasserman (1992), in a study of suicide based on data from the General Social Surveys, found that members of churches with strong social networks had lower rates of suicide ideation. They also found that members of churches with conservative ideologies, nonecumenical orientation, Presbyterian polity, or teachings that were in conflict with the wider society had lower levels of suicide ideation. These authors interpreted their findings as support for the network theory—that is, individuals in churches that require extensive participation are more connected with their churches and these rich social networks serve as a buffer against despair and, ultimately, suicide. Similarly, Hoelter (1979) obtained significant results indicating that a lower percentage of religious people considered suicide as a means of problem solving than did nonreligious people. Contradictory findings were reported by Medoff and Skov (1992). They found that although strong religious beliefs among fundamentalists may explain sexual morality (abortion, birth rates, and marriages), such beliefs have not only been unsuccessful in reducing social deviance (divorce, murder, and suicide) but may actually increase such behaviors. The authors credit these findings to the fact that fundamentalists tend to be authoritative and extra-punitive in personality—that is, they react to inner frustration by outward aggression. It should be noted that these two studies are discussing differences among churches and not the relationship between active/nonactive church participation and suicidal ideation/suicide attempts. When Bainbridge (1989) entered into a regression equation the variable of the proportion of those who moved to a different house in the past five years, an indication of an objective stressor, the impact of religion on suicide collapsed.

Suicide is a significant factor among the young (those who are fifteen to twenty-four years old). It is the third leading cause of death, after accidents and homicide, in this age group. In a study of university students, Salmons and Harrington (1984) found that students who reported a religious affiliation were significantly less likely to have suicidal ideation than those who did not. Stack (1983b) found that the effect of unemployment and military participation (two variables usually associated with increased likelihood for suicide) as risk factors in suicide was significantly diminished when religious behavior was included as a variable. Stack's study included the United States as a whole over a long period of time. He concluded that "the elasticity coefficients indicate that a 1% increase in church attendance decreases suicide by .59%" (p. 246). Donahue and Benson (1995), in a study of some thirty thousand adolescents, concluded: "After gender (girls are more likely to attempt suicide than boys), religiousness is the second strongest inhibitor of both suicide ideation and suicide attempts" (p. 155).

The overall trend in the literature is to support Durkheim's original thesis that active participation in religious groups deters suicide. There appears to be a consensus that religion, with the exception of the cases of extreme cults, has a positive influence on suicidal ideation and suicide attempts, even though this influence is not fully understood. Given the strong relationship between religion and suicide, Kehoe and Gutheil (1994) have raised the issue that none of the commonly used scales to detect suicidal ideation includes a religious or spiritual element. These authors have proposed that these scales should include such an item so that patients' religious and spiritual dimensions will no longer be neglected by psychiatric clinicians.

MENTAL HEALTH AND RELIGION

In a review of the literature on mental health and religion, Payne et al. (1991) concluded that while religion is correlated with self-esteem, well-being, personal adjustment, and suicide, there is "little evidence supporting religious influence in the prevention of serious clinical diagnosis like bipolar disorders, major depression, schizophrenia, obsessions, and panic disorders" (p. 11). In other words, religion helps in personal adjustment and daily interactions, but it is not a preventive against severe mental illnesses. In the case of personal adjustment, Spilka and his colleagues (1987) found that children from religious families who had cancer and their families exhibited better ability to cope with death than did nonreligious children and their families. These authors found that upon diagnosis, religious children exhibited questioning and depression, whereas nonreligious children exhibited anger, fear, and denial. Religious families also became stronger and mother-child relationships strengthened among religious families as compared with nonreligious families. Similarly, in a review of the literature Spilka, Hood, and Gorsuch (1985) found that twenty-four of thirty-six reviewed studies of adults "reported that stronger faith or afterlife views are affiliated with less death concern and fear" (p. 131).

Caplan (1972), who pioneered the study of social support systems, concluded that next to families, religious groups and communities provide the strongest and most common of all support. As such, religious groups are an important source for primary prevention of mental health problems. Additionally, cohesive religious groups provide individuals not only with support but also with clear directions and instructions on group norms and codes of behavior, thus minimizing their level of confusion and doubt.

In a study of 836 outpatients of a university geriatric clinic (mean age over seventy), Koeing, Kvale, and Ferrel (1988) found that all types of religious activity (congregational participation, personal praying, and intrinsic religiosity) were positively correlated with morale. The only variable that contributed more to morale among older people was physical health. Interestingly, congregational participation and intrinsic religiosity explained morale better than personal praying did. Similar findings were reported by Worthington (1989) in a literature review on old age, life satisfaction, and religion. However, these findings are not unexpected, as many elderly people tend to find solace in God and to prepare themselves for the possible afterlife. Willitis and Crider (1988) studied a large sample of people in their fifties. This is a cohort of people who are in the prime of their life economically and professionally and generally in good physical health. These authors concluded that "religious attitudes positively related to overall well-being and community and marital satisfaction of both men and women and to job satisfaction of men. Present church attendance was positively associated with overall and community satisfaction but not with the other dependent variables" (p. 281). In fact, the strong association between religion and morale, subjective well-being, and life satisfaction was supported by numerous studies with minor variations. They were also strongly shown in a meta-analysis of studies in this field carried out by Witter, Stock, Okun, and Haring (1985).

Johnson (1995) studied 122 extreme-aged (eighty-five-plus) black individuals in the Bay Area (San Francisco/Oakland). She found that many expressed high levels of contentment with their lives, especially if their social integration with their family, the black church, and the community was high. Thus, this study indicates that participation in the black church is associated with subjective well-being.

When more serious mental illnesses were considered, the results seem to be either contradictory or of little effect. For example, Bergin (1983) performed a meta-analysis of 24 studies covering 1951 to 1979. He found that 23 percent reported a negative (more religious/more ill) association between religion and mental health, while 47 percent reported a positive association. The overall meta-analytic correlation was extremely low (-.09) indicating that, in severe mental illnesses, the contribution of religion as a mental health buffer disappears. Similarly, Judd (reported in Payne et al. 1991), in a meta-analysis based on 116 studies, found that in the final analysis, the positive and negative results canceled each other out and accepted the null hypothesis of no relationship. Gartner, Larson, and Allen (1991) in a review of the literature, noted ambiguous or complex relationships between religion and anxiety, psychosis, self-esteem (others report different results on this issue), sexual disorders, and prejudice. These authors also noted that the literature suggested a negative impact of religion on issues such as authoritarianism, dogmatism, suggestibility, and self-actualization.

One study that suggests an association between religion and mental health was performed by MacDonald and Luckett (1983). They studied some ten thousand people who had been treated at a Midwestern community mental health center between 1977 and 1980. They found that clients who reported they had no religion were more likely to be substance abusers and/or paranoid schizophrenics, hostile and aggressive, and less likely to be diagnosed with a neurosis. These authors suggested that people who have no religion in their lives "simply are not a neurotic group, and appear to avoid sustained interior reflection on emotional stress" (p. 33). A similar study of high school students in Texas was conducted by Wright, Frost, and Wisecarver (1993). They found that students who attended church frequently and viewed their religion as providing meaning for their lives scored significantly lower on depression compared with other students. These authors interpreted their findings as consistent with Carl Jung and Victor Frankl's theories on religion, namely, that religion provides purpose to life and therefore the religious person is less likely to despair. Similarly, in an earlier study from World War II, Arnold Rose (1956) found that soldiers who prayed regularly while in combat were less likely to experience psychoneurotic trauma than those who did not pray.

Religion can play an important role in the care for and adaptation of mentally ill people in the community. Chu and Klein (1985) reported that a sample of people with schizophrenia who had been referred to and attended church services demonstrated significantly lower rates of rehospitalization, compared with those who did not attend church. Their findings suggest that congregational support and newly acquired spiritual beliefs were keys to this positive outcome.

PHYSICAL HEALTH AND RELIGION

The mind-body link has been well established in the last two decades. While many illnesses are the result of well-defined biological causes, susceptibility to illness and coping abilities are often affected by mental outlook. Furthermore, the mind's ability to overcome physical ailments seems to be enhanced when one has a group of supportive friends. We would therefore expect religious people who are supported by their congregations to be healthier and better able to cope with problems than those who do not have such a support system. Levin and Vanderpool (1987) in a review of the literature noted:

> Twenty-two out of 27 studies found the frequency of religious attendance to be significantly associated with health in a positive direction, and in four studies reporting insignificant associations, the authors presented data revealing strong salutary trends for attendance. In short, it seems clear that frequent attendance is a proscriptive factor against a wide range of illness outcomes. (p. 590)

These authors also reported that, as a group, religiously committed people live longer. Hannay (1980) and Zuckerman, Kasl, and Ostfeld (1984) also reported that regular church attendance and strong religious beliefs are associated with improved physical health and reduced mortality. In a later literature review, Levin (1994) examined more than two hundred published empirical reports in medicine and epidemiology. In general, these reports showed significant statistical associations between religion and health in such conditions and illnesses as "cardiovascular disease, hypertension and stroke, cancer (especially uterine cancer), colitis and enteritis, overall and site-specific mortality, general health status, physical symptomatology, and self-rated health as well as dozens of illnesses" (p. 5). Religion was found to be beneficial among cancer patients as it was associated with decreased levels of pain, anxiety, hostility, social isolation, mortality rates, and higher levels of life meaning and satisfaction (Acklin, Brown, and Mauger 1983; Jenkins and Pargament 1995; Kaczorowski 1989). Bourjolly (1998) found that religiousness helped women cope better with the trauma of and treatment effects of breast cancer. African-American women who were more religious than Caucasian women used religion to better cope with the disease.

Religious faith is significantly related to the ability of individuals and families to cope with disaster, injury, and illness. Clearly, the nexus between physical health and emotions is relevant here. If individuals see these events as God's will, then their anger decreases and their ability to cope increases, especially if they are members of a supportive religious congregation. Pollner (1989) reported a significant positive association between prayer and individuals' perceptions of their health and well-being. He found that those who prayed were more likely to feel healthier and less dependent upon health services.

Walsh (1980) noted that immigration and assimilation are stressful life changes. Immigrants who experience the most difficulty in assimilating, for example, usually evidence higher blood pressure levels than those who experience less difficulty. To determine whether immigrants with a religious outlook on life are better able to cope with assimilation, Walsh studied data on seventy-five immigrants living in Toledo, Ohio. He found that those with lower blood pressure levels were those who had a religious outlook.

It is not clear whether findings from these studies are valid, as only a few studies controlled for potential confounding variables. It is possible that church members are less likely to smoke and drink and hence are healthier. It is also possible that religious people are less engaged in risk behavior and hence are less likely to become ill. In sum, the independent variable that contributed to the results noted above is not clearly identified. In their study of the relationship between religion and health, Ferraro and Koch (1994) include gender, race, social support systems, and social integration as variables. Their findings suggest that neither social support nor social integration mediates between religion and health. Race, however, was an important factor, as was religion. They concluded:

> In sum, the effects of social support on health appear quite similar for black and white people, despite the generally higher levels of religious identification and participation among black persons. The link between religion and health is stronger for African Americans than whites on two counts. First, those who practice their religion appear to reap positive benefits to health. Second, black adults in poor health--regardless of their levels of practice--are more likely than whites to turn to religion as a coping resource in the face of physical suffering.   (p. 373)

Wrigley and LaGory (1994) reviewed the literature on rehabilitation, the process by which biological, psychological, and social functions are restored or developed after injury. They concluded that religion and spirituality play an important role in both the adjustment to the injury and the process of rehabilitation. Religion helps people attribute a meaning to the injury and regain a positive outlook.

In sum, religion cannot substitute for a good health system. Nevertheless, there is supportive evidence that religious people who are part of a religious community are better able to cope with health problems, may engage in fewer health-risk behaviors, and may even live longer.

WELL-BEING AND RELIGION

Moberg (1984) noted that religion has a preventive and adjustive influence on the believers. Religion provides them with a social support network and principles of living that both guide and minimize doubts and worries. "Prayers can help conquer neurotic attitudes, heal conflicts, overcome loneliness, and renew the sense of belonging to a larger whole" (p. 465). The belief that all is due to God's will also helps those who are coping with changes and stresses. Griffith, English, and Mayfield (1980) studied a Wednesday-night prayer meeting in one black church in New Haven, Connecticut. These authors found that, during an eight-week period, one-quarter of the church members attended these meetings. The meetings involved praising the Lord, providing personal testimonies, and blessing people who shared personal problems. The authors noted that these were very intense meetings, attended by only a few members of the congregation. For those who participated, however, the meetings served as a mental health resource. Members reported feeling better about themselves and their problems and being able to cope more effectively when new crises arose. The prayer meetings provided a positive frame of mind by constantly referring to the goodness of the Lord and encouraging members to celebrate their God-given life.

Ellison and Smith (1991) reviewed the literature on religion and well-being. Overall, they found strong association between religion and well-being, especially among the elderly. This general trend supported the findings of Rogalski and Paisey (1987), who found among the elderly a positive relationship between religious commitment and well-being. Ruffing-Rahal and Anderson (1994) studied well-being among 161 elderly women in a Midwestern state. After regressing various explanatory variables, they concluded that "according to the regression model, well-being increases when women (1) are able to practice their religious beliefs; (2) are of a younger chronological age; (3) have a minimum of a completed high school education" (p. 10). They also reported finding two ecological contexts of well-being. The stronger context was the older women's perceived ability to practice their religious preferences; the weaker context was an association between length of residence in the community and the number of health concerns. It is evident that the only context in which practitioners can help elderly women improve their sense of well-being is by helping them remain in touch with their religious community of choice. This may include transportation, outreach to the religious community, and education for change in the way family members and neighbors are assisting the elderly.

Another study that focused on the well-being of women examined the effects of religion and spirituality on fifty homeless women in Los Angeles (Shuler, Gelberg, and Brown 1994). The authors found that 88 percent of the women reported praying, 70 percent reported attendance at religious services, and 68 percent reported reading the Bible. They also found that 42 percent of these women reported that their religious beliefs and practices gave them the strength to cope and survive, while 20 percent said their beliefs gave them hope that things would get better. Prayer was reported as an effective strategy by almost half of the women (48%), and a small percentage (8%) said that referral for a spiritual or religious consultation would have been helpful. Shuler, Gelberg, and Brown concluded that "spirituality/religion appears to be an important resource area for inner-city homeless women" (p. 110).

It should be noted that religious commitment in this discussion included attendance at religious services, personal praying, and high levels of religious beliefs (intrinsic religious motivation). Ortega, Crutchfield, and Rushing (1983) studied the relationships between race, social contacts, and well-being among 4,522 adults in Alabama. They measured well-being in three ways: general life satisfaction, relative life satisfaction, and happiness. Their findings suggested that race itself is a factor of little consequence in explaining all three forms of well-being. They noted that "the relationships between race and relative life satisfaction and happiness are reduced to unimportance when church-related friendships are considered" (p. 111). In other words, it is this unique primary group of people who are not relatives but who share in values and life perspective that contributes to one's relative life satisfaction and happiness at an old age. Ortega, Crutchfield, and Rushing explained the reason why church friends are so much more important than kin or nonchurch friends in three ways. First, the church may serve as a moral integrating agency, and its members are part of the moral community, which is more important at later life stages. Second, often the church is a community of faith and sharing that reaffirms one's own faith and sense of belonging. Finally, the church may also serve as an extended family. Children and other relatives may emigrate away, but church friends are close spiritually and geographically; thus they can serve as a surrogate family. Whether all or some of these reasons can be generalized is not clear. However, the emerging picture is that participating in a religious community and befriending its members contributes to well-being in old age.

Phillip Shaver, Michael Lenauer, and Susan Sadd (1980) reported the result of a readers' survey regarding religion conducted by the women's magazine *Redbook* in September 1976. From the more than 65,000 replies, a random sample of 2,500 was used for analysis. The findings supported William James's (1902) concept of "healthy-minded" religion—that is, religious beliefs that benefit mental and physical health. The assumption is that the absence of firm beliefs is related to uncertainty and misguided behavior. In other words, value conflicts and indecisiveness contribute to unhealthy-mindedness. Indeed, Shaver and his colleagues found that "in general religiousness correlated most strongly (.64 and .57) with what might be considered indicators of healthy-minded religion" (p. 1565). They also found that both religious women and antireligious women scored high on all measures of healthy mind and quality of life, while those in the center (slightly religious) scored the lowest on all measures. They found that converts were, for the most part, more religious than other women, and while converts tend "to have gained in health and happiness" they also "seek authority for their beliefs beyond experience and may be somewhat intolerant of alternative beliefs" (pp. 1565–66).

Quite a few studies suggest that religious people demonstrate higher levels of marriage satisfaction (Schumm, Bollman, and Jurich 1982) as well as stability and longevity of the marriage (Larson and Goetz 1989). This is not surprising, as most religions advocate and teach the importance of the family and raising children. Further, most religions discourage—if not forbid—divorce, and couples to be wed are instructed that marriage is a commitment for life. Hence, the level of disappointment and unmet expectations is somewhat minimized. The fact that many religions are hostile toward divorce introduces the potential effect of "cognitive dissonance," in that people may overstate their level of marriage satisfaction to avoid the stigma or social pressure involved in a divorce. Religious people who contemplate divorce often have to get the permission of both the state and their religious community. Generally, the religious community will not give permission until the couple has made every attempt to reconcile their differences. In some orthodox religious groups, this can place undue pressure on one spouse (usually the woman) to remain in the marriage; however, it is often a means to salvage the marriage rather than let it end too quickly (Hunt and King 1978).

A population whose feelings of well-being can be jeopardized by organized religion is that of single fathers with custody of their children. Greif and

DeMaris (1990) studied 1,132 single fathers to assess what factors might explain their comfort or discomfort in their role as a single parent. They found that men who were members of a religious congregation experienced more discomfort in this role, compared with those who had no religious affiliation. These authors explained this finding as a result of the emphasis that organized religion places on a family structure with two parents of opposite sex and the negative attitude of religion toward separation and divorce.

CRIME AND DELINQUENCY

While no one would claim that religious people do not commit crime, it is still a major news item when a well-known religious person is accused of a crime. The reason is that religious people are significantly less likely to commit a criminal act than nonreligious people are (Lester 1987) because such behavior contradicts all religious teachings. It should be noted that these findings are based on the actual practice of religion and not on feelings of religiosity (Ellis 1987; Gartner, Larson, and Allen 1991). Similarly, Bainbridge (1989), using a unified ecological database from 1980, found that in seventy-five U.S. metropolitan areas, "many forms of crime and cultism are deterred by religion, whereas the influence of religion on suicide and homosexuality appears to be indirect" (p. 288). More specifically, he found that religion is associated with decreased assault, burglary, and larceny. He also noted that the association for robbery was nearly significant. In an international study, Ellis and Peterson (1996) found that adult religious practice (especially church attendance and membership) was significantly associated with lower levels of crime, especially property crimes in the thirteen studied countries.

The study of the relationship between religion and criminal behavior among adolescents is most contentious. In 1969, Hirschi and Stark published a landmark article, titled "Hellfire and Delinquency," that paved the way to a series of studies in the field. These authors studied both reported and recorded criminal behavior with three measures of religion (belief in hell, church attendance, and parental religious involvement) and found no significant association between criminal behavior and religion. Their explanation was that those who attend church are no more likely to act on ethical principles than those who do not attend church. This study initiated numerous replications, which did find significant associations between religion and criminal behavior among the young. Tittle and Welch (1983) reviewed sixty-three studies on the relationship between religion and criminal behavior among youth and noted that only 10 percent failed to report a significant negative association between these two variables.

A series of regional studies found that juveniles involved in church activities are less likely to be involved in vandalism and other delinquent behaviors (Beit-Hallahmi 1974; Cochran 1989; Singh 1979). Cochran studied a series of self-reported delinquent acts and found a strongly negative correlation of religion with premarital sex, auto theft, assault, weapon use, major theft, all drug use, beer drinking, and liquor drinking. The only variables not to be associated with religion were vandalism and wine drinking. Singh measured religiosity on a seven-point semantic scale in which church attendance was only one item, on the premise that one can be highly religious yet seldom attend religious services. He also measured antisocial behavior on a scale that included forty-eight items, such as stealing, vandalism, property damage, and abusive behavior. Singh concluded that "individuals who considered themselves as religiously involved tended to engage less in anti-social behavior than those who consider themselves as non-religious" (p. 158). Chadwick and Top (1993) found delinquency rates lower among adolescent members of religious communities, including more-liberal and nonevangelical communities. They concluded that peer pressure is the strongest explanatory variable for delinquency, followed by religiosity. Their findings regarding lower rates of criminal and antisocial behavior support Durkheim's assertions.

Several highly debated explanations have been offered regarding the relationships between religion and delinquency among adolescents: (1) the arousal theory; (2) the social control theory; (3) sequence of events (religious withdrawal followed by criminal behavior or vice versa); (4) denominational effects (greater likelihood of delinquent behavior among Catholics); and (5) social and economic status (greater likelihood of delinquency among poor children with less supervision and less encouragement by family and friends to attend church). In addition, the ecological explanations suggested that religion has an effect on delinquent behavior only in cities and towns where a large part of the population is religious and laws reflect this religious culture. For example, Olson (1990) found that the religion-delinquency nexus is not empirically supported either for Catholics or for those in the northeast region of the United States. Yet, he reported, "for all 1,586 counties for which we have crime statistics, the correlation between Index crime and church attendance is -.38" (p. 399).

The arousal theory offered by Ellis (1987) suggests that people who become bored quickly seek constant stimulation and are attracted to risk-taking behaviors rather than to religious activities. Ellis contended that the relationship between religion and crime is largely a spurious correlation of biological (neurological) origin. This finding, however, was not replicated by other studies. Social control theory seeks to explain the religion-delinquency relationship by stating that individuals in a religious community are held accountable for their actions by other members, which deters them from antisocial behavior. Cochran, Wood, and Arneklev (1994) controlled for these two theories and assessed their impact on various criminal behaviors. They concluded that "the answer to our question, 'Is religiosity-delinquency relationship spurious?' must be a qualified yes. It appears to be spurious with regard to assault, theft, vandalism, illicit drug use, and truancy. However, religious participation and religious salience maintain significant negative effects on alcohol and tobacco use after controls for arousal and social control have been added to the model" (p. 114).

Benda (1995), in a survey of more than 1,000 adolescents in rural and urban areas, found that "results do not support the hypothesis that anti-ascetic behaviors are more affected by religiosity than are criminal behaviors or that religiosity is an antecedent factor that has effects fully mediated through other more proximate elements of social control" (p. 464). In a later article, Benda and Corwyn (1997) suggested that many findings regarding an association between religion and juvenile delinquency are the result of a reverse process—namely, that adolescents involved in criminal behavior gradually reject the religious culture and teaching in favor of a new culture of risk taking and criminal behavior. In a study of some 1,500 high school and college students, they found a positive correlation between religious practice and reduced crime rates. Nevertheless, when they added the variables of arousal and control to the models, the impact of religion declined dramatically. They concluded that "the effect of religiosity was reduced to insignificance for assault, theft, vandalism, illicit drug use, and truancy" (p. 92).

On the other hand, Sloane and Potvin (1986) argued that low or insignificant relationships between religion and delinquency among adolescents occur because of insensitive statistical methods, noting that "when odds ratios and more sensitive tests of significance are employed, strong effects of religion on all offenses are found" (p. 87). Using a sophisticated method of data analysis, they concluded, "with somewhat greater confidence than previous research has allowed, that there is an association between religion and delinquency that is not confined to certain offenses or to certain sub-groups or social contexts, and that is not readily accounted for by the types of controls that seemed reasonable to introduce" (p. 104).

In a study comparing African-American males who had a history of incarceration with those who were not in prison, Parson and Mikawa (1991) found that those who did not go to church, or had stopped going by age ten, were much more likely to be imprisoned, compared with those who attended church regularly. Interestingly, those in prison also reported deviant behavior by age ten or earlier, first manifested by behavior problems in school. Those not in prison were more likely to report a belief in working hard to support themselves and also were more likely to report being "born again." Again, the findings should be viewed with caution. It is not demonstrably clear whether people who practice religion are those less likely to engage in crime. Nor is it clear whether the practice of religion per se is associated with lower crime rates. It may be that the failure of a family to encourage church attendance is actually an indication of the family's dysfunction and inability to care for its members. Another reason for caution is that the study participants were not randomly selected, and each group consisted of only thirty men. Nevertheless, the two groups were controlled on many variables and thus better suited to elicit meaningful findings for African-American males.

Religious-based services provide hope and a sense of connectedness with a higher power that can give meaning and direction to those in need. Recent reviews of studies have shown a strong correlation between religious participation and avoidance of crime and substance abuse (Dilulio 1994; Young et al. 1994). Furthermore, Werner and Smith (1982) in a longitudinal study of at-risk youth, found that youth with strong religious faith who drew support from religious personnel (teachers, ministers, or members of the religious community) had significantly more positive life outcomes than those without these religious resources. The possibility of selection bias must be considered in this study—namely, that the less seriously at-risk are those who are willing to be influenced by religious personnel (the arousal theory). Nevertheless, this finding deserves serious consideration if we are to direct young people toward more positive life outcomes.

DRUGS AND ALCOHOL

Ruth Engs and David Hanson (1985) collected data from 6,115 college students in 107 departments at 81 colleges. Of these, 81.9 percent drank at least once a year, while 20.2 percent were defined as heavy drinkers (those who drank six or more alcoholic drinks at any one sitting more than once a week). Heavy drinking was significantly associated with being male, white, first-year student; having a low grade-point average; being Roman Catholic or uncon-cerned with religion; and attending college in the north-central United States. While these findings indicate that many explanatory variables account for heavy drinking in early adulthood and none can be singled out, they also sug-gest that, except for Roman Catholics, those involved with a religious congre-gation are less likely to be heavy drinkers.

Amoateng and Bahr (1986) found that people who were religiously active consumed substantially less alcohol than those who were not religiously active. Gorsuch (1995) reviewed the literature on substance abuse and religion sepa-rately for adolescents and adults. He found that for both groups religion was consistently associated with substance nonabuse but that the association was stronger for adults. He also reported that "religious activity at one point in time predicts substance nonabuse at later points in time" (p. 71).

A correlation between religiosity, especially church attendance, and lower levels of drug abuse has been found in many studies (Adlaf and Smart 1985). In this respect, the combination of religious teaching, internalized values, and the social control of the religious community are all credited for the low con-sumption among those who are religious. Similarly, Lorch and Hughes (1985) found that among 14,000 youths, those who were religious were significantly less likely to abuse or try drugs. These authors found that the importance of religion to the adolescent, rather than fear of peer pressure, was the most important variable in explaining drug abstinence. Again, there were varia-tions, drug-abuse rates were lowest among (a) the more-religious adolescents in each denomination and (b) the more-proscriptive denominations. Similar findings were reported by Resnick and his colleagues (1997), who studied 12,118 adolescents from across the country. Of the sample, 88 percent reported a reli-gious affiliation. Those who considered religion and prayer to be important were less likely to use drugs and alcohol. In this respect it is important to note that Kutter and McDermott (1997) found that adolescents in proscriptive denominations (those that prohibit drinking) have lower rates of alcohol and drug consumption. Adolescents who break the denominational taboo against drinking, however, are much more likely to engage in binge drinking (five or more drinks in a single episode).

We should also mention here that religion has been an important force in substance-abuse rehabilitation. Those who are familiar with Alcoholics Anonymous (AA) and Narcotics Anonymous (NA) readily recognize that their Twelve Steps programs are based on religious principles. The programs also call for reliance on a "higher power" and carrying out a "moral inventory," which are central to many religious traditions. In effect, it has been argued that AA, and other Twelve Steps-based programs, have replaced alcohol dependency with dependency on God's power and daily acknowledgment of one's own weakness (Slagle and Weibel-Orlando 1986). The religious bent of the Twelve Steps program explains why AA groups are often welcomed by the host congregations and meet in religious properties.

Maton and Rappaport (1984) conducted an ethnographic study of a non-denominational Christian fellowship that emphasized personal transformation and interpersonal development. They found that members, many of whom had a history of drug abuse and antisocial behaviors, were encouraged to come to Jesus via the fellowship and reported dramatic transformation. Considering themselves to be reborn spiritually, the members abstained from drug or alcohol use and lived productive and prosocial lives. Maton and Rappaport attributed these positive changes to the following factors: (1) an organizational culture that fosters the ideal of personal development in Jesus' image (love and care of others); (2) extensive and intensive experience of prayer-based sharing, guidance, and support that ranged from one-to-one relationships and small-group interaction to interaction with the whole congregation; (3) the intuitive and emotional experience of God's love, forgiveness, and caring; and (4) many opportunities for meaningful contributions to the congregation and its activities. Whatever the causes, the Maton and Rappaport study demonstrated, the religious community is not only deterring antisocial activities such as alcohol and drug abuse, it is helping in the rehabilitation of individuals with substance abuse and behavior problems and assisting in reintegrating their lives into mainstream society.

In a quasi-experimental study, Mitchel, Hu, McDonnell, and Swisher (1984) assessed the impact of three curricula—health, religion, and/or social studies— on substance consumption by 250 ninth-grade students in a private school. The religious program reduced the consumption of cigarettes, beer, wine, and marijuana, whereas the health and social studies programs did not. While these authors failed to report the nature of the religious curriculum and the sample was not randomly selected, this is one of the few studies available that is not cross-sectional but intervention-based. The findings suggest that religion can be used for prevention of substance abuse and/or reduction of substance consumption. Similarly, Barrett, Simpson, and Lehman (1988) found a positive effect of religion (self-reports of church attendance) on 326 Mexican-American teenagers in four separate drug intervention programs in Texas. The authors reported that success (short-term reduction in substance use and legal/school problems) was associated with positive peer group (non–substance users), family support, and background of religious involvement. The program tried to encourage the religious involvement of these adolescents, and it was suggested that being religiously involved while in the program may enhance involvement with more-positive peer groups and contacts with family, the other predictors of success. This study suggests that introducing religion as part of the substance rehabilitation program may contribute to the overall success of substance abuse treatment.

Finally, El Azayem and Hedayat-Diba (1994) reminded us that the Qur'an, the source of all Islamic law, prohibits the use of alcohol. This religious prohibition explains low rates of alcoholism in Islamic countries and Islamic communities in non-Islamic countries.

INTEREST IN COMMUNITY AFFAIRS

Benson, Williams, and Johnson (1987) found that importance of religion (measured by church attendance, orthodoxy, and personal religiosity) among adolescents was consistently correlated with measures of caring (concern for the poor and other helping behaviors). They also found significant correlations between altruism and religion, ranging from importance of religion in an adolescent's life (.27) to church attendance (.11). Overall, these findings indicate that young people who are deeply religious are more concerned with the well-being of others. Similarly, Donahue and Benson (1995), in a sample of 34,129 cases, drawn from a study of 250,000 public school students in thirty-two states, found that religion is the best predictor for altruistic behavior. Religion was more strongly correlated with altruistic behavior (.27) than with altruistic values (.16). The authors, however, suggested that the high rate of altruistic behavior may be a by-product of church attendance and compliance with the congregational expectation for participation in social services provided by the congregation. Regardless, it is evident that religion does affect adolescents' actual contribution to the welfare of others.

Congregations are similar to many civic and voluntary groups in that they are places of belonging, but belonging to a religious community has a moral weight not always granted to other membership organizations (Ammerman 1996). Congregational life is not limited to religious worship, studying, and teaching. In fact, congregational life spans many spheres of social and cultural activities that are organized and carried out by members (Heilman 1976). Some have also argued that religion has a political dimension because many congregations are actively involved in serving community needs. An important aspect of civic service is the teaching of social and community skills.

Brady, Verba, and Schlozman (1995) defined civic skills in terms of concrete activities, specifically letter-writing, participation in decision-making meetings, planning and chairing meetings, and giving presentations or speeches in public forums. The authors found that religious communities are one of the key places where people can acquire these civic skills. These skills can also be acquired in the workplace and the nonpolitical organization. However, these environments attract and favor white middle-class-to-upper-class members of society, and as such they perpetuate the power imbalance in society. It is in religious organizations that women, people of color, and the poor are provided with the opportunities to acquire skills of political participation. The congregational member who learns to write letters to support religious activities or collects money to pay for special holiday services can use those skills to actively participate in political life from local to federal levels. The authors concluded that religion is the predominant institution working against the class bias in American civic engagement—namely, the economically privileged also control a greater portion of the resources needed for democratic participation.

Membership in a religious congregation or a small religious group means belonging to a network of social relations. People who join groups, especially religious congregations, are likely to internalize the norms and activities prevalent in these groups. Involvement in the social life of a congregation increases the likelihood that an individual will engage in church-related activities with other members. Because many congregations provide social services, members have more opportunities for volunteer work and political participation.

Wilson and Janoski (1995) found that churchgoers, especially adults, are more likely to volunteer than those who do not attend church. Frequency of church attendance was less important when compared with attendance/nonattendance. Of those attending church at least a few times a year, 48 percent reported themselves as volunteers, while only 34 percent of those who did not attend church reported themselves as volunteers.

Wuthnow (1992) has suggested that, although the religiously active participate in many groups and get involved in community issues, those groups and activities tend to be insular and lead to greater separation by race and class rather than to social integration of society. Wuthnow emphasized that congregations tend to be places where people of the same race and social class come together to worship; thus, their social activities are also part of a segregated and exclusive group.

We have discussed in this chapter many of the positive contributions that religion makes to people's lives. We need, however, to keep in mind that religion has also generated or tacitly supported many evils. Among them are religious crusades, support of dictatorships, oppression (particularly sexism and racism), and the perpetuation of class structure that oppressed most members of society. Yet, to their credit, organized religions have also been a constructive force for the social good—a fact that needs to be acknowledged by social workers.

The findings discussed here demonstrate that religion has a strong effect on people's well-being and, for many, serves as a buffer against mental and physical adversity. In some instances, improved quality of life has resulted from religious beliefs; in others, from actual participation in a religious community. Belief and participation in a religious community do not always go hand in hand, although participation is indicative of one's beliefs. And in some instances, religion has had a negative effect, leading to antisocial behavior. But overall, the literature suggests that religion is strongly associated with good citizenship and improved physical and mental health. As such, it should be included in social work practice as a source of strength and as part of social work education.

As noted above, Bergin (1983) tested the pathology hypothesis of religion and behavior through a meta-analysis of twenty-four empirical studies carried out between 1951 and 1979. He found no across-studies correlation between these two variables. Yet this was a period during which the American Psychiatric Association Diagnostic Statistical Manuals referred to religious issues as a form of pathology (Lukoff, Lu, and Turner 1992), and therapists were prone to view religion as either incidental to the therapy or a source of the client's problem. As noted, Bergin found that 77 percent of these studies failed to show a negative effect of religion on people's lives, and some found no significant relationships at all. Bergin concluded that psychology has had a value bias against religion and has been too quick to interpret people's values and beliefs as psychopathological. In fact, as Lehr and Spilka (1989) and Paloutzian and Kirkpatrick (1995) noted, psychology of religion, very much like social work, has never received much attention in "mainstream" psychology and is relegated to a few specialized journals that are read by only a few in the discipline. The leading journals in psychology ignore this field almost completely. Interestingly, Ellis (1996) and Stack and Kanavy (1983) suggested that the vast majority of texts in criminology also completely avoid discussing religion.

Most religious communities serve as support groups for members and as places where people can obtain emotional and tangible support in times of need. Although religious teaching and practice help most people to cope more effectively with adversity, religion is neither a panacea nor a miracle cure-all. Religious people do get sick and suffer from stress just as nonreligious people do, and religious beliefs and participation apparently have better-demonstrated effects on some health and mental health problems. Negative side effects of organized religions range from authoritarianism and dogmatism to support of nationalistic crusades. The preponderance of the evidence, however, suggests that religion is modestly helpful in the areas of prosocial behavior, personal and social adjustment, life satisfaction and well-being, and physical symptomatology.

The implications of this literature review are that social work should view religion as an ally that enhances the quality of life and improves certain outcomes. If, as the literature suggests, religion benefits community tenure and stability, then social work needs to consider enlisting the help of organized religion in addressing personal and social issues. For example, practitioners might consider eliciting information regarding the religious affiliation and religious needs of clients; linking interested clients with a religious community; and including representation from the relevant religious community in the circle of care, particularly when a client is in crisis, as is the case when a spouse or a child dies.

The findings discussed in this chapter demonstrate that religion has a strong effect on people's well-being and, for many, serves as a buffer against mental and physical adversity. It is important to remember what Bourjolly (1998) found in her study of women who had been diagnosed with breast cancer. In her words, "unless one is encouraged to openly discuss her use of religion, she may be reluctant to do so, therefore limiting the use of interventions that are culturally relevant" (p. 33). The evidence of church groups' rebuilding lives indicated in this chapter is very promising, particularly for social work. We strongly believe that it is time for social work to consider a limited partnership with the religious communities of this nation.

CHAPTER 8

RELIGION AND SOCIAL SERVICES PROVISION AT THE END OF THE TWENTIETH CENTURY

The full extent, depth, and range of religious-based social services provision in the United States have yet to be addressed in the social work literature. Currently, there are no aggregate statistics regarding the overall contribution of the religious community to the welfare of Americans. Wilensky and Lebeaux (1965) analyzed data for 1952 regarding the social welfare and health expenditure of the nonprofit sector (excluding governmental expenditures). Total health expenditures were $675 million, of which religious organizations contributed $375 million (55.6%); total welfare expenditures were $1,610 million, of which religious-based organizations contributed $235 million (14.6%). Although current data of this nature are not available, anecdotal and descriptive studies suggest that many services are provided under religious auspices and that social service constitutes a major part of clergy and lay-leader activity. In this section, we highlight findings from these studies, to be followed later by findings from our own studies. Our intent in this chapter and the following three chapters is to show that social services in religious communities in the United States are involved in social services provision to a degree unimagined and unacknowledged in the social work literature.

As an introductory note, it is important to point out that the major reason for exempting nonprofit organizations from taxation is the assumption that these organizations confer benefits to society as a whole and not just to those who operate the corporation. Brown (1990:1634) went further, noting that:

Congress grants section 501(c)(3) status to organizations that it believes convey these significant beneficial externalities. The government forgoes tax revenue to encourage production of the public benefits these organizations convey. The Supreme Court has held that the public benefits conferred by religious organizations are a "beneficial and stabilizing influence in community life" and encouragement of diversified views and perspectives which contributes to vigorous, pluralistic society.

People expect the religious community to be engaged in welfare provision and to provide direct services to people in need. Ammerman (1996), for example, found that "eighty-eight percent of the congregational members interviewed said that helping the needy is very important or essential to living the Christian life, and ninety-two percent said that service to the needy is very important or essential to the ministry of their congregation" (p. 8). At the same time, people in need are expected to approach religious institutions as sources of help.

FAITH AND PHILANTHROPY

An important corollary to understanding religious-based social services provision is understanding that people with religious commitment tend to contribute to charities of all kinds. The Russ Reid Company (1995:2), in conjunction with the Barna Research Corporation, carried out a study of donors (those who gave money to a nonprofit organization other than a church or place of worship in the twelve-month period preceding the study). They found that "the best predictor of people's giving behavior relates to the intensity and nature of their spiritual commitment. Eighty-two percent of the people who give to nonprofit organizations also give to churches or places of worship." They went on to state that "no other characteristic is so predominant or defining [of donors] as religious giving" (p. 3). Among the regular donors in the study, 60 percent had attended a church or another religious service in the past month; 37 percent had volunteered at their place of worship in the past month; and 84 percent agreed that religious faith was very important in life. This high correlation between giving to charities and involvement in religious organizations is not coincidental. For many people, giving to others is central to their religious beliefs. Given this historical chain of charity, it is evident that giving is rooted in religious belief.

The Independent Sector biannual survey of volunteering and giving (Hodgkinson et al. 1994) found a strong correlation between volunteering and giving. This national survey, carried out by the Gallup organization, also found that religious communities are a main source of volunteers. When volunteers were asked how they were recruited, the majority (56%) reported they had been recruited by friends involved (as staff or volunteers) in the organization. Others reported recruitment by religious institutions (26.4%), family members or relatives (18.7%), coworkers (10.9%), employers (6%), and others (13.8%). It is important to note that the options in this questions were not exclusive and that people could answer with more than one option. Hodgkinson and her colleagues also found that the average hours of volunteering per week rose from 1.6 hours for those who do not attend church to 3.4 hours for those who attend church weekly.

The correlation between volunteering and the organized religious community suggests that people who worship together form a community and are more likely to volunteer as a group or as a representative of the group. For example, in Council Grove, Kansas, once a month each local religious congregation provides the local thrift store with volunteers who sort out clothing, mend and sew whatever is needed, shelve items, and assist customers. Wymer (1999) reported that a key factor distinguishing church volunteers from nonvolunteers was regular attendance at religious services: volunteers attended 6.7 services per month, compared with 2.4 services per month for nonvolunteers. This finding suggests that those who attend church services more frequently feel more connected to the religious community and are more willing to volunteer. Robert Wuthnow (1994) noted that "religious organizations tell people of opportunities to serve, both within and beyond the congregation itself, and provide personal contacts, committees, phone numbers, meeting space, transportation, or whatever it may take to help turn good intentions into action" (pp. 242–43).

The link between church membership and volunteering should be qualified, as Wilson and Janoski (1995) have found that members of conservative Protestant congregations are less likely to be involved in secular volunteer activities. Their focus is more on the interior spiritual life than on the community at large. Although congregants do learn social skills, they use them primarily for evangelical purposes and not for social and secular causes. Furthermore, these authors found that only 38 percent of conservative Protestants who never attend church were volunteers, as compared with 71 percent of those who do attend church. Hence, religious activity is associated with willingness to help others in the community.

Marilyn Dickey and her colleagues (1997) reported in the *Chronicle of Philanthropy* that in 1996 the Salvation Army raised more than $1 billion from private sources, far more than any other charity in America. It was ranked first in public donations, followed by the Red Cross ($480 million). Other religious-based organizations in the top ten charitable organizations were Catholic Charities ($385 million), Second Harvest ($351 million), YMCA of the USA ($340 million), and Habitat for Humanity International ($334 million). The ranking of five religious-based charities among the nation's top ten charities indicates strong and generous public support for religious-based social service organizations.

In our opinion, the devolution that started in the early 1980s has given rise to uninformed rhetoric by conservative politicians and scholars regarding an expanded role for the religious community in the provision of social services. Because there are no hard data to support their claims that welfare services delivery would improve under religious auspices, practitioners have no real criteria by which to judge the directions that service development should take in this new era. To date, scholars concerned with social welfare and nonprofit organizations have tended to concentrate solely on the secular aspects of service delivery. Yet findings suggest that many religious people are willing to help others in need and that their support of nonprofit organizations goes beyond financial contributions (Hodgkinson et al. 1994; Wineburg 1996; Wuthnow 1994). The religious community has the potential to be a partner with secular services, but unfortunately the scholarly community and the social work leadership continue to ignore this important resource. We believe that this approach is detrimental over the long run, because systematic research is necessary to provide a basis for new services and new partnerships. Without systematic studies, service approaches will develop haphazardly.

Bellah (1991) asserted that religion is the force that ties together community members and the community at large: people join together for religious purposes and, in the process, form associations that benefit the community in several ways. Local congregations provide physical/social space where people can come and meet others like themselves, pray with them, and often receive help for their problems. These congregations are more than service agencies; they are places where people can organize to care for their communities (McDougall 1993).

EXAMPLES OF RELIGIOUS-BASED SOCIAL SERVICES

One example of the role played by religious organizations in the social welfare arena is in the field of homelessness. On May 17, 1994, the federal government released its report *Priority: Home! The Federal Plan to Break the Cycle of Home-*

lessness. While acknowledging the government's lack of significant progress in alleviating the problem, the report gave credit to the nation's churches, synagogues, and other nonprofit organizations, which responded to the crisis in the early 1980s, long before the federal government even conceded that there was a problem (Alliance 1994).

A specific example will illustrate this trend: New York City's Partnership for the Homeless, which was founded in 1982. The Partnership was created by a handful of religious leaders from the city's major faith traditions who were distressed by the lack of services to meet the burgeoning needs of the homeless. The Partnership became one of the premier service organizations of its kind, mobilizing some 150 churches and synagogues and more than 11,000 community and congregational volunteers to provide a new community of comprehensive care for the homeless (Cohen and Jeager 1994). A similar example was reported by Bonne and Ronne (1990). Oakhurst Baptist Church in Atlanta started a homeless ministry, even though the church's building was not in the center city. The church van picks up homeless men and takes them to the church, where they are fed and offered a place for the night. These authors note that, before the Oakhurst ministry, Atlanta had three thousand homeless people and bed space for only thirty. Currently, some seventy other congregations, inspired by Oakhurst's example, shelter homeless people, some of them year-round.

It is often assumed that conservative or evangelical religious groups are not interested in social services provision because their emphasis is on proselytizing. This is not always the case. The International Union of Gospel Missions (IUGM), an evangelical group, is a major player in serving the homeless. Founded in 1913, IUGM supports some 250 inner-city rescue missions across the United States (Burger 1996). The combined activity of these missions is very impressive. In 1997 they provided 12 million nights of lodging, 24 million meals, 30 million items of clothing, almost a million items of furniture, and "graduated more than 20,000 homeless men and women into productive living" (Burger, personal communication, December 2, 1997). IUGM makes it clear that they firmly believe that spiritual renewal is the fountainhead for personal transformation. As Burger noted: "The homeless need an environment in which they are challenged to acknowledge and consistently renounce unhealthy behaviors; otherwise, they won't acquire the practical or emotional skills they need to succeed" (p. 24). These missions stress personal contacts between church members and homeless people, which are predicated upon Christian teaching and transformational experiences. Providers and volunteers pray and read the Bible with clients, while providing quality care that ranges from basic needs of food, clothing, and shelter to permanent housing and drug and alcohol rehabilitation. IUGM boasts a 70–80 percent rate of success among those who graduated from the program. Clearly, this program is not for all clients. IUGM providers screen potential clients to identify those with higher chances of success, and the organization's statistics do not include those who drop out. Still, the numbers of those served and the range of services provided are impressive because IUGM's rescue missions do not expect or accept any government support. The overwhelming majority of funds come from individual members, participating congregations, and corporate sponsors. Whether or not one approves of IUGM's evangelism, it is impossible to ignore its impressive, ongoing commitment to assist the neediest members of our society.

It is ironic that the religious community, the first to acknowledge and cope with homelessness, may also be the last. In response to a public backlash against helping the homeless, most cities have cut back services, and only the religious community has taken up the slack. Kress (1994) reported how residents in a Washington, D.C., neighborhood used zoning regulation and city support to prevent a religious group from offering shelter, a soup kitchen, and other services for the homeless. Burger (1996) also reported how cities and zoning boards are restricting increases in homeless services by religious groups, despite their private funding. In chapter 13, we discuss the case of Pastor Wiley Drake, whose congregation, First Southern Baptist Church of Buena Park, California, was ordered by a judge to stop housing homeless people on the church's patio. The congregants insisted that the patio was much better suited to sleeping than the streets, but the judge disagreed. These examples are indicative of changing attitudes toward the homeless over the past fifteen years. They also demonstrate how the religious community has moved from being the pioneer to being the last fully committed actor in helping America's homeless people.

Serving the homeless is but one example of how the religious community has taken the initiative in developing new and innovative modes of service delivery. When there were no public services available to people with AIDS, members of religious groups were among the first to assist, even if they disapproved of the moral behavior of those who had contracted AIDS. Susan Chambre (1991) found that AIDS volunteers in the New York metropolitan area were either people from a religious community or people who had firsthand experience with the disease and its effects. One example is God's Love We Deliver (GLWD), an organization formed by Ganga Stone, a Hindu follower (originally a Presbyterian). As a volunteer, she had brought canned food to a person with AIDS but realized that he needed freshly prepared food. GLWD, the non-profit organization that she started in 1994, serves more than eight hundred people daily with fresh and highly nutritious lunches and dinners (Bender 1995). Many volunteers who serve in GLWD do so because it resonates with their religious and spiritual beliefs of healing through feeding. A service like GLWD is particularly beneficial because it helps to meet the nonmedical needs of AIDS patients that hospitals and physicians tend to ignore. Food distribution significantly depends on the religious community. In Forest Hills, Queens, for example, two synagogues share in running a food distribution center. The synagogue member who initiated the "partnership" approached her rabbi and social service committee about the project after witnessing the death of a friend's child from AIDS (Bender 1995:35).

Religious denominations have provided a vast array of health and social services. For example, Wittberg (1994) noted that Catholic orders alone maintain some 645 orphanages and 500 hospitals in the United States. Filinson (1988) documented how a mental health center trained and used church volunteers from an interfaith coalition to provide services to people with Alzheimer's disease, and Hendrickson (1987) reported health services provided by congregations. Art Moore (1998) discussed the role of religious-based organizations in the child welfare system. Accordingly, religious groups have organized to provide better foster care services and to offer responsible and caring adoptive parents. One such example is Child Save, of Glendale, California, a Christian organization that works in collaboration with local child welfare services. Moreover, it links the public system with foster and adoptive families from some 250 religious congregations, representing numerous denominations. In each church, members may serve as the foster parents or as support to the foster parents, providing baby-sitting and respite care. Similarly, in Texas the placement of minority children in homes of similar backgrounds is provided through a collaboration between public services and religious organizations. Through a network of churches, Project Hustle, for example, provides homes for African-American children who are considered hard to place. These are just a few examples of a national trend that saves millions of dollars annually and enhances the quality of foster care provided for children who must be removed from their biological parents.

An example of how devolution is taking form on Main Street can be seen in the case of the First Baptist Church of Philadelphia, one of the oldest congregations in the country. Many outside groups use the church's spacious facilities for their programs. A minimal rental fee helps the small membership to meet the costs of operating this historic building. The building needs major repair, but the congregation is ineligible for government funding because of the principle of separation of church and state. It is therefore somewhat ironic that, when the City of Philadelphia was forced to cut a publicly funded AA program to which the courts had referred offenders with substance abuse problems, probation and parole officers began referring their clients to First Baptist's AA and NA programs. They simply told their clients to attend the AA or NA meeting at the church and bring back a signature from the group leader.

As a result, for the first time in its history, the First Baptist Church has had to hire a security firm to protect the facility from the vandalism that has occurred in conjunction with the church-housed rehabilitation programs. By late 1994 the number of those attending the AA and NA programs averaged five hundred a day. As the population of recovering substance users and offenders grew, so did thefts and damage to the church property. Whatever was not nailed down was stolen, and church volunteers who staffed the doors and building complained of abusive behavior by clients. The First Baptist congregation decided not to ask for reimbursement, even though these clients had been shunted into their program without any advance warning from city officials. The closing of the public program by the City of Philadelphia also ended entitlement for service. Continued availability of the service depends on how long the congregation is willing to support the program and to assume the financial burden. With devolution, we may expect more such blurring between public and private functions of the religious community. Consequently, we may also expect corresponding debates about the use of public funds to refurbish a religious structure that serves both public and private functions.

A recent phenomenon in the religious community is a new form of religious congregation, the mega-church, also known as the "next church." In this kind of congregation, thousands of individuals attend a concert-like service in a mall-like building. Even in these large institutions, volunteerism and social services are central (Trueheart 1996). "Willow Creek, for example, is famous for its active car-repair ministry, in which weekend grease jockeys fix up the cars of fellow parishioners who can't afford professional service or restore clunkers to life and donate them to the poor" (Trueheart 1996:56). In 1993 alone, this ministry gave away eighty-five vehicles to poor single mothers who had no means of transportation. This congregation also feeds 350 people a month with its food pantry and donates more than $250,000 annually to local charities (Maudlin and Gilbreath 1994).

RELIGION AND ETHNIC MINORITIES

Lincoln and Mamiya (1990) noted that the black church has given birth to numerous social institutions that have strengthened the African-American community and helped community members. Among these were mutual aid societies, fraternal lodges, benevolent societies, burial associations, and other mutual-help organizations. During the period 1950–1960, the black church discovered its political voice and harnessed its energy to the social justice movement. All these initiatives contributed to empowering the African-American community. Aldon Morris (1984) noted the extensive role played by black churches in the South in developing and spreading the civil rights movement (see also Webber 1964).

Less well publicized is the role of the Black Muslim movement in working for prisoners' rights in the early 1960s. The philosophy and actions of the prisoners' rights movement coincided in many ways with those of the civil rights movement. Many of the early legal cases for prisoners' rights were filed by Black Muslims with the support of the movement. Consequently, prisoners won the right to practice their religion without fear of punishment and to file civil rights suits against prison officials (Smith 1993). The most important cases filed by Black Muslims were *Sostre v. McGinnis* (1971), which helped establish the principle that prisoners can receive monetary compensation for deprivation of constitutional rights, and *Cooper v. Pate* (1964), which enabled prisoners to file suits against officials of state correctional facilities under the Civil Rights Act of 1871. Smith noted that in the twelve months preceding June 1987, 23,697 civil rights cases were filed by prisoners based on the precedent set in the *Cooper v. Pate* case.

Verba, Schlozman, and Brady (1995) found that churches attended by African Americans, regardless of denomination, were more likely to impart civic skills, promote political participation, and provide social services to the community. For example, Chang et al. (1994) noted that African-American congregations in New Haven, Connecticut, offered a remarkable range of programs and services:

> These programs included education, substance abuse, child abuse, parenting, domestic violence, job training/unemployment, adoption/foster care, homeless shelters, soup kitchens, youth programs, elderly programs, long-term illness, AIDS, food and clothing distribution, counseling, spiritual outreach, day care, recreation, social and political activism, finances, and various volunteer programs. . . . What is even more remarkable about them

[African-American congregations] is that almost all of them reported that their programs are financed entirely through church funds with no external forms of support.   (p. 93)

Testimony to the importance of the black church is provided by Thomas et al. (1994) and by Rubin, Billingsley, and Caldwell (1994). These researchers studied some 634 Northern black congregations and found that 67 percent had family support programs. Of these programs, only 28 percent were expressive (personal support without services), while 46 percent were instrumental (services) and 26 percent were both instrumental and expressive. Other programs reported by congregations included youth programs (28%), parenting/sexuality (27%), substance abuse (27%), youth-at-risk (25%), role-modeling (14%), and job training (13%).

One underreported fact is that many middle-class African Americans who have joined the "white flight" to the suburbs still remain active in their inner-city congregations. They not only return every weekend to their inner-city neighborhoods for worship and fellowship, but they also work to improve the quality of life in their churches' home community (Cnaan 1997). This contribution of the suburban African-American community to inner-city life is seldom discussed either in the media or in the professional literature. Indeed, the complex relationships between suburban residents and center-city congregations have received little attention (Mukenge 1983). It is important to note that this continued concern and involvement by those who have left the neighborhood stands in opposition to Morris Janowitz's (1967) notion of "communities of limited liability"—namely, that local religious congregations are associations in which members not only worship but also invest their families, wealth, and concern. Some leave the old neighborhood for larger houses, more-rewarding jobs, or better amenities. Mukenge's findings showed that, for many middle-class African Americans, the transition upward is not necessarily at the expense of abdicating responsibility to the welfare and well-being of their former inner-city community.

Anna Waring and Susan Sanders (1997) reported the case of Englewood, a Chicago neighborhood on the decline over the past twenty years in terms of number of residents, economic viability, and safety. In April 1993, the mayor and the police superintendent identified five police districts as experimental prototypes for Chicago's Alternative Police Strategy. In Englewood the strategy centered on using the neighborhood's three hundred churches as the focal point of a joint police and community campaign to reduce crime. Because the police had little credibility with the neighborhood's 108,000 residents, they sought the support of local clergy, who knew the community's needs, were trusted by the residents, and could assemble large numbers of people. The program included sixty ministers, and all meetings took place in congregational buildings. There the agenda focused on crime prevention but was also imbued with the culture and spirit of the church. Waring and Sanders noted: "Churches were stable entities in a community that had experienced a large amount of turnover among residents and businesses. As stable institutions, these churches could serve as locations for services and activities unlike some of the other institutions that disappeared as financial resources declined" (p. 19). Thus the churches were the entry point into the community, and the church culture helped bring community residents and the police together in new joint initiatives to reduce crime.

C. Eric Lincoln and Lawrence Mamiya (1993), after considering the historical role of the black church from the days of slavery to the post–civil rights movement, noted that if the black church is to sustain its role in the community, then it must be ready to adapt to new needs, given the reality of urban decay. They concluded: "Now the black church faces the gravest challenge of all: [t]he challenge to sustain with economic empowerment the hard-won freedoms that came with open access to education and the legal availability of civil rights." Lincoln and Mamiya also noted that the black church is, economically speaking, the largest institution in the black community. The black church annually takes in more than $2 billion in offerings, donations, and charitable giving. It takes in even more in the form of volunteer service and in-kind support from members and community residents. As such, religion is a major social, political, and economic force that enhances the quality of life in the black community.

In the Hispanic community many congregations are active in refugee resettlement and in helping members become part of the community (Orr et al. 1994). Many of these congregations offer classes in English as a Second Language (ESL) and other educational and vocational training. Similarly, Delgado and Humm-Delgado (1982) noted that in Hispanic communities the dominant religions (primarily Catholicism and some Protestant denominations) are the key social and welfare service providers. These authors also noted that the extended family, folk healers, merchants' and social clubs, and religious organizations are key sources of social support in the Hispanic community.

Two examples that demonstrate the power of local coalitions to represent the needs and political will of the Hispanic community are Oakland Community Organizations (OCO) and Nueva Esperanza, in Philadelphia (described in detail in the next chapter). OCO is a federation of eighteen churches in Oakland, California, representing some 25,000 residents, most of whom are of Hispanic origin. OCO is a religious organization that seeks to meet the social and political needs of community residents. OCO has succeeded in persuading the city to improve neighborhood street lighting, established an aviation academy in the public school system, and helped persuade Montgomery Ward to give up a large old store building that the company closed but did not sell or redevelop.

IMMIGRANTS AND RELIGIOUS ORGANIZATIONS

As early as 1951, Oscar Handlin had noted the importance of the religious community to numerous immigrant groups throughout American history. People who come to a new country with a different language, different norms and expectations, and few kinship bonds tend to experience higher levels of anomie and less successful adaptation. Immigrants who do not have a broad social network that can assist them must find an alternative support system. For many, an ethnic congregation or religious community is the answer (Gelfand and Fandetti 1986). One reason that these congregations can be so supportive is that they are highly segregated. As one might expect, people are more likely to join in efforts with others who are more like themselves. Moberg (1984) noted: "The most segregated hour of the week may still be 11:00 A.M. Sunday, the customary Protestant worship hour, but most of it is by the minorities' choice" (p. 451). It is the choice of immigrant minorities because the congregation serves as an assimilation center where newcomers are provided both practical information and emotional support by those who share their native culture and language. Church members who immigrated a few years earlier, for example, give newcomers advice on how to adapt to the new culture and often make them loans, as most new immigrants are unable to secure loans from commercial banks.

Mohl and Betten (1981) studied the immigrant history of Gary, Indiana. They found that the first Polish, Croatian, Slovak, and Lithuanian Catholic churches were all founded at the initiative of laypeople, in an effort to preserve their ethnic heritage and to foster a sense of belonging. Consequently, parochial schools as well as church sermons tended to support ethnic traditions. These churches established a sense of ethnic identity that distinguished insiders from outsiders, members from nonmembers. Immigrant Protestant, Orthodox (Greek, Romanian, and the like), and Jewish congregations also emerged and served as sources of acculturation and support. Mohl and Betten observed that over time, with the growing Americanization of the second generation, the ethnic parochial schools created by immigrant groups began to decline and were replaced by Sunday schools.

Immigrants frequently use religious congregations as a means of reestablishing a sense of community in a strange, and sometimes hostile, host society, maintaining ties with their home culture, and enhancing adaptation to American culture. For example, Kim and Kim (1997) showed how Korean churches are serving both as religious centers and as community centers. These churches are the places where help is provided, where Korean classes are held for children, and where new families form friendships. Kim and Kim suggested that "to most Korean immigrants, churches are the kind of organization with which they need to be affiliated for a meaningful living in the United States. Collectively, the Korean ethnic churches are indispensable" (p. 12).

Similarly, Menjivar and Agadjanian (1997) studied Salvadorian immigrants in Washington, D.C. They found that those who attend church started doing so immediately after arriving in the United States and that, for many of them, the church is their only form of social interaction other than the family. They noted that the local Catholic and Protestant churches provide the immigrants with assistance including job referrals, legal help, medical care, family support, and English as a Second Language classes. The Catholic Church, through the cardinal, even protested the Personal Responsibility and Work Opportunity Reconciliation Act of 1996, which will certainly hurt many in the Salvadorian community. These are not ethnic churches, but to accommodate the many immigrant congregants, the worship service is largely bilingual and in the Salvadorian tradition.

Bankston and Zhou (1995), who studied the adaptation process of 403 Vietnamese high school students, found that religious participation contributed significantly to ethnic identification. Religious participation, in turn, facilitated positive adaptation to American society by increasing the probability that adolescents would do well in school, set their sights on future education, and avoid some of the dangers that confront young people today.

Kegley and Doob (1984) noted that aiding illegal immigrants who are denied political asylum poses an ethical dilemma for many congregations, missions, and other religious organizations. These authors raised the issue of civil disobedience and identified eight criteria that justify its use in specific cases. They also noted that ethnic congregations are more likely to help illegal immigrants and that these congregations often must choose between breaking the law and holding themselves responsible for the eventual torture or murder of those who are deported.

HEALTH CARE AND RELIGIOUS ORGANIZATIONS

Quinn and Thomas (1994) reported that the black church was the first to cope with AIDS within the African-American community. They noted that African Americans, who constitute 12 percent of the American population, represent 32 percent of AIDS cases. These authors reported a project by the Southern Christian Leadership Conference Center that provided AIDS education in five cities. This project is not unique, as African-American clergy across the nation are heavily involved in community health education, and AIDS prevention is a key issue.

Eng, Hatch, and Callan (1985) described a project to institutionalize health-related activities through the black church in the rural South. The goal was to improve the fit between recommended health behaviors (diet, exercise, immunization, risk reduction, hypertension control, checkups, and so on) and the social support network of the congregation. The expectation was that "members will not only be able to persuade one another to effect change but will also be able to offer social support for sustainable change" (p. 83). Church members, trained by experts, became "lay health advisers," who identified risk factors in their communities and helped people cope with health problems. Because of the shortage of medical staff in rural communities and the lack of professional services, the lay health advisers became the link to health sources and promoters of public health and prevention in their communities via their respective churches.

In a review of the literature on church-based health promotion programs, Ransdell and Rehling (1996) reported on the history and growth of church involvement in health promotion, factors contributing to program success, barriers to implementation, problems during implementation, and implications for practice. They concluded that churches are taking on more-complex and sophisticated roles, as evidenced by their growing involvement in health promotion.

Brashears and Roberts (1996) reported the case of the Second Baptist Church in Kansas City, which has a long history of helping its members. In 1987 the church hired one of its members who held an M.S.W. degree as a part-time social worker. This arrangement made church members and their families eligible for many social and health-related services. Free services included case management for elderly and disabled members; support for homebound and institutionalized members; and support for members and families experiencing health crises, distress, or death. "The social worker also served as coordinator of the various worship and missionary groups who had contact with shut-in or elderly members to see that their needs were met in a balanced, inclusive way" (p. 188). The social worker also worked with other health-related groups in the community, such as hospice, and produced a fifty-two-page guide detailing some 280 community social and health resources available to members and their families in the community.

COMMUNITY ORGANIZATIONS AND RELIGIOUS ORGANIZATIONS

Industrial Areas Foundation (IAF) was begun by Saul Alinsky in 1940 (Horwitt 1989). IAF had its origins in Alinsky's "Back of the Yards" organization, a coalition between Catholic congregations and labor/Communist Party organizers to enhance the quality of life in Chicago's neighborhoods by means of advocacy and lobbying. Alinsky is often credited as pioneering social action and empowerment strategies. Today IAF is the most prominent national organization dedicated to community-based organizing. Its network of affiliates includes those in New York, Connecticut, Illinois, Tennessee, Georgia, Texas, and California. IAF, which considers itself an "organization of organizations," provides professional organizers with expertise in the workings of metropolitan political economies as well as in social movement dynamics. IAF does not determine political agendas at the local level, but encourages the local coalitions, who pay fees to IAF and the salaries of lead organizers, to do so.

Michael Byrd (1997) described the work of IAF in Nashville. In 1993 a convention was held to form Tying Nashville Together (TNT). In the months following the founding convention, TNT visited schools, conducted public hearings on nursing homes, and held School Board Candidates Accountability Night and Metro Council Candidates Accountability Night. Leaders also formulated an after-school K–8 program and a "strategy for labor force development and economic development," both based on IAF initiatives in other communities. In addition, TNT members convinced the mayor's office to open and fund a Neighborhood Justice Center for mediating disputes without police intervention as a means of fostering a sense of community. That so much has been accomplished so quickly is attributable to the organization's large membership. By 1995, TNT included forty-three congregations and associations representing about five thousand people. Attendance at TNT meetings, actions, and assemblies is remarkably high. At all TNT activities, members pray together and emphasize that their raison d'être is to fulfill their religious calling. TNT is one of more than two hundred community-change projects supported by the Campaign for Human Development of the Catholic Church.

Oakland Community Organizations (OCO), which was discussed above, is a chapter of a larger national religious organization, Pacific Institute for Community Organization (PICO). PICO is a national network of urban community-organizing federations based in religious congregations (Wood 1997). PICO is one of four national church-related organizations committed to community organizing. The other three are the Industrial Areas Foundation (IAF), Gamaliel, and Direct Action and Research Training Center (DART). As Boyte (1989) noted, this type of community organizing, currently under way in some 120 urban centers in the United States, is the most extensive and successful effort by low-income people (citizens and unregistered aliens) to influence the social, economic, and political sphere in which they reside. Each local federation is composed of ten to forty congregations or religious groups. These local federations are affiliated with and supported by the national organization. As noted above, Tying Nashville Together (TNT) is a member organization of IAF. In all these cases, organizers meet with individuals and small groups to identify needs and ways to cope with them. Once a need and a solution strategy are agreed upon, the group selects the target person/group for facilitating the change, be it city hall, an individual politician, a utility company, a transportation authority, or a private company. The fact that a federation of religious congregations can galvanize large numbers of people to advocate an initiative is a compelling reason in itself for politicians and business owners to listen and to attempt to cooperate.

The involvement of a congregation in political action is strongly associated with the congregation's religious life. In a study of thirteen individuals from three congregations, Wood (1994) found that the most politically successful congregation is not the one with the most politicized faith but rather the one whose liturgy leads to rich religious experience and who interprets its religious symbols in this-world terms.

One important point must be stressed: religious congregations are among the last community institutions still functioning in American's neighborhoods. Peter Dobkin Hall (1996) found that in New Haven, Connecticut, the number of local voluntary associations remained stable from 1850 to 1990. What is of interest is that during this period, the number of fraternal/sororal organizations dramatically decreased, almost to the point of extinction, while the number of religious congregations dramatically increased. His findings provide further evidence that the one community institution still active and visible in most American communities is the local religious congregation. These congregations meet the criteria for a community institution in that their locale and activities provide a focal point for fostering and expressing feelings of community. Large numbers of people can also be recruited to work on behalf of causes important to the community through local congregations.

HOUSING FOR THE POOR AND ELDERLY

Providing housing for the poor and elderly is another social service role of the religious community. This relatively new service, which can range from minor renovations to rehabilitation of an entire block, is intended to help the community and its members (Mares 1994). A specific example is provided by Sengupta (1995:B1) in his report on the work of the Allen A.M.E. Church in Queens, New York. This church built a three-hundred-unit apartment complex for the elderly in 1980 with federal housing loans. Another 50 two-family homes are currently being built with city and state housing dollars. An additional seventy-six houses are either being developed by the church or have already been sold to private home buyers. The church also owns a strip mall that houses a pizzeria, a beauty shop, and a home health care agency. Sengupta (1995:B1) concluded: "In the church world, Allen A.M.E.'s real estate ventures are nothing new. . . . Over the last decade, many Black churches have taken up the task of building housing and running neighborhood businesses at a time when the federal government has largely abandoned urban economic development." Allen A.M.E. is not unique in this respect. As DePriest and Jones (1997) noted, many black churches across the country are serving as catalysts for the creation of black enterprises, jobs, and economic development. These authors provided additional examples of churches that use available public resources to enhance the lot of African-American people in their community. One such example was the Northwest Community Baptist Church in Houston:

> Northwest has engineered the construction of a 36,000-sq-ft. shopping center, home to several small businesses including the Deliverance Grocery and Deli Institute Inc., a grocery store training initiative. The church also owns a drug rehabilitation center, and in 1990 purchased 22.6 acres of land, at a price of $955,000, on which it will build a 3,000 seat sanctuary, community life center and Christian educational facility.   (pp. 197–98)

Another example is the Vine City Housing Ministry, Inc., in Atlanta, a coalition of eleven churches representing the residents of the Vine City community. The organization was established in the mid-1980s as a community response to a plan to build a state office building on a nine-acre parcel designated for redevelopment. The eleven churches, their clergy, and their congregants served as the catalyst and the leaders in this campaign. After several months of planned and well-organized demonstrations, the office building project was canceled, and a new land plan was approved for a mixed use of the property. What it is crucial to understand in this case is that the only local infrastructure the community had for organizing itself was its churches. It was to the churches that local residents looked for a solution, and indeed these local institutions managed to defeat the plan (Ward et al. 1994).

From its role as a housing advocacy organization, the Vine City Housing Ministry moved into the business of building. In 1988, with support from private foundations, Habitat for Humanity, and other volunteer groups, the coalition built its first home, for a resident from public housing and her children. In the following years the coalition received $10.5 million and built twenty-eight houses for low-cost and low-mortgage sale and was a partner in the rehabilitation of a twelve-unit apartment complex in the neighborhood. Clemetson and Coates (1992) assessed the housing success as follows: "The success of the funding efforts to date has depended greatly upon the church leaders' effectiveness in relationship-building and in using the moral and political force of the churches to attract attention and resources to the venture" (p. 12).

Although there are no national statistics on the scope of housing development by religious groups, numerous case studies indicate that it is a national phenomenon. The Allen Temple Baptist Church in Oakland, California, for example, sponsored a seventy-five-unit housing development for the elderly and fifty-one additional unrestricted units (McCarthy 1995). Housing projects are also often run by coalitions of local congregations, as we have noted in chapter 2. In Brooklyn, the Bridge Street African Methodist Episcopal Church joined with ten local churches to redevelop a forty-block area. The church collected $1.3 million in tithes and offerings in 1992, with $600,000 going to renovation and construction. The effort included renovating forty housing units and building twenty-two duplexes in partnership with the Enterprise Foundation and the New York Partnership. One national statistic is provided by the Special Committee on Aging United States Senate (1984), which reported that a national survey of Section 202 housing for the elderly and the handicapped found that religious groups sponsored 59 percent of all 202 developments for the aged.

In Indianapolis, the Mid-North Church Council, working with the Mapleton–Fall Creek Neighborhood Association, established the Mapleton–Fall Creek Housing Development Corporation in 1985. With a grant from Lilly Endowment, the corporation works with residents on housing rehabilitation. To date, more than two hundred homes have been repaired, remodeled, or renovated. The council has also implemented job training in construction trades, personal counseling, and other social services. For low-income purchasers, one-on-one counseling sessions are required to help families learn how to improve their credit record and design a budget (Kriplin 1995).

Another example of religious-based housing development can be found in the East Brooklyn Churches (EBC), a coalition of churches that joined with the Industrial Areas Foundation (IAF). The goal was to redevelop Brooklyn, a deteriorating neighborhood with little financial stability, many abandoned properties, and outmigration of most working-class families. IAF agreed to participate, on the condition that EBC first raise $200,000, which it did.

The first campaigns were well organized and were chosen to assure success. As a result, street signs were replaced, food quality and sanitary conditions in local supermarkets were improved, long-abandoned buildings were demolished, smokeshops (places for selling illegal narcotics) were closed, and a voter registration campaign boasted an increase of ten thousand new voters in 1984. When EBC devised its housing project—building a thousand new homes in Brooklyn—it was estimated that the cost would be $7.5 million. Support for the plan, named the Nehemiah Project, came from Missouri Synod Lutherans ($1 million), the Catholic bishop of New York, who became an avid supporter of the coalition ($2.5 million), and the Episcopalians of Long Island ($1 million). Pressured to support the Nehemiah Project, the City of New York donated the land, paid for landfill removal, and provided $10,000 in interest-free loans for new homeowners. EBC is still in operation, building new houses and representing itself vis-à-vis the city. It is a true local coalition, with each congregation represented by its clergy and three or four lay leaders. EBC has no president, and decisions are made by consensus. In a review of EBC, Gittings (1987) accounted for the success of this advocacy and housing coalition as follows: "In an area bereft of banks, civic clubs, industry, and professionals, the churches were the only organizations—apart from the rackets—that remained alive amid the wreckage of the community" (p. 10). Pastors of these churches were forced to become the entrepreneurs of the community, since they were the community's only organized cohesive social organization that remained intact. As such, they spearheaded the civic campaign to improve services as well as to found the Nehemiah Project.

OTHER PUBLIC ROLES OF CONGREGATIONS

Day Care

The religious community plays an important role in the field of day care. This service has become even more crucial since the drastic cuts in AFDC under the 1996 Personal Responsibility and Work Opportunity Reconciliation Act (P.L. 140). Single mothers of young children, who now must find work, would find the availability of day care even more limited were it not for congregations. A third of all day care in the United States is housed in religious buildings, making the religious community the largest provider of day care in the country. Half of these programs are provided by the congregations themselves, the other half by independent, usually not-for-profit organizations (Lindner, Mattis, and Rogers 1983; Trost 1988). Cnaan (1997) found, in a national study of 111 congregations housed in older properties (built before 1940), that one-quarter of them housed a day care center. Churches, synagogues, and other religious communities offer special advantages in that they generally have ample space and well-equipped kitchen facilities that are available during the week. The potential for more congregations to be sites for day care centers could be fully realized with the encouragement of and collaboration with social service agencies.

Ammerman (1996) noted that congregations "provide meeting space and transportation, bulletin boards and public address systems, copying machines and paper. The material resources of congregations and other voluntary organizations provide an infrastructure for doing the work of the community, an infrastructure often most visible in times of crisis" (pp. 7–8). She further noted: "The material infrastructure of gymnasiums and kitchens and telephones and vans is a critical part of the social capital contributed to the rest of society by voluntary organizations, especially congregations" (p. 8).

Social Action

Burch (1965) discussed the different types of social welfare services in which religious organizations were involved. One type of social service—direct care to individuals, families, groups, and sometimes communities—has already been discussed in this chapter. The other type of service is social action, which is characterized by involvement in social policy/planning/change; informing members of social needs, problems, policies, and community changes; organization of members and others for action; and attempts to

effect changes in the power structure that will affect present and future policies. The distinction between these two types of religious involvement in
social welfare can be viewed as macro practice versus micro practice. It can
be best understood by the words of Bishop Dom Helder Camara (cited in
Simon 1987): "I brought food to the hungry, and people called me a saint; I
asked why people were hungry, and people called me a communist." The issue
of social action on the part of the religious community, especially regarding
empowerment, is discussed more fully in chapter 9, but some elements of it
are important here.

Biblical injunctions to help the traveler and the refugee are at the heart of
the Sanctuary Movement: a recent example of social involvement by religious
congregations, especially those with a strong ethnic identity (Cunningham
1995). The Tuscon Ecumenical Council—Task Force for Central America
serves as central headquarters for this church-based movement, which began
in the early 1980s. The goal is to shelter refugees, primarily from Guatemala
and Salvador, who are at risk for deportation by the U.S. Immigration and
Naturalization Service (INS). The INS views these undocumented aliens as
seeking economic success rather than political asylum, whereas sanctuary
activists believe that many meet both international and U.S. criteria for political refugee status. In addition to providing shelter, sanctuary members actively protest these deportations as a violation of human rights, claiming that the
government has failed to consider the civil and religious unrest in many
Central American countries (MacEoin 1985).

The exact number of congregations involved in the movement is not
known. Most members carry out their activities with little or no publicity
because they are at risk of arrest for violating federal immigration laws. This
risk was made clear in the indictments of sanctuary activists in Arizona, New
Mexico, and Texas. In the highly publicized 1985–1986 trial of the "Tuscon 11,"
the defendants were indicted on seventy-one charges, all punishable by fine
and prison sentences (Wiltfang and McAdam 1991). Eight of the eleven defendants were indicted on at least one charge.

In San Francisco, the San Francisco Organizing Project (SFOP), which is
made up of twelve religious congregations, twelve labor organizations, and
one community group, was instrumental in the process that led St. Theresa
Catholic Church to become the first Catholic sanctuary in San Francisco. St.
Theresa and SFOP worked with Salvadorian families and were politically
involved in monitoring the Simpson-Rodino Refugee Act (Burks 1987).

Nancy Ammerman and Wade Roof (1995) documented the massive
involvement of churches in assisting families and communities faced with

severe economic dislocation and hardship. In times of natural disaster or tragedy, for example, churches and synagogues provide not only consolation to those in crisis but also tangible support that ranges from temporary shelters in religious properties to food, clothing, and other needed supplies. This support comes not only from local congregations but also from congregations across the nation.

Economic security is another issue addressed by the religious community. The concept of religious-based loan societies (discussed in chapter 5) is being continued in religious-based credit unions. For example, the Cory United Methodist Church in Cleveland, Ohio, under the leadership of the Reverend Orlando Chaffee, has established a credit union with some $1.7 million in assets and 1,100 members. The credit union provides financial services to neighborhoods without banks. It also helps people in areas that have been redlined by the banking industry to acquire basic financial and organizational skills and provides them with funds to avert crises or to start small businesses (Delloff 1995). In Oakland, California, Allen Temple Baptist Church established a credit union with $1 million in assets, a blood bank, and other initiatives that are vital to community service (McCarthy 1995). In south central Los Angeles, First African Methodist Episcopal (FAME) Church, working with a $500,000 grant from the Walt Disney Company and a similar grant from the Atlantic Richfield Company, has set up a program to make low-interest loans to minority entrepreneurs and finance the creation of jobs for community residents. FAME is also helping local residents become entrepreneurs by providing workshops and contracts.

A research team led by John Orr from the University of Southern California studied how Los Angeles "began to heal" after the 1992 race riots in the wake of the not-guilty verdict in the Rodney King trial (Orr et al. 1994). His team was surprised by the extent to which the religious community in L.A. was involved in community-based social services. They noted: "The vastness of the social service infrastructure that has been created by the city's religious institutions rarely becomes visible. . . . The religious social service infrastructure has become vast, because the needs of the city have been vast and because California's publicly supported infrastructure has been cut back in the face of the state's tax revolt and of its long lasting recession" (p. 16). One interviewee explained that "there certainly was an infrastructure that could be activated at a moment's notice" (p. 16).

The work of the Society of Friends, whose doctrine of the "inner light" holds that all persons are of immense value and should be treated accordingly, is recognized worldwide. This egalitarianism has been evidenced in Quaker support of pacifism, care for the poor, prison reform, and opposition to slavery. The American Friends Service Committee, perhaps the best-known Quaker social service organization, was founded in 1917 to provide assistance for conscientious objectors and to send relief workers overseas. In 1947 the organization received the Nobel Prize for its outstanding work with refugees following World War II (Leonard 1988). Similarly, the Brethren Peace Fellowship actively opposed the war in Vietnam and any military solution for conflicts. The World Conference on Religion and Peace, an ecumenical organization with headquarters in New York City, is devoted to the promotion of peaceful solutions to world conflicts and is a powerful lobby against the arms race. The organization is especially active in pressuring the United Nations on behalf of the worldwide religious community.

In chapter 5 we referred to the historical and ongoing role of some Catholic orders in helping people. This role continues anew in our day, as evidenced by the work of Little Brothers of the Gospel (established by René Voillaume, a French priest, in 1965) and Little Sisters of the Gospel (established by a French nun in 1964). The orders consist of small contemplative communities (three or four members) who live and work among the poor. Members of these worldwide orders first arrived in the United States in the late 1960s. The Brothers and Sisters work in rural areas such as Appalachia and urban areas such as New York City. Their service ranges from helping people with AIDS and working in shelters for the dually diagnosed homeless to advocacy for low-income housing (Anderson 1994). In comparison with Catholic Charities and its $1.9 billion budget, this is a very modest order, yet it is indicative of the innovation that is found in today's religious-based social services system.

SCOPE AND BREADTH OF SOCIAL SERVICES

An example of the scope and breadth of religious-based social services can be found in a study conducted by the Community Workshop on Economic Development (1991). The study, based on a random sample of 152 synagogues and churches in Chicago, found that 77 percent of the sample housed at least one community program or organization and 59 percent housed two or more. The average religious congregation had two programs and served four hundred persons per month, 70 percent of whom were not church members. Most congregations (83%) provided space free of charge to other groups, such as

AA and food and/or clothing distribution centers. More than half of the congregations (59%) funded their own social service programs. These programs included meals for the hungry or frail elderly, counseling, youth services such as latchkey programs, tutoring for immigrant children, sports programs, and day care programs. Nowak (1989) found similar results for Philadelphia; 92 percent of AA groups, 80 percent of Police Athletic Leagues, and 55 percent of Boy Scout troops were housed in religious congregations.

In the only national survey of local congregations, Hodgkinson et al. (1993) found that in 1991 nearly 92 percent of congregations reported one or more programs in human services and welfare; 90 percent reported one or more programs in health (mostly visitation of the sick); and 62 percent reported involvement in international relief. These congregations also reported programs for public or societal benefits (62%), educational activities (53%), activities in arts and culture (50%), and programs for the environment (40%). In the same year, these congregations alone spent $4.4 billion for human services, $4.0 billion on health and hospitals, $1.3 billion for arts and culture, $0.7 billion on human justice and community development, $0.5 billion for environmental programs, $0.5 billion for international welfare, and $2.1 billion on other programs to benefit the community. Similar findings have been reported by La Barbera (1991), Salamon and Teitelbaum (1984), and Wineburg (1990–1991, 1994).

Thomas J. Harvey is the former president of Catholic Charities USA, a network of more than 1,200 social service agencies. Recently Harvey (1997) noted that when he came to Catholic Charities in 1982, the system served 3.5 million clients, of whom 23 percent needed basic immediate services such as food, clothing, and shelter. The remainder required specialized services, mostly a one-time type of help such as adoption, marital counseling, resettlement support, and personal guidance. When Harvey left office in 1992, the Catholic Charities system served some 12 million clients, of whom 68 percent needed the basics of food and shelter. This dramatic threefold increase in clients and the need for basic services over a ten-year period underscores the challenge imposed by the devolution begun in the early 1980s by the Reagan administration. As we noted earlier, it took the public sector much longer to acknowledge and come to terms with the advancement of homelessness as a social problem that needs massive social and fiscal intervention.

It is very difficult to assess the overall impact of the religious community in the field of social and community service delivery. One attempt was made in 1985 by the Council on Foundations (1985), which identified 2,700 religious-based social service agencies that the council termed *charities* and mailed questionnaires to them. (This number is an underestimate, as it does not include church-based services.) The response rate was 19 percent (N = 485), which was reasonable for this type of study. The support represented by these 485 organizations in 1985 came to more than $1 billion in grants, loans, and services to individuals and communities in need. Based on this sample, the researchers estimated the total impact of organized religion in these areas to be between $7.5 billion and $8.5 billion. Obviously, that figure has increased since 1985. This study adds further support to the case that the religious community is in the forefront of social services provision.

Were this 1985 estimate to be adjusted for 1996, allowing for cost-of-living adjustments and increased social services provision by the religious community, the estimated annual contribution of organized religion would exceed $10 billion. Yet even that figure would not reflect the contributions of local congregations. An estimate of their overall contribution has been made by Cnaan (1997), who studied 111 congregations in six urban areas (Chicago, Indianapolis, Mobile, New York, Philadelphia, and San Francisco/Oakland). The study assessed the value of congregational support for social programs, including financial subsidies; in-kind support; utility costs; hours contributed by clergy, staff, and volunteers; and value of space provided for the programs. For the sample as a whole, the value of congregational support was estimated at $12,053.62 per congregation per month, or $144,643.47 per congregation per year. Given that there are some 250,000 religious congregations in the United States, it is not unreasonable to estimate the total contribution of organized religion to social services as being close to $36 billion annually. While this figure may initially seem excessive, later studies that are regionally based confirm these numbers. It should also be noted that Protestants are the majority in the United States and, as a group, they provide more social services at the local (congregation) level and fewer services through national umbrella organizations than do Catholics and Jews.

Cnaan also asked these 111 congregations what percentage of their annual operating budgets they allocated for social services that they provide directly and what percentage is allocated to those that they support, such as denominational international relief. For the total sample, the mean percentage of the operating budget allocated to social ministry was 17.40 percent (SD = 14.15 with a range of 0–80%). This indicated that community support by congregations was above the traditional charitable tithing of 10 percent.

RELIGIOUS-BASED SOCIAL SERVICE: AN
INTERNATIONAL PERSPECTIVE

Although America is unique in the role played by the religious community in social and community services provision, there are many examples of religious-based social services in other parts of the world. In most of these cases, the religious groups are community-based and use the local culture to provide services. One such example is the Universal Church in Brazil. This is a relatively new denomination, and it is indicative of the growth of Protestantism in a country that until some fifty years ago was almost totally Catholic.

The Universal Church (UC), founded in Rio de Janeiro in the 1970s by Bishop Edir Macedo, has spread rapidly and now has branches throughout the world. In the United States, for example, the church is gaining widespread popularity among Brazilian immigrants. One reason for its rapid growth is that the UC uses a wide range of initiatives to meet the psychological, social, and emotional needs of its members.

The UC membership, which has significantly more women than men, consists primarily of the poorest classes, including the "lumpen" (the lowest category of the proletariat). The UC operates the Beneficent Christian Association, a social services organization that distributes soup, food, and basic life necessities to the poor, even those who are not members of the church. Religious worship is part of this service. UC religious services are very expressive and are based on local Brazilian traditions rather than on European liturgy. The minister functions as a therapist, and the liturgy is specifically designed to help members cope with their poverty and strengthen them morally and emotionally.

The UC also provides free legal services. Part of the ministry is in prisons and orphanages. The church, which has a right-wing orientation in social and political matters, is active in politics. Its goal is to end the rampant political corruption in Brazil that emanated from unethical political behavior.

It should be noted that the religious community is often a reluctant companion to social causes, but an important one. Traer (1988), in an assessment of the response of the religious community to the United Nations Universal Declaration of Human Rights in 1948, noted that most religious groups, with the exception of mainline Protestants, opposed the declaration for various reasons. Today, however, most religions not only support this universal declaration but also claim that it comes from their own theological teaching— namely, that human rights come directly from God and that people have duties toward one another. Thus, while organized religion was displeased with the declaration when it was first introduced, it is now one of the strongest proponents of it.

TESTIMONY OF CLIENTS

Since the 1950s, social work has deliberately divorced itself from the field of public support. This separation of cash from social services has moved social work away from Social Security, AFDC, and local welfare assistance programs. The end result is that many services are provided by bureaucrats in a formal manner that alienates clients. Shapiro and Wright (1996) quoted a mother on welfare who had been assisted by both church and state programs: "The personal contact was better than anything. When you apply for welfare, you are a case number. But the church officials would call me, and we'd talk" (p. 48). A woman who received job training from both state and church programs called the government training programs "impersonal." In contrast, the authors suggested: "In the Joy of Jesus (program), there were daily Bible lessons to talk about diligence, responsibility and other values that make good workers. And there was prayerful discussion of the loneliness and financial woes in her life" (p. 52). The point here is that the human touch in many public services was lost when social work gave way to bureaucracy. People in need seek not only material support but also affirmation of themselves as worthy people. Many religious-based services provide care for individuals in the context of such affirming relationships. As Hall (1990) noted, "Christian charity involves far more than the economical provision of services. As, if not more, important was the creation of a community feeling, a set of human bonds, which are in themselves far more valuable than the service" (p. 52). An overburdened bureaucracy cannot successfully cater to both the need and the person as a whole, whereas religiously motivated professionals and volunteers can.

Studies have shown that consumers have greater confidence in nonprofit organizations with a religious affiliation than in those with no such connection (Mauser 1993; Weisbrod 1993). It is not our intent to bring either social work or the religious community under the umbrella of the other. It is our intent, however, to point out that if religious social resources were to be added to the public and secular-private resources available to people in need, the scope and impact of care would be significantly broadened. Hence, social services provision by the religious community ought to be taken seriously by social work leaders and scholars.

The information provided in this chapter reflects the knowledge in the field. It underscores the remarkable variety and scope of services under religious auspices. Yet the data regarding the scope and overall contribution of the religious community in the field of social welfare are difficult to assess. As noted in chapter 2, defining what is and what is not a religious auspice in social services is a complicated issue. For example, is the Red Cross a religious organization? While its symbol and origin are clearly religious, many would rightly argue that today's Red Cross is a secular organization. Another problem is that of religious-based organizations whose social service work is unpublicized and therefore unknown outside their communities. These kinds of organizations fall through the statistical cracks. Furthermore, some organizations may have a set of ministries under the same hierarchical structure and budget, not all of which are welfare-related. Thus, understanding the net contribution by the religious community to social welfare requires a level of accounting that is beyond the expertise of most studies.

While we cannot publish irrefutably reliable statistics on the actual scope and breadth of social services provided by the religious community, we believe we have made the case for the magnitude of these services by using available statistics, case studies, and reports from a wide variety of sources. Even though a few of these sources may be less than objective, all of them, taken as a whole, point to a single conclusion: the role of the religious community in the provision of social services is enormous and secondary only to that of the government.

In the next chapter, we concentrate on an often-neglected role of the religious community—empowerment. As noted in chapter 3, social work and social provision can be divided into direct service (provision of care and goods to maintain the person in need) and social change (working with people in need to change the power structure so that the disadvantaged will gain more access to means and better control over their environment). Social action is epitomized by empowerment. After reviewing the role of the religious community in empowerment, we will discuss in detail two local case studies, one in Greensboro, North Carolina, and one in Philadelphia, to demonstrate the role of the religious community in the social welfare arena.

CHAPTER 9

EMPOWERMENT AND ORGANIZED RELIGION

Barbara Solomon (1976) first introduced the concept of empowerment into social work in her book *Black Empowerment*. She saw the process of empowerment as a means of increasing personal, interpersonal, political, and economic power so that people could take action to improve their life situations. As her ideas took hold, social work professionals began to make the case for empowerment as the best means of assisting the needy and the disfranchised. Although social work scholars have yet to agree on a single definition of *empowerment*, there is general consensus that the term implies a dual commitment by the profession to (1) assist clients in solving problems of immediate concern and (2) assist individuals and groups in asserting their needs and bringing about change in social systems and power relationships. Before discussing the role of organized religion in empowerment, it is appropriate to consider how the literature has defined and addressed the issue.

The literature provides several definitions of empowerment. Parsloe (1996) described empowerment as "users of social services having greater control over the services they receive" (p. xvii). Rappaport (1987) defined empowerment as a process or mechanism "by which people, organizations, and community gain mastery over their affairs, and involve themselves in the democratic processes of their community and their employing institutions" (p. 122). To Osborne and Gaebler (1992), empowerment meant that the locus of control shifts from the agency to the community. Cohen and Austin (1997) offered a broader interpretation, noting that "despite its widespread acceptance, the concept of empowerment has been applied almost exclusively to the relationship between professional social workers and their clients" (p. 37) and suggesting that empowerment be extended to service providers as well. They also pointed out that empowerment is not limited to helper/service relationships but is relevant to all aspects of social life. This perspective agrees with that of Saleebey (1992), who wrote that empowerment "requires a deep belief in the necessity of democracy and the contingent capacity of people to participate in the decisions and actions that define their world" (p. 8).

Underlying these definitions is the assumption of an imbalance in power relationships in society. Empowerment helps rectify this imbalance by providing the weak with the means to counteract the oppression that can stem from power relationships, whether they be that of helper and client, rich and poor, or dominant culture and government. The goal of empowerment in all instances is to have individuals assert their preferences, assume an active role in the change process, and have control over their environment. The literature cites a number of different means to achieve this goal, yet neglects the role of the religious community in empowering people.

In this chapter we discuss relationships between the powerful and the powerless, as well as the tenets common to organized religion in America that call for support and equality for the oppressed. We present four illustrations of empowerment facilitated by organized religion, among populations that have been identified by social work as being in need of assistance: African Americans, a Philadelphia-based Hispanic community, women, and gay and lesbian people. In addition, we document the contributions of religious-based coalitions and the contribution of liberation theology to empowerment. Finally, we suggest that cooperation between organized religion and social work may significantly advance the cause of empowerment.

POWER AND POWERLESSNESS

Gaventa (1980) raised the issue of why nonelites fail to challenge the domination of elites in certain social relationships. He called this type of situation "quiescence." Logically, people should resist domination and exploitation. Yet, if it is assumed that the elite elicit the cooperation of the non-elite by a process of bargaining in a mutually agreed-upon field, such as public hearings or negotiations, then non-elites may be unaware of either their right to refuse cooperation or the long-term effects of the power relationship. Robert Dahl (1961), in an attempt to solve this paradox, claimed that people have different interests. He distinguished between the *homo politicus*, the social activist, who is involved in planning and decision making, and the *homo civicus*, the nonactivist, who is involved in work, family, leisure, and personal matters and rarely, if ever, in social issues. As many social workers can attest, this model reflects empowerment and civic participation in our society. On the one hand, we have the middle and upper classes, who are seldom the victims of powerlessness. On the other, we have the disadvantaged, whose low income, job insecurity, poor housing conditions, and low-level education are significantly associated with political apathy, minimal civic participation, alienation, and passivity. Thus the role of the so-called *homo civicus* for many disadvantaged people is not a choice but is the result of circumstances over which they have no control.

What Dahl and many others have failed to see is that gaining power is a dynamic process and keeping power is a means of perpetuating the powerlessness of others. Once a certain group gains control, their interest lies in maintaining the power relationship. One way to maintain the status quo is to create complex and intimidating procedures that forestall any action or grievances on the part of the powerless. Faced with these formidable barriers, those seeking redress of power imbalances are likely to retreat long before the process can gain momentum and lead to mobilization for change.

The status quo and established power structure, which is primarily rich, white, and male, can also be maintained by social processes that deter any challenge to them. This implicit social pressure immediately puts the individual or group with a grievance at a severe disadvantage. Under the aegis of established norms, sanctions, rewards, political structures, due processes, and laws created by those in power, the weaker segment of society lives almost normally with the power imbalance, or is, at least, unwilling to rock the boat (Solomon 1976). Those who would challenge the power imbalance are viewed as un-American and too liberal, even by those who are the victims of the imbalance. When the powerless attempt to change the power balance, they are almost always defeated, and their defeat becomes a lesson to others—namely, that attempts to overturn power relationships are costly and futile. Evans (1992) noted that powerlessness sets in motion a cycle of self-reinforcing defeats, also known as "learned helplessness." This is why Gaventa (1980) concluded that "a sense of powerlessness may manifest itself as extensive fatalism, self-deprecation, or undue apathy about one's situation" (p. 17). Gaventa further noted:

> Continual defeat gives rise not only to the conscious deferral of action but also to a sense of defeat, or a sense of powerlessness, that may affect the consciousness of potential challengers about grievances, strategies, or possi-

bilities for change. Participation denied over time may lead to acceptance of the role of non-participation, as well as to a failure to develop the political resources—skills, organization, consciousness—of political action.

(p. 255)

How then can power imbalances be rectified? How can people raised in an environment that stresses obedience and conformity change their way of thinking and become actively empowered? Scholars have argued that one way to bring about change is through the involvement of people who know the importance of political participation in the political process. As Pateman (1970) noted, however, political learning and awareness are dependent, to a certain degree, on political participation. Those who have had the opportunity to engage in a political process in at least one area are more likely to use the skills they have acquired in other political contexts. However, those who are denied participation, even if they are politically conscious, are unable to actively engage in any political activity. Salamon and Van Evera (1973), for example, found that low voting rates among African Americans in the South were due more to fear of the local power elite than to political apathy. This showed that some patterns in power relationships result from fear of repercussions, if and when resistance, or "unaccepted" and "un-normative" behavior is expressed. In this chapter we will observe how organized religion can challenge such power relationships and how it has done so.

EMPOWERMENT AND ORGANIZED RELIGION

The major monotheistic religions in the United States share the belief that all human beings are created by God and are equal in God's sight. This belief in equality and dignity is expressed in religious tenets that call for equal and respectful treatment of all—poor and rich, young and old, man and woman, black and white—without exception. Yet one of the many contradictions between religious teaching and daily life is that many professedly religious people consider themselves to be superior to others. Nevertheless, the emphasis on the equality and dignity of all God's people by the religious community gives the concept of empowerment a powerful moral and ethical underpinning.

Unfortunately, the role of organized religion in individual and group empowerment has been widely overlooked and undervalued. As Warner (1993) pointed out, congregations socialize members from a young age to recognize that they are not the victims of circumstances and that they can solve personal and collective problems. Warner further noted that ethnic groups in America have historically used organized religion as a means of creating a sense of community, sharing the adaptation experience, and assisting one another financially and emotionally. This same scenario is being played out today among many Southeast Asian immigrants to the United States. Many who are neither Christians nor religious people have become active church members because the church represents to them a base of support and communal life that goes beyond religious beliefs. This is true for many other groups in America. Haddad and Lummis (1987) and Chazanov (1991) found that among Sunni Muslims, the Imam, traditionally a member elected as prayer leader, has become a de facto community leader. The Imam represents his people in public forums (such as an ecumenical coalitions or vis-à-vis city hall), conducts marriages and funerals, visits the sick, and counsels families. Like Asian churches, mosques in the United States have become centers for education, social services, social activities, and cultural events, as well as religious worship. These roles are unique to America and stem from the fact that the nation's churches and mosques are both a source of mutual support and a power base for people who share the same ethnic, socioeconomic, and religious heritage.

As noted earlier, Rappaport (1987) defined empowerment as conveying both a sense or feeling of personal control or influence and actual influence of both individuals and groups. In line with this definition, Strader and his colleagues (1997) reported that church volunteers who participated in a program of church-based drug-abuse prevention reported significantly higher levels of empowerment after the project than before the project. Their findings indicate that individuals who learn participation skills through church work are able to apply their knowledge and skills to other social arenas and demonstrate involvement in local power relationships.

Brady, Verba, and Schlozman (1995), in a major national study, found that religious organizations are key teachers of political and civic skills. They defined these skills in terms of concrete activities such as letter-writing, participating in decision-making meetings, planning and chairing meetings, and giving presentations or speeches in public forums. These activities represent the most rudimentary skills needed to transform and change power relationships. When the authors asked respondents where they had gained these skills, a significant number cited their church work. The authors concluded that church members who learn how to write letters in support of religious activities, collect money for a social ministry, or organize weekly Bible study groups can use those same skills to participate in political life. It is interesting to note that these investigators considered their findings so surprising that they rechecked their survey data.

In the next section we would like to demonstrate how religious groups, institutions, and theologies have helped people in the United States and in other countries gain control over their lives. The following six examples show that religion can be a key force in the quest for empowerment: African Americans, a Philadelphia-based Hispanic community, women, gay and lesbian people, religious-based coalitions, and the contribution of liberation theology. Each one serves as an interesting case in and of itself, yet combined they weave a tapestry of religious contributions to human empowerment.

EMPOWERMENT OF THE AFRICAN-AMERICAN COMMUNITY THROUGH ORGANIZED RELIGION

Historically, the black church was the only place where the African-American community could gather for mutual aid and support. This was particularly true in the years prior to the Civil War when African Americans were held as slaves and forbidden any education. White churches of the day would not accept them because their members considered slavery to be acceptable and blacks to be inferior. For these oppressed people, the black church became a refuge where they could learn to read and write and develop a sense of community. Thom Moore (1991) described the activities of black church members as follows:

> What followed for them was among the earliest empowering activities of the slaves. They began organizing their own worship services. After a day's work or on Sunday evenings, at a prearranged time they would meet in a slave's home for an evening of singing, preaching, telling of Bible stories, and praying. At other times they would meet in open fields, which became known as "hush harbors," where they could be relatively safe from detection.   (p. 153)

According to Raboteau (1978), the black church was the place where slaves experienced communal support, developed a sense of group, and gained spiritual sustenance. Even today, as Sarfoh (1986) noted, the black church remains the only institution that seeks to foster a sense of personal identity as well as group unity and solidarity among ghetto residents.

W. E. B. Du Bois (as discussed in Marable 1985) attacked all Christian denominations not only for their support of slavery in the past but also for their indifference to racial segregation and discrimination in his own time. Nevertheless, he considered the black church of his day to be the social center for the African-American community and the most distinctive expression of the African-American character. Du Bois (1903) wanted black clergy to have a prophetic voice for the community and to be politically radical in the antebellum tradition of the slave preacher and rebel Nat Turner because their congregations viewed them as community leaders. And rightly so. The black clergy generally were better educated. They offered hope and were genuinely concerned with people's lives and struggles. Most important, they were neither selected by nor dependent upon the powerful white elite.

According to Baer and Singer (1992), the black church is more than a place of worship. It is a multifunctional institution that has developed many communal institutions for African Americans, such as schools, credit unions, banks, insurance companies, and low-income housing projects, some of which are discussed below. Equally important, black churches and mosques are the hub of political training and political participation. Lincoln and Mamiya (1990), in a survey of black clergy, found that 92 percent advocated church involvement in social and political issues. According to Caldwell, Greene, and Billingsley (1992), the social and political involvement of clergy in black churches is both significant and expected. This is important for empowerment because, as the literature notes, many in the African-American community are unaware of or uninformed about political news and issues. Reese and Brown (1995), for example, reported that members of black churches are likely to hear two messages from the pulpit. One message stresses civil awareness, which leads to a heightened sense of racial identity. The other message stresses political activity, which leads to a clearer perception of the power imbalance among groups. As discussed previously, both identity and the perception of a power imbalance are crucial to the evolution of empowerment.

The institution that is most influential in making African Americans politically aware is the black church. A national survey by the Pew Research Center for the People and the Press (1996), for example, found that black church members were much more likely to have heard from their ministers about health care reform (62%) than were white church members (19%), while the same percentage of black and white church members (about two-thirds) reported hearing about abortion. In other words, the black church is active, both theologically and politically, in issues relevant to the quality of life of African Americans.

In a comparative study of white and black congregations, Chaves and Higgins (1992) found "compelling evidence that black congregations are more likely to be involved than white congregations in *certain kinds* [emphasis in original] of traditionally non-religious activities: civil rights activities and those activities that are directed at disprivileged segments of their local communities." They also found that "this race effect is not explainable by the organizational or environmental variables available" (p. 438). As such, political education and empowerment are by-products of participation in organized religion. People come to attend religious services and, in the process, become more politically aware and more prepared for political participation (Wilcox and Gomez 1990). Wilcox and Gomez also found that regular church attendance and participation in church organizations and clubs increased political participation by African Americans.

Further evidence of empowerment by organized religion can be found in the civil rights movement. Black churches provided the social base that helped make the movement possible and served as the training ground for many of its leaders. Jesse Jackson, for example, said, "The church was like my laboratory, my first actual public stage, where I began to develop and practice my speaking powers" (quoted in Frady 1996:59). Dr. Martin Luther King Jr. was another example of the outstanding leaders produced by the black church (Battle 1988). These churches did more than train leaders; they served as the local suppliers and headquarters of the civil rights movement. As Aldon Morris (1984) observed:

> Churches provided the [civil rights] movement with an organized mass base; a leadership of clergymen largely economically independent of the larger white society and skilled in the art of managing people and resources; an institutionalized financial base through which protest was financed; and meeting places where the masses planned tactics and strategies and collectively committed themselves to the struggle.   (p. 4)

Following the civil rights movement, African-American congregations became active in urban renewal, black business enterprises, economic redevelopment, and housing projects. DePriest and Jones (1997) noted that Christian capitalism encourages African Americans to pool their dollars and invest in one another's enterprises and local communities. African-American clergy encourage members to support black-owned businesses as a means of creating financially viable and stable communities. This collective approach to addressing the socioeconomic conditions of African Americans establishes a power base for the community. This model is in contradiction to that of white businesses, whose support for the community is generally limited to charitable donations or services such as soup kitchens—types of support that, although they may help meet community needs, have no effect on rectifying the power imbalance.

Another important religious force in the African-American community is the Nation of Islam. Under the leadership of Elijah Muhammad and the influence of Malcolm X, the Nation of Islam is credited with transforming the self-perception of African Americans. Feelings of inferiority to white people gave way to a new spirit of racial identity evoked by such terms as *black power*, *black pride*, *black consciousness*, and perhaps most important, *black is beautiful*. This approach is known as "reverse superiority." The fact that these messages were endorsed by religious authority empowered African Americans, who, for generations, had seen themselves as powerless in white America and now experienced a sense of pride and self-importance. This change in perception invigorated and strengthened the civil rights movement and energized a generation of young African Americans (Battle 1988; Lincoln and Mamiya 1993). Battle (1988) noted that, although the Islamic movement in the United States began in response to racism, the Nation of Islam taught its members to focus on education and economic development. The Nation of Islam, especially under Elijah Muhammad's leadership, purchased numerous businesses and used them to train African Americans as employees and potential owners.

Currently, black churches have been expanding their efforts and advocacy in new directions. Tapia (1996) noted: "There is a rising class of black churches that are energizing whole communities through economic empowerment projects, effective work at getting kids off drugs, keeping them out of jail, and sending them to college" (p. 27). Black churches, more than any other group of churches, are also involved in acquiring properties in their communities and/or building new ones. DePriest and Jones (1997) highlighted a few such cases. Wheat Street Church in Atlanta, for example, owns real estate valued at $33 million. The holdings include a senior citizens home and a low-income family development. Although both were built with public money, the church initiated the projects and, through its subsidiary nonprofit organization, has revitalized the community and provided local people with jobs and a sense of pride. The Wheat Street congregation also has a credit union with approximately a thousand members and more than $1 million in assets. This credit union, an institution common to many black churches, provides financial help to people who often are refused loans by commercial banks (a means used by the elite to maintain power). The empowerment offered by a credit union is attested to by a member who said, "You become an owner and share in the proceeds through interest dividends" (p. 196). This is but one example of how proactive African-American congregations build an economic infrastructure in their community that provides employment opportunities, services, and sense of ownership as well as social, political, and economic skills for African Americans. Without the church, it is likely that far too many consumers of the financial system would be provided services at the lowest end of the spectrum.

Similar success stories of economic development in dilapidated urban areas have been reported for Hartford Memorial Baptist Church in Detroit, Allen African Methodist Episcopal Church in Los Angeles, and St. Edward's in Chicago (Stodghill 1996). A story less often told is that of economic empowerment in rural America. Gite (1993) reported the case of Mendenhall Bible Church in Mississippi. Established in the 1970s, this nondenominational church, which has only 125 members, purchased a long-abandoned school building and remodeled it with the help of two hundred volunteers from Aurora, Illinois. The building, now a business complex, houses a health clinic, law office, thrift shop, elementary school, and recreation center.

The two-hundred-member Greater Christ Temple Church in Meridian, Mississippi, is another success story. The church, whose members were near or at poverty level, now owns three restaurants, a bakery, an auto repair shop, and four thousand acres of farmland with seven hundred head of cattle and two meat-processing plants. The holdings of the church are under the auspices of its nonprofit corporation REACH, Inc. (Research Education and Community Hope). According to Gite, Greater Christ Temple Church enabled its two hundred members to exit the welfare system by pooling their resources.

EMPOWERMENT OF A HISPANIC COMMUNITY THROUGH ORGANIZED RELIGION: A CASE STUDY

Our discussion to this point has centered on the role of organized religion in empowering African Americans, but we wish to stress that many other minority groups in America have been, and continue to be, empowered through organized religion. Jews in America, for example, formed mutual help associations, free loan societies, and other religious-based mechanisms of support and enhancement that made their transition into mainstream society easier and faster (Tenenbaum 1993).

Of necessity, we have limited further discussion of other ethnic groups to one case study: Nueva Esperanza, a religious-based nonprofit organization in Philadelphia serving the Hispanic community. Nueva Esperanza, the idea of the Reverend Luis Cortes, is one of the few ecumenical grassroots Hispanic agencies in Pennsylvania (Blake 1991). Cortes first came to Philadelphia from New York in the early 1980s as a theology professor at Eastern Baptist Theological Seminary. Deeply disturbed by the fragmentation, underrepresentation, and political weakness of Philadelphia's Hispanic community, he pushed for the formation of the Hispanic Clergy of Philadelphia and Vicinity, an ecumenical coalition. The coalition, in turn, formed Nueva Esperanza, which means "new hope."

Through Nueva Esperanza, religious leaders working with the local Hispanic community have made enormous strides. They have built five housing units for senior citizens in North Philadelphia. They also developed Villa Esperanza, a home ownership project consisting of 14 three-bedroom town houses, and a twenty-one-unit housing development. Local residents, predominantly Hispanic, were hired to work on both development projects. These housing projects have enabled people with very low incomes to obtain $100,000 houses for $35,000, with mortgage payments of only $300 a month. The goal of Nueva Esperanza is to empower people as residents, as homeowners, and as employees in local businesses. In collaboration with a local businessman, the organization has also developed a full-service community laundromat (La Lavanderia del Pueblo), which handles 2,500 loads of wash daily. La Lavanderia also serves as a community center, with a small library and classrooms for GED classes and Bible study. In addition, Nueva Esperanza provides mortgage counseling, tenant assistance, financing, architectural reviews, and after-school tutoring.

In 1997 Nueva Esperanza received a $656,000 grant from the Commonwealth of Pennsylvania to expand its job-training program. The fact that such a large grant was awarded to a religious-affiliated organization indicates that organized religion is currently the main representative and advocate for the Hispanic community in Philadelphia. It should be emphasized that neither the grant nor the need to work closely with city officials has diminished the advocacy role of the Hispanic Clergy of Philadelphia and Vicinity. They have successfully lobbied against riverboat gambling in Philadelphia, which had the support of the mayor, and have successfully advocated for increased representation and recognition of Hispanics on Philadelphia's police force.

In 1994 the City of Philadelphia, in collaboration with Camden, New Jersey, applied to the federal government for empowerment zone status and funding. Even before the government had made any decision, fierce competition erupted among many neighborhoods in the city as to which one should be awarded the status and the money. The Hispanic Clergy of Philadelphia and Vicinity, Nueva Esperanza, and Rev. Luis Cortes fought hard and publicly to have American Street, where most Latino people reside, included in the empowerment zone. Finally, in 1995, Mayor Ed Rendell allocated $29 million of Philadelphia's share of $79 million in empowerment-zone funding to American Street (Twyman 1995). Despite the allocation, Cortes, Nueva Esperanza, and the Hispanic Clergy of Philadelphia and Vicinity have remained at odds with city hall as to what businesses will be approved for American Street. The mayor's office, for example, has suggested locating a beer distribution center on an empty lot, while Nueva Esperanza has pushed for a commercial center that would house a Taco Bell, Pep Boys, and classrooms. The stalemate is yet one more indication that organized religion is the sole voice speaking out for Hispanics in Philadelphia. Through the efforts of organized religion, the social, political, and economic rights of Hispanic people are currently being protected and advanced.

EMPOWERMENT OF WOMEN THROUGH ORGANIZED RELIGION

It is no surprise to most people that the more a modern American woman is identified with feminism, the less she is identified with organized religion (Wuthnow 1988). This view, however, is mitigated by the influence of the extreme religious right and ignores the historical contribution of organized religions, whether intended or not, to promote the rights and equality of women.

For many generations, organized religion had provided women with the opportunity to assert themselves and to work for the public good outside the home. The fact that religion in all societies helped reinforce societal structures that kept women powerless, dependent, and with minimum rights is well acknowledged, but what is seldom discussed is the fact that religion was also an avenue and a means for their empowerment (Harrison 1984). During the nineteenth and early twentieth centuries, for example, more than half of all missionaries were women (Xi 1997). Missionary careers enabled women to train for professions such as medicine, nursing, and teaching. Women like Pearl Buck, the author who wrote of China and its people, became nationally and internationally known for their work in the mission fields.

Spurred on by the example of women missionaries, other women began to form moral reform organizations. These organizations provided many women with their first opportunity to act outside the realm of home and community (Brereton 1989). As Carol Smith-Rosenberg (1985) noted: "Using religion to develop extra-domestic roles, [women] created powerful local and national single-sex organizations expressive of women's particular angers, anxieties, and demands" (p. 142). Before 1835, all women's associations were allied with churches (Cott 1977). These were primarily educational groups, prayer groups, auxiliaries, and benevolent societies. That churches supported organizations whose leaders and members were women is remarkable considering the social inequality of women at this time. By the end of the Civil War, these church-based women's organizations had begun to assert themselves as autonomous entities, and women began to gain a public voice outside the church.

Organized religion has produced many organizations that have worked with female victims of violence or sexual harassment in a nonpatronizing manner. One example is the settlement houses of the Salvation Army. Magnuson (1967) reported that the staff in "Army homes" never referred to the women as "fallen women" or "cases," but rather as "sisters," "our girls," or "sisters who have stumbled." Similarly, among Catholics, devotion to Saint Jude caused women to feel "empowered in new ways. They broke off relationships with 'mean' boyfriends [and] rejected unwanted medical treatments" (Orsi 1991:159).

A church-affiliated project to empower women in Gilpin Court, an inner-city neighborhood in Richmond, which was reported by Amy Sherman (1996), is one such example. Victory Christian Fellowship developed a program to get women off welfare and out of housing projects with the help of a church-based ministry called STEP (Strategies to Elevate People). STEP has an academy where Gilpin Court residents can study and complete their GED or transfer into a community college. The program is offered at times convenient for the women and provides each of the fifty participants with a "Family Sharing Team." Each team is composed of three to six white suburban women who provide emotional, spiritual, and, often, practical support to program participants, many of whom are trying to raise children and advance their education and job opportunities at the same time. The program, which seeks to empower women on welfare, represents a collaborative effort by an inner-city church and suburban ministries.

Membership in a religious congregation has helped women assimilate and adapt to a new society even though they may not fully adhere to its religious tenets. Winland (1994), for example, reported on a group of Laotian Hmong refugee women in Ontario, Canada, who became Mennonites. The Mennonite Church provided these women with a sense of empowerment in their new environment while respecting their social practices and values as Hmong. Kim (1996) noted that Korean-American women are finding it difficult to be equal in the church. According to Kim, the Korean-American church is a male-dominated institution that is also the focal point of sociocultural integration and the center of community life. This leaves Korean-American women in limbo because they are not equally valued in the church. While the Korean-American church still has a long way to go to achieve gender equality, Kim noted that Korean-American women are using techniques defined as "micro-manipulative skills" to become more active in their church and thus use the church as a means of support and strength.

In recent years, the struggle for gender equality has permeated the sphere of organized religion. Although women are more religious than men (Wuthnow 1988), historically they have been denied access to formal positions of religious leadership, particularly clerical ones (Baer 1993). According to Ozorak (1996), the reason for this inequality is that most religions in the past did not advocate equality between genders. Ozorak found that women, despite their lower status in official church circles, are able to empower themselves through affiliation and collaboration with those of higher status.

Recently, a growing number of denominations have begun to ordain women and appoint them to leadership positions. These include many mainstream Protestant and Jewish (except Orthodox Judaism) denominations. Wallace (1992), who reported on a group of Roman Catholic women who served as pastors in small, unstaffed churches, noted that these women felt spiritually empowered because of the acceptance and recognition of their leadership by parishioners. In contrast to male priests, the women pastors knew each parishioner personally, encouraged all of them to become involved in parish life, and tended to empower them to claim ownership of their parish. While denominations that are more conservative and evangelical do not accept women as religious leaders, it is likely that the trend toward more female clergy will continue, as church attendance by women is much higher than that by men. Women are enrolling in seminaries in record numbers even as the number of male applicants is down. For example, seminary enrollment for women in mainline Protestant denominations grew from 4.7 percent of total enrollment in 1977 to 25.4 percent in 1992 (Association of Theological Schools 1993). While ordination of women is viewed as a recent phenomenon, what in fact is recent is the magnitude of it, not the practice itself. Once women were accepted as lay leaders in the church, denominations that did not require a wider church approval for ordination were open for women clergy. The first woman ordained by a large Protestant denomination was Antoinette

Brown, who was ordained in 1853 by a small Congregationalist church in South Butler, New York.

Lehman (1985), however, believed that women pastors have little chance of being accepted in large, wealthy congregations or of being promoted to high ecclesiastical positions. But the road has already been paved, and the growing presence of women clergy in many churches will doubtless influence young women in the future. Purvis (1995), however, discussed in detail the cases of two female ministers in Atlanta who were appointed in the mid-1980s to be the senior clergy in two large Protestant churches. In both cases a process of change and learning occurred that strengthened the churches and their ministries.

The ordination of women is not the end of the road in the struggle for equality of the sexes within religion. A cautionary example is that of ordained women in the Methodist denomination. Nearly forty years after women received full rights as ordained elders in the Methodist denomination, they are still hitting the "stained-glass ceiling" when it comes to appointments as lead pastors in local churches (Collier 1997). "Lead pastors" are defined as pastors whose staff includes at least one other ordained minister. Statistics based on data from the denomination's finance agency show that, of 81 churches with membership of more than three thousand, none is served by a woman lead pastor. Other statistics show that, of 1,119 churches with membership of one thousand or more, 17, or 1.5 percent, are served by women lead pastors. However, women elders constitute approximately 11 percent of all ordained elders in the church, while 16 percent of district superintendents and 15 percent of active bishops are women. The latter positions are appointed by the denomination itself and not by local congregations.

This finding has disturbed the Methodist leadership. In an effort to find out why there is a ceiling for women pastors, the section on elders and local pastors of the Division of Ordained Ministry is offering an ongoing consultation for women serving as lead pastors. The consultation will assist these women with their needs and concerns, examine specific issues, provide a network, and develop new models of ministry (Gilbert 1997).

In the Jewish tradition, women were highly valued, and at the time when the Jewish texts were written, the role and rights of women were considered very liberal. In the present day Orthodox Judaism is highly gendered, whereas Conservative and Reform Judaism are not. Comet (1995) noted that the Reform and Conservative movements of Judaism in the United States adopted and incorporated democratic policies that called for full gender equality in Jewish life, including the acceptance of women as rabbis and cantors. Some groups even rewrote the Jewish Bible in a nonsexist voice and revised texts such as the Passover book of Haggada to make them nonoppressive and non-sexist. It should be emphasized that such an egalitarian approach is stronger among the least orthodox and among those who are more in contact with the non-Jewish community.

Empowerment of women through organized religion is a global phenome-non. De Sousa (1995), for example, described a church-sponsored program in which poor Brazilian women, in three groups of twenty-five each, received training in health and sexuality issues. The women, in turn, were expected to teach others. According to De Sousa, the program empowered the women psychologically, cognitively, and physically, as indicated by their increased positive self-perception, extensive community health work and a campaign for change, and broader knowledge regarding sexuality. This type of program obviously could have succeeded elsewhere, but the fact that the program was operated in Brazil under the auspices and support of both the Catholic Church and the Methodist Church made it culturally acceptable to the women and to those in their social network. Additionally, Drogus (1990) reported that, as the result of liberation theology in Brazil, most communities of believ-ers were staffed by women. While most women were involved in charitable work and not in politics, other women, not always in line with the church expectation, used these religious communities to get involved in politics, chal-lenge gender roles, and oppose discrimination.

Fernea (1998) studied the role of women in Islamic countries. She found great variability in these countries as to the role of women in society. But regardless of the country, she found that Islamic feminists find their convic-tion for gender equality in the Qur'an. It was these women's perception that gender inequality in Islamic countries is the result of erroneous interpretation of the Qur'an, and they find their strength and hope in the religious tenets of the Qur'an.

EMPOWERMENT OF THE GAY COMMUNITY THROUGH ORGANIZED RELIGION

Empowerment of the gay community visibly began under religious auspices when Troy Perry established the Metropolitan Community Church in Los Angeles in the early 1970s. The church quickly became a center where gay peo-ple could, for the first time, express themselves publicly. Perry founded the church for two reasons. One was to organize the gay community. The other was to actualize his Pentecostal-inspired belief that he was created gay by a benevolent personal God (Perry 1972; Perry and Swicegood 1990). Gay people today can find many organizations in which they can express their own sexual identity, but for the times, Perry's church was considered revolutionary.

Perry's work has led to the Universal Fellowship of Metropolitan Community Churches, a national denomination for gay, lesbian, and bisexual people. The new denomination, which has 312 congregations and 22,000 members, is based on an orthodox Trinitarian theology with overtones of pentecostalism (Warner 1989). The public opposition of many evangelical and conservative denominations to gay behavior and gay rights should not detract from our appreciation of the church structure that allowed gay people their first public and open organization. As Dennis Altman (1982) noted, "In many places, the church is the only form of the gay movement that exists" (p. 123).

While Perry chose to establish a new denomination, others, like Barry Stopfel, decided to change the religious establishment from within. Stopfel became the second openly gay man to be ordained in the Episcopal tradition. With the help of his partner, Will Leckie (Leckie and Stopfel 1997), Stopfel wrote a very moving autobiography about his struggle to be accepted and his efforts to lead congregants and the church to accept his sexual preference. Stopfel concluded that although much remains to be done, the church had helped him and many others find a place where they can affirm themselves within mainstream America.

The United States is not the only country in which gay people have found support and power in organized religion. Sweet (1995) reported that in 1982 groups of gay people began to affiliate themselves with Protestant churches in the former (East) German Democratic Republic. These congregants have become a fast-growing nucleus of the gay emancipation movement. Although infiltrated by the Stasi (secret police), the gay community within the German church grew so rapidly that the state eventually embarked on a program to integrate gay people into socialist society. What is of relevance here is that the East German Protestant churches, although under total state control, were the first institutions that enabled gay people to organize and work together.

The rise of gay religious institutions in the post-Stonewall era has accelerated the process of gay empowerment in organized religion. Gay congregants have begun to press for greater tolerance within mainstream religious denominations, thereby counterbalancing the increased influence of the religious right. Gay houses of worship have also filled a variety of religious, political, and social needs within the gay community. Shokeid (1995), for example, conducted an ethnographic study of Congregation Beth Simchat Torah (CBST), a gay synagogue founded in 1973 in New York's Greenwich Village. The synagogue has more than a thousand members and recently hired its first ordained rabbi. Membership in CBST has enabled gay Jews to gain a sense of personal and collective identity in a world that regards them as anathema. CBST has affirmed the full personhood of its members through a process of continual negotiation designed to ensure that synagogue practices reflect both Jewish values and gay values.

Gay empowerment through organized religions is not limited to the right to be ordained (in some denominations) or form a new denomination. In her study of congregations in changing communities, Ammerman (1997) found that members of congregations that included gay people were more likely to be active in their support for gay rights. One example cited by Ammerman is that of St. Matthew's Catholic Parish in Long Beach, California. In 1986, Cardinal Mahoney had asked parishes in his diocese to establish formal programs to meet the needs of their gay members. These programs were related to, but not limited to, the rise of the AIDS epidemic. St. Matthew's responded by sponsoring a Mass of healing for people with AIDS. This initial program step led to the formation of Comunidad, a group of gay people who met monthly. These individuals eventually joined the church and became members of the parish. Ammerman reported: "Comunidad members are quick to point out that they are integrated into all areas of parish life as lectors, altar servers, Eucharistic ministers, choir members, song leaders, and members of other parish committees, especially the Peace and Justice Committees" (p. 167). In this case, gay Catholics not only fully participated in parish life but also received the support of the parish for their social action organization Comunidad. Ammerman posed an interesting question: Why has the parish been so hospitable to people whose sexual preference is at odds with traditional Catholicism? A likely explanation, she offered, is that "they may not understand why some people are homosexual, but they are convinced that if God made them that way, they should be treated with the respect every part of creation is due" (p. 171).

Another congregation that opened membership to gay people is the First Congregational Church in Long Beach, California. This church is part of the United Church of Christ, a denomination that has formally designated several of its congregations as "open and affirming." According to Ammerman, this is a "designation for congregations who not only are open to lesbians and gays, but affirm them by supporting them for leadership positions and taking their concerns seriously as a congregational issue" (p. 175). The United Church of Christ not only permits the ordination of gay people but also encourages congregations to employ gay ministers, although this decision is left to the discretion of the local congregation.

The level of inclusion and support for gays evident in "open and affirming" congregations exceeds that of many secular social groups and organizations. The entire congregation, for example, will participate in campaigns and programs relevant to its gay members. Ammerman described the sense of total inclusion in the congregation as follows: "Gay and lesbian persons . . . find here a home, a reconnection with church traditions they thought lost, a place that acknowledges their spiritual longing *and* accepts them for who they are. As well, parents of gay and lesbian children find here a place where they can talk about their children's lives (and deaths) without censorship" (p. 181). It should be made clear that no one in the congregation wants the place to become a "gay church." Members are happy with the present mix. This and similar congregations constitute one of the very few arenas where gay people can come and celebrate their differences while being fully accepted by traditional society. The only other alternatives are gay bars and bathhouses, where the primary purpose is dating and sex.

At a time when the armed forces and many public organizations adhere to a policy of "don't ask, don't tell," a growing number of religious organizations, denominations, and congregations are opening their doors to gay people, supporting them as individuals, and assisting in their cause for equal rights. While the gay lifestyle is vehemently criticized by some religious conservatives (both individuals and organizations), who argue that religion and homosexuality are incompatible, the gay community is finding empowerment in organized religion. Congregations across the nation are providing arenas where gay people can assert themselves without fear of sanction, where they are respected for who they are, and where social action on their behalf is supported.

Even among evangelical groups, gay men and women are beginning to come to terms with their sexual identity. Thumma (1991) described one such group, called Good News, in Atlanta, Georgia. Following a long process of redefining themselves, members of the group managed to resolve the dissonance between their extreme religious beliefs and their homosexual lifestyle. Yet, as Clark, Brown, and Hochstein (1989) reminded us, organized religions, and especially the Judeo-Christian tradition, has historically kindled homophobic feelings on the part of their followers, thereby fostering anti-gay oppression.

EMPOWERMENT OF THE DISENFRANCHISED THROUGH
ORGANIZED RELIGION

Participation in organized religion empowers members socially, economically, and politically as well as spiritually. Belonging to a proactive organization helps members learn the skills and means of advocacy and working for change. Belonging to a collective that is often in contact with political and community leaders helps members to become knowledgeable about issues and involved in protecting their interests. In this way, religion forms group identification and a collective engagement in the process of change. Moreover, young and inactive members are encouraged to participate and become assertive members of society (Warner 1993).

Pertinent to the discussion of empowerment is the religious right movement of the 1980s. Movement organizers have clearly shown how the disenfranchised can be empowered once they learn the skills needed to work for change. Although many may disagree with the ideology of the religious right, the movement's organizational methods and attempts to control local boards of education provide an effective "how-to" guide to empowerment and community organization. Its members have been able to move into positions of power because they have learned and applied organizational strategic skills. Their methods and success should serve as a model for anyone concerned with community organization and empowerment.

Maton and Rappaport (1984) studied an evangelical Christian, nondenominational congregation to assess empowerment among its members. The congregation of 150–200 members had originally begun as a fellowship. Using multiple data-collection methods and sources, the authors concluded: "Those who were perceived by both themselves and others to have become empowered in the direction of desired interpersonal behavior change are also described by themselves and others as deeply committed to God and to the particular local setting of which they are part" (p. 67). In other words, those with a high religious commitment were more likely to have attained a higher level of empowerment, acquired a psychological sense of community, and actualized their life goals.

The Industrial Areas Foundation (IAF), previously discussed in chapter 8, which has its roots in organized religion, is a powerful catalyst for the social and economic empowerment of poor neighborhoods. The IAF provides professional organizers, while local churches provide institutional bases, linkages, members, and moral support (Boyte 1984).

In addition to the aforementioned church contributions to the civil rights movement, we should also acknowledge that the movement challenging U.S. immigration policies toward Central American refugees was rooted in religious groups (Wiltfang and McAdam 1991). On the labor front, Dwight Billings (1990) asserted that only organized religion helped Appalachian miners achieve solidarity against mine owners. Referring to "religion as opposition," he noted that "the repetition of collective symbols and their ritualized expression in sermons, prayers, and group singing helped to sustain miners' commitment to the sacred cause of unionism and solidarity" (p. 20).

Some members of congregations live in the same neighborhood where their congregation is located. These local members often form residents' groups similar to secular neighborhood associations. In a study of citizen organizations in a Midwestern city, Speer et al. (1995) found that church-based organizations were more likely to be more intimate and less controlling than other organizations and that their members were more likely to feel empowered.

There are a few congregations in America that are experiencing the empowerment of both individuals and a community challenged by intense drug activity, high crime rates, and extreme poverty and homelessness. For example, empowerment through the Glide United Methodist Church in San Francisco is through faith and resistance: faith in church, family, and community; resistance to slavery of body, mind, and spirit. The pastor of Glide, the Reverend Cecil Williams, calls upon his own African heritage of community and village to emphasize the interdependence involved in the empowerment process. That is, the welfare of the individual is viewed as dependent upon the welfare of the community, and in the same way the welfare of the community depends on the welfare of the individual. Hence, the empowerment programs of Glide are based on an extended-family model that welcomes all races, classes, ages, genders, sexual orientations, and conditions. It is in the context of vital relationships that people embrace their own God-given uniqueness and differences and can love and accept others as they love and accept themselves.

Those who come to Glide are encouraged to tell their own story and reclaim themselves and their special identity. This, too, is a powerful process that allows individuals to affirm their power—the power of faith, hope, and God that propels people forward for themselves and their community. This church offers agape—unconditional acceptance and love—to those who feel most unacceptable and marginalized by society. For those searching for a community and wholeness, Glide is a spiritual, social, emotional, and physical home.

Spirituality is at the center of Glide's message of liberation. Accordingly, to be spiritual is to be authentic, to define oneself, to choose freedom. Spirituality gives us the power of a community that believes in us and the power to move forward with that community to bring about justice and the empowerment of others. With this spiritual awareness those who once had no face, no voice, and no power are acknowledged as whole people, worthy of help and capable of healing and recovery. Glide recognizes the need to first meet people where they are in the circumstances of their life. To be truly spiritual, the whole of the person's experience is acknowledged: the conditions of poverty, homelessness, drug abuse, sexual abuse, domestic violence, incest, rape, divorce, lack of education, and joblessness. The choice of life over death and destruction is the basis for spirituality that produces a transformed and empowered life.

Through a network of innovative culturally and gender-sensitive services, Glide addresses the social, economic, and spiritual conditions and causes of the problems that are a part of every community. Glide serves more than one million free meals each year, provides programs to test people for HIV/AIDS, offers health care, women's programs, men's programs, crisis intervention, literacy and computer training, job training and placement, and educational programs. Glide also works in collaboration with the Haight Ashbury Free Clinic to provide addiction recovery and health services.

EMPOWERMENT OF THE OPPRESSED THROUGH LIBERATION THEOLOGY

Liberation theology is a form of political reform that originated in and embodies religious tenets, especially those of the Catholic Church. Liberation theology, unlike other theologies learned and speculated upon in seminaries and universities, is a social movement whose purpose is to bring about radical social, economic, and political change (Smith 1991). The movement, which originated in Latin America and Brazil, is most often associated with Central and South America. Liberation theology was directly influenced by the work of the Second Vatican Council held in the 1960s. Council members issued an official Vatican document that, for the first time, placed social issues on a equal footing with religious issues. This socially oriented doctrine brought about major revisions in Catholic theology and was responsible for the rise of Catholic social activism (Ryle 1989; Scherer-Warren 1990). The cause of liberation theology received further impetus when Pope John Paul II issued *Populorum Progressio*, an encyclical specifically directed to Latin America and the issue of social justice for a society long exploited economically and politically. The Vatican's calls for action and involvement were received with rapt attention on the part of many concerned Catholic theologians in Latin America.

Scherer-Warren (1990) summarized the goals of liberation theology as follows:

> In the material sense, the Church must work for liberation from several forms of oppression: economic (classes and foreign exploitation), political (both internal and external), racial, ethnic, sexual, age and so on. In the spiritual sense, it aims to liberate people from alienation, false consciousness, lack of courage and encourages self-determination. It aims to recuperate the loss of dignity of the human person, and transform the oppressed into agents of their own history, supported by their faith in God.
>
> (p. 17)

Larrea (1994) identified three key tenets of liberation theology: (1) the historical liberation of people, classes, races, and cultures that are economically, politically, and socially oppressed; (2) an understanding of the ethical implications of an anthropological approach (helping by outsiders); and (3) a theological tenet that accepts total liberation as redemption from sin. Regarding the second tenet, Breton (1992) noted that social workers should use the same resources available to the poor and oppressed, including their support systems, in their efforts to bring individuals and groups together into larger communities. The idea behind liberation theology is not to have outside helpers study people's needs and offer solutions but to have the oppressed and the helpers live together. Through joint efforts, the oppressed people learn how to assess their own situation and formulate and implement their own plans for nonviolent action. By forming several small groups in close proximity to one another and to the larger community of those experiencing similar difficulties, members are able to extend their influence beyond their own groups and achieve greater cooperation.

It is interesting to compare these tenets of liberation theology with the way empowerment is conceptualized in social work literature. Simon (1990), for example, suggested that empowerment decreases feelings of alienation from the dominant culture, helps individuals to develop the capacity for collective action, and leads to the development of a sense of community and a sense of responsibility for and ability to resolve problems. The similarities in the approaches of social work and liberation theology to empowerment are indeed striking.

Pena (1994) reported that only the Catholic clergy were able to get different protest groups in Peru to cooperate with one another. By preaching liberation theology from the pulpit and in small group sessions, the Catholic priests and sisters presented the idea of protest as acceptable to God and hence justified as a means to a better Christian life and the advancement of justice on earth. In fact, the liturgical texts of the Roman Catholic Church in Central America were changed to embody the local social context so that the religious symbols became more accessible to believers and made them aware of the injustice of their sociopolitical situation (Samson 1991). Smith (1991) noted that this theology was disseminated through thousands of Base Christian Communities (Comunidades Eclesias de Base [BEC]). This method is also used in Central and Southern America. Boff (1985) described BEC as groups of fifteen to twenty families that meet a few times a week to hear the Word of God and share their problems through the inspiration of the Gospels. A pastoral staff, consisting of priests, sisters, and laity trained by a small number of itinerant liberation theologists who are at risk of torture, imprisonment, exile, and death for their activities, work together to keep the movement going.

Young (1980) reported that a movement based on liberation theology principles began in Brazil in the early 1950s, before the Second Vatican Council. The movement started in a local Catholic church and soon spread throughout Brazil via church-related groups and teaching. The success of the movement led to concessions by the ruling party, but it was brutally suppressed following the 1964 coup d'état. Since then, members of the movement have adopted more subtle strategies to combat political oppression. The Catholic Church, in turn, has become the sole institutional opposition to the government, which fears its power among the poor. For example, when news of the murders of Brazilian street children began to surface, the Catholic Church spearheaded the campaign to stop the killing and to press charges against those responsible. Similarly, the church in Guatemala has been the key institution for community development and the teaching of political skills, consciousness-raising, and self-reliance (Gondolf 1981).

The influence of liberation theology has moved beyond Central and South America. As Hatjavivi, Fostin, and Mbuende (1989) noted, Namibia's transition from a colony to a quasi state is, in large part, the result of the efforts of the church and the remaining German clerics who, under British rule, fueled hope for independence with their message of liberation theology. In September 1997 some one million Filipinos marched to protest the decision by President Fidel Ramos to stay in power for a second term (Alabastro 1997). These peaceful rallies were organized by the Roman Catholic Church. The church's political stance against dictatorship demonstrated both its influence and its intent to advocate for the 68 million Filipino citizens, the majority of whom are Catholics.

Given the radicalism of liberation theology and the rigid hierarchical structure of the Catholic Church, opposition to the movement was inevitable. Many church leaders, especially the most conservative and those closest to the regimes in power, have attempted to undercut the influence and appeal of liberation theology. Lynch (1994), for example, noted how orthodox Catholics sought to diminish the appeal of liberation theology by accusing liberation theologists of missing sacred text and precepts in their teaching. *Sensus Fideli*, a document issued by the Magisterium (the teaching authority of the church), included advice on how opponents of the movement could demonstrate the weaknesses of its theological underpinnings. The liberationists have continued to espouse their traditional philosophy but have had to change some of its precepts.

Regardless of its opposition, liberation theology has been a vital force for emancipation and empowerment in Latin and South America and worldwide. It is so progressive in its tenets that many view it as a semi-Marxist movement within the church (Evans 1992; Pottenger 1989). In fact, Dussel, Hodgson, and Pedrozo (1992) argued that liberation theology and Marxism are very similar, except for one major difference: liberation theology universally rejects "dialectical materialism." It is not surprising, then, that many social work leaders today have urged that liberation theology be adopted by the profession (cf. Breton 1992; Campfens 1988; Evans 1992). In many ways, it complements the work begun by Saul Alinsky that laid the foundations of current day community practice. Thus, the Catholic Church, through its liberation theology, has become a major contributor to personal, social, economic, and political empowerment in an unprecedented manner.

In this chapter we have juxtaposed empowerment, social work's most proactive principle, with the work of organized religion in America and abroad. Our argument is that empowerment goes beyond the relationships of client and social worker or consumer and agency. Empowerment is necessary when there are power imbalances, and the disenfranchised have neither the perception nor the skills needed for change. As we have shown, many religious organizations and congregations are actively involved in assisting the powerless to advance their position in society. In this respect, we concur with Maton and Wells (1995), who suggested: "Concerning group empowerment, religion has the potential to facilitate groups' critical awareness of oppressive forces, to offer compelling alternative visions and cultural values, and to mobilize human and institutional resources" (p. 177).

It is important to reemphasize that organized religion has been a source of repression and intolerance as well as empowerment. The same religious-based mechanisms and structures used to empower the disenfranchised and the disadvantaged can also be harnessed to work against them. This is all too evident in religious history, which is replete with instances of clerics' working against the powerless and in the service of dictatorships. The forces of organized religion can also be used to deny the rights of others who disagree with church teaching. Religious-sponsored antiabortion protests, for example, may empower those opposed to abortion, but they also are an attempt to abridge the rights of others. The new religious right is reported to be using empowerment techniques to impose its opinions and values on school boards, local government, public media, and the arts. In a similar vein, Baer (1993) noted that in African-American churches men had full access to positions of control and influence that were unavailable to women. This imbalance empowered male members at the expense of female members. Our point is that organized religion is not a monolithic, cohesive institution but rather a diversity of institutions, organizations, and congregations, some of which actively support empowerment while others are neutral or even hostile with regard to it.

Belonging to a proactive organization helps members learn the skills and means to advocate for change. Such a collective often maintains contact with political and community leaders, which helps members to become knowledgeable about issues and involved in protecting their interests. In this way, religious organizations form group identification and collectively engage in the process of change. Moreover, young and inactive members are encouraged to participate and become assertive members of society (Warner 1993). When such a collective embraces a process of social change, it is already equipped with personal ties, basic resources, leadership skills, and a strong sense of virtue. Many religious groups, from congregations to denominations, have the capacity to assist in empowering the neediest members of society but are waiting to be asked. As such, they are a potential resource that social workers can tap into in order to successfully campaign for increased empowerment in society.

We have documented the efforts and contributions of organized religion to empower four groups of people identified by social work as in need of assistance, as well as two empowerment interventions based on religion. The groups included African Americans, other minorities, women, gays and lesbians, the disenfranchised, and the oppressed. We have also noted that findings regarding the efforts by organized religion to empower these people have been largely underreported and undervalued. It is our contention that religious organizations, denominations, and congregations are, in fact, doing more for the powerless than many social services organizations are. It is important to remember Durkheim's (1954) assertion that religion provides direction and expectations as to the meaning of human existence and defines the obligations of its members to themselves, their families, and the broader society. This suggests that the efforts of organized religion to empower people should be recognized, supported, and expanded. We are firmly convinced that social service organizations should not only focus on empowering clients in the consumption of services, but also adopt a broader societal perspective to combat power inequalities, a perspective such as that proposed by Breton (1992), Evans (1992), and Moore (1991). Social work and the religious community need to teach and learn from one another. The religious community can learn a great deal from social workers about how to care for and deal with needy people, while social work can cooperate with religious organizations in an effort to empower clients in all aspects of life, from understanding who they are and how society is treating them, to their contact with service providers. By working together, social work and the religious community can help counteract the power imbalance that is so pervasive in the world today.

CHAPTER 10

RELIGIOUS-BASED SOCIAL SERVICES PROVISION: FINDINGS FROM LOCAL STUDIES—GREENSBORO

As a corollary to examples of religious-based social services, we offer findings from surveys we conducted in Greensboro, North Carolina (1989–1996). The Greensboro study examined provision of social services by local congregations and use of congregational resources by public and private secular social service agencies. The findings from Greensboro are similar to those reported by other researchers (Hodgkinson et al. 1993; Orr et al. 1994). This in-depth look at one community provides empirical support for our thesis—namely, that places of worship serve as important social service centers and as cornerstones of service development, innovation, and social stability. Two things make this possible. One is that congregations provide volunteers, space, and money. The other is that their facilities serve as sacred spaces for house worship and as human spaces where faith is expressed through social and community service. Without these congregations, social and community activities in many of the nation's neighborhoods would be significantly curtailed.

DEMOGRAPHIC BACKGROUND

Greensboro is a city located in the Piedmont area of central North Carolina. The county is part of the eleven-county Piedmont Triad region, which has a population of 1.2 million people. Greensboro, the third-largest city in North Carolina, has a population of just over 200,000 people. It is the county seat of

Guilford County, which has a population of 379,000 and is the third-largest county in the state. The population is 72 percent white, 26 percent black, and 2 percent other racial/ethnic groups. Guilford County is centered along the Piedmont industrial crescent that stretches from Raleigh to Charlotte. The county's traditional employment base of textiles, apparel, and furniture has diversified greatly in the last fifty years and now encompasses more than three hundred concerns with a wide range of products.

In the following sections, we first present findings from two studies in the Greensboro series. The first study (1989) offers a community portrait of 128 of the major white and black religious congregations in Greensboro during the Reagan/Bush era of the late 1980s. The study describes the kinds of social services provided by these congregations and how they assisted service organizations in the Greensboro community. The 1992–1995 study examined how the religious community supported public and private social service agencies during the early Clinton years.

CONCEPTUAL FRAMEWORK

Before presenting our findings, we wish to clarify several points relevant to our research. First, the Greensboro studies were exploratory in nature. The road maps and knowledge bases we used to conceptualize our research studies were basically our own. This was not because we were closed-minded but because we were the first to consider religious social services activity. Second, to guide our research, we categorized the social and community service provision of religious congregations as: (1) in-house services and (2) outreach assistance. In-house services were broadly defined as the social services (counseling, food pantries, or night shelter, for example) that congregations frequently offer at their place of worship. Outreach assistance was defined as services that members of congregations offer to community-service providers, such as money, volunteers, goods, or use of congregational facilities. No major distinction was made in either category between services offered to members and those offered to nonmembers. While we are keenly aware of the overlap and intricacies of provision of service within these categories, we believe that they provide a useful conceptual framework for understanding the dimensions of service that are discussed in this chapter.

The basic assumption underlying our research is that the religious community is much more involved in social services provision than is acknowledged by social work practitioners and academicians. Although the early research of Salamon and Teitelbaum (1984) and Wineburg and Wineburg (1986; 1987) documented the significant involvement of the religious community in social service provision, we firmly believe that additional research is required if this area of investigation is to gain credibility with the gatekeepers of knowledge and attract the support of funders. Given the present intersection of politics, religion, and social services, such studies are going to be crucial to the future directions of social service in the years ahead.

In this chapter we will focus on the role that religious congregations play in their communities, as a means of (a) understanding the impact of large-scale policy decisions on the operation of local human service systems and (b) reinterpreting social work practice in light of the activities of faith communities in helping their neighbors.

SURVEY OF GREENSBORO CONGREGATIONS (1989): STUDY ONE

Sample Characteristics and Study Design

The sampling frame consisted of 330 religious congregations within the city limits of Greensboro, a city with a population of 200,000. Lists of congregations were obtained from the telephone book and a mailing list provided by the Greensboro Urban Ministry. Surveys were sent to pastors of 330 congregations in November 1988. Nonrespondents were sent a second survey and were also contacted by phone. The number of completed surveys totaled 128 (38%). The high nonresponse rate (62%) was not a major limitation because the respondents represented most of the community's mainline black and white congregations. These who did not respond were mostly very small evangelical congregations with itinerant pastors.

Findings

Table 10.1 lists all in-house services and community outreach reported by the congregations surveyed. As noted previously, "community outreach" referred to services provided by congregations to nine agencies in Greensboro. Of these agencies, five had been established during the 1980s: Lutheran Family Services, Hospice, Project Uplift, Habitat for Humanity, and South East Council on Crime and Delinquency. The remaining four—Greensboro

Urban Ministry, Salvation Army, Guilford Native American Association, and United Services for Older Adults—predated the Reagan budget cuts.

Study Instrument

The survey instrument elicited information from respondents (clergy) regarding: (a) the use of their congregation's facilities, staff, and members for thirty-one social service activities (family counseling, soup kitchens, day care, Alcoholics Anonymous, shelter, referral to other agencies, legal assistance, and so on) and (b) the nature and scope of services provided by their congregation. For each program offered by the congregation, respondents were asked to indicate whether the program was formal or informal; restricted to members only or open to the community; offered free or at a charge; and started after 1980 (to determine the number of services offered after Reagan cuts). The survey instrument also measured community outreach over time and in terms of volunteer services, money, and goods for twenty-seven programs administered by nine service agencies.

IN-HOUSE SERVICES HIGHLIGHTS

Below are key findings from the first Greensboro study, some of which have been published elsewhere. Our purpose is to present a clear, but broad, picture of social services delivery in a small Southern city.

   Of the 128 responding congregations, 107 (84%) offered at least one in-house service, such as counseling, transportation to appointments, telephone reassurance, and the like.

   Overall, the responding congregations provided a total of 632 services for an average of about 5 (4.93) formal/informal services per congregation.

   Of the 632 services, 248 (39%) were offered to members of the community. Half of the respondents (64 congregations) offered in-house programs to the community.

   At the time of the survey, 114 (89%) of the 128 congregations had counseling services. Forty-six (36%) congregations provided those services through a formal counseling program, while 68 (53%) congregations provided counseling services on an informal basis.

   Forty-four (34%) of the responding congregations housed Alcoholics Anonymous, Narcotics Anonymous, Al-Anon, Alateen, and/or Overeaters Anonymous programs.

Only 12 congregations reported starting after 1980. Of those, most had an
average of fewer than 5 services and 47 were food, clothing, and cash
assistance services.

Services provided by congregations and reported by both congregants and
residents of the surrounding community are listed in table 10.1. Two findings
are of particular interest. One is the number of clothing and cash assistance
programs ($N = 47$) that came into being following the Reagan budget cuts of
the early 1980s. The other is both the range and the number of services that
the religious community was already providing before the Reagan era. The
findings indicate that congregations did respond to the drastic budget cuts in
government programs, and more important, they were prepared to do so
because they were already involved in provisions of services.

Congregations also reported a significant number of services provided on
an informal basis. This finding suggests that congregations are resilient, in
that they respond to new needs and continue to meet ongoing needs in a fluid
and dynamic way (Jeavons and Cnaan 1997). This openness may explain how
congregations become catalysts for new agencies, a development discussed in
chapter 11. When in-house and outreach assistance provided by religious congregations is considered as a whole, the religious community emerges as a
vital player in social services provision.

COMMUNITY OUTREACH SERVICES HIGHLIGHTS

Of the 128 responding congregations, 111 (87%) provided volunteers or other
in-kind support for one or more human service activities in the Greensboro community.

Members of 22 congregations (17%) of the responding 128 congregations
volunteered at the shelter for homeless adults at Greensboro Urban Ministry. Members of 43 (33.6%) volunteered at the agency's community
feeding program.

Fifty-one congregations (40%) gave food to the Urban Ministry food bank.

Forty-one congregations (32%) provided volunteers for Habitat for
Humanity.

Seventeen of the congregations (13%) provided volunteers for the Lutheran
Family Refugee Resettlement Program.

One hundred and four congregations (81%) reported that they would
participate in community-based programs in the future.

Fifty-seven congregations (44%) worked with neighborhood groups.

TABLE 10.1

1988–89 Survey of Services Offered By 128 Greensboro Congregations

Service	Formal	Informal	For Members	Charge a Fee	For Community	Charge a Fee	Begun After 1980
Emergency Food Asst.	18	56	5	1	39	2	22
Clothing	20	40	7	2	30	2	15
Congregate Meals	8	6	9	2	6	2	2
Soup Kitchen	7	4	4	1	1	1	4
Emergency Shelter	3	11	2	2	2	2	2
Cash	30	31	12	0	27	0	10
Mobile Meals	22	8	1	0	9	0	8
Personal Counseling	27	37	17	0	25	0	7
Family Counseling	19	31	16	0	19	0	3
Phone Reassurance	11	21	12	0	11	0	5
Transportation	3	15	11	1	8	0	3
Housework for Disabled	2	8	7	0	1	0	3
Housework for Elderly	2	9	7	0	1	0	3
Home Health Asst.	4	3	2	0	2	1	1
Food Preparation	6	11	6	1	3	0	5
Legal Help	3	7	5	0	2	0	2
Help Finding Services	12	23	7	0	11	0	3
Child Care	16	4	4	2	8	6	3
After-School Care	12	4	3	2	7	5	5
Adult Day Care	1	1	1	0	1	0	1

TABLE 10.1 (*continued*)

1988–89 Survey of Services Offered By 128 Greensboro Congregations

Service	Formal	Informal	For Members	Charge a Fee	For Community	Charge a Fee	Begun After 1980
Tutoring	6	4	1	0	6	0	1
Employment Help	5	12	4	0	4	0	3
Pregnancy Counsel	7	8	4	0	5	0	1
Foster Care	3	1	0	0	2	0	2
Alcoholics Anonymous	23	3	2	0	10	2	3
Alateen	6	0	2	0	1	1	3
Narcotics Anonymous	8	0	0	0	3	0	3
Overeaters Anonymous	4	1	0	0	3	0	2
Mental Health	4	0	0	0	3	0	3

The first Greensboro study illustrates the social services provision of congregations beyond those services provided on their premises. Findings showed that these congregations also provided volunteers, money, and/or goods to secular, sectarian, and interfaith agencies at the community level. This combination of in-house and outreach services demonstrates that the religious community is more than an adjunct service provider in the system of services. Organized religion functions over time as the "social glue" that holds neighborhoods and communities together through its social services provision. Nevertheless, we do not agree with the suggestion of the religious right that public programs be totally replaced by a faith-based system of services. What we are suggesting is that the faith-based system of services be understood for what it is: a constantly changing and essential link in the system of public and private nonprofit service delivery at the local level. In the following discussion, we provide overviews of several Greensboro agencies and examples of congregational support and involvement during the 1980s.

Greensboro Urban Ministry: This agency warrants discussion as an example of an organization that has attracted enormous interfaith support. Greensboro Urban Ministry, a professional social service agency with trained MSWs and BSWs in key leadership roles, represents what can happen when social services shift from government programs to local congregational initiatives. Greensboro Urban Ministry grew from a storefront operation in 1980 to a multiservice operation housed in a new $3.5 million facility at the end of the 1990s. From its beginnings with six paid staff and volunteers representing fewer than one hundred congregations, this agency now has fifty-nine paid staff and more than a thousand volunteers from more than two hundred congregations. Its annual operating budget is $2 million, much of which comes from local congregations.

A health clinic, originally established by Greensboro Urban Ministry, now operates as an independent nonprofit organization called Health Serve Ministry. Its facility is located next door to Greensboro Urban Ministry. The board of Health Serve Ministry is equally divided between congregational representatives and representatives from a local hospital that uses the clinic to serve indigent clients. This clinic serves the needs of the clients and cuts health care costs by using volunteer nurses, doctors, social workers, and other members of local congregations.

Greensboro Urban Ministry is an example of how devolution is taking form locally. This can be seen in the "spotter" strategy that the agency uses to maintain its network with local congregations. The spotter is a volunteer who checks the bulletin boards in Greensboro's more than three hundred congregations to identify any changes in ministerial leadership. When changes are noted in a congregation that has a relationship with Greensboro Urban Ministry, staff members initiate steps to continue the institutional connection. Greensboro Urban Ministry is an object lesson in how organizations can learn, cope, and sometimes thrive in changing times, despite devastating policy changes.

Seven of the nine programs offered by the Greensboro Urban Ministry started after the Reagan budget cuts in the early 1980s. These programs are night shelter, food bank, soup kitchen, project independence, housing rehabilitation, family shelter, and cheese distribution. Congregations supported the Urban Ministry in all programs. Most notably, 30 percent of the 128 studied congregations financially supported night shelters, food bank, emergency assistance, and soup kitchen. One third of the congregations also provided volunteers to the soup kitchen, and two-fifths of the congregations provided goods to the clothing room and food bank. It should be noted that all programs provided by the Urban Ministry were supported by at least ten congregations.

Salvation Army: The Salvation Army itself is a church and one that has been most active in social services delivery since its inception. Given that the mission of local Salvation Army corps is to address unmet needs, it is not surprising that during the 1980s the Salvation Army in Greensboro pursued new service areas as Greensboro Urban Ministry grew to become the dominant faith-inspired service agency. The Army began to focus on night shelters, soup kitchens, thrift shops, and youth programs. Most of the support from other congregations came in the form of nine congregations supporting the thrift shop. In general, assistance from other congregations to the Salvation Army during the 1980s was minimal.

Lutheran Family Services: Lutheran Family Services in the 1980s provided two major programs: refugee resettlement and youth programs, primarily adoption and foster care services. Greensboro became a national model for refugee resettlement when Lutheran Family Services established a program for Southeast Asians in the early 1980s. They used a private network of congregational sponsorship programs in which local congregations adopted one or more Southeast Asian refugee families and set up support networks to help them find employment, learn the language, get medical care, and become self-sufficient. Sixteen of the 128 studied congregations (12.5%) provided volunteers to the refugee resettlement program, and most of these congregations also supported the program with money and goods.

Other Agencies: Both Habitat for Humanity and Hospice received tremendous outreach support from Greensboro's religious congregations in the 1980s. Of the 128 studied congregations, one-third provided volunteers for

Habitat for Humanity and one-fourth provided volunteers for the local hospice. Most of these congregations also supported these programs with money.

AGENCY USE OF CONGREGATIONAL RESOURCES (1996): STUDY TWO

Since our initial findings indicated significant congregational support for selected agencies in the Greensboro community, we decided to study the entire social service system in Greensboro to determine the magnitude of the relationships between the religious community and public and private nonprofit agencies. The following summary outlines our results of the 1992–1996 study in which we surveyed local agency directors in Greensboro to determine how their agencies used volunteers, money, and facilities of local religious congregations. In addition, we examined six agencies in depth to observe the inner workings of the congregation-agency relationship.

Sample Characteristics and Study Design

We mailed survey questionnaires to 193 public/private social agencies and self-help groups listed in the United Way's directory of Greensboro's agencies. Of these, 147 (76%) agencies responded to the mail survey. The statistical margin of error was ± 3 points.

Of the 147 responding agencies, 28 percent classified themselves as public agencies and 72 percent, as private agencies. Further analysis showed that 9 percent of the responding agencies reported a religious affiliation and 14 percent reported a United Way affiliation. Twenty percent of the agencies classified themselves as independent organizations, and 14 percent classified themselves as self-help organizations. Thirty-six percent of the responding agencies were affiliated with national agencies. Of the 147 responding agencies, 31 percent reported annual budgets of less than $100,000; 40 percent, budgets between $100,000 and $1 million; 30 percent, budgets of more than $1 million.

The major services reported by these agencies included: community education (50%), individual counseling (44%), information and referral (42%), family counseling (36%), youth counseling (25%), service to the elderly (15%), substance abuse counseling (14%), financial counseling (13%), and telephone counseling (12%). The number of full-time employees was as follows: 1–4 employees (38%), 5–20 employees (35%); and more than 20 employees (26%).

The number of part-time employees was as follows: 1–4 employees (52%), 5–20 employees (32%); and more than 20 employees (16%).

Findings

In the following section we report findings from the second Greensboro study (1996) regarding the use of congregational resources by the entire social services system.

Greensboro Agencies and Volunteer Support: Of the 147 responding agencies, 78 percent reported using volunteers to support their operations. Of these, 50 percent reported having more than 45 volunteers working in various capacities. Large agencies, such as the Boy Scouts, Girl Scouts, and Red Cross, reported more than 1,000 volunteers. The annual dollar value of volunteer services was calculated by 16 percent of the agencies, and another 11 percent reported their estimates. The annual value was $1,554,003. Half of the agencies claimed more than $45,000 in volunteer contributions. Another 12 percent that do not regularly calculate the dollar amount of volunteer services estimated $3.8 million in volunteer service.

Agency Use of Congregational Volunteers: Sixty (49%) of the responding agencies reported using congregational volunteers. Thirty-nine percent of those who reported they did not use congregational volunteers nevertheless noted that their volunteers included members of religious congregations who volunteered as individuals and not as representatives of their congregations.

This finding suggests a strong formal and informal relationship between the religious community and the social service community. Of the agencies that gave reasons for not using congregational volunteers, 17 percent noted that they had not yet developed congregation-agency contacts. This finding suggests that some agencies saw the potential for an expanded volunteer relationship in the future.

The number of congregations reported by the sixty agencies was as follows: 1–25 volunteers (54%); 26–50 volunteers (15%); and more than 50 volunteers (31%). This finding, combined with the breakdown of full-time and part-time employees noted above, suggests that a substantial portion of Greensboro's agencies and social service organizations relied heavily on part-time employees and volunteer labor (and a significant number of volunteers from religious congregations).

At the time of our survey, each of the following eleven agencies in Greensboro was using more than 100 volunteers from religious congregations: Red Cross, Girl Scouts, Greensboro Jewish Federation, Greensboro

Crisis Pregnancy Center, Shepherd's Center of Greensboro, Greensboro Youth Council, Greensboro Urban Ministry, Boy Scouts, Lutheran Family Services, Voluntary Action Center, and AGAPE. Close to 10 percent of the public/private agencies have been dependent on the religious community for their pool of volunteers. This finding reinforced the 1988–1989 finding that congregations support the operations of many community agencies with volunteer assistance.

Years of Agency Use of Congregational Volunteers: More than half (58%) of the sixty agencies that reported using congregational volunteers had been doing so for more than ten years at the time of the 1992 survey. This finding indicated that use of congregational volunteers was already under way before the Reagan budget cuts of the 1980s. Other reported lengths of congregational volunteer use were as follows: 6–10 years (14%); 1–5 years (26%); and less than one year (2%). The last three categories reflect the time periods when the budget cuts of the Reagan era were taking effect.

Monetary Value of Congregational Volunteer Service: Only a small number of agencies calculated the financial worth of services performed by their congregational volunteers, probably because this task is time-consuming and not a high priority in most agencies. Greensboro Urban Ministry, as previously mentioned, documented 60,000 hours of volunteer service in 1992. At $5.35 per hour, that represents more than a $300,000 contribution in volunteer labor from the religious community. If we were to use the Independent Sector valuation of $11.58 an hour for volunteer service, the contribution of the religious community to this agency would be valued at $694,800. Considering that doctors, lawyers, accountants, and other professionals donate their time to Greensboro Urban Ministry and other agencies, the $300,000 figure is conservative. It is reasonable to conclude that the religious community contributes significantly to reducing the labor costs of local agencies that use congregational volunteers. Yet when we discuss the contributions of the religious community to the social services and nonprofit sector, we often fail to discuss the role of religious volunteers.

Denominational Volunteering: Half of the sixty agencies that used congregational volunteers at the time of the survey estimated the number of congregations represented by their volunteers as follows: 1–5 congregations (38%); 6–10 congregations (24%); 11–20 congregations (14%), 25 or more congregations (21%). The rest (3%) did not respond. These findings, together with the previous findings, suggest that congregational volunteering was on the rise in the early 1990s and that agencies were seeking and using the service of volunteers from multiple congregations.

Fifty-three percent of these agencies reported organized recruitment of volunteers from congregations. Those involved in initiating the agency-congregation relationships were as follows: agency staff members (50%); board members (31%); volunteers (6%). The rest (13%) did not respond. Ninety-eight percent of the agencies reported that they did not train congregational volunteers differently than they trained other volunteers.

The primary contact person for recruiting congregational volunteers was reported as follows: pastor/spiritual leader (41%); community members (33%); member of the agency who was also a church member (20%); and a volunteer or church staff member (7%). When asked to rank the key elements in brokering the volunteer relationships, the agencies gave the highest ratings to personal contacts (78%) and the reputation and track record of commitment of the congregation (78%).

To build relationships with local congregations, agencies reported as the key methods: sending newsletters to congregations announcing volunteer opportunities at their agency (54%) and using other initiatives, such as speakers' bureau or working through the local Voluntary Action Center (70%). Note that the respondents could identify more than one method, hence the methods add to more than 100 percent. This clearly suggests that the agencies rely on a two-pronged process of resource development from the religious community that requires (a) the development of individual relationships and (b) the nurturing and sustaining of institutional bonds. These are important findings for community practitioners.

Agencies reported the most frequent activities performed by congregational volunteers as follows: direct services, such as counseling and transportation for clients (43%); administrative activities, such as planning, fund-raising, or board participation (20%); secretarial assistance (5%); custodial services (3%). The rest (29%) did not respond.

In sum, the findings indicate that congregational volunteers are and have been extremely important to the operations of Greensboro's social service agencies. The agencies used various methods of recruiting volunteers, ranging from newsletters to personal contacts. The agency–congregational volunteer link appears to be dependent on an agency employee who is also a congregation member and uses personal contacts to broker the relationship between his or her congregation and the agency.

Financial Support by Congregations: Of the 147 responding agencies, 40 percent reported that they had sought financial support from local religious congregations. At the time of the study, 30 percent were receiving financial support from congregations. Twenty-two percent reported previous congregational support, although they were not currently receiving funds. To our surprise, only 48 percent of the responding agencies reported that they had never received funds from religious congregations. Twelve percent reported that they did not seek money from congregations but had received funds. Our finding that public agencies received funds from the religious community was unexpected. It is of interest that the respondent from the Greensboro Public Health Department noted that congregations contributed funds indirectly. As an example, the respondent cited the agency's Adopt a Mom program, in which a local congregation adopted a pregnant mom who could not afford prenatal care and "[paid] her pre-natal cost and transportation costs etc." The respondent also noted that she and a member of her staff brokered the relationships with the congregations.

The number of congregations that provided funds to the sixty-one agencies reporting direct congregational support were as follows: 2–10 congregations (48%); 11–30 congregations (13%); 31–100 congregations (8%). The rest (31%) did not respond. This finding suggests that agencies are using congregations as informal grant-making sources, in that they are seeking and receiving funds from multiple congregations.

Forty-seven percent of the responding agencies use board members to broker the financial arrangement with the congregation; 39 percent use a member of their staff to do so. Forty-three percent of the responding directors reported that they are the ones who broker the financial arrangements with congregations. The main contact person named by agencies in seeking financial contributions was as follows: pastor/spiritual leader of the congregation (45%); community leader who is also a member of the congregation (26%); and employee of the agency who is also a church member (22%).

Thirty percent of the responding agencies reported that they request money through annual solicitations to all congregations in the local community. Other methods of solicitation reported were as follows: informal requests to selected members of a selected group of congregations (31%); informal requests to a specific person from a selected group of congregations (33%); and formal proposals to selected members from selected congregations (26%). Twenty-nine percent of the agencies reported that they did not request congregational support. A small number of the agencies in this group were approached by the congregations.

Use of Congregational Facilities: Just as congregational volunteers and financial support are important to community agencies, so is the use of congregational facilities. Of the 147 responding agencies, 62 percent reported that they had sought the use of congregational facilities; 66 percent reported they had used such facilities; and 34 percent reported they had never used these facilities. At the time of the study, 36 percent were using congregational facilities, and 30 percent were not using congregational facilities but had used them in the past. Of the agencies that were using congregational facilities, 73 percent did not pay rent. Of those that did pay rent, 70 percent paid a reduced rate of rent. Only 6 percent of the agencies paid fair-market rent for use of congregational facilities. Congregations therefore make a significant contribution to the community agencies by allowing them to use facilities at reduced rates or, usually, at no rent at all.

Agencies reported using congregational facilities for the following purposes: educational programs (26%); agency meetings or retreats (17%); community meetings (11%); services for the developmentally disabled, blind, or elderly (7%); and office space (7%). Of the agencies reporting use of congregational facilities, 46 percent reported they have used them for less than ten years, and 54 percent reported using them for more than ten years.

Frequency of agency use of congregational facilities was reported as follows: daily (15.5%); weekly (12%); monthly (21%); and yearly (52%).

Ninety-five percent of the agencies initiated the arrangement to use the facilities of religious congregations. Those serving as agency brokers were as follows: agency staff member (56%); agency director (38%); and agency board member (25%). In contrast to the finding regarding congregational financial support, this finding shows that building use is usually solicited by a staff member. This is an important finding for the practitioner who wants to use congregational facilities for agency programs.

Significance of Agency-Congregation Relationships: The overall findings in the solicitation and use of congregational resources strongly suggest that very deep and intertwined relationships between the social services and religious communities have developed over time in Greensboro. Congregations have been and still are providing volunteers, giving money, and offering the use of their facilities to local agencies. To reiterate a point made earlier, 49 percent of the agencies used congregational volunteers; 52 percent have received congregational money; and 66 percent have used the facilities of congregations. The relationships go far beyond the mere solicitation, distribution, and receipt of goods and services. Religious congregations not only enhance the services of local agencies such as Greensboro Urban Ministry, the Red Cross, the Girl Scouts, the Boy Scouts, and the Jewish Federation, but they also underpin agency operations by providing thousands of volunteers, money, services, and buildings.

This exchange is not just a one-way street. The local agencies serve as conduits or as the organizational structures (Berger and Neuhaus 1977) between the charitable impulses of members of religious institutions and the people they want to help. This is an important concept because it speaks directly to the question of what holds civil society and community together. And the answer—from Tocqueville to the present day—has been the same: voluntary associations and religious institutions. The information presented in this book underscores this fact time and time again: voluntary associations and the religious community are the social glue that holds communities together. As the two studies reported in this chapter show, congregations have been slowly but steadily simulating agency development since 1917 (Wineburg 1996). Cnaan (1997) found a similar phenomenon on a national level.

Historically, congregational initiatives have always been part of the broader community's philanthropic efforts, while creating an underlying community ethic of concern and assistance. Today, congregations do not necessarily have to start an agency to display their care and concern. Existing agencies provide numerous opportunities to help, and congregations are responding generously, as evidenced by the findings from Greensboro.

These findings also show a surprisingly strong interdependence. Agency use of congregational volunteers, money, and facilities, as well as use of part-time employees, demonstrates both prudent fiscal management and concern for clients. With the continual pressure on agencies to use charitable contributions efficiently and effectively, the religious and social service communities would benefit by adopting documented methods that have proved successful in such cities as Greensboro.

Clearly, one of the most noteworthy findings of this study is the relationship between an agency's use of a congregation's facility and the likelihood of additional congregational resources. The data demonstrate a trend in which facility use leads to a more comprehensive set of agency and congregational relationships. One reason for this development may be that when a congregation offers its facilities to a community social agency, it also acknowledges its own institutional commitment to the broader community.

Underneath the facts, figures, descriptions, and accounts in this chapter, we believe, is a picture of a community's spirit. While we realize that there are no statistical tools that can measure a community's spirit, we believe that the breadth and depth of that spirit can be sketched in part by the community's daily efforts to put its concern for others into practice. It has been our intent to present a more detailed picture of the partnership between the social work community and the religious community as it exists in one small city. It is our hope that these studies of Greensboro will stimulate a new set of questions for demographers who study American religion and nonprofit agencies, and for social work scholars and practitioners as well. Without consideration of this partnership any analysis of either the social work community or the religious community will necessarily be incomplete.

RELIGIOUS-BASED SOCIAL SERVICES PROVISION: FINDINGS FROM LOCAL STUDIES—PHILADELPHIA

In the previous chapter, we presented findings from a study on congregational and religious-based social services in one midsized southern city. In this chapter, we present a corollary to examples of religious-based social services: findings from studies carried out from 1996 to 1998 in Philadelphia, a major northeastern urban area. The findings represent two related studies. The first was an in-depth survey of twenty-four congregations in Philadelphia. This survey was conducted as part of a larger study to assess the role of local religious congregations in the provision of social and community services. The second was a survey, conducted specifically for this chapter, of noncongregational religious-based organizations involved in social services provision in Philadelphia. The sample of thirty-three noncongregational religious-based organizations included coalitions, denominational organizations, paradenominational agencies, and religious-affiliated social service agencies.

THE SOCIAL AND COMMUNITY INVOLVEMENT OF LOCAL RELIGIOUS CONGREGATIONS

Study Design and Sample Characteristics

The findings of Philadelphia local congregations are taken from a larger in-depth study of local religious congregations in six urban areas: Chicago, Indianapolis, Mobile, New York, Philadelphia, and the San Francisco area (including Oakland). For each of these cities, we obtained from a local historic preservation or assistance organization a list of all congregations housed in historic properties. The term *historic properties* is used in this context to mean churches built before 1940 and still used as places of worship. In some cases, the current congregation has no affiliation with the denomination that originally built the place of worship. In Philadelphia, we generated a random list of 25 congregations housed in historic properties from a list of 699 congregations. One congregation refused our invitation to participate in the study, and so the sample for Philadelphia included 24 congregations.

In carrying out this study, we used a comprehensive range of research instruments to determine the congregation's membership, history, governance, budget, future plans, physical layout, and—most important—social and community services. To obtain the required information we interviewed clergy, lay leaders, and service directors/providers. We employed three research assistants, who were trained by the principal investigator. To assure the validity of our findings, we administered the study instruments to more than one person. For example, we posed the same questions to the pastor and to a lay leader of the congregation.

Membership varied widely among the congregations; it averaged 920 persons, with a range from 40 to 11,000 individuals ($SD = 725$). Membership average was 482 when the 11,000-member congregation was excluded. Active membership, defined as attending services at least monthly, averaged 263. The ethnic composition of congregations in the sample revealed an interesting finding. In Philadelphia, all but two congregations (92%) have 75 percent or more of their members belonging to one ethnic group. Of the twenty-four congregations, 58 percent were dominated by African Americans, 21 percent by Caucasians, 8 percent by Asian Americans, and 4 percent by Hispanics.

Most congregations in our study were older congregations. Among Philadelphia congregations, the average date of founding was 1892. The oldest congregation was founded in 1681, the newest in 1991 ($SD = 81.7$). Similarly, most congregations in the sample reported that they have been at the same location for many years; the length of time a congregation has been housed in the same property averaged 66 years. The time span among congregations ranged from two to 234 years ($SD = 64.3$). Baptist and Episcopal congregations were overrepresented in this sample.

Social Services Delivery

We used two methods to determine the extent to which congregations provided social and community services. First, the interviewees were asked whether their congregation had provided, within the past twelve months, any of the programs listed in our instrument. The list consisted of some two hundred programs that had been identified from congregational literature, previous work of the research team, and consultation with many experts in the field. We included only nonreligious programs. That is, the program could not be dependent upon the faith tradition, as in communal prayers, Bible classes, or worship services. Second, we asked the interviewees to select up to five social programs that best represented their congregation's involvement in the community. For each such selected program we administered a four-page instrument assessing the nature of the program, its beneficiaries, cost, location and time of service, income, and other people or organizations involved in its implementation.

Using the first method, we referred only to formal programs operated by the congregation, officially supported by the congregation, or carried out on the congregation's premises by a third party. We emphasize that the number of programs listed does not represent the actual number of programs provided by local religious congregations but rather a tabulation of the types of services offered. In some cases, one program was broken down into several components in the study instrument. For example, the instrument might list a program to visit homebound and sick people as both hospital visitation and visitation of sick people (buddy program). For some congregations, these services are two distinct programs; for others, they are a single program. Similarly, shelter for homeless people may include a soup kitchen and a mental health care unit. Although all of these services may be considered a single program by a congregation, the instrument required that they be identified separately. After-school programs provide another example. Such programs can be either/both recreational and educational and either/both for children and teens. In all such cases, we encouraged respondents to identify separately the services offered under the aegis of the program.

We found wide variability in the types of programs offered by congregations in Philadelphia. This finding supports the premise that congregations meet the unique and specific needs within their communities by implementing a wide and varied spectrum of programs. We were informed that congregations that wish to be socially active assessed local needs, compared them to services offered, and developed a program to fill existing voids in services. Thus, congregations covered a wide range of human needs and together formed an impressive network of social services.

The programs in Philadelphia that were carried out by more than 25 percent of the congregations are presented in table 11.1, which constitutes an impressive list of areas of social and community involvement of local religious congregations. The table strongly illustrates that congregations are not focusing primarily on their own members but are attuned to the social needs in the community around them.

TABLE 11.1

Social and Community Programs in Philadelphia

Social and Community Programs	Percentage of Congregations with Program
Food pantries	58.35
Summer day camp for children	58.35
Scholarships for students	54.17
Summer programs for teens	54.17
Holiday celebrations	50.00
Recreational programs for children	50.00
Scholarships for students in need	50.00
Clothing closets	45.83
Cooperation with police	45.83
Recreational programs for teens	45.83
Tutoring for children and youth	45.83
Visitation of sick people (buddy program)	45.83
Advocacy for civil rights	41.67
Advocacy for social justice	41.67
After-school care (recreational)	41.67
Hospital visitation	41.67
Space for police/community meeting	41.67
Choral groups	37.50
Health programs for the sick and homebound	37.50
Latchkey/after-school homework	37.50
Music performances	37.50
Programs for race reconciliation	37.50
Education for family values	33.33
Interfaith collaboration	33.33
Prison ministry	33.33
Adult literacy program	29.17
Collaboration with neighborhood associations	29.17
Drug and alcohol prevention	29.17
GED classes	29.17
Intergenerational programs	29.17
International relief	29.17
Neighborhood cleanup	29.17

(continued on next page)

Social and Community Programs	Percentage of Congregations with Program
Single-parent programs	29.17
Sport activities	29.17
Working on interfaith relations	29.17
AA meetings	25.00
Advocacy for peace	25.00
Communal (on site) meals for senior citizens	25.00
Education on women's issues	25.00
Health care for the elderly (physical and mental)	25.00
Historic preservation	25.00
Site for Cubs/Boy Scouts/Brownies/Girl Scouts	25.00
Soup kitchen	25.00
Tutoring for adults—computer literacy	25.00
Voter registration	25.00

Information on Selected Programs

In the second method we asked each congregation to identify *up to five programs* that were most representative of their social and community involvement. For each of these programs, respondents were asked to identify what was the nature of the program, how it was funded, who were the beneficiaries, where it was carried out, and whether the congregation derived any income from the program. It should be noted that we limited the number of programs to five, as data collection became too lengthy. However, there were many congregations that had more than five social programs. Using this method, our report underestimates the social and community services provision of local religious congregations.

In all, 89 programs were reported by twenty-four congregations in Philadelphia, for an average of 3.71 programs per congregation. The national average was 4.04. Of the twenty-four congregations, twenty-three offered at least one service (95.8%), and eleven (45.8%) reported five or more programs. The only congregation reporting no social/community programs was St. Martin Episcopal, a Korean congregation founded in 1990 and preoccupied with issues of survival and growth. It was also one of two congregations that was considering moving to a larger facility. While this congregation did not offer programs for the wider community, it did serve as a community center for and a source of support for 175 members who were first-generation Korean immigrants striving to acculturate into American society.

Spinoff organizations: One of the objectives in our study was to identify any past program offered by a congregation that had become an independent, freestanding program. Our reasoning was that members of a congregation are often the first to notice a new need in the community and attempt to meet it. As requests for services grow, other congregations or local groups may become partners with members of the community in service provision. It is thus highly likely that such partnerships will eventually evolve into independent organizations, and secular ones at that. For example, MANNA, an organization (discussed later in this chapter) that distributes meals to people with AIDS/HIV, originated in the basement of a Presbyterian church and is now a major independent nonprofit organization.

Of the twenty-four congregations, nine (37.5%) reported programs that became independent organizations. One congregation, Arch Street Friends Meeting House, reported the incubation of more than one hundred programs. Exclusive of this congregation, each congregation reported, on average, a little more than two spun-off programs. The congregations and the spin-off organizations are listed in table 11.2.

Who benefits (Cui bono)? To determine whether the programs reported by congregations (data from our second instrument) were intended primarily for members or for those in the larger community, we asked the respondents to indicate for each program (a) the total number of individuals served monthly and (b) the total number of nonmembers served monthly. The mean number of participants per program was 96.37. The number of members benefiting per program ranged from one to 500. The mean number of members benefiting per program was 15.54. The mean number of nonmember beneficiaries was 80.83, for a total of 96.37 beneficiaries and a ratio of 5.20:1 in favor of serving others. The number of members providing service outnumbered that of nonmembers (15.64 and 7.03, respectively), a ratio of 2.22:1. Overall, these findings indicate that local religious congregations should be viewed not merely as organizations that serve the church's members but rather as charitable organizations concerned with the welfare of others. The focus of most congregations in our sample was the betterment of community life. They not only provided services to others directly and in partnership with other organizations but also made their facilities available for a wide range of community activities.

In most cases, membership is not a criterion for receiving the services provided by the congregational program. Yet it is important to note that even when a congregation's members are being served, the program is important for society as a whole. If the congregation helps its elderly members (or their

TABLE 11.2

Agencies, Organizations, and Associations Emerging from Historic
Religious Congregations

Philadelphia: Of the 24 congregations, 8 (37.5%) reported programs that became independent organizations. One congregation reported the incubation of more than 100 programs. Exclusive of this congregation, each congregation reported, on average, a little more that two programs. The congregations and the spin-off organizations were as follows:

Arch Street Friends Meeting House	140 organizations
Episcopal Church, Germantown	Germantown Women's Ministries Vocational Educational Project Interfaith Hospitality
First Reformed Church	Civic associations Boys' Choir of Philadelphia Philadelphia Committee for the Homeless
Episcopal Church of Atonement	new congregation spun off from this place "Grand Old Gospel" radio show
Sacred Heart Church (Camden, N.J.)	day care center in new building
St. Andrew's and St. Monica's Episcopal Spanish Baptist Church	Powelton Village Civic Association Norris Square Senior Center Hispanic Clergy of Philadelphia Nueva Esperanza CIEBA UN
Phillipian Baptist Church	Progressive Convention Under Martin Luther King
Hugh of Cluny Roman Catholic Church	Catholic Credit Union

Source: Cnaan's 1997 six-city study commissioned by Partners for Sacred Places.

relatives) by providing them with transportation or assistance with shopping, cooking, and cleaning, it is helping these members not only to live better in the community but also to postpone or eliminate the need for nursing care. It is also a service that saves the public purse the expense of caring for these homebound elderly. For some people, assistance from a congregation may be the first and last line of defense before seeking assistance from the public or private sector. Furthermore, the above findings also suggest that the people being served by these congregational-based social services were probably not getting those needs met adequately by public or private sectors of society. Hence, congregational support of members and their relatives in and of itself saves the public sector and serves as the front line of social care.

Program costs incurred by congregations: Program costs incurred by congregations in our sample varied greatly. We asked the respondents to assess, to the best of their ability, the following types of program costs: monetary support by the congregation; type of space used, its assessed value, and amount of time used; total hours worked by staff and volunteers; in-kind support; and utilities. In all cases, we asked respondents to assess the monthly cost of the program, regardless of whether the program was offered daily, weekly, monthly, or annually.

Monetary support: Relatively few congregations reported direct financial support of any of their programs. Of the 89 programs reported by the twenty-four congregations, 51 programs (57.3%) received direct monetary support from the congregation. Two programs were omitted from further analysis, since we limited the amount to be reported to $5,000 a month so as not to bias the findings. The total monthly allocation was $30,608.34, with a mean of $624.66 per program.

Space provision: Of the 89 reported programs, 61 (68.54%) were provided solely in-house, while 7 others were provided both in-house and in the community. Congregations reported an average of 41.13 hours of space use per program per month. To determine the monetary value of the space provided by congregations for social and community service, we asked the respondents to assess the market value of the space that they provide to the programs. Although some found it difficult to assess the value, many were familiar with property values in their community (some even studied the market value of their properties in a process of planning to offer space for rent). Of the 68 programs that provided on-site services, we obtained only 33 (48.53%) responses to this question. The average monthly value of space provided per reporting program was $829.33. The total monthly assessed value of property used was $27,367.89 or $328,414.68 a year for congregations that answered this question.

We strongly believe that the program's values of property used were largely underestimated by the congregations in our sample. On one hand, this was a result of the low response rate regarding the market value of the space. On the other hand, many respondents noted that comparable space was not available in the community, and thus they based their assessment on the values of available properties in the community that are inadequate for the needs at hand.

Volunteer work: Local religious congregations have an important advantage in that their members generally know one another quite well and share a commitment to the same values. Another is that they are able to mobilize their members as volunteers for worthy causes. Our findings show that volunteers are an important resource to congregations in providing community service. Of the 89 programs, 57 (64.04%) reported use of volunteers. The previous figures indicate a very high rate of volunteer hours on behalf of community service. These data do not reflect volunteer activities of individual church members, a small subset of congregation members acting on their own (not as a congregation-related program), nor do they reflect services that are informal, provided within or for church members, and they do not reflect volunteering for the congregation itself (such as lay leadership, music, or Bible class teaching). In 1991, the Independent Sector, a national organization studying volunteer activity nationwide, assessed the value of a volunteer hour to be $11.58 (Hodgkinson et al. 1992). If we apply this conservative estimate to the above findings, the estimated monetary value of the 4,485.9 volunteer hours per month was $51,946.72, or $623,360.66 a year.

Impressive as these numbers are, they would have been even more so had all the congregations in our sample provided information on volunteer hours. Still, volunteers were not the only people to serve and assist in carrying out congregational social and community programs; others included clergy and congregational staff.

Clergy and staff hours: We asked respondents to indicate the number of programs in which clergy and other staff were actively involved. Clergy were involved in 40 (44.94%) of the 89 programs; staff, in 37 (41.53%). Another issue relevant to congregational involvement was the number of hours per program per month contributed by clergy and staff. We found that the mean hours by clergy per program per month averaged 26.1 and those by staff averaged 63.05. It is estimated that the monthly value for clergy per reported program is $522.00 per month, or $6,264 a year; for staff per reported program the figure is $6,305.00 per month, or $75,660.00 a year.

In-kind support: In addition to monetary and labor support, congregations in the sample assisted the numerous programs that they provided/housed in many ways; congregations also bore indirect costs in terms of such services as cleanup, maintenance, extra utility use, security, and so on. The most commonly reported types of in-kind support were use of phone, printing, photocopying, and postage. We asked respondents to assess the cost of the in-kind support they provided to the programs. In-kind support was reported for 33 (37.08%) of 89 programs at a mean cost of $184.70. The total in-kind support for the 33 programs reported was $73,141 per year.

Cost of utilities: Religious congregations are housed in properties that are often centrally located and perceived as nonthreatening. Thus, a large variety of community groups and organizations use the congregational building for meetings.

These groups usually pay no rent or only a small fee, yet keeping the building open for programs costs money in terms of heating, cleaning, supervising, and wear and tear. We asked respondents to assess the cost of utilities. Of 89 programs, 28 (31.46%) reported a mean utilities cost of $298.57 per month. The total utilities cost for the 28 programs reported was $100,319.52 per year.

Average monetary value of a congregational program per month: In determining the average monetary value of a program provided by a congregation per month, we used traditional economic methods for imputed values. We assumed that respondents had reported for each program the total cost of its operation on all dimensions (financial support, value of space, value of volunteer work, in-kind support, etc.). We calculated the *average monetary value* by adding the total reported costs for programs and dividing the result by the number of all programs whether or not they reported such costs. For example, as noted above, for Philadelphia, 28 of all 89 programs (31.46%) reported the cost of utilities. Among these programs, the mean cost per month was $298.57. Thus, the total mean utilities cost per month was $8,359.96 ($298.57 x 28 programs). In order to obtain a *conservative* cost estimate that would be applicable for all programs, we assumed that the programs that reported no costs for utilities had zero utilities cost. Thus we calculated the average monthly cost of utilities by dividing the total average cost per month ($8,359.96) by the total number of programs (89). This gave us an average monthly utilities cost of $93.93 per month per program. We carried out similar calculations for all dimensions of costs incurred by the congregations in services provision: financial contribution, space value, volunteer work, clergy and staff work, and in-kind and utilities costs. We summed these means to assess an average program's cost. The average monetary value of a program in the Philadelphia sample was $2,025.28 per month. It should be noted that this was the lowest mean for any city in our sample. The national mean was $3,176.98. When we deducted from this mean the income that some programs generated, the net congregational contribution was $1,863.44 per program per month. The national mean was $2,983.57.

How much a congregation gives: As was indicated above, the analysis in this section was based on social programs as the unit of observation. To assess the average contribution of congregations, we need to remember that on average each congregation in Philadelphia reported that it offered 3.71 programs. Thus, we multiplied the financial values reported above by the average number of programs to obtain the imputed values of the monthly congregational contribution to society. The average monetary value per congregation is estimated to be $6,913.63 per month, or $82,960.35 per year.

Another way to assess the contribution of congregations to their community is the percentage of the annual operating budget allocated to social ministry—also known as social action, social outreach, and social settlements. The mean percentage of the operating budget allocated to social ministry was 21.17 percent (SD = 15.12 with a range of 5–75%). The mean percentage allocated to social ministry was therefore higher than that of tithing (10%). Indeed, collectives such as congregations are not theologically expected to tithe, as tithing is an individual obligation. Yet many of our interviewees, clergy and lay leaders alike, expressed a collective desire to tithe by allocating a certain amount of the congregational budget and staff work time to support the needs of others locally or globally. This indicated that congregations directly support their community even above the expected charitable giving level of tithing.

While there is a definite trend toward generous support for social and community services, some congregations are struggling financially, and their support for such programs is below the 10 percent level. At the same time, other congregations donate a large share of their annual operating budget for social and community services. In order to understand the high percentage (21.17%) reported here, it is important to note that the *Yearbook of American and Canadian Churches* (Bedell 1996) reported that American congregations use 21 percent of their contributions toward benevolence. While Bedell's method of analysis differs from ours, the findings support each other and lend credibility to our data from Philadelphia.

How and why do congregations get involved? A congregational decision to assist needy members or nonmembers is not a random one. Social ministry requires that a need be identified and that someone, usually a leader in the congregation, advocate for a service to be developed and delivered. Those most influential in initiating social services were the clergy (49.44%) and individual members and groups (33.71%). Others initiating social services included congregational committees (16.85%) and staff members (14.61%). Fewer than 5 percent of the programs were initiated in response to requests from those outside the congregation, entities such as other congregations, diocese/judicatory, neighborhood coalitions, human service organizations, and government agencies. Thus, it is the internal participants and those affiliated with the congregation that influence the decision to embark upon a new social program. In keeping with this pattern, respondents identified internal dynamics as the most relevant in initiation of new programs. That is not to say that external changes did not affect congregational decision making. In fact, congregations reported taking collective action to provide services in instances where the public sector failed. However, the initiative to act was internal. In such cases, a member of the congregation observed the external changes and increasing needs and brought the matter to the attention of other congregants.

An interesting finding emerged when respondents were asked why their congregation had initiated new programs, other than as a response to an evident need. Six (6.74%) of the 89 programs had been initiated in response to cuts in local spending and the same number as a response to cuts in state spending. Seven (7.87%) programs were reported to have been initiated as a response to cuts in federal spending. It should be noted that these few programs overlap each other. Twenty (22.47%) programs were reported to be initiated as a response to a change in the community and none as a response to the redlining of the community. The overwhelming majority of programs were reported not to be the result of external changes in the community, although they were geared to the needs of the homeless and poor people who were affected by changes in welfare policies. Again, the same mechanism was in place. Although the observed need was the result of a public cut in spending, it was brought to the attention of the congregation as a testimony of one member who witnessed a need. Thus, the internal process and the decision to act were unrelated to the changes in public spending; rather they were a direct reaction to the people affected by the need.

What can we learn from these findings? Overall, we found that the majority of the congregations are well established in their respective communities and have been in the same location, on average, for more than sixty-six years. Furthermore, only a few in the sample have considered relocating. In this respect, congregations, along with public schools and liquor stores, are the last social institution to stay in all urban areas. However, they are unique in that they care for the needs of individuals in their community throughout the life span and across generations.

In an era in which mutual aid societies are practically vanishing and the traditional lodge and fraternal orders are rapidly declining (Hall 1996; Putnam 1995), there is one community institution that is still active and visible in most American communities. The local religious congregation still fosters and strengthens feelings of community through its activities. Congregational members are either neighbors or people who commute especially to be at their congregational property and thus are invested in the quality of life in the community around the congregation. The fact is that most congregational members commute to their place of worship, yet provide services to people who reside in the immediate vicinity of the congregational building. Such a deliberate choice to maintain the property in its current location, coupled with the fact that people within a congregation know each other and are easily accessible for recruitment, makes the religious congregation a natural leader or a partner for local coalitions and initiatives. We found congregations to provide an array of social services that are not necessarily coordinated. Yet, within any geographical community one can find congregational-based services to meet almost any human need. One may have to travel between a few congregations during one week to acquire the needed goods and services, but congregations as social institutions are in the forefront of social services delivery.

Of the twenty-four congregations in the sample, twenty-three (95%) reported providing at least one social service. This high percentage is consistent with the findings of the Gallup organization in a study commissioned by the Independent Sector (Hodgkinson et al. 1993). The congregations studied reported 89 specific programs with an average of 3.71 programs per congregation (this is an underreported estimate). The congregations are involved in numerous programs for children, the elderly, the poor, the homeless, and many others. The majority of beneficiaries are people that live in the community but are not members of the congregation.

The mean percentage of the operating budget allocated to social ministry was 21.17 percent. For our sample, the monthly value of congregational support is estimated to be $6,913.63 per month, or $82,963.56 per year. Multiplying these numbers by 2,100, the estimated number of congregations in Philadelphia, yields an estimated contribution of $14,519,253.00 per month, or $174,231,036 per year. This is definitely an impressive estimate of the contribution of local religious congregations.

One question that the reader may pose is to what extent these findings from Philadelphia compare to congregations in the rest of the country or even to others in the City of Philadelphia, given that these results are based on twenty-four congregations housed in historic buildings (the pre-1940 building). An answer to this question is found in recent studies that used different methodologies and studied other geographical regions. First, the findings from other cities in this study (Chicago, Indianapolis, Mobile, New York, and San Francisco) document similar situations, and Philadelphia often reported a lower rate of congregational social and community involvement (Cnaan 1997). The Independent Sector, in a national survey using mailed questionnaires, studied more than 1,000 congregations and found that 89 percent of them provide at least one social service to the community (Hodgkinson et al. 1993). Grettenberger and Hovmand (1997) studied, again through mailed questionnaires, United Methodist churches in Michigan and found that half of the churches provide more than seven different social programs, and of

444, only about 30 (6.7%) did not provide any social program. Maxie Jackson and his colleagues (1997) studied black churches in Michigan. With a limited return rate of 22 percent, they found that 93 percent (141) of the churches provided at least one social service with a range of no services to 47 services and a mean of 13 programs. Jackson and his colleagues also found that the initiative to carry out programs was basically internal and was most often the result of a pastor's vision or the laity's concern. Finally, Tobi Printz (1997) studied the service capacity of religious congregations in Washington, D.C., and that city's Maryland and Virginia suburbs. This study, conducted by the Urban Institute, had a 25 percent rate of response, using mail questionnaires. Printz reported that almost 95 percent of the congregations offer some type of program or service. While most congregations provided one to four programs, one in seven offered seven or more programs. The picture evolving from these studies strongly supports the Philadelphia findings, which are based on in-depth interviews with the clergy and lay leaders. In particular, the types of programs conducted in all of the cited studies confirmed our findings.

NONCONGREGATIONAL RELIGIOUS-BASED AND RELIGIOUS-AFFILIATED ORGANIZATIONS

The difficulty in defining what is a religious-based social service organization is historically puzzling. As early as 1908, Amos Warner, a pioneer social welfare researcher, complained that there was no formal definition to the term *sectarian*, and he further wrote:

> There are few institutions that will admit its [sectarian] applicability to themselves, and there are few to which it is not applied by someone. Many institutions having no trace of sectarianism in charter, constitution, or by-laws are yet administered in the interest of a sect. A willingness to admit beneficiaries of all denominations is frequently less an evidence of non-sectarianism than of a tendency to make proselytes.   (pp. 407–8)

Jeavons (1993) also attempted to assess what defines an organization as "religious." He acknowledged the ambiguity and suggested four ways to identify organizations as religious: (1) their purposes and activities are sacerdotal; (2) they identify themselves as religious through their commitment to fields of work "typically and appropriately associated with religious endeavors"; (3) their participants, resources, products or services, and decision-making processes are religious in nature; or (4) they participate in formal or informal networks of organizations in which religion plays a major role. Each of the organizations listed below meets at least one of these four criteria, and many meet more than one. Still, the level of religion in each of them varies; in fact, we categorized as "secular" some organizations that started with a religious base and over time shifted toward secularism.

Identifying religious-based social services in a large metropolitan area such as Philadelphia was a difficult task. Defining what is meant by *religious-based organization* was our first challenge, followed by assessing whether or not the organization offered social and community services. Diversity among organizations with respect to their interpretation of religious affiliation presented several problems. In some cases, we found organizations such as the YMCA and St. Mary's Respite Center, whose name and founding suggest religious affiliations. However, such organizations have become relatively more and more secularized and now serve a wide constituency. Other organizations were less familiar and hence difficult to identify as religious-based organizations, especially since they did not appear in any directory as a religious organization. For example, our identification of Nueva Esperanza and Esperanza Health Center came as a result of building relationships with clergy and lay leaders in the Hispanic community. Obtaining information about such organizations was not a simple matter of knowing about the organization but a complex process of gaining the trust to access data. We suspect that we have missed several other religious-based organizations that provide social and community services in Philadelphia because we did not have the knowledge, access, or time to discover the networks that would lead us to them. Most notable among the probable omissions are addiction programs, counseling services, and community development corporations that were not listed or identified as religious-based organizations.

We were also confronted with the methodological problem of limiting the unit of analysis to large and established organizations. Choosing this method, we excluded such organizations as ministerial coalitions, which are involved in community projects, and we omitted as well the religious organizing committee against the death penalty as a chapter of Pennsylvania Abolitionist. Another difficulty was narrowing the scope of service. We did not include the following religiously affiliated organizations: (1) more than fifty day care centers that operate outside the governance of congregations, (2) the nine homeless shelters of the Office of Services to Homeless Adults (OSHA) that are managed by congregations or religious-based organizations, (3) soup kitchens, (4) thrift stores, and (5) services to prisoners and their families. Hence, by restricting the size and scope of the religious-based organizations, we have grossly underestimated the magnitude of services provided by religious-based and religious-affiliated organizations in Philadelphia. We have limited the following discussion to 33 larger organizations that were identified and were able to provide information regarding the nature of their religious affiliation, the extent of their collaboration with other organizations, the scope of their services, and/or the cost of operating these services. At least another 45 religious-based organizations were identified, but information was not available to document their services.

In the following sections, we present the thirty-three religious-based and religious-affiliated social service organizations in Philadelphia that we selected. These organizations are discussed separately, as they operate outside the governance of congregations and include additional types of organizational models, as presented in chapter 2: (1) interdenominational coalitions and ecumenical organizations; (2) citywide or region-wide sectarian agencies; (3) projects and organizations under religious auspices; (4) paradenominational organizations; and (5) religious-affiliated organizations. We have also added secularized organizations to capture those entities that were established in affiliation with religious groups like the Jewish Community Centers of Greater Philadelphia but are now nonsectarian organizations. These organizations illustrate the breadth of services and issues that religious-based organizations address. Most important for our discussion, these organizations demonstrate the expansive public- and private-sector partnerships that religious-based and religious-affiliated organizations use to maximize their service delivery.

Coalitions and Interfaith Organizations

1. The African-American Interdenominational Ministries (AAIM), formerly Black Clergy, Inc., is a nonprofit organization that seeks to empower black congregations in addressing the cultural, economic, psychological, and spiritual needs of urban neighborhoods. AAIM was founded in 1989. One of its primary missions is to fill in the gaps created by continued cutbacks in social services. AAIM receives its funding from the following sources: the philanthropic community (60%), the corporate community (30%), and religious congregations (10%).

In an effort to provide vital community services, AAIM has developed programs in the following areas: youth, violence prevention, economic development, health, and evangelism/discipleship. AAIM has provided community support and technical assistance for Rites of Passage programs for 180 teenagers annually. It has also participated in the Philadelphia Project for Youth Ministry, a program preparing adults and students for leadership in youth ministry and funded by the Pew Charitable Trusts. AAIM also cosponsors the Empowering Christian Leaders for Reconciliation with Justice Program of Philadelphia. This two-year program trains pastors and lay members in mediation skills and increases their awareness of human diversity. Another violence-prevention program supported by AAIM is the Safe Corridor initiative. This program stations adult volunteers on street corners so that children can travel to and from school in safety. The Family Economic Empowerment Project, another AAIM initiative, links families with congregations that provide training in financial management, debt reduction, taxes, insurance, real estate, planning, and investments. AAIM also fosters collaboration between church groups and outreach programs of health care organizations as a means of increasing community access to health resources and services and helping clergy better understand health-related issues. AAIM's Philadelphia Urban Education Institute provides biblically based, Afrocentric, urban-focused leadership training in discipleship and evangelism. This training is an important aspect of AAIM's mission, as its philosophy holds that evangelism is a way "to lead members of the community to faith, a sense of well-being, and connectedness" and discipleship expressed in active participation in helping the community.

2. The Northwest Interfaith Movement (NIM) is an alliance of Protestant, Jewish, and Catholic congregations engaged in advocacy, community service, networking, and training. Since 1969, NIM has grown from eight to thirty-two congregations. The mission of NIM is to "build a more just and sensitive community" by being a "catalytic and facilitative agent for change" in Northwest Philadelphia and the wider community. NIM's efforts are largely focused on the needs of low-income and at-risk communities.

Since its founding, NIM has responded to issues of community welfare by building coalitions to advocate for reform in the school system, address the energy needs of low-income residents, and provide low-interest loans for low-income housing and small businesses. NIM has also created five independent organizations: Northwest Meals on Wheels, Deane House (house for runaway children), Central Germantown Council (organization for business development and job creation), Germantown Interfaith Housing (housing for elderly/disabled persons), and Northwest Victim Services. NIM also sponsors an oil-purchasing group to assist congregations in lowering their fuel costs.

NIM has six major programs. The Early Childhood Collaborative, supported by the William Penn Foundation, provides training to child care staff, advocates for child care, maintains six resource rooms in underserved neighborhoods, makes grants to improve child care programs/facilities, and assists day care programs in accessing health care for the children served by these programs. In 1996 this program awarded 102 grants, totaling $29,617, to center and home-based child care providers. The Neighborhood Child Care Resource Program provides training, resources, technical assistance, and a support service line to center and home-based caregivers and parents of young children. This program also publishes the *Directory for Children, Youth, and Families.*

The Long-Term Care Connection (LTCC) serves residents in nursing homes and personal care homes as well as their families and care providers. The LTCC has three ombudsmen who respond to the complaints and requests of residents. This program also links volunteers with nursing homes, publishes a consumer guide for nursing homes in Philadelphia, trains care providers and staff, and provides technical assistance and resources. The School Age Ministry Program (SAM) works with congregations to address the need for safe and nurturing after-school programs. SAM's goal is to create forty-five licensed after-school programs in less-advantaged neighborhoods. To achieve this goal, SAM provides technical assistance, financial resources, and training. Other initiatives include organizing neighborhood support networks and disseminating information through the SAM link newsletter.

The Philadelphia Religious Leadership Development Fund makes available grants to train clergy and lay leaders and support congregation-initiated outreach programs in less-advantaged neighborhoods. This program publishes a newsletter that is distributed to the participating congregations. To date, the fund has awarded grants to 380 congregations through funding from the Pew Charitable Trusts in excess of $1 million. In 1996 grants totaling $192,335 were awarded to 174 congregation-initiated community outreach programs. The Pastorius Child Health Watch program sponsors health education events and assists families in accessing no-cost/low-cost health insurance. The Reverend Richard Fernandez, executive director of the program, describes the program as "helping Philadelphia congregations lead with their head as well as their heart, and helping them to fulfill their obligation to be good stewards of their blessings."

NIM receives the support of congregations, individuals, foundations, corporations, and public agencies. For the 1996 fiscal year, NIM received $1,602,174 in support and revenue. Seventy percent of these funds were from foundations, as compared to 19 percent from public agencies. The expenses for 1996 totaled $1,597,634.

3. The Northwest Philadelphia Interfaith Hospitality Network (NPIHN) is a nonprofit corporation supported by eleven Philadelphia churches and synagogues, as well as individuals, corporations, and foundations. Members of the religious community work in partnership with other community organizations to address the needs of homeless families. National IHN headquarters is located in Summit, New Jersey, and was founded in 1986. NPIHN is one of thirty networks in six states with more than four hundred congregations and 30,000 volunteers serving 6,000 families each year.

The Northwest Philadelphia Interfaith Hospitality Network was founded in 1990. The NPIHN program provides "home-like" shelter accommodations, meals, support services, and referrals to social service agencies. Host families provide shelter and meals to homeless families on a rotating basis through a network of congregations. The program also provides an opportunity for the religious community to advocate on behalf of the homeless, raise awareness of the problems related to homelessness, and build support for permanent solutions. The primary goal of the program is to assist families to locate permanent housing within ninety days. NPIHN reported a higher than 70 percent success rate in assisting families to find permanent housing.

Citywide and Region-wide Sectarian Agencies

4. In the Philadelphia area are six social service agencies of the Southeastern Pennsylvania Synod of the Evangelical Lutheran Church in America: Lutheran Settlement House, Artman Lutheran Home, Paul's Run services for older adults, Silver Spring Lutheran School, Ken Crest Services, and Mary J. Drexel Home.

The Artman Lutheran Home (ALH) is one of three Lutheran social agencies in the Philadelphia area that provide care for older adults. ALH has been faithfully serving the church and community since 1912. In 1997, ALH provided homes for four hundred residents and membership for more than five hundred at the Becoming Center. ALH provides high-quality services to clients, with professional and caring staff and a combination of exercise programs, weight management, traditional medicine, and alternative therapies to promote wellness. ALH received approximately $17.9 million in annual funding in 1997 and $17.4 million in 1996. In 1997, total direct gifts increased 77 percent ($383,805).

ALH has cultivated partnerships with several community citizens and organizations and has the regular support of seventy-seven volunteers. The special events and fund-raising activities support such programs as Special Olympics and the annual golf outing. In addition, ALH promotes intergenerational activities between residents and school-age children through activities with students of Shady Grove Elementary School and children from the Lutheran Ken Crest Child Development Center.

5. Baptist Children's Services (BCS), a licensed social service agency, was established in 1879 to care for the needs of dependent and neglected children. The origin of this agency has been traced back to the bequest of a dying girl to have her savings of ninety cents donated to care for homeless children. This gift inspired the establishment of the Baptist Orphanage, which offered a family-like environment based on a cottage system with live-in housemothers. This structure was progressive for its time. Over the past twenty years, BCS has expanded its services and continued to create a family-like atmosphere and programs that provide a moral and spiritual foundation. The primary goals of all services are family reunification and the development of the children served in Pennsylvania, New Jersey, and Delaware.

BCS offers a continuum of care that reflects its commitment to providing services that respond to the changing and varied needs of children and their families. These services include a family resource center, services to children in their own homes (SCOH), family reunification services, emergency shelter service, crisis intervention services, drug and alcohol counseling, juvenile probation assessment program, a community-based twenty-four-hour residential program, a group home program, and a supervised independent living program. BCS operates nine facilities in the tristate region: Alternatives group home, Alternatives shelter, Avondale group home, Alternatives Family Resource Center, Germantown Avenue group home, Lewis Road shelter, Meridian group home, Spring Garden Street group home, and Thornsbury group home.

BCS recognizes that the problems of today's children and families are too large for any one agency to tackle alone, and it has been effective in mobilizing social services providers and coordinating community-based services. The agency uses all available resources—public and private, spiritual, medical, mental health, educational, and recreational—to provide the most comprehensive and holistic services. The BCS family center has developed partnerships for prevention-oriented strategies that promote coordinating community-based services. Through collaborative efforts with organizations such as the Montgomery County Youth Council, Montgomery County Housing Authority, Pottstown Medical Center, Visiting Nurses Association of Pottstown, March of Dimes, and Ursinus College, BCS has improved access to existing services and expanded services. These services include prenatal education, transportation to prenatal clinic appointments, parenting-education workshops, new-parent discussion group, teen parenting classes, in-home postdelivery services, self-esteem program for children, after-school tutoring, drug and alcohol prevention education, drop-in counseling programs, and therapy for survivors of abuse. BCS also contracts to provide on-site comprehensive prevention, education, and intervention services to families and youth of the Bright Hope Estates and Rolling Hills housing communities. On-site services include: parent/child play groups, a drop-in/outreach center, information and referral services, intervention services, drug education, a tenants association/youth committee, and volunteer opportunities. BCS youth and families services provides drop-in and outpatient drug and alcohol counseling, juvenile probation assessments, family counseling, and supervision for family visitation through referrals from the Office of Children and Youth, Juvenile Probation, and Drug and Alcohol Services.

BCS received $2,584,680 in annual funding in 1996 from the following sources: fees and grants for children services (68.3%), contributions, legacies, and trust fund income (16.0%), endowment fund and interest (12.5%), and Chapter I funds and interest, nutrition program, and miscellaneous services (3.2%). These funds are distributed to support children's programs (70.6%), counseling programs (16.9%), and management and general services (12.5%). BCS has a professional and program staff of thirty-three members that includes social workers, case managers, outreach counselors, chaplains, psychologists, psychiatrists, therapists, tutors, teachers, and a corporate staff of seventeen. With more than one hundred years of service to children, Baptist Children's Services has gained the recognition of public figures such as former first lady Barbara Bush for its commitment to providing homes to countless children and families.

6. Catholic Social Services (CSS) of the Archdiocese of Philadelphia is a multiservice agency established under the authority of the Archbishop of Philadelphia to assist him in providing for the poor and needy committed to his care. As an arm of the Catholic Church, it embraces all people, particularly the hungry and homeless, the elderly and disabled, the imprisoned and those displaced from their countries. These services are based on the belief that all human beings are created in the image of God. Hence, professional

services are provided to protect and enhance the dignity of every person and family. Catholic laity have cared for the children of Philadelphia since 1797. The Catholic Children's Bureau was incorporated in 1919, and care was extended to the physically and mentally impaired and the poor of all ages. In 1964 the name Catholic Social Services was adopted to reflect the diversity of services offered.

CSS provides an array of family-centered services to support emotional stability and financial independence in families. Core services include family and marriage counseling, pregnancy services, foster child care, adoption, case management, immigration assistance, senior centers, shelters, emergency services, services to Hispanics, parish social ministry, parish nursing, criminal justice program, AIDS ministry, and community organizing. CSS works with the community to offer activities and services that address the unique needs of the communities it serves. CSS continues to be a pioneer as a service provider to more than 160,000 Spanish-speaking clients, as well as those affected by HIV/AIDS and those in the criminal justice system. CSS's family-living program links mentally handicapped teens and adults with families that are willing to provide a home and long-term personal care. The organization also participates in a cooperative program with Catholic Health Care Services to assist elderly clients and their families when placement in a nursing facility is unavailable, unwarranted, or inappropriate. A collaborative effort with the Nutritional Development Services has expanded the ability to serve children and families with food, food preparation and nutrition classes, and the SHARE food program.

CSS fulfills its mission by bringing hope and services to thousands. Each year, more than 250,000 people are served, including 80,000 families, 15,000 mentally or physically impaired individuals, and 20,000 children. Of the children, 18,000 are served in their own homes, and 2,600 are children with special needs who are served in foster homes, group homes, shelters, and institutions. Catholic Social Services also provides care for more than 110,000 adults over sixty-five years of age. Of the elderly clients served, 21 percent are over eighty years of age. Six hundred of the clients are active and participate in the Retired Senior Volunteer Program, and 35,000 participate in senior clubs. A staff of five hundred professional and support employees serve at seven family centers, two satellite centers, two housing facilities for older women, four senior adult centers, four residential facilities for homeless men and women, a child care center and adoptions services. CSS staff are also available to train parish representatives and community groups to deliver social services.

7. Episcopal Community Services (ECS) has been "ministering to the poor and sick" of all faiths since 1870. The mission of ECS includes advocacy, technical assistance, leadership development, and community organizing. ECS is one of the largest social service agencies in the Philadelphia area. The staff includes social workers, nurses, home health aides, administrators, support staff, and more than five hundred volunteers.

ECS provides services in three major categories: children and family services, adult services, and church and community ministries. In 1996 the children and family services program served some 140 families. These programs included services to children in their homes (SCOH program), foster care and kinship care, services to homeless families (Project SAFE), services to HIV/AIDS-affected families (STARR program), and the "grandparents as parents" support/advocacy program. ECS also provides social services and community programs (crisis intervention, referrals, counseling, mentoring, and after-school programs) at the Church of the Advocate. The Madeira Family Center, a collaborative project with the Children's Aid Society, provides an environment that fosters family interaction, problem-solving, enhancement of parenting skills, health awareness, and community involvement.

In 1996 the adult services program provided homemaker services to 134 elderly clients and 324 people with AIDS, case management services to 25 elderly clients and 38 people with AIDS, meal delivery to 514 elderly clients and 184 people with AIDS, transportation to nonemergency medical appointments for 120 people with AIDS, and companions for 25 elderly clients. ECS is also under contract to provide case management services for homeless men with AIDS at the Good Shepherd Program of St. John's Hospice.

As part of its church and community ministries, ECS provides chaplaincy services to correctional institutions, hospitals, and nursing homes in Philadelphia. In 1997 ECS secured a contract from the city to provide chaplaincy services at the Youth Study Center, a division of Juvenile Justice Services. These services are in accord with their mission, as Reverend Barbara Duncan, coordinator of the criminal justice program, explains: "Faith is a friend and advocate for the children. By reaching these kids early we hope to be able to intervene and stop the revolving door of crime. We want to help them see that their lives have value." ECS is also a founding member of the New Alliance for Child Welfare and Behavioral Health, a collaborative venture to reform the child welfare system.

ECS receives approximately $5 million a year from the following sources: government (52.3%), endowment (21.5%), private contributions (11.2%), corporations and foundations (7.0%), United Way (1.3%), Episcopalian Diocese of Pennsylvania (2.5%), client fees (.9%), parishes (1.0%), and other sources (2.3%). These funds are distributed to the following programs and services: children and family services (48.0%), adult services (29.6%), nonoperating expenses (8.0%), fund-raising (5.2%), chaplaincy (5.2%), advocacy (2.0%), and volunteer services (2.0%). ECS has an endowment fund of more than $1.5 million.

8. Jewish Community Centers of Greater Philadelphia (JCC) is a nonprofit organization guided by Jewish values that assists people from all backgrounds to find their place in the community. Its primary mission is to "build community" that prepares Jews to participate in and build a pluralistic American society while maintaining a sense of Jewish identity. To accomplish this mission JCC has maintained and expanded many of its programs. Seven Philadelphia-area locations are sites for JCC programs: Charles and Elizabeth Gershman YMHA and YWHA, Kevy and Hortense M. Kaiserman Branch, Raymond and Miriam Klein Branch, David G. Neuman Senior Center, Jacob and Esther Stiffel Senior Center, Bucks County JCC Without Walls, and JCC Bux-Mont Region. Their services include the following: programs for single-parent families, programs for early retirees, informal Jewish education, community education through African-American and Jewish dialogue, after-school enrichment program, adopt-a-grandparent program, kosher meal service, coordination of Jewish organizations serving teenagers, health and nutrition programs, citizenship classes for elderly Russian immigrants, community theater, and mentor/cash assistance for disadvantaged families.

Building community and expanding services to reach a wider range of people and needs have led JCC to forge partnerships beyond synagogues and other Jewish organizations. With more than 271 partnerships with congregations, foundations, corporations, agencies, and organizations, JCC has maintained and increased its service delivery. These partnerships have included such organizations as the Free Library, Habitat for Humanity, Pennsylvania Department of Education, C.A.R.I.E., People's Emergency Shelter, Public Private Ventures, Salvation Army, United Way, and area universities and hospitals. The partnership with the school system places senior volunteers in elementary schools to mentor students. A project in collaboration with the Philadelphia Corporation on Aging and the Albert Einstein Medical Center provides education on nutrition and exercise for senior center participants.

Equal to these partnerships is the service of hundreds of JCC volunteers.

The JCC provides volunteer opportunities for families and individuals of all ages, who serve through painting, repairing and building homes, cooking meals, tutoring/baby-sitting children, visiting the sick and older adults, fundraising, creating agency policy, participating in planning, and other community services. The volunteer opportunities of JCC connect people with the needs of the community and increase access to and availability of services. The JCC recognizes that without the partnership of these volunteers and organizations, its ability to serve would be significantly diminished.

The Jewish Community Centers of Greater Philadelphia received $10,250,000 in annual funding in 1996 and $10,900,000 in annual funding in 1997. Income came from the following sources in 1996: program fees (31.0%), membership dues (21.0%), Jewish Federation base allocation (20.9%), Philadelphia Corporation for the Aging (9.5%), foundation, corporations, and individuals (5.0%) supplemental fundraising (3.8%), miscellaneous income (3.7%), Jewish Federation special grants (3.6%), and government agencies (1.8%).

9. Jewish Family and Children's Services (JFCS) of Greater Philadelphia is a constituency agency of the Jewish Federation of Greater Philadelphia. JFCS was established in 1983 when Jewish Family Services of Philadelphia (1869) and the Association for Jewish Children of Philadelphia (1855) merged to strengthen their mission to support the needs of Jewish children and families, particularly the elderly, the poor, and the disabled. This mission is grounded in a commitment to the values of *tzedakah* and *mitzvot*. JFCS also continues to develop programs to assist individuals in integrating tradition, faith, and Jewish identity. JFCS provides a wide range of family and children's services in collaboration with other communal agencies to enhance the quality of life in the Jewish community and promote the social welfare of the entire region.

Like many sectarian agencies, JFCS has broadened and modified its services as a result of a merger and in response to the changing needs of its clients and the context of a managed-care service-delivery system. The core components of the JFCS system are counseling services, resettlement services, services to older persons, family education and group services, teen education services, crisis services, adoption services, and volunteer services. In 1996, Jewish Family and Children's Services served 16,904 individuals.

The following specialized counseling programs served 2,187 individuals: neighborhood counseling for individuals, families, and groups, drug and alcohol abuse counseling, child and adolescent counseling, school consultation, employee assistance program, case management for persons with developmental disabilities, and domestic violence services. In collaboration with federal and local agencies, JFCS also served 690 recently arrived Jewish immigrants by providing acculturation assistance and counseling, financial assistance, translation services, and case management services to aid in accessing housing, employment, and health care. The services for older persons served 2,588 individuals. The service achieved greater stability and adjustment by providing a range of community-based support services, crisis intervention services, care management, and volunteer opportunities. Through family life education and group services, 1,837 individuals were assisted in addressing issues such as interfaith questions, bereavement, gay and lesbian identity, separation/divorce, and living with HIV/AIDS. Project PRIDE (Positive Results in Drug Education) effectively uses small groups to raise awareness among school-age children on issues of violence, pregnancy, sexuality, suicide, and drug and alcohol abuse. The PRIDE project served 9,081 children in 1996. The adoption services assisted 89 individuals in various stages of the adoption process. JFCS also contracts with the Department of Human Services to provide foster care and services to children in their own homes. In 1996, sixty families received home-based services and 135 families were supported through foster care services.

In 1996 Jewish Family and Children's Services received $8,465,000 in revenue from the following sources: government agencies (39%), Jewish Federation general allocation (25%), investment and fund-raising (9%), program services (8%), other Federation allocation (7%), contributions (6%), and Federation resettlement program (6%). These funds were allocated to personnel costs (62%), client expenses (20%), occupancy cost (6%), office supplies (2%), and other expenses (8%). Resources also include a host of volunteers and a professional staff of social workers, psychiatrist, psychologist, and case managers.

10. Lutheran Children and Family Service (LCFS) is an accredited social service agency of the Evangelical Lutheran Church in America. LCFS was founded in 1922, based on the tradition of caring that emanates from a faith in God that shows itself in service to the human family. During its seventy-fifth year of service (1977), LCFS provided foster care placements for 581 children, after-school care for 74 children, social and community activities for 184 veterans, facilitation for 80 adoptions and 184 reunifications with family of origin, counseling and case management to 210 children, resettlement assistance to 231 refugees, English as a Second Language and GED instruction for 268 students, assistance to 51 refugees in obtaining employment, assistance to refugees and immigrants in establishing 43 new businesses, entrepreneurial training

services to 406 people, case management and other services to 487 families in public housing, free resources to 23 child care providers and training to 227 individuals, HIV prevention training for 556 at-risk youth, and computer training to 83 people receiving government benefits. While LCFS continues to expand its services to meet changing needs, it also monitors the quality of its care through its team-based quality-improvement plan, which includes case review, client grievance procedures, client satisfaction surveys, and personnel review. LCFS received approximately $3.4 million in annual funding in 1997 and $2.7 million in 1996.

LCFS has forged several partnerships in recent years. In 1995, Michigan's Charles Stewart Mott Foundation and the federal government provided funding for the creation of the Neighborhood Development Project (NDP) in West Philadelphia. NDP is a national demonstration project to enhance intercultural community relations and reduce racial conflict through community economic development. NDP works with individuals from a variety of ethnic backgrounds through the Micro-Enterprise Institute and the Neighborhood Visioning Institute. These programs promote multicultural relationships through entrepreneurship and cooperative projects. Of particular note is the West Philadelphia Artisans' Project, which receives technical assistance from NDP on effective marketing and how to organize exhibits. LCFS also collaborated with the Emanuel Lutheran Church in South Philadelphia to establish Bethel House community center. The most significant partnership is its contract with the Commonwealth of Pennsylvania to administer the state refugee program.

11. The Lutheran Social Mission Society/Lutheran Settlement House (LSMS/LSH) is a Philadelphia-based organization that has its roots in the first Lutheran Inner Mission Society (1902) and the first Lutheran Settlement House (1906) in the United States. Its mission is "to empower individuals, families, and communities to achieve and maintain self sufficiency through an integrated program of social, educational and advocacy services." LSMS/LSH is a citywide organization that targets the Fishtown and Kensington neighborhoods for its services.

LSMS/LSH, which has a staff of 106 and numerous volunteers, offers a wide range of programs. These include a bilingual domestic violence program, counseling, a homeless transition/life skills project, adult education, including tore. Each year, LSMS/LSH provides services and programs to more than 8,500 individuals.

LSMS/LSH received approximately $3.2 million in annual funding in 1996 from the following sources: government (74%), corporations/foundations (11%), United Way (9%), private contributions (2%), Lutheran sources (1%), and other sources (3%). These funds are distributed to the following programs and services: senior adults (33%), employment and training (25%), domestic violence and counseling (18%), education (13%), and administration and support service (11%).

12. Methodist Home for Children and Bennett and Simpson Enrichment Services (MHC/BASES) is a nonprofit, multiservice agency for children, youth, and families. The agency opened with three orphaned children as the Methodist Episcopal Orphanage on October 6, 1879. Over the past 115 years of service, MHC has provided education, advocacy, and referral on behalf of thousands of children and their families across the Delaware Valley region. In 1994, the Methodist Homes for Children spawned the Bennett and Simpson Enrichment Services (BASES) to serve as resources, advocates, and partners for children, youth, and families within their communities. The name Bennett and Simpson Enrichment Services (BASES) is in honor of the founders of the organization.

MHC/BASES services include foster care, day care, counseling, before- and after-school programs, summer day camp, three group homes, the Bridge House transitional-living residence, and outreach programs. The foster family care program, established in 1960, and the group homes program, established in 1970, are the primary placement services of MHC. Bridge House, established in 1987, is a residential program to assist homeless young men aged eighteen to twenty-eight in acquiring the skills necessary for independent living. In 1996 MHC served more than 800 children and families: 103 children placed with 43 foster care families, 12 adolescents in group homes, 13 young men at Bridge House, 80 in Educare, 12 in the before-school program, 63 in the after-school program, and 100 per week in summer camp.

The commitment of MHC/BASES to children, families, and their communities is best demonstrated in the agency's outreach programs: Genesis of Tamaqua and Genesis of the Slate Belt. These community-based programs target families affected by domestic and child abuse, drug and alcohol abuse, and depression and other mental health issues. In addition to individual, group, and family counseling, at Tamaqua a drug and alcohol program and a pilot teen parent program are offered. At Slate Belt, collaborative efforts with the school are aimed at keeping adolescents in school. Genesis of the Slate Belt also partners with local congregations to assist clients with basic needs such as food, clothing, and shelter. In 1996, 110 families were served at Tamaqua and 109 families at Slate Belt, and both programs have a waiting list. MCH/BASES is working in collaboration with Kensington Area Ministries and Shalom Zone to establish a Genesis-type program in a section of West Kensington.

In 1996 MCH/BASES received $4,635,112 in revenue. MCH/BASES contracts with the Philadelphia Department of Human Services to provide foster care and residential care for children and youth who are in the custody of and referred by the city. Government support, fees, and contracts covered 70 percent of the agency's operating costs. One-third of the congregations in the Methodist denominational conference financially support this agency. MCH/BASES received income from the following sources in 1996: program service fees (64%), tuition and fees (14%), investment income (11%), Bridge House grant (4.3%), rental income (2.7%), private contributions (1.7%), grants (1.2%), Golden Cross (.56%), designated gifts (.26%), women's auxiliary (.22%), memorial and special funds (.02%), and miscellaneous sources (.07%). These funds are distributed to the following programs and services: foster care (29%), Elwyn (28%), Educare learning center (13%), group homes (9.5%), Bridge House (5.4%), after school program (3.5%), Genesis of Tamaqua (3.7%), Genesis of the Slate Belt (2.9%), management and general services (2.5%), summer day camp (2%), and college special (.04%).

13. The Salvation Army of Greater Philadelphia is part of an international movement and evangelical church. As a Christian ministry, its work is to preach the Gospel and to serve the needs of individuals without discrimination. Worship services and attendance are central to the Salvation Army's programs. In the Philadelphia area there are nine corps community centers, seven day care locations, nine adult rehabilitation centers, one developmental disabilities program, one service center, four shelters, and five residential facilities. In 1996 the Salvation Army of Greater Philadelphia received $20,450,617 in income from the following sources: fees and grants from government agencies (46.5%), contributions and foundation grants (13.7%), special events (.17%), in-kind gifts (.24%), membership dues (.05%), program service fees (11.2%), sales of supplies and services (.07%), adult rehabilitation center sales (14.1%), investment income (.02%), contributions by associated organizations (2.5%), United Way (7.2%), grants from headquarters (2.3%), and miscellaneous (2.0%). These funds were allocated to casework, emergency, and special services (6.3%), correctional services and emergency lodging (17.8%), developmental disabilities programs (22.4%), day care centers (6.4%), foster care

(5.9%), corps community centers (14.4%), adult rehabilitation centers (16.9%), management and general services (.94%), fund-raising services (3.2%), and payment to supervisory headquarters (5.8%). The Salvation Army has 12,588 volunteers, who served 94,207 hours in 1995–1996.

The Salvation Army of Greater Philadelphia has assisted many who experience homelessness, unemployment, and alcohol or drug dependency. The corps centers are known as "one-stop life shops." These centers provide services that include day care, parenting classes, health counseling, drug and alcohol counseling, job training, recreational activities, life skills workshops, and seniors' activities. The new corps community center in the North Philadelphia ("Badlands") area offers programs for seniors, parents, and youth; it is the largest private capital investment that the Salvation Army has made in any one Philadelphia community in more than twenty years. Services at this center address the unique culture and needs of the Latino community. The Gateway center also serves the special needs of homeless adults through a program that is a collaborative effort between Philadelphia's Office of Services to Homeless Adults and the Salvation Army. This program includes residential program and day services, educational programs, veteran's administration outreach, legal services, recreational activities, life skills services, employment referral and placement, and medical services by Thomas Jefferson Hospital staff. In 1996 the Salvation Army of Greater Philadelphia provided 284,740 meals, 191,400 nights of lodging, 51,067 visits to homebound senior citizens, 3,976 senior citizen camp guests, 6,116 children camp days, 128,326 counseling sessions for individuals, 11,019 counseling sessions for families, 630 rehabilitative services with 216 successful completions, 90,067 days of care for 1,142 children in day care, and 38,685 senior citizens' day care activities. During 1995–1996 there were 247,079 Corps community visitors.

Projects and Organizations Under Religious Auspices

14. The Bridges Youth Project/Friends Neighborhood Guild is a program designed to foster cooperation and equality among teens and adults in the Philadelphia area from diverse racial, class, ethnic, and national backgrounds. The Bridges project began in 1989 under the auspices of the Friends Peace and Social Concerns Committee. Since 1996 the program has been under the sponsorship of the Friends Neighborhood Guild. The paid program staff consists of a director/social worker, a fund-raiser, and an administrative assistant. The advisory committee consists of fourteen community members and teen par-

ticipants from diverse backgrounds. Plans are currently under way to incorporate Bridges as a nonprofit organization.

This program aims to (1) expose participants to new environments and different cultures; (2) break down stereotypes and encourage conflict resolution strategies using the consensus process; (3) expand the creativity, flexibility, and communication skills of participants; (4) practice cooperative leadership and mutual learning; (5) enable participants to learn about the life experiences and differences of others; (6) encourage participants to cross boundaries of class, culture, and neighborhood; and (7) improve relations among socioeconomic, racial, ethnic, and national groups.

Program participants, who are recruited through community organizations, represent three different groups: Puerto Ricans and African Americans from disadvantaged neighborhoods and middle-class youth from throughout the Delaware Valley. There is a Bridges teen program for those aged twelve to fifteen and one for those aged fifteen to seventeen. Participants are encouraged to serve on program committees and to assist in planning activities as a means of establishing ownership of the project. The program consists of small groups that are based on a research experiential educational model designed to foster equality among participants of the groups. The teens meet bimonthly from January to August in small groups. Each meeting has a theme, such as cooking, art, or career planning.

Group mentors for the program receive training in group process, intergroup relations, work with adolescents, and history of communities, as well as ongoing support. Mentors are selected from among members of the Philadelphia Quarterly Meeting, community organizations, and parents of participants. This project has received a wide range of support from foundations, community organizations, and corporations, including the Bread and Roses Young People's Fund, the Pennsylvania Abolition Society, Emergency Aid of Pennsylvania, the Marianist Sharing Fund, the Connelly Foundation, the Wertz Fund, Meridian Bank, and the Lawrence Sanders Fund. Since the inception of this project, the annual budget has grown from $9,000 to $26,000.

15 Peace Mission Movement in Philadelphia was founded in 1942 by the Reverend M. J. Divine, also known as Father Divine. Early in the century Father Divine began providing clothing, shelter, and meals to those in need in Brooklyn, New York; he moved to Philadelphia in 1942. From the 1940s through the 1970s, this organization was best known for serving the community through its hotels, cafeterias, food markets, apartments, dress shops, bar-

bershops, gas stations, shoe repair shops, and dry-cleaning businesses. These services were provided at below market value as a means of extending the Gospel through affordable services. They were also among the first integrated services in Philadelphia. During the 1930s and 1940s, before substantial government programs were established, the services of the Peace Mission Movement are reported to have benefited thousands of people from all walks of life through its businesses and congregations.

In 1974, the Peace Mission Movement's Poplar Hotel was donated to Trevor Ferrell's campaign for the homeless and now is the homeless shelter known as Trevor's Place. Today the only Peace Movement businesses that remain in operation in Philadelphia are the Tracey Divine Hotel and the Keyflower Dining Room and the Peace Democratic Garage. The Tracey Divine Hotel offers fax, notary, income tax preparation, copying, typing, and auto plate services at minimal cost. The Peace Mission churches have been active in providing after-school classes, tutoring, and recreational programs in collaboration with the Police Athletic League. The Peace Mission Movement also offers free courtesy employment agencies as a deterrent to public welfare and to promote full employment for all able-bodied adults.

16. Frankford Group Ministry (FGM) was founded in 1979 by St. Thomas, Rehoboth, Frankford Memorial, and Central United Methodist churches of Frankford to address the increasing poverty, ethnic/racial diversity, and declining resources in their community. Since that time, FGM has developed a network of community-based organizations and comprehensive social service programs: the Frankford Human Relations Coalition to promote positive race and cross-cultural relations, Frankford Style for artistic and cultural training and experiences for residents, and the Community Development Corporation of the Frankford Group Ministry for economic and housing development.

One of the goals of FGM is to build strong families and a vital community. To this end, FGM provides emergency assistance to families in need of food, clothing, or utility assistance. The Neighborhood Parenting Program provides workshops, support groups, and play groups for parents, caregivers, and their children. Services to families in their homes is provided by social work staff for local families and those referred by the Department of Human Services. In collaboration with the Greater Philadelphia Federation of Settlements and the Department of Juvenile Justice, FGM's Youth Corps provides case management, counseling, tutoring, and recreation for adjudicated and at-risk youth.

FGM also provides fun clubs, summer day camp, and summer youth employment training and placements. The programs of FGM are supported by the four FGM congregations, other local congregations, United Methodist denominational affiliated groups, foundations, corporations, government contracts, and individual contributions.

17. Habitat for Humanity (HFH) is a nonprofit grassroots organization that works in partnership with homeowners and community members to provide affordable housing and strengthen commitment to rebuilding neighborhoods. HFH has five independently incorporated U.S. affiliates located in the Philadelphia area: West Philadelphia, Germantown, South Philadelphia, North Central Philadelphia, and the University of Pennsylvania campus. These are among the 1,400 U.S. and Canadian affiliates and 73 international projects of Habitat for Humanity International. The work of HFH encompasses working within the larger context of community renewal and revitalization, establishing partnerships with existing community-based organizations to develop the particular necessary skills and structures for community renewal and revitalization, and creating opportunities for constructive interaction between urban neighborhoods and communities outside the city. HFH receives no government funding and relies on the generous contributions of volunteers and donors. This policy refrains from increasing our national debt and keeps the renovation budget low.

The West Philadelphia Habitat for Humanity was organized in 1986. A partnership was formed with the Cathedral Park Association (CPA) and First African Presbyterian Church to reverse the decay and abandonment of homes and other neighborhood property. When HFH-WP was formed, 80 percent of the seventy-nine properties on Stiles Street had been abandoned. Since then, HFH-WP has completed fifteen houses, a community garden, and several grassy open spaces. The restoration of these homes has been made possible through the partnership of families who "invest 500 hours of sweat equity into each house." Each year, 1,500 to 2,000 volunteers from local churches, schools, synagogues, and corporations contribute to the renewal and revitalization of this Philadelphia neighborhood. Construction costs are lowered by using the volunteer labor of carpenters, electricians, and heating contractors.

HFH-WP has developed the Stiles Street 2000 Plan to guide their community efforts. By the year 2000, HFH-WP plans to complete all home renovations, a community house, parking and play areas, and community space. The

University of Pennsylvania campus chapter works in conjunction with HFH-WP to achieve these goals.

A small group of volunteers from St. Paul's Church who had been volunteering at West Philadelphia Habitat for Humanity recognized the need for HFH in their own community, and Habitat for Humanity/Germantown was incorporated in April 1994. They work in partnership with the Westside Neighborhood Council, several civic groups, congregations, corporations, foundations, schools, and universities. These organizations also provide the support and the sense of community necessary for families to become successful homeowners and citizens.

18. Nueva Esperanza, Inc. (New Hope), discussed previously in chapter 9, is a nonprofit community development corporation dedicated to meeting the spiritual, educational, and social needs of low- and moderate-income families and young people in Philadelphia's Hispanic community. The corporation, which was founded in 1987 by the Reverend Luis Cortes and the Hispanic Clergy of Philadelphia and Vicinity, is associated with more than fifty local Hispanic institutions.

With the support of neighborhood groups, businesses, and churches, Nueva Esperanza has created several housing units and businesses in the North Philadelphia Hispanic community. These include Casa Esperanza (a senior citizens' residence), Villa Esperanza I (fourteen town houses), Villa Esperanza II (fifteen town houses), Lehigh Park I (twenty-nine subsidized apartments), La Lavanderia del Pueblo (a laundromat), and community offices. The corporation was also selected to pilot a Redevelopment Authority program to renovate and sell homes to low-income first-time home buyers. Other services provided by Nueva Esperanza include mortgage counseling, tenant assistance, financing, architectural review, and after-school tutoring. In 1996 Nueva Esperanza assisted ninety-three families in obtaining mortgages.

Nueva Esperanza has many other successful initiatives to its credit. In conjunction with the Hispanic Clergy of Philadelphia, the corporation established the Hispanic Century Fund, the first Hispanic foundation in Pennsylvania. Its highly successful Beta Job Training Program is the only state-contracted job training/placement program based in a Latino agency. Nueva Esperanza has also been instrumental in founding United Neighbors Against Drugs, Puerto Rican Justice Defense Coalition, Ceiba (Hispanic Association of Community Development Corporations), and the Hispanic Institute for Mental Health. Projects currently being explored include the possibility of establishing a community college, radio station, and retreat center/campground. In 1995, at the invitation of Hispanic clergy from New Jersey, a Nueva Esperanza was established in Camden. As Nueva Esperanza expands its service and influence across the Delaware Valley, it is dramatically transforming the community known as the Badlands.

19. The Shefa Fund (TSF) is a Philadelphia-based organization to promote *tikkun olam*—Jewish social responsibility and spirituality innovation. Established in 1988, TSF is an American Jewish foundation committed to the value of *tzedakah*, sharing resources to create social justice for the whole community; concern for the environment, dignity and compensation for laborers, and stewardship that emphasizes communal obligations over ownership of wealth. Through grant-making, low-income community investment, and funder education, TSF performs *tzedakah* at the highest level—that is, creating partnership between funder and recipient.

The Shefa Fund has three major initiatives that express these values: donor-advised grant-making, *tzedek* (justice) economic development, and funder education. The donor-advised grant-making is a lending program, similar to a bank in that it receives charitable contributions that are later allocated to grantees with the recommendation of the funder. Funds were allocated to support low-income community development in the United States, the Middle East, and Central America ($158,720), feminism and gender issues ($99,591), and Middle East peace work in North America ($109,323). Such projects include Yachad, Inc., a community development program working with African-American churches to rebuild abandoned housing, funding an institute to train poor communities in El Salvador to design self-sufficient strategies for economic development, implementation of marketing plans for the Marketing for Jewish Nonprofits program, and education of American Jews about the Middle East peace process through the Jewish Peace Lobby. The Tzedek Economic Development Campaign is an investment program that promotes social responsibility by investing in low-income community development and integrating concerns for equity and justice in the decision-making process of investors and shareholders of stocks. Funder Education brings the principles of Judaism and socially responsible investing to the broader public through consultation, technical services, and the publication of a newsletter, *Wealth and Covenant, and the Highest Degree of Tzedakah*, a guide to low-income community development for American Jews and Jewish communal institutions. The goal of each program is to support responsibility to the whole community, particularly direct investment in low-income communities.

In 1996–1997, TSF received more than $1.25 million in total revenue. Shefa funds were received from the following sources: contributions (59%), *tzedek* (14%), donor-advised accounts (9%), managed projects (6%), pooled funds (4%), investment income (4%), grants (3%), and honoraria and other services (1%). These funds were distributed to the following sources: personnel (28%), nonpersonnel (11%), and grants paid (61%).

Paradenominational Organizations

20. The Association of Concerned Christians for Emerging Social Services (ACCESS Services, Inc.) is a social service agency that provides specialized services for persons with cognitive, emotional, and behavioral disabilities. ACCESS primarily serves families in the communities of Lehigh, Northampton, Schuylkill, and Philadelphia counties. Services are based on a Christian philosophy of service that seeks to empower and support each individual so that he or she can function at the fullest potential. ACCESS, founded in 1976 by local members of the National Association of Christian Social Workers, is funded by five foundations, fourteen churches, and more than twenty-one businesses.

Services provided by ACCESS include employment training and placement, community-living homes, family-living homes, in-home support services, life planning and consultative services, professional development for staff, training for host families, respite program, specialized family residential living, specialized foster care, and wraparound (early periodic screening, diagnosis, and treatment) services. The agency collaborates with the Office of Mental Health/Mental Retardation and the Department of Human Services, both of which recognized ACCESS for its Host Family Respite Program.

ACCESS also partners with the community by providing volunteer opportunities in administrative support, landscaping, home repairs, and visitation.

21. Bethanna Christian Services to Children and their Families is a nonprofit agency that serves abused, neglected, and medically needy children in the Philadelphia area. Bethanna began in 1934 with the response of two Christian women to the needs of a child and his family. This program developed as an extension of the Christian conference, fellowship center, and summer camp program. Bethanna is one of several private agencies that contracts with the Philadelphia Department of Human Services to provide foster care, kinship care, and residential care for children and youth who are in the custody of and referred by the city.

Bethanna continues to offer services that demonstrate the love, compassion, justice, and mercy of Christ on behalf of children and families. The agency is also committed to supporting the strengths of the family's community. Bethanna serves over a thousand children annually. It provides the following social service programs: services to children in their own homes (SCOH), traditional foster care, family-to-family foster care, kinship care, foster parent mentoring, therapeutic foster care, residential treatment, adoption, and the Green House school program. Services are provided in partnership with several congregations and Christian families that serve as foster care and respite care families.

22. The Sunday Breakfast Rescue Mission (SBRM) was founded in 1878 to provide Sunday breakfast and Christian influence to the poor and needy. This organization began with the support of Christian businessmen, such as John Wanamaker, John B. Stetson, William M. Shoemaker, and former Governor James Pollock. In the 1930s SBRM expanded its efforts to include sleeping facilities for the homeless and a chapel. In 1942 it established a work program for men and women and a thrift store. Over the years the programs have changed to meet the changing needs of the homeless and poor. Today the Sunday Breakfast Rescue Mission programs provide meals, shelter, clothing, Christian counseling, addiction recovery, employment programs, life skills training, financial planning, and day care for mothers.

For the 1996–1997 fiscal year, the Sunday Breakfast Rescue Mission received $1,220,838 in revenue. The operating costs for the year's programs, administration, and fund-raising were received from the following sources: individual contributions (80%), program fees (5%), thrift store sales (14%), investment income (.09%), and gains on investments (.01%). The funds were distributed to program services for men (49%), program services for women (22%), administration (15%), and fund-raising (14%), for total expenditures of $1,228,792.

23. The Center for Urban Resources (CUR) is a nonprofit organization that provides technical assistance and training to urban churches in the development of social and community programs. The organization was founded in 1987 with a vision to support churches as a primary source for community betterment. Hence CUR recognizes that many churches lack information regarding resource availability, accessibility, and development, and it acts as a bridge between urban churches and the philanthropic community and other private-sector organizations in the development of programs for low-income

urban communities. Additionally, private-sector organizations are unfamiliar with the organizational functions, structure, and needs of inner-city churches that are serving their communities. CUR assists churches in forging partnerships and securing resources from private-sector organizations in addressing urban problems. The success of such partnerships and resource assistance has resulted in an increase in programs in urban communities such as preschools, day care centers, job training centers, youth programs, homeless crisis centers, programs for the elderly, food programs, family and community programs, literacy programs, and housing and economic development programs.

The primary services of CUR include: Inner City Impact Institute (ICII) training programs, ICII replication project, resource services, the Philadelphia Project for Youth Ministry, and Project News. The Inner City Impact Institute offers a sixteen-week training curriculum, a technical assistance fair with panels of grantmakers, a special workshop series on resource and program development, and the Urban Church Banking Project seminar. More than 630 pastors and church leaders representing 320 churches have participated in the ICII since 1987. CUR also provides churches with information through the resource library, resource fair, resource packets, directory of community service programs, and the quarterly *Inner City Impact News*. CUR makes referrals for technical assistance to such organizations as Community Accountants, Community Design Collaborative, the Homeless Advocacy Project free legal services, Preservation Alliance's Historic Religious Properties Program, the Foundation Center at the Free Library, and the United Way. CUR is developing a resource bank using a case management model that would assess technical assistance needs and oversee agreements between urban churches and graduate interns, technical assistance agencies, professional volunteers, consultants, and other churches. CUR consults with leaders in Detroit and other cities interested in replicating the Inner City Impact Institute. A proposal is under consideration for a five-site demonstration project.

The Center for Urban Resources also functions as the liaison between church-based community programs, grantmakers, and organizations launching new programs. As of 1999, it manages the Scott Educational Initiative, an after-school project for boys in public elementary schools, and Project Light, a literacy program. With Kingdom Works, CUR is co-managing the Philadelphia Project for Youth Ministry, an initiative funded by the Pew Charitable Trusts to develop a long-term youth ministry movement. CUR also oversees Project News, a cooperative initiative of the *Philadelphia Inquirer* and the *Daily News*, the West Philadelphia Enterprise Center, and the youth programs of six Philadelphia congregations. In working with youth a common ground is discovered that allows each partner to gain from this venture. Participating youth develop entrepreneurial skills through learning about the newspaper industry and career opportunities, selling subscriptions, and earning income. The participating congregations learn to develop job readiness programs and receive a grant to support the administrative cost of this project. The *Philadelphia Inquirer* and the *Daily News* target new subscribers through the congregation and youth by investing in the future labor force.

24. The Esperanza Health Center is a nonprofit Christian organization that provides a wide range of health care services to the Hispanic community of North Philadelphia. Esperanza uses a holistic approach that integrates Christian counseling with social work. Outreach workers, health educators, and lay staff provide home visits and community health education and prevention programs. These initiatives are essential to Esperanza's efforts to break down the bureaucratic, cultural, language, and financial barriers to health care encountered by this low-income population. The Esperanza Health Center has three full-time doctors, one full-time counselor, one part-time B.S.W., one part-time doctor, two full-time and one part-time master's-level Christian psychotherapists (two are bilingual), one psychiatrist, three volunteer doctors, and one volunteer specialist in HIV-risk reduction.

Each year, Esperanza enlists the assistance of more than two hundred medical students from the Summer Medical Institute to provide immunizations to community residents. As of 1997, 3,244 children had been immunized and 4,872 adults had received tetanus shots. Esperanza works in partnership with Christian rehabilitation programs to provide primary health care. It has also provided health care and coordinated services for more than 320 persons with HIV. Mental health services are provided by staff familiar with the culture, language, and needs of the Hispanic community. In keeping with its philosophy that health care is 20 percent medical care and 80 percent spiritual, social, emotional, and physical care, Esperanza provides financial support to local churches, trains the laity in how to promote health issues, and encourages churches to adopt patients from Esperanza and assist them in maintaining healthy lifestyles.

25. InterVarsity Christian Fellowship is one among several campus religious-based organizations that provide students with the opportunity to participate in a faith community and engage in community service projects.

Other organizations include the Newman Center, Hillel, and Campus Crusade for Christ. InterVarsity Christian Fellowship has Philadelphia chapters on the campuses of the University of Pennsylvania and Temple University. Its primary purpose is to establish a community of Christians among students and faculty. Philadelphia is one of the twenty cities where InterVarsity has established an Urban Project. This project creates opportunities for students to explore issues of justice, poverty, racism, racial reconciliation, and violence in relation to their faith commitment. Students may serve in homeless shelters, build houses for Habitat for Humanity, assist in a church day camp, or work at a food pantry or clothing closet.

26. The Philadelphia Family Policy Council (PFPC), founded in 1981, is a progressive, urban-based, interracial, pro-family, pro-life, and public policy organization. Its mission is to strengthen families by winning the city back to Judeo-Christian values and by influencing policy-making decisions in Philadelphia. To these ends, PFPC informs policy makers and the media on current issues, educates the public on the policy process and participation, researches social issues, encourages citizen involvement in the policy process, builds interracial/multiethnic coalitions to provide leadership to other groups, develops networks of community impact groups to address social needs, and provides technical assistance to Christian organizations. In addition, PFPC has collaborated with the Black Clergy of Philadelphia in establishing the Safe Corridors Initiative in North Philadelphia, previously described.

27. Teen Challenge of Philadelphia is a "Christ-centered" drug-and-alcohol-treatment program that was established in Philadelphia in 1964. This program, founded by David Wilkerson in 1958, is one of 120 Teen Challenge programs in the United States and 250 worldwide. The Philadelphia program targets the Germantown and the Delaware Valley areas. The theme is to proclaim "liberty" from the bondage of drug and alcohol addiction to all who will embrace it. Each year this program serves approximately 175 people. Teen Challenge offers a long-term, biblically based, residential treatment program for men and women eighteen years of age or older. The program consists of group classes, individual counseling, personal studies for new Christians, devotional times, group prayer, group counseling, and church attendance. During the treatment the residents do not work in order to focus all their attention on learning how to live a life free of addiction.

In addition to the residential program, Teen Challenge has outreach teams that present to schools, juvenile halls, prisons, jails, and on the streets. The program also offers weekly support groups to assist local churches in establishing small-group ministries to help people overcome addiction and maintain a drug-and-alcohol-free lifestyle. Teen Challenge reports that more than 70 percent of the graduates of their program remain free of drug and alcohol dependency.

28. Whosoever Gospel Mission and Rescue Home Ministries is an evangelical, nonprofit social service organization dedicated to serving men who are homeless and/or addicted. The mission's purpose is to proclaim the Gospel through service and to rehabilitate substance abusers through a holistic approach to recovery. The organization was founded in 1892 by William A. Raws, a recovered alcoholic. It is affiliated with the Christian Addiction Rehabilitation Association and the International Union of Gospel Missions (see chapter 8 for more details). Services are maintained by more than fifty volunteers and a ladies' auxiliary organization. The mission is unique in that it does not charge for its services, nor does it receive government funds. It is wholly dependent on the generosity of supporters.

Located in the Germantown section of Philadelphia, the Whosoever Gospel Mission is the largest transitional, residential facility of its kind in Philadelphia. Over the past hundred years, it has helped more than 700,000 of Philadelphia's most vulnerable and needy homeless men. Among the services provided is the New Life in Christ program, a rehabilitation/job readiness/ career track learning program. New Life in Christ consists of a three-month residential program and a three-month halfway house program. Program facilities include a computer lab and resource center. A vocational specialist, certified teachers, and learning program director assist participants in developing the social, educational, financial, professional, and work skills necessary for productive and independent living. In 1996, 247 men participated in the New Life in Christ program. Of these, 25 graduated from the program, 78 obtained full-time employment, 23 worked toward their GED, and 19 participated in off-site vocational programs.

Among other services provided to the community by the mission is a thrift store and a recycling operation, which provide in-house training for program participants and a source of income for programs. The mission also provides food, shelter, clothing, and chapel to transients. In 1996, it provided more than 20,600 overnight lodgings and served more than 58,900 meals. In collaboration with the Canaan Baptist Church of Germantown, the mission operates a community food cupboard. It also provides educational and service opportunities for churches, schools, and youth groups to help them become informed and involved with issues related to homelessness.

Religious-Affiliated Social Organizations

29. The Bethesda Project is a nonprofit organization established by individuals and faith-based groups committed to serving the poor, homeless, and disabled. This project began in 1979 through the initiative of the Body of Christ Prayer Community from Daylesford Abbey of Paoli, Sisters of Mercy, and others, who rented an apartment in Center City Philadelphia to care for a group of homeless women with mental illness. Bethesda provides professional social, counseling, and health services through a social worker, a certified addictions counselor, a caseworker, and a host of volunteers. Increasing support from other individuals, corporate donors, and religious groups has allowed the Bethesda Project to expand its services to six residential communities. For example, Upper Darby Plymouth, Congregation Rodeph Shalom, the Wharton School of Business, Villanova University, the Connelly Foundation, and Old First Reformed Church provided volunteer and/or financial support. In 1997, donations supported 18,000 nights of shelter for more than three hundred men, 75,000 meals, and 20,000 changes of clothing.

The mission of Bethesda is unique in that it seeks out the abandoned poor and provides a caring and family environment to those without family. As such, outreach to the poor and homeless on the street is a central part of the services offered. Bethesda Project has the capacity to serve 120 men and women in one of seven residences and three satellite shelters, which include Bethesda Spruce Street, Bethesda Bainbridge Street, Bethesda Christian Street, Bethesda North Broad Street, Mary House, Domenic House, and My Brother's House. Three local congregations provide space for the satellite shelters: Trinity Memorial Episcopal, Old First Reform United Church of Christ, and St. Mary's Episcopal. My Brother's House (MBH) provides overnight shelter and twenty-four-hour hospitality services that include showers, clean clothing, mailboxes, counseling, and referral to social service agencies. MBH is also the home of the Sanctuary program for homeless men with HIV/AIDS and other chronic health conditions. The other six residences are also based on a community-living model that fosters social support and encourages participation in housekeeping and maintenance of facilities. Homeless men and women find permanent homes and a supportive community at the Bethesda residences.

Bethesda Project works in partnership with several public and private agencies. In particular, it collaborates to provide field placements to clinical and health professionals from the Philadelphia Health Management Corporation, Hall-Mercer Community Mental Health Organization, Temple University School of Social Administration, the University of Pennsylvania School of Social Work, Graduate Hospital community outreach department, Episcopal Community Services, and Horizon House Addiction Services Unit. Also incorporated under the auspices of Bethesda is Nazareth Housing, which provides construction, rebuilding, and home maintenance trades to residents and neighbors who are in danger of losing their housing.

30. Project H.O.M.E. (Housing, Opportunities, Medical Care, Education) is a nonprofit organization that works in partnership with chronically homeless men and women to provide housing and social services. It also addresses the causes of homelessness through community building and relationship building in low-income neighborhoods and through education and advocacy on issues of homelessness, housing, and poverty. The mission of Project H.O.M.E. (PH) is to empower persons to break the cycle of homelessness and poverty, to address structural causes of poverty, and to enable all individuals to reach their fullest potential as members of society. PH grew out of the work of the Bethesda Project, Women of Hope, and activist Sister Mary Scullion. In the winter of 1988–1989, these organizations pooled their resources and expertise to establish the Mother Katherine Drexel Residence. During the initial four months of operation, they experienced the remarkable success of assisting thirty-seven men to enter substance abuse programs, nine to enter mental health programs, two to enter dual diagnosis programs, and several others to reenter the workforce. After two years of providing FEMA-funded winter shelter, Project H.O.M.E. opened its first transitional house and broadened its program to include support services. The work of Project H.O.M.E. is rooted in a strong spiritual conviction of the dignity of each person and commitment to a more just society.

From 1991 to 1998, PH developed a comprehensive program to assist homeless persons in their transition from the streets. This program reflects the understanding that homelessness is not an isolated phenomenon but rather a complex set of problems that require interrelated solutions. The available services include homelessness prevention, street outreach, emergency residence, transitional residences, permanent residences, employment programs, and adult learning and arts programs. Homelessness prevention efforts target at-risk neighborhoods through two community centers, focusing on affordable housing, anti-graffiti efforts, adult learning, after-school programs, mentoring, public safety, neighborhood gardening, home repairs, community health, and education and advocacy issues related to homelessness. Street outreach teams conduct outreach to homeless persons five days a week. PH also coordinates public and private efforts for homeless persons through the Outreach Coordination Center. The three emergency residences and three transitional permanent residences are the entry point of services for chronically homeless adults. These facilities supply communal shelter or private rooms, meals, support services, referrals for health care, and case management. PH also has a specialized residential program for homeless persons with drug and alcohol addictions. PH believes that all persons are entitled to affordable housing and maintains 124 permanent units at seven sites.

Through partnerships with various agencies, programs, and neighborhoods, Project H.O.M.E. provides shelter, health care, mental health care, recovery services, educational and recreational programs, employment training, and home-ownership opportunities. Working in conjunction with the City of Philadelphia's Office of Mental Health and Mental Retardation, PH established a transitional residence and independent living program to address the needs of homeless persons with mental illness. It also received grant support from the U.S. Department of Housing and Urban Development's Shelter Plus Care program to expand its transitional residence program and renovate permanent housing units. In December 1997, PH received a $5.6 million grant from HUD for development of thirty new units for women and children and operation of Women of Change and St. Columbia's emergency shelter programs. PH is also participating in the Philadelphia Plan, which will allow it to expand its community development efforts in the neighborhoods of its community centers. Mercy Health Plan funded the development of the on-staff Job Skills Training Program. The employment and education initiative has expanded to include the Back H.O.M.E. Cafe, Our Daily Threads thrift store, a cottage industry program, and a joint venture— the Cornerstone Community Book and Art Center. In addition to providing employment for residents, these for-profit businesses financially support the continued work of Project H.O.M.E. PH and the Honickman Foundation are collaborating with the mayor's office and local religious leaders to target congregations that can join efforts in creating solutions to homelessness.

Secularized Organizations

31. Metropolitan AIDS Neighborhood Nutrition Alliance (MANNA) is the only nonprofit organization providing freshly cooked, home-delivered, and congregate meals for persons living with HIV/AIDS, nutrition education, and counseling to providers and consumers of HIV-related services. This organization began in the basement of the First Presbyterian Church in Philadelphia in 1990. Since then, MANNA has provided more than 1,000,000 meals to 45,000 people and nutrition counseling and education to 24,000 people. Meals and other services are offered at the main office in downtown Philadelphia, as well as at thirteen satellite locations. In 1995 MANNA developed and began publishing *Eat Well, Think Well, Feel Well*, a low-literacy nutrition guide for persons living with HIV/AIDS. This publication has been distributed nationally and selected by NIH as the national standard for HIV nutrition education.

In many ways MANNA has been a ministry of feeding and a place of healing for those who serve and those who are served. In 1997 the agency provided 823 home-delivered meals, 4,518 congregate meals, 291 individual nutrition counseling sessions, 421 group nutrition counseling sessions, and 134 professional training sessions. At least nine modified meal plans are available to accommodate special dietary needs and religious-practice dietary restrictions. The clients served are predominantly people of color living on low incomes. More than 37 percent of the clients are women and children. A small staff of chefs and registered dietitians along with more than six hundred volunteers carry out the meal preparation, delivery, administration, fund-raising, and governance.

In 1997 MANNA received $1,199,899 in revenue. The operating costs for programs, administration, and fund-raising were received from the following sources: individual contributions (46%), foundations and corporations (26%), government grants (20%), fee-for-service (4%), communities of faith (3%), and other (%1). The funds were distributed to program cost (79%), administration (9%), and fund-raising (12%), for total expenditures of $1,387,618.

32. Saint Mary's Respite Center is a nonsectarian, nonprofit social service agency that was founded in 1991. This community-based organization was established through the ministry of the Episcopal Church in Philadelphia. St. Mary's Respite Center is housed in the Cathedral Church of the Savior in Philadelphia. The constituency and supporters of St. Mary's reflect diverse

religious, socioeconomic, ethnic, and cultural backgrounds. In addition to the support of volunteers, individual donors, churches, and private foundations, St. Mary's receives funding from the City of Philadelphia AIDS Activities Coordinating Office, the Philadelphia AIDS Consortium, Philadelphia Health Management Corporation, the AIDS Fund, the Philadelphia Foundation, and Women's Way. The support of volunteers and financial contributors allows St. Mary's Respite Center to provide respite care at no cost to the families. Meals are contributed by the Metropolitan AIDS Neighborhood Nutrition Alliance (MANNA).

St. Mary's is the only out-of-home respite program in Pennsylvania for HIV-infected and -affected children. It provides a safe, stimulating, and developmentally appropriate child care program for children aged five weeks to five years who are HIV-infected themselves or living with someone who is HIV-infected. This unique program gives the caregiver five to six hours off and gives the child an opportunity for structured learning and creative play with other children. One day of care per week is available, with children enrolled for one of the four service days, a schedule that allows the center to serve forty children per week. The center's preschool curriculum enhances the social, physical, emotional, and cognitive development of the children in order to prepare them for full-time day care, Head Start, or kindergarten. Six professional staff members and several volunteers provide initial assessments and monitoring of each child's progress.

33. Young Men's Christian Association (YMCA) of Philadelphia and Vicinity is a nonsectarian, nonprofit organization that continues to be guided by the Christian ethics and family values on which it was founded. The YMCA translates its Christian heritage into programs that "nurture children, strengthen families, build strong communities and develop healthy spirits, minds, and bodies for all." The YMCA of Philadelphia and Vicinity has eleven branches and thirty-two program sites within the Delaware Valley.

Today the YMCA's services are geared predominantly toward families and children. The programs at each site are designed to reflect the unique needs and character of that community. For example, the Central office, West Philadelphia, Abington, Rocky Run, and Columbia North YMCAs have expanded youth programming to include a Black Achievers program to provide leadership training and role models for black teenagers. The Christian Street center collaborates with ten public schools to provide aquatic programs.

West Philadelphia YMCA has demonstrated a commitment to community needs by developing five collaborations with the medical community, universities, and schools, and has targeted twenty-five congregations for collaboration. The Community Development department has prepared fifty individuals to transition from public assistance to jobs in child care and has assisted others to develop the skills to open home day care centers. The Columbia North YMCA established home day care in a public housing development and sponsored fifty children from the housing development to go to camp through a HUD grant. Also unique to Columbia North is the Child Readiness Center Day Care to expose preschool-age children to reading, foreign language, and swimming. The West Philadelphia and Mainline YMCAs offer Active Older Adult programs. This is only a sample of the wide range of services provided by the staff and volunteers.

The YMCA of Philadelphia and Vicinity received $18,226,582 in annual funding in 1996 from the following sources: membership (33.02%), child care (27.12%), day camp (8.73%), youth programs (7.08%), United Way (5.07%), adult health (3.22%), government grants (2.34%), and other sources (7.78%). These funds were distributed to the following sources: personnel (56.17%), programs (20.96%), occupancy (13.83%), debt reduction (8.10%), national dues (.94%), and other (5.64%).

In this chapter we have briefly surveyed the involvement of religious organizations in social and community service delivery in Philadelphia. As noted above, we had to make some decisions about definitions: What is a religious-based organization? What is a social and community activity? We decided to take a conservative approach about what a religious-based social services agency is and, using this approach, included a small sample of organizations. Clearly, the task of identifying and tabulating the involvement of religious-based organizations, from local congregations to national headquarters, is a new terrain. Yet our findings do suggest that religious-based organizations are involved in social and community services that go beyond the well-noted congregational soup kitchens and include business incubators and community organizing for welfare rights. Such activities reflect a significant investment of religious communities, totaling millions of dollars and tens of thousands of hours in labor annually.

These religious organizations represent a major part of the American welfare system. Tens of thousands of people in the Philadelphia area are being helped by all kinds of programs, from soup kitchens to housing services, from job training to educational enhancement classes. One can only imagine what would happen to the collective quality of life if these religious organizations would cease to exist. To go one step further, what *could* happen to our welfare system if there were more recognition and understanding on the part of religious communities and social work as to what unique contributions each can make to the network of social services? It is obvious that our public system depends on the complementary existence of a religious-based welfare system that enables the public sector to provide limited assistance without public outcry. A close look at the Philadelphia landscape reveals that many religious-based buildings exist in every part of the city, each of them offering a slightly different array of the services required for human development and subsistence. Furthermore, the staffs of these religious-based organizations include a large number of qualified social workers. Indeed, religious-based social services are one of the largest employers of social workers in the Philadelphia region and possibly nationwide.

These findings, along with those from Greensboro, North Carolina, reported in chapter 10, suggest that religious organizations play an important role in the local social service arena. In fact, they are second only to the government in the magnitude of their investment in social and community services. It should be noted, however, that larger organizations tend also to contract with the government and hence receive a substantial part of their revenue from public sources. Much of the work of congregations and religious-based organizations is conducted in collaboration with community volunteers and other community-based organizations. The notion of partnership is not a foreign concept for religious-based organizations but an approach that is often employed when their goals for human and community development are aligned with those of potential partners.

PART 3

THE CHALLENGE AHEAD

CHAPTER 12

POLITICAL AND SOCIETAL TRENDS IN SOCIAL SERVICES PROVISION

Murray's notion of a clergyman was somebody who worked among the poor, not as efficiently, perhaps, as a trained social worker, but doing his best and doing it cheaply.
—Rev. Darcourt on Murray Brown the politician, in Robertson Davies, *The Rebel Angels*

The American social welfare system is in flux. Unlike European countries, the United States is not a welfare state, yet the federal government at times has assumed a greater role in caring for the poor and needy. This can be seen in the New Deal of the 1930s and, to a lesser extent, in the War on Poverty of the 1960s. But things have changed. Government support for social welfare has been steadily eroding since 1981.

We are now in an era of devolution. Responsibility for the poor and needy is being shifted from the federal government to the state, and from the state to the local level, primarily to the private and nonprofit sectors. What started as contracting-out has become planned cuts in services, with the expectation that others will fill the gap left by the government's decreasing participation in social services provision. In the past, once a person's eligibility for services was verified, it was federally protected and legally guaranteed, despite the ups and downs of the economy or the opinions of local residents.

With devolution and block grants, entitlements no longer exist. Social service and welfare programs are limited to their earmarked budgets. It has taken almost two decades for the picture of this new welfare scene to develop, and now its key features are evident. It is not a pretty picture. It is a picture of government carelessness and apathy, of restricting eligibility criteria to such a point that fewer people are assisted and costs are minimized. Yet it is also a picture of greater community involvement.

Why, then, are we advocating that social work seek a rapprochement with the religious community?

The answer to the above question has to do with change—a rapid change in the social service terrain that is dramatically shifting the balance between public secular services and sectarian private services. It is a time when most Americans, not only Republicans and conservatives, assume that the state has failed to provide adequate welfare and that what has been provided has been too bureaucratic and demeaning. Media, political leaders, foundations, and the public discourse are of one voice: The balance of social services provision is shifting, and the religious community will be a central actor in the new social arrangement.

Powerful political and social trends already under way suggest that the United States is ready for a paradigm shift in which the religious community will become a major player in the delivery of social services. Most Americans, for example, consider helping the needy to be a religious virtue, and they expect religious organizations to be engaged in service provision (Ammerman 1996; Wuthnow 1994). If these trends continue to gather momentum, social work as a profession and secular human service organizations nationwide will have to reassess their practices and orientations.

PERSONAL RESPONSIBILITY AND WORK OPPORTUNITY RECONCILIATION ACT OF 1996—CHARITABLE CHOICE

One of the most startling developments in this era of devolution may well be the passage of the Personal Responsibility and Work Opportunity Reconciliation Act of 1996 (P.L. 104–193). This act, signed into law by President Clinton on August 22, 1996, ended Aid to Families with Dependent Children (AFDC) and made welfare entitlements much more difficult to obtain and to keep. This law claimed to introduce antipoverty measures, but it immediately captured the attention of social work professionals and social services leaders, who believed that many of the poor would face new and greater hardships. Nevertheless, the new welfare reform law contains an important section that has a significant bearing on the future relationships of the religious community and social services. As stated in section 104:

> The purpose of this section is to allow States to contract with religious organizations, or to allow religious organizations to accept certificates, vouchers, or other forms of disbursement under any program described in subsection (a)(2), on the same basis as any other non-governmental

provider without impairing the religious character of such organizations, and without diminishing the religious freedom of beneficiaries of assistance funded under such program.

As such, this section of the law has three objectives. It seeks to: (1) encourage states to increase the participation of nonprofit organizations in the public antipoverty campaign, with specific mention of religious-based organizations; (2) protect the religious integrity of participating religious-based organizations; and (3) safeguard the religious freedom of participants.

Section 104, for the most part, refers to the Temporary Assistance for Needy Families (TANF) programs that have taken the place of AFDC. Money for these programs comes directly to the state as block grants. Section 104 also applies to food stamps, Medicaid, and Supplemental Security Income (SSI). This means that any state or county can now contract with a religious-based organization to provide services in the following areas: food (such as subsidized meals, food pantry, nutrition education, or soup kitchen); work (such as job skills training, on-the-job training, vocational education, GED and ESL programs, job-search help, and job-readiness preparation); medical and health services (such as abstinence education, drug-and-alcohol-treatment centers, health clinics, wellness centers, and immunization programs); and maternity homes (such as residential care, second-chance homes, and supervised community housing). By law, religious-based organizations may not only provide such services but are also encouraged to take a larger role in the provision.

Many religious-based organizations that are interested in greater involvement in social services provision have refused to contract with the government because they fear losing their religious character and independence (Esbeck 1996; Monsma 1996). Until very recently, contracting with the government meant that a religious-based organization had to remove all religious symbols from the room where service was provided; forgo any religious ceremonies (such as mealtime prayers); accept all clients, even those opposed to the beliefs of the providers; and hire staff who reflected society at large and not the organization's spirit and belief system. The new welfare reform law has effectively ended these restrictions. The law specifically states:

A religious organization with a contract described in subsection (a)(1)(A), or which accepts certificates, vouchers, or other forms of disbursement under subsection (a)(1)(B), shall retain its independence from Federal,

State, and local governments, including such organization's control over the definition, development, practice, and expression of its religious beliefs. Subsection (d)(1)

Provisions noted in section 104 mean that religious-based social services will neither become providers in the sense of a state sector nor lose their religious autonomy. Religious-based providers will not be required to alter their internal governance or add outside members to their boards in order to be eligible for participation. Furthermore, they will not be required to remove from their property any "religious art, icons, scripture, or other symbols" [Subsection (d)(2)].

Congregations and religious organizations have been exempt from compliance with employment policies mandated by the Civil Rights Act of 1964 and the Americans with Disabilities Act of 1990. However, religious-based, publicly funded social service organizations, considered to be a separate legal entity, have not been exempt. Under the new welfare reform law, religious organizations are no longer required to incorporate social services separately, although they must have a separate accounting system for the contracted services. The law also exempts the social service arms of religious organizations from compliance with the employment policies mandated by the Civil Rights Act:

> A religious organization's exemption provided under section 702 of the Civil Rights Act of 1964 (42 U.S.C. 2000c-1a) regarding employment practices shall not be affected by its participation in, or receipt of funds from, programs described in subsection (a)(2). [Subsection (f)]

The welfare reform law is as yet unchallenged. It may be that the Supreme Court will rule it unconstitutional because of its very broad interpretation of the First Amendment. The law is also vague in defining the rights of clients. For example, a state may contract solely with a religious organization, but it must also provide for clients who prefer nonsectarian services. Such services must be of equal quality and in close proximity to the client, but these are terms that are difficult to define concretely. How this will be accomplished and how much influence religious providers will have over services are aspects of the law that are yet to be determined. Some states may choose not to contract with any religious organizations, while others may give them preference.

It is most interesting to note that while the Personal Responsibility and

Work Opportunity Reconciliation Act of 1996 was being debated, President
Clinton was already advocating for church involvement in welfare. In a
speech delivered during the 1996 election campaign at the 116th annual
session of the National Baptist Convention U.S.A., President Clinton asked
churches to do what Governor Fordice had asked Mississippi churches to
do:

> Under this law [P.L. 104–193], every state, when it becomes effective, every
> state in the country can say: If you will hire somebody off welfare, we'll give
> you the welfare checks as a supplement for the wages and the training. It
> means, folks, when you go back home, your church can receive a person's
> welfare check and add to it only a modest amount of money to make a liv-
> ing wage, and to take some time to train people and bring their children
> into the church, and make sure their children are all right and give them a
> home and a family.
>
> I just want every pastor in this audience to think about it. Just think
> about it. If every church in America hired one person off welfare, if every
> church in America could get some work to do that, it would set an example
> that would require the business community to follow, that would require
> the charitable and other non-profit organizations to follow. We cannot cre-
> ate a government jobs program big enough to solve this whole thing, but if
> everybody did it, one by one, we could do this job.

President Clinton made clear his expectations: religious organizations
would assume a greater role in welfare, and in turn, those who were assisted
would undergo a radical life transformation. Ideally, those who were helped
would join the church that assisted them, become productive citizens, and
help others as they had been helped. That an American president, while still in
office, would challenge the traditional boundaries between state and church
under the auspices of this law can likely be construed as an official call for a
new and larger welfare provision system in which religious organizations
would play a primary role.

The trend represented by the welfare reform law is unmistakable. The Congress and the president of the United States are seeking greater involvement in
social services delivery by the religious community. Given the provisions of
this law, it is likely that religious-based organizations will assume a larger and
more central role in local social services. This will be an enormous change
and one that will have a major influence on social service organizations as we
know them today.

MEDIA COVERAGE

While academic researchers have been slow to recognize the importance of the changing role of the religious community in local service development from the early 1980s to the present, the media have been quick to see the implications and have gone ahead with their own story—a story that tells how political decisions have catapulted religious organizations into services provision, both on-site and by providing community agencies with volunteers, money, and space. It was the media's story that helped shape public opinion and ultimately led to the decision of policy makers to reform the welfare system—the most dramatic social policy shift since the New Deal. Central to this reform was the idea that the religious community would, could, and should solve problems locally, especially those left unsolved by the new reform.

Our area of study—religious-based social services—has become a hot news story, a sure sign that the field is changing and that academic social work needs to play catch-up. For example, in a recent *U.S. News and World Report* article with a cover page teaser reading "The Faith Factor: Can Churches Cure America's Social Ills?" Shapiro and Wright (1996) summed up the issue as follows: "With President Clinton and Congress agreeing to end welfare as we know it, there is talk of a second welfare revolution: let churches and charities, not government, provide more of the safety net."

Similarly, *Time* magazine published an article by Adam Cohen in 1997 titled "Welfare: Reaching Out to the Poor," in which the author discussed the fact that the new welfare reform contains a little-noticed provision that paves the way for religious organizations to become government agents. After discussing the welfare services provided by the Reverend Floyd Flake and his Allen A.M.E. Church in Queens, New York, Cohen noted:

> The future of America's antipoverty efforts may look a lot like Allen A.M.E. As the nation wrestles with how to reform a failed welfare system, and as more than 35 million Americans continue to live below the poverty line, government is increasingly asking churches to succeed where social workers and bureaucrats handing out checks have failed. State and local welfare departments are starting up innovative partnerships with religious institutions.   (p. 47)

His message is clear: social work and welfare bureaucracy have missed the boat. It is time to call upon the religious community to do what others have failed to do. It is not a question of whether religious-based social services are more effective. It is a question of whether this nation can find an alternative to a system that seems doomed, anachronistic, paternalistic, and impersonal. The pendulum of public opinion is now swinging toward the religious community, and the national media are only echoing national sentiment.

Even the *New Yorker* (Klein 1997) has had its say on this issue. Klein's article, like many others in the popular press, acknowledged the achievements of religious-based social service organizations. He singled out two in particular: Chuck Colson's prison fellowship ministry and a Boston youth ministry that police credit with reducing crime in the Dorchester area. These programs are based on mentoring, one-to-one support, and the personal influence of church members who are willing to share their religious fervor and social commitment with others. Klein assessed the new urban reality as follows: "Indeed, more than a few cities, Boston among them, have come to see the churches as the most reliable institutions in poor neighborhoods, and have been able to smudge the line between state and church by quietly funding various church-run programs" (p. 42). What Klein underscored is that, in these cities, secular social service agencies, public as well as private, seem incapable of preventing urban decay, and to some extent, are even being blamed for it.

In his article, Klein quoted Gary Bauer, a leading religious conservative and president of the Family Research Council: "We certainly agree [with liberal Protestants] that government solutions have fallen short and that you can't successfully address the problems of the poor without addressing the spiritual aspect of their needs." Thus, Klein argued, the faith-based movement is politically inconvenient for liberals. However, Kramnick and Moore (1997) in the liberal journal *American Prospect*, argued that "American religion is a crucial national resource for addressing social problems, and liberals need to say so in accents that don't sound partisan" (p. 48).

These reports are only the tip of the iceberg. The material presented above is taken from a few national magazines of 1996–1997. We have compiled a much larger file of daily newspapers, ranging from the *New York Times* and the *Wall Street Journal* to community newspapers, reporting similar stories and highlighting the successes of social ministries carried out by religious-based organizations. What is common to these hundreds of reports is that they contrast the highly personal and caring services provided by religiously motivated organizations and volunteers with the impersonal services provided by a bureaucratic system. The reader ultimately gets the message that the solution to "welfare as we know it" is to make the religious community the national social service arm of the state.

NEW PROPOSALS IN WASHINGTON

Much of the current political rhetoric about social services and welfare reform has been aimed at the religious community. National and state politicians, eager to convince exasperated voters that they are attacking social decay and government largesse, have raised the stakes, not to mention their voices, for greater involvement by the religious community in solving local social problems. Newt Gingrich, impressed by the volunteer spirit expressed in the home-building efforts of Habitat for Humanity, supported legislation introduced by Representative Rick Lazio (R-N.Y.), for a $50 million federal grant for Habitat and other organizations that build homes for the poor. Similarly, in 1996, Republican senator John Ashcroft of Missouri proposed that states use federal block grants to contract directly with religious-based charities for delivery of social services to the poor. The grant money would go straight from the U.S. Treasury to local charities without passing through any federal or state agency.

The Democratic governor of North Carolina, Jim Hunt, in a speech at Highland United Methodist Church in Raleigh, called on the religious community to "pitch in and make this happen." By "this," he meant the Work First Program, a North Carolina welfare reform program (*Greensboro News and Record* 1996a). As we noted previously, President Bill Clinton, in his 1996 address to the National Baptist Convention U.S.A., which represents 33,000 primarily black churches, urged the nation's churches to take the sting out of the tough new welfare bill by hiring people off the public rolls (Associated Press 1996).

Another indication of the political and social changes taking place is the use of vouchers. In 1996, Ohio became the first state to issue school vouchers. This gave parents and students the right to choose the school they wanted and to pay part of the cost with public money, even if they choose a religious school. If this program withstands all legal challenges, it will pave the way for vouchers for welfare recipients and social service clients. Although Ohio's voucher system is geared to education, the implications for the social service system cannot be ignored. As noted previously, it is quite possible that welfare recipients may receive vouchers to pay for social services, and that they will be allowed to use them at any social service agency, including religious-based organizations. Should these religious-based services prove to be cheaper and more enthusiastic and accommodating about their work, they may attract a large number of clients. This, in turn, would diminish the client load of private secular social service agencies.

It is not only Republicans who are calling for the involvement of the religious community in the provision of welfare services. Henry Cisneros (1996), the former secretary of Housing and Urban Development (HUD), publicly advocated a partnership between government and religious organizations in the field of community housing and building. Cisneros cited examples such as Chicago's Antioch Missionary Baptist Church, which, with HUD assistance, rehabilitated and developed 177 apartments and 120 town houses.

In a booklet titled *Higher Grounds: Faith Communities and Community Building*, written while he was still at HUD, Cisneros (1996) asked why faith communities have such a special role to play in inner-city communities. He answered his own question by listing four features that characterize the religious community. He also noted that other institutions may have two or three, but not all, of these features. These characteristics, which give the religious community its special role in the inner city, are as follows: (1) Faith communities, unlike other social institutions and populations, did not flee to the suburbs but stayed rooted in the inner cities. (2) Community is central to the mission of charity (see chapter 5), and all religions stress social service to others. (3) While some faith communities have financial resources, all have a unique resource—namely, a collective of people willing and ready to assist others. (4) Faith communities touch the soul and provide more than mere financial assistance or material goods. For these reasons, Cisneros argued that it is reasonable for the religious community to use public funds to restore the quality of life in inner cities. He invited them not only to build houses but to fill these houses with spirit and faith.

Cisneros, who saw the potential for the role of the religious community in building/renovating inner-city housing, worked to bring that role into the government. Soon after he came to HUD, he established the Religious Organizations Initiative in the Special Actions Office, Office of the Secretary. The mission of this initiative was to provide extensive outreach to the faith community and to engage religious institutions as partners in forwarding the priorities he established for HUD.

NEW APPROACHES TO SERVICE DELIVERY

We have noted two important trends emerging in the welfare arena. One is greater religious involvement. The other is destandardization of service delivery, with numerous local variations. An example of this new welfare revolution is under way in Mississippi. In 1995, Mississippi, under the leadership of Governor Kirk Fordice, began experimenting with a new welfare reform called Faith and Family. The program is based on Marvin Olasky's (1992) idea that charities and voluntary organizations, many of them churches, are better equipped than government to deal with helping the poor. Governor Fordice pushed for this program, in which 5,500 congregations were asked to adopt poor families and help them get off public assistance by helping them find jobs after initial job training. Congregational volunteers help welfare families with transportation, résumé preparation, child care, loans, personal advice, and other needs, but are not expected to proselytize. Harrison (1995) reported that none of the welfare families helped by one Mississippi Baptist church had been asked to attend worship services, yet all had chosen to do so. Of the 59,343 eligible families and 5,500 religious congregations in Mississippi, in 1997, 165 families and 55 congregations were actively involved in the program.

Governor Fordice was not alone in this trendsetting approach. In 1991 Governor John Engler of Michigan called for shifting the responsibility for helping the poor from the government to civil institutions, particularly religious ones, which can address the moral and cultural aspects of chronic dependency. Engler later approved a multimillion-dollar contract with the Salvation Army to care for the state's homeless population (Sherman 1995). In Cleveland, the Methodist church was contracted by the city to provide all services to the homeless. Similarly, in Illinois, Catholic Charities was contracted to operate most of the state's foster care services. In North Carolina the state's Department of Human Services is examining ways to form partnerships with the religious community (Britt 1996).

In Texas in the mid-1990s, Governor George W. Bush promoted a voucher system for welfare recipients. Noting that some of the best antipoverty programs come from private and religious organizations, Governor Bush has suggested that people eligible for welfare receive vouchers redeemable for services by any public, private, or faith-based organizations. Under the voucher system, those in need could choose for themselves the type of service organization that they preferred. Although this proposal faces strong opposition, it is in line with Ohio's use of educational vouchers. The point is not whether Bush's program will work or whether it will work well; the point is that the State of Texas is willing to broaden the mix of service providers by including faith-based services.

THE PRESIDENTS' SUMMIT FOR AMERICA'S FUTURE

In 1997, shortly after the signing of P.L. 104–193, the Presidents' Summit for America's Future was convened in Philadelphia. This was a media-hyped event in which a call for volunteerism was raised by President Clinton, former presidents Bush and Ford, Nancy Reagan (representing the ailing Ronald Reagan), and former general of the armies Colin Powell. Some 250 religious leaders and activists were among the invited guests, so it was no surprise that one of the designated tracks was religion and its impact on volunteerism. A major theme of the Summit was that nobody knows the needs of a community better than its churches, mosques, and synagogues do, and nobody has more financial resources to meet these needs than government and business do. This, the attendees agreed, was what society needed: a new partnership of church, government, and business.

Governor Don Sundquist of Tennessee, a key speaker, said that America needed partnerships with the religious community. He suggested that, with proper safeguards, community-based religious groups might do a better job of redistributing financial aid and providing community services than government does. Religious leaders attending the Summit tended to agree with the governor. For example, Joan Campbell, president of the National Council of Churches, noted that community religious institutions have the needed infrastructure in place and added: "So the question is not: How can we get around the First Amendment separation of church and state, but how can we work creatively with government to meet human needs?"

THE RELIGIOUS COMMUNITY AND SOCIAL SERVICES

Many churches and religious groups are not waiting for the government. They have already begun to expand their social services delivery, and more of them are beginning to partner with social workers. Bonne and Ronne (1990), who reported on the work of several inner-city congregations, described the social worker/church partnership of Oakhurst Baptist Church in Decatur, Georgia, as follows:

> Another unique ministry of Oakhurst is their involvement in a social work-er/church partnership that is being implemented in many churches around the country. The partnership involves the pairing of a particular social worker with a particular church. If the social worker runs across a need that the government or other subsidy programs are not able to take care of, he brings it before his partner church. The church then steps in to help meet these needs that would otherwise fall by the wayside. These needs range from throwing a nine-year-old a birthday party, to helping someone find a job.   (pp. 45–46)

The scope of these partnerships is impossible to measure because they are often informal. One reason is that a formal arrangement might be challenged as a violation of church-state separation. What is important is that such part-nerships show that one bridge already exists at the local level for cooperation among social workers, social service agencies, and organized religion.

A group called the Working Group for Religious Freedom in Social Ser-vices, composed of key national groups such as the American Jewish Com-mittee, the Anti-Defamation League, People for the American Way, and the Baptist Joint Committee on Public Affairs, has encouraged religious organiza-tions of all kinds to take part in the new welfare reform act. However, the Working Group also cautions potential providers that, if the government begins to pay for services that have traditionally been funded and carried out by congregational members, such payment will make providers even more dependent on government support and, consequently, on government poli-cies and preferences. The Working Group cites Art Smith of Volunteers of America, who said that government funding "impairs your impetus to go out and raise funds. That's a real danger all non-profits face—just sitting back and figuring the government will take care of you." They also warn their members that the welfare reform law will have unintended consequences and that gov-ernment regulation will inevitably follow government dollars: "If religious programs are funded, the government will inevitably become entangled in the affairs of otherwise autonomous religious groups, thereby jeopardizing their religious liberty." It should be noted that this statement comes from a liberal group, not from an ultraconservative antigovernment group. Hence, both sides of the religious community fear charitable choice and need to be per-suaded that it can work.

MIXED SIGNALS FROM THE RELIGIOUS COMMUNITY

The trends discussed above are not being embraced wholeheartedly by all players in the religious community. One reason is that a more prominent role for religious-based social services in the provision of welfare means a tighter linkage between religious organizations and the state. Many in the religious community view such a linkage as a threat.

Joe Loconte (1997), in an article titled "The 7 Deadly Sins of Government Funding," gave seven reasons why government funding should be opposed: (1) government regulations force providers to waste resources; (2) government regulations cripple commonsense caregiving; (3) government squeezes providers into its caregiving mold; (4) government focuses on delivering services, not results; (5) agencies that chase public dollars confuse their mission; (6) politics often drives caregiving decisions; and (7) government tends to secularize religious programs. Some of Loconte's fears are common to most nonprofit service providers, but the last three are mostly relevant to the religious community. Religious-based groups provide social services not only to meet a need but also, and at times more so, to express their faith. If government funding for social service curtails some or all of the religious tenor of these services, then the gift is unwelcomed. Amy Sherman noted: "At its heart, a religion-based service provider aims to transform lives" (Sherman 1995:61). She further warned the religious community that "religious nonprofits that contract with the state may, as a result, shift their purpose from the transformation of lives to the mere delivery of services" (p. 58). In one of the congregations we studied in Philadelphia in 1999, we were informed that after receiving a $15,000 grant from the Department of Public Welfare, the congregants decided to return the money. The grant was for an after-school program, yet the congregants did not want to be entangled by the state.

Another call from the religious right is that of Stephen Burger, executive director of the International Union of Gospel Missions, which was discussed in chapter 8. Burger (1996) noted that the government hampers the work of religious-based social services providers by forcing them to hire only licensed employees, enforcing zoning rules that limit the number of clients served in any given place, requiring the service site to be licensed by numerous city and state inspections, and prohibiting their participation in federal food programs. The last point refers to a 1993 ruling by the U.S. Department of Agriculture that USDA commodities were not to be used in meals where individuals were required to attend religious services. For many missions, the choice was clear—give up USDA commodities.

While Loconte, Sherman, and Burger all represent the fundamentalist camp in the religious community, Thomas J. Harvey, the former president of Catholic Charities, does not. Yet Harvey also is suspicious of public and political expectations that the religious community will succeed where the government has failed. In a 1997 publication titled *Government Promotion of Faith-Based Solutions to Social Problems: Partisan or Prophetic?* Harvey explains why the role of the religious community should be debated and challenged. He noted that the recent popularity of the term *faith-based* is coming from partisan politics. "As such, it may be being used in an attempt to co-opt and misuse the best of the religious idealism to relieve or lessen the government's responsibility for alleviating poverty and the social woes which surround it for the well being of society" (p. 8).

Social workers should remember that the religious community does not exist to do social work or to help the needy. The primary role of the religious community is what Lincoln and Mamiya (1990) refer to as its "privatistic" function—that is, serving the religious needs of members. No religious group or organization can survive if that function is not primary and seriously adhered to. A growing number of organizations in the religious community have an additional function, a "communal" one. However, that communal function, which is the focus of our book, is only secondary in the religious community. If it comes to pass, as Loconte, Sherman, and Burger have warned, that the communal function threatens the primacy of the religious function, then the choice of the religious community is obvious: relinquish the communal function to preserve the privatistic-religious function.

It is our view that, were the religious community to withhold its social and communal involvement, no other force would step in to fill the void. Others in the profession may disagree and say that this is a nonissue and that only public nonsectarian services should be provided in a modern democracy. Such a stance, however, would be at the expense of the needy and disadvantaged members of our society, and we doubt if any conscientious social worker would countenance this viewpoint.

Barbara Solow (1997) reported on a meeting of some two hundred leaders of churches, nonprofit, and governmental social service agencies in Raleigh, North Carolina. The conference, titled "Faith and Welfare Reform," focused on the impact that welfare reform may have on the religious community. It was clear to all participants that welfare reform means more social involvement by that community. Solow noted that the clergy were critical of the state's call for support from religious-based institutions. Most felt that the state's efforts to soften the blow of welfare reform were putting the churches at risk of straying from their broader scriptural mission to fight poverty. Although most participants were not members of the Christian Coalition or the religious right, they were in accord with this sentiment.

The signals from the religious community are indeed mixed. There are those who are preparing to take on new social responsibilities, while others vehemently oppose any public funding. There are also others who represent a different agenda. One such group is Call for Renewal, a national coalition of religious organizations. This coalition, established in a small conference in May 1995, calls for the religious community to provide the moral accountability that is lacking in the country's social debate. Call for Renewal, which had an impact on the 1996 election, advocates for just state legislation and is leading the way in identifying new ways of overcoming poverty.

Call for Renewal includes a variety of religious leaders. Among them are evangelical pastors and the founders of successful church-based urban programs; diocesan social action directors and Catholic sisters in social service ministries; conveners of local coalitions and leaders of national networks, such as the Christian Community Development Association (with more than 250 affiliates in a hundred cities), Pax Christi, Bread for the World, Evangelicals for Social Action, Seminary Consortium for Urban Planning Education (SCUPE) (the largest urban ministry network in the country), InterVarsity Christian Fellowship, and the Leadership Foundations (building faith-based partnerships in twenty-one cities), and more. The widespread appeal of Call for Renewal is evident in that it has attracted representatives from the full spectrum of the religious community, all eager that a voice other than that of the Christian Coalition be heard.

It is interesting to read Call for Renewal's statement of its spiritual politics. In this document, Jim Wallis (1997), the founder of Call for Renewal and the editor of *Sojourners*, gives an indication of how interwoven religion and social politics have become at the end of the twentieth century:

> We serve a God who upholds the dignity and hope of the poor and a Savior who loved the little children. We must save all our children and not punish the disadvantaged. We follow the One who called us to be peacemakers and gave his life to reconcile a broken humanity. We must stop the violence that has overtaken the nation and address its root causes in the distorted spiritual values and unjust social structures for which we all share complicity. We have a faith that invites us to conversion. We must revive the lapsed virtues of personal responsibility and character, and repent for our social sins of racism, sexism, and poverty. We love a Creator who calls for justice

and stewardship. We must begin to judge our economic and environmental habits and policies by their impact on the next generation, rather than just our own. We are compelled to a lifestyle of service and compassion. We must seek healing from the materialism that has made us less caring and more selfish, isolated us from one another, enshrined the power of money over our political processes, wounded our natural world, and poisoned the hearts of our children—rich and poor alike. We are led by our faith into community. We must rejuvenate the moral values and political will to rebuild our disintegrating family systems, our shattered neighborhoods, and our divided nation.

While opposing abortion on theological grounds and concerned with teenage pregnancy and the breakdown of families, Call for Renewal offers practical solutions that can be appealing to many social workers. The coalition asks: Why can't we be committed to public policies that discourage abortion and actively seek alternatives that save lives, while fostering an environment that protects the equality of women and the well-being of all children? Why can't pro-life and pro-choice people work together to reduce dramatically the number of abortions by targeting teenage pregnancy and adoption reform, for example, instead of endlessly debating a constitutional amendment that is dividing people in our society?

Similarly, Call for Renewal seeks support for traditional two-parent families, but in a way that does not scapegoat or discriminate against gay and lesbian citizens. It also seeks a middle ground regarding poverty by avoiding the all-or-nothing government debate. Instead, the coalition suggests that new partnerships between nonprofit organizations and governments on all levels are likely to create the kind of civil society that will solve many of the nation's social problems.

The coalition seeks to meet its agenda in three ways: (1) by organizing new coalitions that bring together churches and service providers, groups that have not worked together before and that now realize the need for unity to deal with the current situation; (2) by advocating state legislatures to work with churches and service providers in developing welfare plans, so that the least-restrictive rules are implemented under the new federal law; and (3) by providing service. With regard to the last, Call for Renewal acknowledges that although churches and charities cannot, and should not, fill the legitimate roles of government, there are many instances in which support is needed. Thus, Call for Renewal encourages opening churches for shelters and soup kitchens, establishing day care and after-school programs, and assisting in job location.

One activity of Call for Renewal is indicative of the coalition's potential importance as a collaborator with social work. As the provisions of the 1996 welfare legislation went into effect, tens of thousands of Americans lost food stamps on March 1, 1997. Hundreds of thousands more were cut off as of April 1, 1997. On March 5, some three hundred D.C.-area homeless people and their advocates, led by Call to Renewal, met on the U.S. Capitol lawn for a soup and sandwich meal, a press conference, and a prayer service. Their message to the Congress and the religious community was that the people being discarded by society cannot be allowed to simply disappear. As Christians and as members of society, members of the religious community therefore have an obligation both to serve and to witness for justice.

FOUNDATION INVOLVEMENT

A historical trend in the United States is for foundations and private corporations to experiment with social arrangements before they are debated and often embraced by the public and the political system. In line with this tradition, we present an overview of several initiatives by major foundations that focus on the interface between religion and society. In 1993, for example, the Robert Wood Johnson Foundation launched a program called Faith in Action. The program provided $25,000 in start-up funds to each of some nine hundred interfaith volunteer programs across the country. In its first phase, the program assisted coalitions of community congregations in developing local caregiver projects, based on a model Interfaith Volunteer Care Givers Project developed by the Robert Wood Johnson Foundation in 1983.

Faith in Action, funded for $23 million, enlists volunteers from religious-based groups and trains them to assist people with disabilities who otherwise might need nursing home care. The project is helping numerous people maintain their independence despite chronic health conditions. The volunteers assist in shopping, arranging/negotiating health services, providing social contacts, helping with home repairs, and linking the person to his or her spiritual community. The program is open only to interfaith coalitions that are incorporated and have their own tax-exempt status under section 501(c)(3) of the IRS Code.

The Lilly Endowment, a foundation in Indianapolis, has long been concerned with religion and has provided many grants to congregations and theological seminaries. In the past ten years, however, this foundation has been heavily supporting projects that seek to assess the role of religion and religious organizations in enhancing the quality of American life. For example, it has funded projects to assess congregational roles in time of crisis, as in the Los Angeles riots, and the impact of changing neighborhoods on local congregations. In a way, Lilly is moving from "pure" support of religion to the interface of religion and its role in society. This is the reverse of the course that the Robert Wood Johnson Foundation has taken. Originally, this foundation was concerned with health needs, but now it is focusing on identifying religious communities to meet the needs. Yet the two foundations find themselves in the same social domain: supporting initiatives that use religious-based groups to solve human problems in an era of decreased public concern.

The Brookings Institute in Washington, D.C., announced in 1996 an initiative focusing on civil society, especially the role of the government in promoting a civil society. The role of churches was to be part of this initiative, as E. J. Dionne Jr. (1996) noted in the *Brookings Review*:

> Virtually everyone engaged in the civic revival debate underscores the central role churches play in dealing with neighborhood breakdown and problem such as crime and teen pregnancy. Can government help churches carry out their civic role? What First Amendment problems would be raised? Would government engagement with churches limit their autonomy and flexibility? The issue is a tricky one, but in poor neighborhoods, government help can be essential to the success of church projects.   (p. 3)

Such an acknowledgment from one of the country's most respected think tanks is a powerful indication that the balance of welfare provision is at the brink of radical change. The final outcome is still unclear, but increased involvement by the religious community seems a certainty.

Some foundations see the religious community as a vehicle for solving the problems in inner cities and are assisting religious-based groups in sponsoring housing and economic development projects. One example is the Lilly Endowment's Religious Institutions as Partners in Community-Based Development Program, which provides these groups with financial support, information, and networking. Another is the Ford Foundation's support for church-based social justice initiatives (including community development) through the National Congress of Black Churches. The Kellogg Foundation supported projects in which Detroit churches and local religious-based organizations helped low-income families get off welfare and obtain jobs. Finally,

Pew Charitable Trusts have made a large grant to World Vision, the evangelical agency, to foster housing ministries.

The time has come, then, for us to summarize our arguments and state what can be, and should be, done in the future to assure a better and greater array of social and communal services. Although the new social welfare picture in the United States includes government cutbacks, fewer federal standards, and enormous local variations, it also identifies several important trends. As this chapter indicates, the trendsetters in our society—journalists, politicians, foundations, and social leaders—are sending us the same message. That message is that the public views the government's handling of welfare as inept, ineffective, and demeaning and that there is a groundswell of support for social services provided in an efficient, effective, and humane manner. In other words, there is growing support for the type of social services provision that is construed to be the hallmark of the religious community.

The body of evidence presented here strongly indicates that social services in the next generation will largely be provided by, or in collaboration with, religious-based service organizations. As we have shown in chapters 7 to 11, involvement by the religious community is already impressive.

The expected increased involvement of the religious community in social services provision will differ from what is being done now. It will not be merely a matter of more projects being contracted out to religious-based organizations, such as Catholic Charities or Jewish Family and Children's Services, as it was in the 1980s. We predict the change will be much more extensive. We will see more paradenominational organizations and local religious coalitions providing services on their own terms. We will see service delivery with a religious message. We will see both more evangelical fervor and attempts by many religious providers to help people empower themselves via spiritual salvation funded by governmental grants and contracts or vouchers. We will see religious-based social services hiring qualified social workers and serving as sites for field placement of students of social work. We will see all this because church-state boundaries are becoming more blurred, and the public is ready to have the government support the religious community in doing what everyone else has failed to do. In sum, a new type of religious-based social services has emerged. They will be larger in scope and more open and public about the religious message they want to bring to the community. Equally important, these religious organizations will have the resources, financial as well as legitimacy, to become a force in the field that social work has long dominated.

As we have previously noted, our aim in this book has been to document (1) the massive involvement of the religious community in social services provision and (2) the failure of social work to acknowledge this involvement. We believe that we have successfully documented these two issues. What is left now is our argument that cooperation between these two communities is a preferred alternative to hostility and shunning of each other. In the next chapter we will make the case that, to better serve those in need, the religious community and the social work community should join forces. Neither should yield to the other's values and ideology, but both can engage in a limited partnership that eventually will result in better, larger, and more varied social services in the community.

As we conclude this book, the spirit of the newer deal is gaining momentum. In May 1999, then Vice President Al Gore spoke at a meeting with the Atlanta chapter of the Salvation Army. In his speech he outlined a plan charting a new course that would make the social services delivered by the religious community an integral part of the American public welfare system. He promised his audience that if he were elected president, the voice of faith-based organizations would be integral to policies in his administration and Charitable Choice would be expanded to include drug treatment, homelessness services, and youth-violence prevention. His opponent, Bill Bradley, identified religious groups as key players in his committee to make America a more "civil" society. Moving this agenda forward is also Texas govenor George W. Bush, who supports applying the Charitable Choice spirit to the Texas social service system. It seems likely that whoever becomes the next president in the new millennium will call for a significant but limited partnership between religion and social work—a newer deal.

CHAPTER 13

TOWARD A LIMITED PARTNERSHIP FOR
A NEWER DEAL

Before we present our conclusions, a few words about religion in other Western democracies are warranted as a means to understanding the complexity of the religious community's involvement in social services provision. The main function and top priority of organized religion is to provide theological, spiritual, and ritual services. Thus religious organizations offer a variety of religious services, such as worship services, religious education, baptismal and/or other rites of acceptance, marriages, and funerals. In many European countries, these are the only services that congregations provide to their members. The second priority of organized religion is system maintenance. Regardless of location and denomination, most congregations need resources to maintain themselves. Building and staff management demand expenditures of time and money by the congregation. Social services can become a priority only when the basic priorities of religious services and maintenance have been met.

In many Western European democracies, even those that are most socialistic, there is no church-state separation as there is in the United States. In these countries, certain religious groups are "established" and supported by the state. These countries levy taxes or allocate funds from the general revenues to finance the operation, salaries, and buildings of religious communities (Monsma and Soper 1997). In many of these countries, the state often employs many of the clergy and provides major funding for religious congregations. Long before the Civil War, state support for the church was also common in the United States, but since 1830 American religious congregations have been expected to finance themselves. After "disestablishment," congregants bore the cost of religious services, and church leaders had to foster an environment in which members willingly provided the means to pay for the clergy and maintain the building (Warner 1993). Thus, in America the clergy are expected not only to bring the Word of God but also to establish a community of members who voluntarily support the congregation.

Another difference is that European congregations are not expected to provide welfare services because these services are both mandated and provided by the state (Wuthnow 1988). While many European congregations do have social programs, these are generally for members only. If a program is for the benefit of the community, it is expected that the state will assume full responsibility for its operation once it reaches a sufficient level of maturity and growth (Harris 1995).

It is important for any discussion of religious-based social services to distinguish between *social ministry* (a way of serving the community) and *social mission/gospel mission* (a proselytizing vehicle). At times the two may overlap, as when a congregation helps others as a means of spreading the Gospel and saving souls. It is also the case when members heed a call to practice their faith by helping others in need. With few exceptions, most religious groups engage in social and community service provision as a means to witness their faith, fulfill religious teaching and beliefs, or simply "do good" for others in the community. The desire to save souls and spread the Gospel solely through social services provision has proved to be both ineffective and too expensive. It is important to note that efforts at proselytization are minimal when compared with the volume of social services provided by religious-based organizations. This being the case, the religious community and the social work community are more closely aligned than they may appear. While social workers should not embrace the religious motivation, they should embrace any manifestation of caring for people in need as a potential for an effective coalition.

The liberal tradition holds that religion is a private matter that should be excluded from the public and formal spheres. This tradition also calls for government neutrality with regard to religion. Government should neither assist nor hamper religious gatherings and practices, as long as they do not pose a threat to others. Nevertheless, as we have argued in this book, organized religion does have a public face that is very important to the quality of life in our society. Although we have focused only on social services provided under religious auspices, the religious community is also active in providing health services and education, ranging from kindergartens to universities. As such, the religious community cannot be kept outside the public realm. It must be considered as an important actor in our social life and a major contributor to social capital and civic society. Despite all the attempts to separate church and state in the United States, the two are quite interwoven.

We would like to believe that church and state can be fully separated. How-ever, this is not the case. In a country that calls upon the religious community to do more for the welfare of strangers and that willingly pays religious-based groups to do so, church-state separation is merely an ideal. Politicians, as doc-umented in chapter 12, recognize that the separation does not exist. Managers of religious-based social services also know it. After all, more than 50 percent of the budgets of Catholic Charities, Jewish Family and Children's Services, and Lutheran Social Ministries, to name just a few agencies, comes from the public coffers. It is now time for the profession of social work, its leaders, its scholars, and its practitioners to acknowledge the same: the church–social work separation is unwarranted.

If the religious community is to be even more deeply involved in social serv-ices provision, then we must learn how to cooperate with organized religion to improve the lot of those whom we serve and whose interests we represent. We must apply a more pluralistic model, one that enables both sides to maintain their ideological and value stances while collaborating where possible and when beneficial for both.

These are not easy times for either social work or organized religion. Social work and social service agencies have been under attack since the Reagan years of the early 1980s. The religious community is facing a membership decline in traditional denominations, the rise of mega-churches, and the increased pop-ularity of nonmainstream Protestant churches. Thus, the two communities are in a state of flux that could facilitate a new form of cooperation between them. Despite differences of opinion, each camp should acknowledge that there is indeed another camp and should objectively weigh the advantages of cooperation in meeting mutual goals.

THE COMPLEXITY OF THE ISSUE: A CASE EXAMPLE

The complicated partnership between social work and religion can best be understood by a case involving Pastor Wiley Drake. In July 1997, Judge Ran-dall L. Wilkinson ordered Pastor Drake and his First Southern Baptist Church in Buena Park, California, to stop housing homeless people in the church patio. Since the city did not provide services for the homeless in this area, the congregation had decided to provide shelter and food. The judge ruled that the church patio did not comply with city codes for sleeping space. He told the pastor and the church members that they could take the homeless to their own homes to sleep, but they could not let them sleep at the church. Pastor Drake and his congregants decided to fight city hall. They maintained it was their duty as Christians to care for the needy and that the church patio was better suited to sleeping than the streets were. In this case, most social workers would have sided with Pastor Drake and First Southern Baptist Church in their efforts to serve the neediest members of our society.

However, in discussing Pastor Drake the activist, we are also discussing Pastor Drake the flamboyant preacher who gained the national spotlight in 1997 as the instigator of the Southern Baptist Convention's boycott of the Walt Disney Company. The boycott was triggered by the company's provision of benefits to same-sex couples and by objections to the content of some of its entertainment products. In this case, it is safe to assume that the mainstream social work profession would have opposed Pastor Drake's position as reactionary. The National Association of Social Workers Code of Ethics clearly states that any discrimination on the basis of sexual orientation is forbidden and should be protested.

In both cases, the pastor and the church were acting out of religious conviction. Yet their convictions led them to actions that were consistent with mainstream social work ethics in one case, but contradictory in the other. How, then, do we work with religious groups whose convictions and motivations conflict with the social work code of ethics? The answer is: limited partnership. By this, we mean a partnership that is based on service compatible with the other's position. It is a difficult proposition, and in this chapter we will elaborate on ways this limited partnership can be achieved.

WHAT DO OUR FINDINGS MEAN?

What is evident from our study is that religious-based social services are mushrooming and that this new reality needs to be understood. The desire of believers, regardless of creed, to affirm their beliefs by service to others has assumed special significance in the era of devolution. This desire merits broader consideration because of its relevance to religious-based services provision and the future of the American welfare system.

Services provision by today's religious community continues a centuries-old tradition of service by religious organizations in the United States. This voluntary system of service can be likened to the underground economy, little of which is ever officially counted and even less known. Had it not been for the wide divergence in religious and secular approaches to service, perhaps religion and social work would better understand each other. This is certainly true in the academy: most social welfare scholars do not study religion, and most scholars of religion do not study social welfare and services. Consequently, we currently have little if any knowledge of how the social policy of the Reagan era changed the relationships between the sectarian and secular realms of social service.

ORGANIZATIONAL IMPLICATIONS

Our findings indicate that, as far as social services provision is concerned, religious congregations and organizations are not solely member-serving organizations, but rather are other-serving organizations committed to improving the quality of life in their communities. This commitment extends to matters of cost and income. No matter how conservative the calculations, we found that the costs to the congregations (in providing both space and programs) considerably exceed what they charge. In many cases, congregations open their doors to worthy community groups and causes at little or no charge, despite the fact that building use involves wear and tear and utility costs. Rent is rarely charged, lest it compromise the congregation's charitable organization tax status. Thus, the provision of these services is clearly not to benefit members financially. It seems that giving is as important for the members of the congregation as it is for those benefiting from it. The ancient traditions of *tzedakah*, the Good Samaritan, and *zakat* are alive and well.

Chaves (1993) underscored the complexity of religious-based social services by distinguishing between agency authority (such as the bureaucratic authority of the Methodist Board of Pensions or soup kitchen advisory board) and religious authority (such as the prerogatives of a bishop or a parish pastor). The latter represents the mission of the agency, while the former is akin to a board of trustees whose concern is efficiency and accountability. Chaves argued that the preponderance of agency-structure authority has increased in this century and that the major denominations now have essentially the same agency structure regardless of polity. Religious-based social services are, for the most part, willing to be accountable to both agency and religious authorities, even though they are often in conflict. For example, the government may pressure a religious based social service to care for the homeless without requiring it to participate in public prayer, while religious authorities may require prayer, viewing it as essential for social services provision that transforms people's lives. The agency authority is the one with which social work can easily link. The religious authority is the one with which social workers must come to terms regarding their own values and principles. While this is not always easy, understanding this duality of authority is essential to cooperation between social work and the religious community, since a misunderstanding of the dual-authority structure can lead to discord. If religious organizations are coerced by agency authority to adhere to bureaucratic standards, then they may well choose to devote themselves to living their faith, rather than to expressing it through expanded social programs.

Further research should include the study of organizational behaviors and management of religious-based social service agencies. This knowledge will allow social workers, administrators, and policy makers to determine the types of programs and processes that will facilitate collaboration with religious-based organizations. A clearer understanding of the dual structure of religious social services will also help to resolve conflicts between the two authorities. Such knowledge should be incorporated into the macro practice curriculum so that future cohorts of social workers will be prepared for effective practice within and with religious-based organizations.

SOCIAL IMPLICATIONS

Putnam (1995) has asserted that the decline of America's voluntary associations has led to declines in our social capital. While the numbers of fraternal orders and bowling leagues have indeed declined, we hold, along with others (cf. Ammerman 1997; Hall 1996) that Putnam has failed to acknowledge the rise in the scale and scope of organizations not accounted for in current theories of social capital. Among them are large-scale social movement organizations, government-sponsored community organizations, and religious congregations. Nor has he acknowledged their contribution to social capital. Furthermore, as the government continues to abdicate its role in the provision of social services, voluntary organizations and religious congregations in particular are attempting to fill the growing demand for such services. Religious organizations have traditions of civic engagement that produce social capital. This civic engagement, in turn, improves the quality of life in communities and integration of social networks (Greeley 1997; Verba, Schlozman, and Brady 1995). In addition, the assets held by congregations are made available for the maintenance and development of community life. In this respect, we highlight John Orr's (1998) findings in four Los Angeles neighborhoods. He reported that "there is an average of 35 religious congregations and 12.5 religiously-affiliated nonprofit corporations per square mile, far more than the number of gasoline stations, liquor stores, and supermarkets combined" (p. 3). In our study of West Philadelphia, we found in a territory that is estimated to be between six and nine square miles 321 places of worship, a number that is quite similar to that found by Orr in Los Angeles.

ECONOMIC IMPLICATIONS

Making a congregation's space, or that of any other religious group, available to the larger community is much more than a real estate transaction. The sharing of sacred space with the community is a public expression of faith that also gives the congregation the opportunity to be a good citizen and a good neighbor. Holding meetings and services in sacred places gives the groups who hold the meetings a sense of special importance and higher purpose. It is not a coincidence that numerous day care centers, Twelve Step groups, and Scout troops meet in congregational spaces. They do so because the property is available and is perceived as "pure" and positive. Furthermore, congregations provide space to others either at no cost or nominal cost, usually far below market value.

Religious groups not only support community agencies with volunteers, money, meeting space, and other resources, but they also run their own on-site projects, which they fund through individual donations, in-kind contributions, or their operating budgets. Most recipients of service are people from the community rather than members of the congregation. In sum, many congregations both practice and pay for what they preach.

Many religious-based organizations have little or no interest in obtaining public funds for their programs. Congregations fear the risks and regulations that accompany public funding. Just as social work may be reluctant to cooperate with religious organizations, these organizations may be just as reluctant to work with public funds. Religious-based social services are initiated by the clergy or lay leaders, often in response to the changing social environment and the decrease in public services. Nevertheless, they view these services as an expression of faith and not as social service per se. Social workers would do well to recognize that they can benefit the communities they serve by learning how to practice in and with this social, institutional, and religious-based environment.

POLICY IMPLICATIONS

Despite methodological drawbacks in generalizing from our own studies and others we have cited, we believe these findings are strong indicators of an emerging trend. They provide a solid basis for theory development and testing. Although our findings do not constitute the entire picture, they provide a distinct idea of what the final picture may look like once all the pieces are in place. We have, for example, identified an important aspect of today's urban reality as it pertains to social services and religion. Two things are urgently needed. One is for academicians to come to grips with this issue and begin to study it more systematically. The other is for policy makers to stop viewing the religious community as the magic cure-all for ailing local human service systems.

America has witnessed the first two stages in the reshaping of the welfare state. The first stage was marked by budget cuts, mostly under the Reagan administration, and the move for greater local nonprofit involvement in social services provision, mostly during the Bush administration. The second stage was marked by further budget cuts and the targeting of the religious community for greater involvement in local service provision. The latter is evident in legislative proposals such as those sponsored by Representative Lazio and Senator Ashcroft in the mid-1990s, and the use of the political bully pulpit to elicit more service from the religious community, as Governor Fordice has done in Mississippi. In all this, one fact stands out: since 1980, the religious community has become an even bigger player in the delivery of local services than it was prior to the New Deal of the 1930s.

The question is not whether congregations in particular and the religious community as a whole should or should not get involved. The question is how much more can they do? The religious community already carries the double burden of paying for upkeep, security, and maintenance of its properties and making them available to its communities. Grettenberger and Hovmand (1997) noted that there is a limit to what even the most willing congregations can do. Yet politicians continue to push for even more religious-based social services provision as a way to reduce public expenditures and cure all social ills. Meanwhile, many local authorities are adding fuel to the fire by challenging the tax-exempt status of religious charities and threatening to levy property taxes on them. Eventually someone will have to give way. The reason is that at a time of public retrenchment, the religious community has taken on new and expanded importance. It is important to the welfare of local citizens and the careers of politicians who see religious congregations as the means to rejuvenate morality, reduce public expenditures, increase private initiative, and provide programs that work. Yet our social problems are far too complicated, and our system of public and private nonprofit welfare services is too structured and too complex. To expect a major redesign that would make the religious community the main provider of the nation's social services does not mean that the present system should not be changed. It should. That does not mean that religious-based social services will not expand their roles in local service design and delivery. They will.

It does mean that future social welfare historians who compare the social service system of the 1990s pre-welfare reform to that of the 2040s are going to find dramatic differences. They will find that today's trends in social welfare became the norm, paving the way for a new era of even greater devolution and increased religious involvement. They will find that the local system became more responsible for solving, managing, and preventing problems. What they will not find is the religious community serving as the major provider of these problem-solving programs. They will find the religious community highly involved in the provision of social services. The religious community already has enormous social commitments. It provides places for communal worship, helps its own members, offers its facilities to the community, supports community agencies, and gives money and service nationally and internationally. It is unimaginable that the religious community would shift this organizational focus to become the linchpin in the nation's social service system. Religious-based service providers will grow in importance, and they will employ many human service professionals. They will be an integral part in the *community of care* all over America, and they will sit at the table when welfare is discussed. Nevertheless, the public sector will still need to play the leading role in financing and directing social services provision. What is not clear is the role that social work will take in this future and whether public support will be further eroded.

Governor Fordice's Faith and Families program is based on the Reagan/Bush ideology that calls for changing the welfare system from a federal structure to a state structure with a local voluntary delivery system. From the viewpoint of Mississippi's statehouse, such a system is already in place: a statewide web of 5,500 community-based religious organizations that are committed to helping those in need. From our viewpoint, before any state can put such a program in place, every religious-based social service organization should be: (a) asked whether it wants to participate; (b) assessed as to its capability for service provision; (c) reviewed for the types of practical support it can offer; and (d) queried as to whether a requirement for such support would hinge on the recipient's religious affiliation or the lack thereof. Such an assessment in Mississippi, for example, would have provided some sobering guidance for Governor Fordice, whose program has encountered numerous barriers and resistance.

The religious community finds itself in a precarious situation in the midst of devolution. Suddenly and without being asked, it is cast as the last hope for social services delivery. If politicians reduce the fiscal outlay for public sector services by relying only or mostly on religious resources, then social services offered by the religious community will have to expand exponentially. This will put extreme pressure on congregations and other religious organizations to contribute more volunteers, more space, and more money, which they may or may not have. The irony is that if voluntary organizations are pressured by the government, either directly or indirectly, to do something beyond their missions, then these organizations are no longer voluntary. As small as the Mississippi numbers are, they are indeed a wake-up call to social work. The message is not only that the religious community provides welfare services but also that the government is looking to the religious community for more help in providing those services.

The religious community cannot solve the social problems that plague our nation. Conversely, social problems cannot be solved without the active participation of the religious community. If the immediate future is more like what we see now, that is, the religious community as a silent partner in the social service arena, then many changes must occur if we are to maximize the societal benefits from such participation. In the following section, we list our recommendations for a limited partnership between social work organizations and religious-based organizations. These include our recommendations for leaders of religious-based social services, leaders of social service agencies and the social work community, and the broader community.

RECOMMENDATIONS TO LEADERS OF RELIGIOUS-BASED SOCIAL SERVICES

The transition into the twenty-first century opens an era in the relationships between religion and state that we have labeled the Newer Deal. Religious leaders find themselves in the midst of vast changes, most of which they do not control. We call on them to collaborate with social work and public social services as a means to better the lives of people in the community. We recommend to leaders of religious-based social services that they:

1. Assess and determine whether their religious mission is likely to suffer from this new welfare emphasis that is often carried out with public funds and under public scrutiny. Given that government involvement in welfare provision will decrease and that welfare programs will devolve to religious-based organizations and other community-based organizations, leaders of religious-based agencies should carefully assess whether their organizations

are suited to the task. Many may assume this greater social responsibility only to find that they have lost members because of dissent over this issue.

2. Take pride in their service to others and "let their light shine" by publicizing their work and achievements. The impressive role played by religious organizations in social services provision is a well-kept secret that needs to be told. More publicity and public recognition of their accomplishments will make society at large, the media, and politicians more aware of what is being done and will give members of these religious organizations a sense of pride in what they do.

3. Prepare for the challenges of increased responsibility in services provision. This includes review of their organization's capability for expansion (with or without additional fiscal resources), assessment of emerging needs, and strategic planning to meet these needs.

4. Form ecumenical and other broad coalitions as a means of meeting both the increasing involvement of religious-based organizations in the welfare arena and the public expectations of even more service. Intervention by a single religious group may be helpful on a small scale, but the challenges facing religious-based social organizations call for coordination and shared knowledge and resources. There are already local initiatives of urban ministry and local coalitions in action across the nation. These should continue to develop and expand.

5. Identify potential areas of conflict between religious doctrines and state regulations, with respect to accepting public funds. These include such issues as federal hiring guidelines, fiscal and program accountability, tax liability, public reporting, tracking of services, program evaluation, nonsectarian service focus, and inclusion of religious symbols and rituals when providing services such as shelter, soup kitchens, skill training, and the like.

6. Ensure that theological seminaries emphasize issues of social ministry and prepare their graduates to establish, operate, and/or supervise such programs. There are numerous resources available for organizing social ministry, and these should come to the attention of new clergy in their formative years at theological seminaries. Courses should be developed on these topics, and social service professionals should be invited to seminaries to lecture and

talk with future clergy on urban ministries and collaboration between social service agencies and religious groups.

7. Become well versed in the government's new welfare policies so that they can advocate knowledgeably and successfully for people in need and take a proactive role in shaping and designing the new face of local community and social services. As we noted in chapter 12, the welfare reform law has opened the door for religious involvement in social services delivery, while increasing public expectations for such involvement. Religious leaders should study this law carefully, become knowledgeable about its implementation and the successes and failures of other groups across the country, and use it to provide better services for needy people in their communities.

8. Contract with reputable researchers to assess outcomes of their programs so they can identify, understand, and replicate successful practices. Data from religious sources are often discredited because of unorthodox methodology. Religious-based social services would do well to employ social scientists with the credentials to evaluate their work so that their data will be considered reliable. Such openness to standards of social science methods will enhance the credibility of these organizations and will substantiate their case for better outcomes.

9. Make it clear that their services are open to all individuals, families, and groups in the community, regardless of their religious affiliation and their interest in salvation.

10. Send local clergy and congregational lay leaders to study methods of direct service, community organizing, and advocacy in national foundations such as the Industrial Areas Foundation or the Gamaliel Fund in Chicago or in schools of social work that specialize in community practice.

11. Be politically wise and aware. Religious-based social services are currently the ace in the hole for local and national politicians. However, politicians focus exclusively on the role of the religious community as a direct-service provider. When the religious community assumes the role of social change agent and advocate, politicians may be less happy and may try to block the religious community's influence and limit its social service involvement. Leaders of the religious community should be aware of possible consequences and make sure that their services can withstand political attacks.

RECOMMENDATIONS TO LEADERS OF SOCIAL SERVICE AGENCIES AND THE SOCIAL WORK COMMUNITY

We have argued that the social arrangements of the 1930s-era New Deal are being transformed. We are now in a new era, which we call the Newer Deal. The Newer Deal calls for a renewed and limited partnership between social work and the religious community. Such a partnership will, however, necessitate some key changes for social work as a profession and for secular social service organizations. To maximize the societal benefits from the active participation of the religious community in social services provision, we recommend to leaders of the social service agencies and social work community that they:

1. Teach students of social work and related disciplines about the increasing pluralism of social welfare provision and the role of the religious community in the delivery of local social services. The social work curriculum should include courses on practice management in and with religious organizations, fieldwork sites and practice modules that prepare students to work more effectively within religious-based social service organizations, and joint programs of social work and theological studies.

2. Form coalitions with religious-based social services and other religious groups when planning/carrying out community projects as a means of increasing both the resource base of the programs and their legitimacy. Churches, religious organizations, and paradenominational organizations traditionally have the trust of local residents and represent a wide range of people in the community.

3. Develop research opportunities/rewards for social work academicians to study the role of the religious-based social services sector. As noted in chapter 3, too little social work research and publication has been devoted to religious-based social services provision. This void needs to be filled so that a new body of knowledge will be created and made available to future students and practitioners.

4. Enable schools of social work to develop innovative practice programs with religious-based social services without fear of violating the accreditation guidelines of the Council on Social Work Education.

5. Help religious congregations and other religious groups identify, redis-cover, actualize, and/or expand their historical tradition of service to others. Many religious organizations can expand or reorganize their programs with the assistance of professional social workers. These organizations have the willingness and the resources but often lack experienced leadership.

6. Facilitate more employment opportunities for graduates through train-ing programs and consultations with religious-based social services, which is one service sector likely to expand. Career opportunities in religious-based social services should be highlighted by schools of social work, and managers of religious organizations should be invited to present their work and agency to graduating classes.

7. Respect the religious values of social work students; allow them the free-dom to express, integrate, and apply their religious values to practice; and help them set boundaries between the individual self and the professional self.

RECOMMENDATIONS TO THE BROADER COMMUNITY SOCIETY

To maximize the societal benefits from the active participation of the religious community in social service provision, we recommend to research institu-tions, foundations, media, and the public-at-large that they:

1. Understand that the new realities of service provision and their role in society require new kinds of partnerships between secular scholars and scholars of religion. No one in academic circles can underestimate the difficulty of form-ing new communities of inquiry. As we noted previously, most secular scholars rarely study religious institutions and activities, and they tend to treat religion as marginal. Scholars of religion, with considerable justification, fear the reduc-tionist tendency of the secular social sciences. Yet each should venture into the other's territory, and such partnerships should be encouraged by funders.

2. Consider carefully the impact of religious social services delivery on state/church separation over time. Attempts to legalize public prayer are only one example of the further blurring of the boundaries.

3. Assure that the eligibility of nonmainstream religions and denominations to participate in and receive funding for social services provision is protected.

It is unclear how supportive the state and the public will be when sects and controversial religious groups seek to join the circle of social services providers.

4. Engage in a national debate as to the extent of the government's responsibility for the welfare of the disadvantaged in society. If the government abdicates its public responsibility in full, then social chaos will result, and the religious community will be made the fig leaf to cover up this human tragedy.

We have documented the long-standing and very strong connection between the religious community and the social service community. We now call for more research on the aspects of the relationship between the two systems that have resulted in the current rift. Social work and the religious community must work together in mending this breach if we are going to amass resources in the most effective ways on behalf of those in need. The old hostility and envy between secular and sectarian social services should be eliminated, and joint projects in both service provision and advocacy should gain a renewed priority. These collaborations are to be limited to the social services arena, and neither side is expected to approve of the other's morality or values.

Social work today is no longer a semi-profession; it is a strong and recognized profession. Religious-based social services have also evolved to a more professional status. Sectarian service organizations today employ professional social workers, many of whom receive third-party payments. In North Carolina, for example, pastoral counselors are eligible for third-party payments either directly or under the supervision of psychiatrists. Given the increased attention to the mind-body connection in well-being, it may be only a matter of time before the *DSM-IV* lists "spiritual crisis" as a reimbursable diagnosis. In this connection, it is interesting to note that the *DSM* only recently distinguished religious and spiritual problems as a category distinct from any mental disorder (Lukoff, Lu, and Turner 1992). We mention this not out of irreverence but to underscore the point that both the religious and the social service systems have been evolving over time and their approaches to service provision are converging. In some instances, such as the United Way's funding of sectarian agencies, the two systems are now inseparable.

How all this will play out in the academic world remains to be seen. On the one hand, secular scholars resist studying religious institutions and treat religion as marginal. On the other hand, scholars of religion, with considerable justification, fear the reductionism of the secular social sciences. Nevertheless, if devolution continues to translate into a convergence of secular and sectarian service concerns at the local level, it is our opinion that public and private funders will be increasingly interested in identifying and improving the inter-connections between social work and religion. As the pressure on research faculty to obtain external funding increases, we may begin to see some of the disciplinary and theoretical walls of the academy come tumbling down in favor of interdisciplinary applied research. As a consequence, the reluctance of social work to acknowledge its religious roots may be a thing of the past, and its strong footing in both the agency world and the academy may be an oppor-tunity to lead the way in studying and improving the links between the social work profession and the religious community.

Making study topics on religious-based social services more acceptable in social work includes acceptance of papers for academic conferences, soliciting funds by schools of social work from religious sources, seeking faculty mem-bers with expertise in this domain, and encouraging doctoral students to write their dissertations in this field as a means of preparing a new breed of social work researchers with expertise in the field.

Social work education should also pay attention to the interconnections between social work and education. Omitting any references to religious-based organizations in the curriculum can be compared to viewing Leonardo da Vinci's *Mona Lisa* sans her nose. The hair, the face, even the famous smile would still be there. Yet a necessary piece would be missing from the overall picture, resulting in a distorted proportion and meaning. For this reason, we strongly call for full acknowledgment of religious-based social services in social welfare and introduction to social work courses.

We are clearly in the last stages of the post–New Deal era. The welfare pro-grams are shrinking, service development is taking new forms, and religious-based social services are fast becoming every politician's panacea for social ills. If social work is to have any say in how service should be configured at local levels, then members of the field will have to continue what we have begun here: an examination of social work's relationship to religion. It is most important that we develop more research and course content on this important issue, for, as Steinfels (1995:11) reminds us, "the new wisdom in Washington is this: religious institutions, along with other charitable organizations, can provide the nation with a social and economic safety net as well as a moral and spiritual one."

The big question is, Where is social work in all of this? As the late Roy Lubove used to remind his students, social policy is complex despite the simplemindedness of its formulators. It is our responsibility as social work educators, scholars, and practitioners to see that social work charts a wise course in formulating future social policy.

REFERENCES

Abell, Aaron Ignatius. 1943. *The Urban Impact on American Protestantism, 1865–1900*. Cambridge: Harvard University Press.

Acklin, Marvin W., Earl C. Brown, and Paul A. Mauger. 1983. The role of religious values in coping with cancer. *Journal of Religion and Health* 22:322–33.

Adlaf, Edward M. and Reginald G. Smart. 1985. Drug use and religious affiliation, feelings, and behaviour. *British Journal of Addictions* 80:163–71.

Ahlstrom, Sydney E. 1972. *A Religious History of the American People*. New Haven: Yale University Press.

Alabastro, Ruben. 1997. Filipinos march: No 2nd term for Ramos. *USA Today* (September 22):7a.

Allen-Meares, Paula. 1989. Adolescent sexuality and premature parenthood: Role of the black church in prevention. *Journal of Social Work and Sexuality* 8 (1):133–42.

Altman, Dennis. 1982. *The Homosexualization of America*. New York: St. Martin's Press.

Ammerman, Nancy Tatum. 1996. Bowling Together: Congregations and the American Civic Order. Seventeenth Annual University Lecture in Religion, Arizona State University, Tempe, February 26.

———. 1997. *Congregation and Community*. New Brunswick, N.J.: Rutgers University Press.

Ammerman, Nancy Tatum and Wade Clark Roof. 1995. *Work, Family, and Religion in Contemporary Society*. New York: Routledge.

Amoateng, Acheampong Yaw and Stephan J. Bahr. 1986. Religion, family, and adolescent drug use. *Sociological Perspectives* 29:53–76.

Anderson, George M. 1994. The Little Brothers and Sisters of the Gospel. *America* 171 (October 22):4–11.

Associated Press. 1996. Clinton asks churches to hire welfare receivers. *Greensboro News and Record* 106 (September 7):A1–A2.

Association of Theological Schools. 1993. *The Fact Boook on Theological Education*. Pittsburgh: Association of Theological Schools.

Axinn, June and Herman Levin. 1992. *Social Welfare: A History of the American Response to Need*. 3d ed. White Plains, N.Y.: Longman.

Bachmann, Ernest Theodore. 1955. *Churches and Social Welfare*. Vol. 1, The Activation Concern. New York: National Council of the Churches of Christ in the USA.

———. 1956. *Churches and Social Welfare*. Vol. 3, The Emerging Perspective. New York: National Council of the Churches of Christ in the USA.

Bacon, Leonard. 1832. *The Christian Doctrine of Stewardship in Respect to Property*. New Haven: Nathan Whiting.

Baer, Hans A. 1993. The limited empowerment of women in black spiritual churches: An alternative vehicle to religious leadership. *Sociology of Religion* 54:65–82.

Baer, Hans A. and M. Singer. 1992. *African-American Religion in the Twentieth Century*. Nashville: University of Tennessee Press.

Bainbridge, William S. 1989. The religious ecology of deviance. *American Sociological Review* 54:288–95.

Baltzell, E. Digby. 1958. *Philadelphia Gentlemen: The Making of a National Upper Class*. New York: Free Press.

Bankston III, Carl L. and Min Zhou. 1995. Religious participation, ethnic identification, and adaptation of Vietnamese adolescents in an immigrant community. *Sociological Quarterly* 36 (3):523–34.

Barrett, Mark E., Dwayne D. Simpson, and Wayne E. K. Lehman. 1988. Behavioral changes of adolescents in drug abuse intervention programs. *Journal of Clinical Psychology* 44:461–73.

Battle, V. DuWayne. 1988. The influence of Al-Islam in America on the black community. *Black Scholar* 19 (1):33–41.

Bedell, Kenneth B., ed. 1996. *Yearbook of American and Canadian Churches*. Nashville: Abingdon.

Beit-Hallahmi, Benjamin. 1974. Treating the sex offender. *Crime and Delinquency* 20:33–37.

Beit-Hallahmi, Benjamin and Baruch Nevo. 1987. Jews in Israel: The dynamics of an identity change. *International Journal of Psychology* 22:75–81.

Bellah, Robert Neelly. 1991. *The Good Society: Individualism and Commitment in American Life*. New York: Knopf.

Benda, Brent B. 1995. The effect of religion on adolescent delinquency revisited. *Journal of Research in Crime and Delinquency* 32:446–66.

Benda, Brent B. and Robert F. Corwyn. 1997. A test of a model with reciprocal effects between religiosity and various forms of delinquency using 2-stage least square regression. *Journal of Social Service Research* 22 (3):27–52.

Bender, Courtney. 1995. *The Meals Are the Message: The Growth and Congestion of an AIDS Service in Organization's Mission Multiple Institutional Fields*. Yale University, Program on Non-Profit Organizations (PONPO), working paper #221.

Benson, Peter L., Dorothy L. Williams, and Arthur Johnson. 1987. *The Quicksilver Years: The Hopes and Fears of Early Adolescence*. San Francisco: Harper and Row.

Berger, Peter. 1969. *The Sacred Canopy: Elements of a Sociological Theory of Religion*. Garden City, N.Y.: Doubleday.

Berger, Peter and Richard Neuhaus. 1977. *To Empower People*. Washington, D.C.: American Enterprise Institute for Public Policy Research.

Bergin, Allen E. 1983. Religiosity and mental health: A critical reevaluation and meta-analysis. *Professional Psychology: Research and Practice* 14:170–84.

Billings, Dwight B. 1990. Religion as opposition: A Gramscian analysis. *American Journal of Sociology* 96:1–31.

Billingsley, Andrew. 1992. *Climbing Jacob's Ladder: The Enduring Legacy of African-American Families*. New York: Simon and Schuster.

Bisno, Herbert. 1952. *The Philosophy of Social Work*. Washington, D.C.: Public Affairs Press.

Blake, Joseph P. 1991. A man on a mission of hope. *Philadelphia Daily News* (March 9):17.

Blidstein, Gerald. 1975. *Honor Thy Father and Thy Mother: Filial Responsibility in Jewish Law and Ethics*. New York: Yeshiva University Press.

Boff, Leonardo. 1985. *Church, Charisma, and Power*. London: SCM Press.

Bonne, Steffen, amd Amy Ronne. 1990. Cities wrapped in the arms of Jesus. *Christian Reader* 28 (1):10–11, 44–48.

Bourjolly, Joretha N. 1998. Differences in religiousness among black and white women with breast cancer. *Social Work in Health Care* 28:21–39.

Boyd, Beverly M. 1949. Protestant social services. In Margaret Hodges, ed., *Social Work Year Book*, pp. 358–66. Tenth issue. New York: Russell Sage Foundation.

Boyer, Paul S. 1978. *Urban Masses and Moral Order in America, 1820–1920*. Cambridge: Harvard University Press.

Boyte, Harry C. 1984. *Community Is Possible: Repairing America's Roots*. New York: Harper and Row.

———. 1989. *Common Wealth: A Return to Citizen Politics*. New York: Free Press.

Brady, Henry E., Sidney Verba, and Kay Lehman Schlozman. 1995. Beyond

SES: A resource model of political participation. *American Political Science Review* 89:271–94.

Brashears, Freda and Margaret Roberts. 1996. The black church as a resource for change. In Sydney L. Logan, ed., *The Black Family: Strengths, Self-Help, and Positive Change*, pp. 181–92. New York: Westview.

Bremner, Robert H. 1972. *From the Depths: The Discovery of Poverty in the United States*. New York: New York University Press.

Brereton, Virginia Lieson. 1989. United and slighted: Women as subordinated insiders. In W. R. Hutchison, ed., *Between the Times: The Travail of the Protestant Establishment in America, 1900–1960*, pp. 143–67. Cambridge: Cambridge University Press.

Breton, Margot. 1992. Liberation theology, group work, and the right of the poor and oppressed to participate in the life of the community. *Social Work with Groups* 15:257–69.

Britt, Robin. 1996. Personal communication with North Carolina secretary of the Department of Human Resources, November 3.

Brown, Trevor A. 1990. Religious nonprofits and the commercial manner test. *Yale Law Journal* 99:1631–50.

Bruce, Maurice. 1966. *The Coming of the Welfare State*. New York: Schocken Books.

Bruno, Frank J. 1948. *Trends in Social Work as Reflected in the Proceedings of the National Conference of Social Work, 1874–1946*. New York: Columbia University Press.

Bullis, Ronald K. 1996. *Spirituality in Social Work Practice*. Washington, D.C.: Taylor and Francis.

Bullis, Ronald K., and Marcia P. Harrigan. 1992. Religious denominational policies on sexuality. *Families in Society* 73:305–12.

Burch, Herbert. 1965. *Denominations and Councils of Churches: Competitive or Complimentary . . . ?* Ph.D. dissertation, Brandeis University, Waltham, Mass.

Burger, Steven. 1996. Arise, take up thy mate, and walk. *Policy Review* 20 (September/October):22–27.

Burks, Paul. 1987. Putting values—and people—to work. *Christianity and Crisis* (February 2):11–14.

Buzelle, George B. 1892. Charity organization in cities. *Charities Review* 2:1–15.

Byrd, Michael. 1997. Determining frames of reference for religiously based organizations: A case of neo-Alinsky efforts to mobilize congregational resources. *Nonprofit and Voluntary Sector Quarterly* 26:s122–s138.

Caldwell, Cleopatra, A. D. Greene, and Andrew Billingsley. 1992. The black church as a family support system: Instrumental and expressive functions.

National Journal of Sociology 6 (1):21–46.

Campfens, Hubert. 1988. Forces shaping the new social work in Latin America. *Canadian Social Work Review* 5:9–27.

Canda, Edward. 1988. Spirituality, religious diversity, and social work practice. *Social Casework* 60:238–47.

Caplan, Gerald. 1972. *Support Systems and Community Mental Health: Lectures on Concept Development*. New York: Behavioral Publications.

Carey, Mathew. 1942 (1833–1835). *Autobiography*. Brooklyn: Research Classics.

Carter, Stephen L. 1993. *The Culture of Disbelief: How American Laws and Politics Trivialized Religious Devotion*. New York: Doubleday.

Catholic Church. 1994. *Catechism of the Catholic Church (originally in Latin, Catechismus Ecclesiae Catholicae)*. Citta del Vaticano: Libreria Editrice Vaticana, 1994.

Chadwick, Bruce A. and Brent L. Top. 1993. Religiosity and delinquency among LDS adolescents. *Journal for the Scientific Study of Religion* 32:51–67.

Chambers, Clarke A. 1963. *Seedtime of Reform: American Social Service and Social Action, 1918–1933*. Minneapolis: University of Minnesota Press.

Chambre, Susan. 1991. Volunteers as witnesses: Perspectives on AIDS volunteers in New York City. *Social Service Review* 65:531–47.

Chandler, Andrew. 1997. Faith in the nation? The Church of England in the twentieth century. *History Today* 47 (5):97–103.

Chang, Patricia M. Y., David R. Williams, Ezra H. E. Griffith, and John Young. 1994. Church-agency relationships in the black community. *Nonprofit and Voluntary Sector Quarterly* 23:91–106.

Chaves, Mark. 1993. Denominations as dual structures: An organizational analysis. *Sociology of Religion* 54:147–69.

Chaves, Mark and Lynn M. Higgins. 1992. Comparing the community involvement of black and white congregations. *Journal for the Scientific Study of Religion* 31:425–40.

Chazanov, Mathias. 1991. Mosque has a U.S. flavor. *Los Angeles Times* (January 25).

Chekki, Dan A. 1993. Some traditions of nonviolence and peace. *International Journal on World Peace* 10 (3):47–54.

Cherry, Andrew, Beulah Rothman, and Louise Skolnik. 1989. Licensure as a dilemma for social work education: Findings of a national study. *Journal of Social Work Education* 25:268–75.

Chu, Chung-chuo and Helen E. Klein. 1985. Psychological and environmental variables in outcome of black schizophrenics. *Journal of the National Medical Association* 77:793–96.

Cisneros, Henry. 1996. *Higher Grounds: Faith Communities and Community*

Building. Washington, D.C.: U.S. Department of Housing and Urban Development.

Clark, J. Michael, Joanne Carlson Brown, and Lorna M. Hochstein. 1989. Institutional religion and gay/lesbian oppression. *Marriage and Family Review* 14:265–84.

Clark, James and Katherine Amato-von Hemert. 1994. Should social work education address religious issues? *Journal of Social Work Education* 30:7–17.

Clayton, H. R. and S. M. Nishi. 1955. *Churches and Social Welfare*. Vol. 2, The Changing Scene. New York: National Council of the Churches of Christ in the USA.

Clemetson, Robert A. and Roger Coates. 1992. *Restoring Broken Places and Rebuilding Communities*. Washington, D.C.: National Congress for Community Economic Development.

Cnaan, Ram A. 1994. *The Neglect of Religious Congregations and Denominations in Social Service Provision in Social Work Texts and Education*. Paper presented at the 23rd annual meeting of the Association for Research on Nonprofit Organizations and Voluntary Action, Berkeley, Calif., October.

——. 1997. *Social and Community Involvement of Religious Congregations Housed in Historic Religious Properties: Findings from a Six-City Study*. Philadelphia: University of Pennsylvania School of Social Work, Program for the Study of Organized Religion and Social Work.

Cnaan, Ram A. and Shimon Bergman. 1990. Construction of social problems by social work students. *International Social Work* 33:157–74.

Cnaan, Ram A., Toni Goodfriend, and Edward Newman. 1996. Jewish ethnic needs in multicultural social work education. *Journal of Teaching in Social Work* 13 (1/2):157–74.

Cochran, John K. 1989. Another look at delinquency and religiosity. *Sociological Spectrum* 9:147–62.

Cochran, John K., Peter B. Wood, and Bruce J. Arneklev. 1994. Is the religiosity-delinquency relationship spurious? Social control theories. *Journal of Research in Crime and Delinquency* 31:92–123.

Cohen, Adam. 1997. Welfare: Reaching out to the poor. *Time* 150 (8) (August 25):46–48.

Cohen, Burton J. and Michael J. Austin. 1997. Transforming human services organizations through empowerment of staff. *Journal of Community Practice* 4 (2):35–50.

Cohen, Diane and A. Robert Jeager. 1994. Urban congregations and philanthropy. *NY Ragtimes* (Summer):7–10.

Coleman, John A. 1996. Under the cross and the flag: Reflections on discipleship and citizenship in America. *America* 174 (16) (May 11):6–14.

Coll, Blanche D. 1969. *Perspectives in Public Welfare*. Washington, D.C.: U.S. Social and Rehabilitation Services.

Collier, Elizabeth J. 1997. *United Methodist Clergywomen Retention Study*. Boston: Anna Howard Shaw Center, Boston University School of Theology.

Colwell, Stephen. 1851. *New Themes for the Protestant Clergy*. New York: A. M. Kelly.

Comet, Murciano Aviva. 1995. Religious feminism and assimilation in Reform and Conservative Judaism. *Jewish Social Work Forum* 31:75–87.

Community Workshop on Economic Development. 1991. *Good Space and Good Work: Research and Analysis of the Extent and Nature of the Use of Religious Properties in Chicago Neighborhoods*. Chicago: Inspired Partnerships Program of the National Trust for Historic Preservation in the United States.

Compton, Beulah Roberts. 1980. *Introduction to Social Welfare and Social Work: Structure, Function, and Process*. Homewood, Ill.: Dorsey.

Conze, Edward. 1959. *Buddhism: Its Essence and Development*. New York: Harper and Row.

Conzen, Kathleen Neils. 1966. Forum. *Religion and American Culture: A Journal of Interpretation* 6:108–14.

Cormode, D. Scott. 1992. *Toward an Urban Religious History: How Did Gilded Age and Progressive Era Urbanism Shape Religion?* Paper presented at the Center for the Study of American Religion, Princeton University, March.

———. 1994. Review essay: Religion and the nonprofit sector. *Nonprofit and Voluntary Sector Quarterly* 23:171–82.

Cornett, Carlton. 1992. Toward a more comprehensive personality: Integrating a spiritual perspective into social work practice. *Social Work* 37:101–2.

Cott, Nancy. 1977. *The Bonds of Womanhood: "Woman's Sphere" in New England, 1780–1835*. New Haven: Yale University Press.

Coughlin, Bernard J. 1965. *Church and State in Social Welfare*. New York: Columbia University Press.

Council on Foundations. 1985. *The Philanthropy of Organized Religion*. Washington, D.C.: Council on Foundations.

Council on Social Work Education. 1996. *Handbook of Accreditation Standards and Procedures*. 4th ed. Alexandria, Va.: Council on Social Work Education.

Crosson-Tower, Cynthia. 1998. *Exploring Child Welfare: A Practice Perspective*. Boston: Allyn and Bacon.

Cunningham, Hilary. 1995. *God and Caesar at the Rio Grande: Sanctuary and the Politics of Religion*. Minneapolis: University of Minnesota Press.

Dahl, Robert A. 1961. *Who Governs? Democracy and Power in an American City*. New Haven: Yale University Press.

Davis, Allen Freeman. 1984. *Spearheads for Reform: The Social Settlements and the Progressive Movement, 1890–1914*. New Brunswick, N.J.: Rutgers University Press.

Day, Phyllis J. 1997. *A New History of Social Welfare*. 2d ed. Boston: Allyn and Bacon.

Dayton, Donald W. 1976. *Discovering an Evangelical Heritage*. New York: Harper and Row.

Delgado, Melvin and Denise Humm-Delgado. 1982. Natural support system: Source of strength in Hispanic communities. *Social Work* 27:83–89.

Delloff, Linda-Marie. 1995. *Credit Union Links Church with "Money Matters": Religious Institutions as Partners in Community-Based Development*. Indianapolis: Lilly Endowment.

Denton, Herbert H. 1982. Reagan urges more church aid for needy. *Washington Post* (April 14):A3.

DePriest, Tomika and Joyce Jones. 1997. Economic deliverance thru the church. *Black Enterprise* 28 (February):195–97.

De Sousa, Felix Carbal Isabela. 1995. Discussing women's reproductive health, religion, roles, and rights: Achieving women's empowerment. *Convergence* 28 (3):45–51.

DiBlasio, Frederick A. 1993. The role of social workers' religious beliefs in helping family members forgive. *Families in Society* 74:163–70.

Dickey, Marilyn, Susan Gray, Holly Hall, and Dan Morris. 1997. The big bounty for big charities. *Chronicle of Philanthropy* (October 30):7–8.

Dilulio, John. 1994. *Deregulating the Public Service: Can Government Be Improved?* Washington, D.C.: Brookings Institute.

Dinello, Natalia. 1997. *Philanthropy and Religion: Russian Orthodoxy Versus Puritanism*. Paper presented at the annual meeting of the American Sociology of Religion, Toronto, August.

———. 1998. Russian religious rejections of money and *Homo Economics*: The self-identifications of the "pioneers of a money economy" in post-Soviet Russia. *Sociology of Religion* 59:45–64.

Dionne Jr., E. J. 1996. Can government nurture civic life? *Brookings Review* 14 (4):3.

Dolan, Jay P. 1992. *The American Catholic Experience: A History from Colonial Times to the Present*. Notre Dame, Ind.: University of Notre Dame Press.

Doll, William. 1984. Cooperation in Cleveland. *Foundation News* 5:66–70.

Donahue, Michael J. and Peter L. Benson. 1995. Religion and well-being in adolescents. *Journal of Social Issues* 51:145–60.

Dorn, Jacob H. 1993. The social gospel and socialism: A comparison of the thought of Francis Greenwood Peabody, Washington Gladden, and Walter Rauschenbusch. *Church History* 62:82–100.

Dreidger, Sharon Doyle. 1997. Is Jesus really God? *Maclean's* 110 (50):40–47.

Drogus, Carol. 1990. Reconstructing the feminine: Women in San Paulo's COBs. *Archives de Sciences Sociales des Religions* 35 (71):63–74.

Du Bois, William Edward Burghardt. 1903. *The Negro Church*. Atlanta: Atlanta University Press.

Durkheim, Emile. 1897 (1951). *Suicide: A Study in Sociology*. Glencoe, Ill.: Free Press.

——. 1954. *The Elementary Form of Religious Life*. Glencoe, Ill.: Free Press.

Dussel, Enrique, Irene B. Hodgson, and Jose Pedrozo. Liberation theology and Marxism. *Rethinking Marxism* 5 (3):50–74.

Ebihara, May. 1966. Interrelation Between Buddhism and Social System in Cambodian Peasant Culture. In Manning Nash, ed., *Anthropological Studies in Theravada Buddhism Southeast Asian Studies*, pp. 175–96. New Haven: Yale University Press.

The Economist. 1995. The counter-attack of God. (July 8):19–21.

Edwards, Bob. 1995. Mississippi families asked to adopt welfare families. Morning Edition, National Public Radio Transcript #1579–8. April 6.

El Azayem, Gamal Abu and Zari Hedayat-Diba. 1994. The psychological aspects of Islam: Basic principles of Islam and their psychological corollary. *International Journal for the Psychology of Religion* 4:41–50.

Ellis, Lee. 1987. Religiosity and criminality from the perspective of arousal theory. *Journal of Research in Crime and Delinquency* 24:215–32.

——. 1996. Arousal theory and the religiosity-criminality relationship. In Larry J. Siegel and Peter Cordella, eds., *Contemporary Criminology Theory*, pp. 65–84. Boston: Northeastern University Press.

Ellis, Lee and James Peterson. 1996. Crime and religion: An international comparison among thirteen industrial nations. *Personality and Individual Differences* 20:761–68.

Ellison, Craig W. and Joel Smith. 1991. Toward an integrative measure of health and well-being. *Journal of Psychology and Theology* 19:35–48.

Eng, Eugenia, John Hatch, and Anne Callan. 1985. Institutionalizing social support through the church and into the community. *Health Education Quarterly* 12.81–92.

Engs, Ruth C. and David J. Hanson. 1985. The drinking patterns and problems of college students: 1983. *Journal of Alcohol and Drug Education* 31:65–83.

Esbeck, Carl H. 1996. *The Regulation of Religious Organizations as Recipients of Governmental Assistance*. Washington, D.C.: Center for Public Justice.

Evans, Estella Norwood. 1992. Liberation theology, empowerment theory, and social work practice with the oppressed. *International Journal of Social Work* 35:135–47.

Evans, Thomas S. 1907. The Christian settlement. *The Annals of the American Academy of Political and Social Sciences* 30:483–89.

Faver, Catherine A. 1986. Religion, research, and social work. *Social Thought* 12 (3):20–29.

Federal Register. 1990. (March 8):8555.

Feingold, Henry L. 1992. *A Time for Searching: Entering the Mainstream, 1920–1945.* Baltimore: Johns Hopkins University Press.

Fernea, Elizabeth Warnock. 1998. *In Search of Islamic Feminism: One Woman's Global Journey.* New York: Doubleday.

Ferraro, Kenneth F. and Jerome R. Koch. 1994. Religion and health among black and white adults: Examining social support and consolation. *Journal for the Scientific Study of Religion* 33:362–75.

Filinson, Rachel. 1988. A model for church-based services for frail and elderly persons and their families. *Gerontologist* 28:483–86.

Finke, Roger and Rodney Stark. 1992. *The Churching of America, 1776–1990: Winners and Losers in Our Religious Economy.* New Brunswick, N.J.: Rutgers University Press.

Flexner, Abraham. 1915. Is social work a profession? *Proceedings of the National Conference of Charities and Corrections,* pp. 576–90.

Frady, Marshall. 1996. *Jesse: The Life and Pilgrimage of Jesse Jackson.* New York: Random House.

Frame, Randy. 1995. Religious nonprofits fight for government funds. *Christian Century* 39:14, 65.

Galvon, Louis. 1996. Fresno police programs honored. *Fresno Bee* (November 14):B5.

Garland, Diana R. 1992. *Church Social Work: Helping the Whole Person in the Context of the Church.* St. Davids, Pa.: North American Christians in Social Work.

——. 1994. *Church Agencies: Caring for Children and Families in Crisis.* Washington, D.C.: Child Welfare League of America.

——. 1997. Church social work. *Social Work and Christianity* 24 (2):94–114.

Gartner, John, David B. Larson, and George Allen. 1991. Religious commitment and mental health: A review of the empirical literature. *Journal of Psychology and Theology* 19:6–25.

Gaventa, John. 1980. *Power and Powerlessness: Quiescence and Rebellion in an Appalachian Valley.* Urbana: University of Illinois Press.

Gelfand, Donald E. and Donald V. Fandetti. 1986. The emergent nature of ethnicity: Dilemmas in assessment. *Social Casework* 67:542–50.

Ghafur, Muhammad Abdul and Mannan Mollah, A. K. M. A. 1968. *Social Welfare*. Dacca, Pakistan: Pubali Prakashani.

Gifford, Carolyn de Swarte. 1981. Women in social reform movements. In Rosemary Radford Ruether and Rosemary Skinner Keller, eds., *Women and Religion in America*, 1:294–340. San Francisco: Harper and Row.

Gilbert, Kathy. 1997. Women lead pastors in the United Methodist Church. News release by the General Higher Education and Ministry, June 9.

Gite, Lloyd. 1993. The new agenda of the black church: Economic development for black America. *Black Enterprise* (December): 54–59.

Gittings, Jim. 1987. East Brooklyn churches and the Nehemiah project: Churches in communities: A place to stand. *Christianity and Crisis* (February 2):5–11.

Glassie, Henry. 1982. The topography of past time. In *Passing the Time in Ballymenone: Culture and History of an Ulster Community*, pp. 619–65. Philadelphia: University of Pennsylvania Press.

Glock, Charles. 1973. *Religion in Sociological Perspective*. Belmont, Calif.: Wadsworth.

Goldberg, Constance. 1996. The privileged position of religion in the clinical dialogue. *Clinical Social Work Journal* 24Z:125–36.

Goldsmith, Samuel A. 1933. Jewish social work. In Fred S. Hall, ed., *Social Work Year Book*, pp. 255–59. Second issue. New York: Russell Sage Foundation.

Gondolf, Ed. 1981. Community development amidst political violence: Lessons from Guatemala. *Community Development Journal* 16:228–36.

Gorsuch, Richard L. 1995. Religious aspects of substance abuse and recovery. *Journal of Social Issues* 51:65–83.

Greeley, Andrew M. 1997. Coleman revisited: Religious structures as a source of social capital. *American Behavioral Scientist* 40:587–94.

Greensboro News and Record. 1996a. (July 25):A2.

———. 1996b. (Governor Hunt article). (July 25):A4.

Greif, Geoffrey L. and Alfred DeMaris. 1990. Single fathers with custody. *Families in Society* 71:259–66.

Grettenberger, Susan and Peter Hovmand. 1997. *The Role of Churches in Human Services: United Methodist Churches in Michigan*. Paper presented at the 26th annual meeting of the Association for Research on Nonprofit Organizations and Voluntary Action, Indianapolis, December.

Griffith, Ezra E. H., Thelouizs English, and Violet Mayfield. 1980. Possession, prayer, and testimony: Therapeutic aspects of Wednesday night meeting in a black church. *Psychiatry* 43:120–28.

Gurteen, S. Humphreys. 1881. *What Is Charity Organization?* Buffalo: Courier Company Printers.

Habitat for Humanity. 199/. The Economics of Jesus. Source: http://www.habitat.org/how/christian.html. Face Sheet.

Haddad, Yvonne Yazbeck and Adair T. Lummis. 1987. *Islamic Values in the United States: A Comparative Study*. New York: Oxford University Press.

Hall, Peter Dobkin. 1990. The history of religious philanthropy in America. In R. Wuthnow, V. A. Hodgkinson, and Associates, *Faith and Philanthropy in America: Exploring the Role of Religion in America's Voluntary Sector*, pp. 38–62. San Francisco: Jossey Bass.

——. 1996. *Founded on the Rock, Built Upon Shifting Sands: Churches, Voluntary Associations, and Nonprofit Organizations in Public Life: 1850–1990*. Yale University, Program on Non-Profit Organizations (PONPO), unpublished paper.

Hammack, David. 1995. Accountability and nonprofit organizations: A historical perspective. *Nonprofit Management and Leadership* 6:127–40.

Hannay, David R. 1980. Religion and health. *Social Science and Medicine* 14A: 683–85.

Handlin, Oscar. 1951. *The Uprooted*. Boston: Little, Brown.

Harris, Margaret. 1995. Quiet care: Welfare work and religious congregations. *Journal of Social Policy* 24:53–71.

Harrison, Barbara W. 1984. Keeping faith in a sexist church: Not for women only. In *Making the Connections*, pp. 206–34. Boston: Beacon.

Harrison, E. 1995. Churches given welfare role: Mississippi families are adopted out. Some say the state's out of line. *Philadelphia Inquirer* (September 10):A15.

Harvey, Thomas J. 1997. *Government Promotion of Faith-Based Solutions to Social Problems: Partisan or Prophetic?* Washington, D.C.: Aspen Institute.

Hasenfeld, Yeheskel. 1987. Power in social work practice. *Social Service Review* 61:469–83.

Hatjavivi, Peter H., Per Fostin, and Kaire Mbuende. 1989. *Church and Liberation in Namibia*. London: Pluto.

Heilman, Samuel C. 1976. *Synagogue Life: A Study in Symbolic Interaction*. Chicago: University of Chicago Press.

Hendrickson, S. L. 1987. Churches as geriatric health clinics for community based elderly. *Journal of Religion and Aging* 2 (4):13–24.

Hessel, Dieter T. 1982. *Social Ministry*. Philadelphia: Westminster Press.

——. 1992. *Social Ministry*. Rev. ed. Louisville: Westminster/John Knox.

Hinson, E. G. 1988. The historical involvement of the church in social ministries and social action. *Review and Expositor* 85:233–42.

Hirschi, Travis and Rodney Stark. 1969. Hellfire and delinquency. *Social Problems* 17:202–13.

Hodgkinson, Virginia A., Murray S. Weitzman, Stephen M. Noga, and Heather A. Gorski. 1992. *Giving and Volunteering in the United States, 1992.* Washington, D.C.: Independent Sector.

Hodgkinson, Virginia A., Murray S. Weitzman, and Arthur D. Kirsch. 1988. *From Belief to Commitment: The Community Service Activities and Finances of Religious Congregations in the United States: Findings from a National Survey.* Washington, D.C.: Independent Sector.

Hodgkinson, Virginia A., Murray S. Weitzman, Arthur D. Kirsch, Stephen M. Noga, and Heather A. Gorski. 1993. *From Belief to Commitment: The Community Service Activities and Finances of Religious Congregations in the United States. Findings from a National Survey.* Washington, D.C.: Independent Sector.

Hodgkinson, Virginia A., Murray S. Weitzman, Stephen M. Noga, and E. B. Knauft. 1994. *Giving and Volunteering in the United States, 1994.* Washington, D.C.: Independent Sector.

Hoelter, Jon W. 1979. Religiosity, fear of death, and suicide acceptability. *Journal of Life-Threatening Behavior* 9:163–72.

Hoff, Marvin D. 1990. A collaborative model for parish social ministry. *Social Thought* 12 (3):12–21.

Hopkins, Charles Howard. 1940. *The Rise of the Social Gospel in American Protestantism, 1865–1915.* New Haven: Yale University Press.

Horwitt, Sanford D. 1989. *Let Them Call Me a Rebel: Saul Alinsky, His Life and Legacy.* New York: Knopf.

Howard, Johnette. 1994. For Coach McCartney, a leap of faith. *Washington Post* (October 25):E1.

Hunt, Richard A. and Morton B. King. 1978. Religiosity and marriage. *Journal for the Scientific Study of Religion* 17:399–406.

Isaac, Rhys. 1982. *The Transformation of Virginia, 1740–1790.* Chapel Hill: University of North Carolina Press.

Jackson, Maxie C., John H. Schwitzer, Marvin T. Cato, and Reynard N. Blake. 1997. *Faith-Based Institutions' Community and Economic Development Programs Serving the Black Communities in Michigan.* East Lansing: Michigan State University, Urban Affairs Programs.

James, William. 1902. *The Varieties of Religious Experience.* New York: Longmans and Green.

Janowitz, Morris. 1967. *The Community Press in an Urban Setting: The Social Elements of Urbanism.* 2d ed. Chicago: University of Chicago Press.

Jeavons, Thomas H. 1993. *Identifying Characteristics of "Religious" Organiza-*

tions: An Exploratory Proposal. Yale University, Program on Non-Profit Organizations (PONPO), working paper #197.

Jeavons, Thomas H. and Ram A. Cnaan. 1997. The formation, transitions, and evolution of small religious organizations. *Nonprofit and Voluntary Sector Quarterly* 26:s62–s84.

Jenkins, Richard A. and Kenneth I. Pargament. 1995. Religion and spirituality as resources for coping with cancer. *Journal of Psychosocial Oncology* 13:15–74.

Johnson, Colleen L. 1995. Determinants of adaptation among old black Americans. *Journal of Aging Studies* 9:231- 44.

Johnson, D. Paul and Kena Dubberly. 1992. *Local Interchurch Cooperation in Downtown Redevelopment.* Paper presented at the 1992 meeting of the Religious Research Association, Washington, D.C., October.

Johnson, F. Ernest. 1930. *Social Work of the Churches: A Handbook of Information.* New York: Department of Research and Education of the Federal Council of the Churches of Christ in America.

Johnson, F. Ernest and William J. Villaume. 1957. Protestant social services. In Russell H. Kurtz, ed., *Social Work Year Book*, pp. 421–31. Thirteenth issue. New York: Russell Sage Foundation.

Johnson, Louise C., Charles L. Schwartz, and David S. Tate. 1997. *Social Welfare: A Response to Human Need.* 4th ed. Boston: Allyn and Bacon.

Jones, M. G. 1938. *The Charity School Movement.* Cambridge: Cambridge University Press.

Joseph, M. Vincentia. 1987. The religious and spiritual aspects of clinical practice: A neglected dimension of social work. *Social Thought* 13 (1):12–23.

——. 1988. Religion and social work practice. *Social Casework* 69:443–52.

Joubert, Charles E. 1994. Religious nonaffiliation in relation to suicide, murder, rape, and illegitimacy. *Psychological Reports* 75:10.

Kaczorowski, Jane M. 1989. Spiritual well-being and anxiety in adults diagnosed with cancer. *Hospice Journal* 5:105–16.

Katz, Michael B. 1983. *Poverty and Policy in American History.* New York: Academic Press.

Kegley, Charles W. and Leonard W. Doob. 1984. The refugee asylum problem and world peace efforts. *International Journal of World Peace* 1 (1):45–52.

Kehoe, Nancy C. and Thomas G. Gutheil. 1994. Neglect of religious issues in scale-based assessment of suicidal patients. *Hospital and Community Psychiatry* 45:366–69.

Keith-Lucas, Alan. 1972. *Giving and Taking Help.* Chapel Hill: University of North Carolina Press.

——. 1989. *The Poor You Have with You Always.* St. Davids, Pa.: North

American Association of Christian Social Work.

Kilpatrick, Alice C. and Thomas P. Holland. 1990. Spiritual dimensions of practice. *Clinical Supervisor* 8 (2):125–41.

Kim, Jung Ha. 1996. The labor of compassion: Voices of "churched" Korean American women. *Amerasia Journal* 22 (1):93–105.

Kim, Kwang Chung and Shin Kim. 1997. *The Ethnic Functions of Korean Churches in the U.S.* Paper presented at the annual meeting of the Association for the Sociology of Religion, Toronto, October.

Klein, Joe. 1997. In God they trust. *New Yorker* 83:40–48.

Kluth, Brian. 1997. Philanthropy vs. Christian stewardship: Is there a difference? *Stewardship Matters* 1 (1):4.

Koeing, Harold G., James N. Kvale, and Carolyn Ferrel. 1988. Religion and well-being in later life. *Gerontologist* 28:18–29.

Kramer, John W. 1876. *A Manual for Visitors of the Poor.* New York: D. Appleton.

Kramnick, Isaac and Laurence Moore. 1997. Can the churches save the cities? Faith-based services and the constitution. *American Prospect* 35 (November–December): 47–52.

Kress, June B. 1994. Homeless fatigue syndrome: The backlash against the crime of homelessness in the 1990s. *Social Justice* 21 (3):85–104.

Kriplin, Nancy. 1995. Building community beyond "bricks and sticks": Religious institutions as partners in community-based development. *Progressions: A Lilly Endowment Occasional Report* (February). Indianapolis: Lilly Endowment.

Kunzel, Regina G. 1993. *Fallen Women, Problem Girls: Unmarried Mothers and the Professionalization of Social Work, 1890–1945.* New Haven: Yale University Press.

Kutter, Catherine J. and Diane S. McDermott. 1997. The role of the church in adolescent drug education. *Journal of Drug Education* 27:293–305.

La Barbera, Priscilla A. 1991. Commercial ventures of religious organizations. *Nonprofit Management and Leadership* 1:217–34.

Larrea, Gayerre Jose. 1994. The challenges of liberation theology to neoliberal economic politics. *Social Justice* 21:34–45.

Larson, Lyle E. and J. Walter Goetz. 1989. Religious participation and marital commitment. *Review of Religious Research* 30:387–400.

Leckie, Will and Barry Stopfel. 1997. *Courage to Love: A Gay Priest Stands Up for His Beliefs.* New York: Doubleday.

Lehman Jr., Edward C. 1985. *Women Clergy: Breaking Through Gender Barriers.* New Brunswick, N.J.: Transaction Books.

Lehr, Elizabeth and Bernard Spilka. 1989. Religion in the introductory psychology textbook: A comparison of three decades. *Journal for the Scientific Study of Religion* 28:366–71.

Leiby, James. 1978. *A History of Social Welfare and Social Work in the United States*. New York: Columbia University Press.

———. 1984. Charity organization reconsidered. *Social Service Review* 58:523–38.

Leonard, Bill J. 1976. Church and culture: A moral dilemma. *Review and Expositor* 73:145–47.

———. 1988. The modern church and social action. *Review and Expositor* 85:243–53.

Lester, David. 1987. Religiosity and personal violence: A regional analysis of suicide and homicide. *Journal of Social Psychology* 127:685–86.

———. 1991. Social correlates of youth suicide rates in the United States. *Adolescence* 26:55–58.

Levan, Christopher. 1995. *God Hates Religion: How the Gospels Condemn False Religious Practice*. Toronto: United Church Publishing House.

Levin, Jeffrey S. 1994. Investigating the epidemiologic effects of religious experiences: Findings, explanations, and barriers. In Jeffrey S. Levin, ed., *Religion in Aging and Health*, pp. 3–17. Thousand Oaks, Calif.: Sage.

Levin, Jeffrey S. and Harold Y. Vanderpool. 1987. Is frequent religious attendance really conducive to better health? Toward an epidemiology of religion. *Social Science Medicine* 24:589–600.

Levy, Leonard W. 1994. *The Establishment Clause: Religion and the First Amendment*. Chapel Hill: University of North Carolina Press.

Lewis, James W. 1994. Going downtown: Historical resources for urban ministry. *Word and World* 14:402–8.

Lincoln, C. Eric and Lawrence H. Mamiya. 1990. *The Black Church in the African-American Experience*. Durham, N.C.: Duke University Press.

———. 1993. Challenges to the black church: The black church in the twenty-first century. In Kenneth B. Bedell, ed., *Yearbook of American and Canadian Churches*, pp. 1–7. Nashville: Abingdon.

Lindenmeyr, Adele. 1996. *Poverty Is Not a Vice: Charity, Society, and the State in Imperial Russia*. Princeton: Princeton University Press.

Lindner, E. W., M. C. Mattis, and J. R. Rogers. 1983. *When Churches Mind the Children: A Study of Day Care in Local Parishes*. Ypsilanti, Mich.: High Scope Press.

Little, David. 1995. Belief, ethnicity, and nationalism. *Nationalism and Ethnic Politics* 1:284–301.

Loconte, Joe. 1997. The 7 deadly sins of government funding. *Policy Review* 21 (March–April): 28–36.

Loewenberg, Frank M. 1988. *Religion and Social Work Practice in Contemporary American Society.* New York: Columbia University Press.

———. 1995. Financing philanthropic institutions in Biblical and Talmudic times. *Nonprofit and Voluntary Sector Quarterly* 24:307–20.

Lorch, Barbara R. and Robert H. Hughes. 1985. Religion and youth substance use. *Journal of Religion and Health* 24:197–208.

Lubove, Roy. 1965. *The Professional Altruist: The Emergence of Social Work as a Career.* New York: Atheneum.

Lukoff, David, Francis Lu, and Robert Turner. 1992. Toward a more culturally sensitive DSM-IV: Psychoreligious and psychospiritual problems. *Journal of Nervous and Mental Disease* 180:673–82.

Lund, Julia A. 1929. Mormon social work. In Fred Hall and Margaret Ellis, eds., *Social Work Year Book*, pp. 272–73. First issue. New York: Russell Sage Foundation.

Lynch, Edward A. 1994. Beyond liberation theology? *Journal of Interdisciplinary Studies* 6:147–64.

MacDonald, Coval B. and Jeffrey B. Luckett. 1983. Religious affiliation and psychiatric diagnosis. *Journal for the Scientific Study of Religion* 22:15–37.

MacEoin, Gary. 1985. *Sanctuary: A Resource Guide for Understanding and Participating in the Central American Refugees' Struggle.* San Francisco: Harper and Row.

Magill, Robert S. 1986. Social welfare politics in urban America. *Social Work* 31:397–400.

Magnuson, Norris A. 1977. *Salvation in the Slums: Evangelical Social Work, 1865–1920.* Metuchen, N.J.: Scarecrow Press.

Mangold, George H. 1907. The church and philanthropy. *Annals of the American Academy of Political and Social Sciences* 30:522–38.

Marable, Manning. 1985. The black faith of W. E. B. DuBois: Sociocultural and political dimensions of black religion. *Southern Quarterly* 23 (3):15–33.

Mares, Alvin S. 1994. Housing and the church. *Nonprofit and Voluntary Sector Quarterly* 23:139–57.

Marty, Martin E. 1980. Social service: Godly and Godless. *Social Service Review* 54:463–81.

Maton, Kenneth I. and Julian Rappaport. 1984. Empowerment in a religious setting: A multivariate analysis. *Prevention in Human Services* 3 (3/4):37–72.

Maton, Kenneth I. and Elizabeth A. Wells. 1995. Religion as a community resource for well-being: Prevention, healing, and empowerment pathways. *Journal of Social Issues* 51:177–93.

Maudlin, Michael J. and Edward Gilbreath. 1994. The house of God: Bill Hybels answers critics of the seeker-church movement. *Christianity Today* 39 (July 18):21–25.

Mauser, E. 1993. *The Importance of Organizational Form: Parent Perceptions Versus Reality in the Day-Care Industry*. Paper presented at "Private Action and the Public Good," a conference sponsored by the Center on Philanthropy, Indiana University, Indianapolis, November.

McAneny, Leslie and Lydia Saad. 1993. Strong ties between religious commitment and abortion views. *Gallup Poll Monthly*, no. 331, 35–43.

McCarthy, E. Lance. 1995. *A Proposal to Get F.I.T: Economic Empowerment Through the African-American Church: Black America 1995—A New Beginning*. Washington, D.C.: National Center for Public Policy Research.

McCarthy, Kathleen D. 1982. *Noblesse Oblige: Charity and Cultural Philanthropy in Chicago, 1849–1929*. Chicago: University of Chicago Press.

McCarthy, Shawn and Erin Andersen. 1997. Was Jesus divine? U.C. moderator roils his flock. *Globe and Mail* (November 15):D3.

McDonald, Jean A. 1984. Survey finds religious groups strongly favor more collaboration. *Foundation News* (September/October):20–24.

McDonnell, James T. 1949. Catholic social work. In Margaret Hodges, ed., *Social Work Year Book*, pp. 85–92. New York: Russell Sage Foundation.

McDougall, Harold A. 1993. *Black Baltimore: A New Theory of Community*. Philadelphia: Temple University Press.

McLoughlin, William G. 1976. Billy Sunday and the working girl of 1915. *Journal of Presbyterian History* 54:376–84.

Medoff, M. H. and I. Lee Skov. 1992. Religion and behavior: An empirical analysis. *Journal of Socio-Economics* 21:143–51.

Menjivar, Cecilia and Victor Agadjanian. 1997. *Church-Based Social Networks and Everyday Life of Salvadorian Immigrants in Washington, D.C.* Paper presented at the annual meeting of the Association for the Sociology of Religion, Toronto, August.

Merline, J. 1995. Who is fighting the budget cuts? *Investor's Business Daily* (May 30):1–2.

Midgley, James. 1981. *Professional Imperialism: Social Work in the Third World*. London: Heinemann.

Milofsky, Carl. 1997. Organization from the community: A case study of congregational renewal. *Nonprofit and Voluntary Sector Quarterly* 26:s139–s160.

Misner, Barbara. 1988. *Highly Respectable and Accomplished Women: Catholic Women Religious in America, 1790–1850*. New York: Garland.

Mitchel, Margaret E., Teh-wei H. Hu, Nancy S. McDonnell, and John D. Swisher. 1984. Cost-effectiveness analysis of an educational drug abuse prevention program. *Journal of Drug Education* 14:271–92.

Moberg, David 1984. *The Church as a Social Institution.* 2d ed. Grand Rapids, Mich.: Baker Book House.

Mock, Alan K. 1992. Congregational religion's styles and orientation to society: Exploring our linear assumptions. *Review of Religious Research* 34:20–33.

Mohl, Raymond A. and Neil Betten. 1981. The immigrant church in Gary, Indiana: Religious adjustment and cultural defense. *Ethnicity* 8:1–17.

Mollat, Michel. 1986. *The Poor in the Middle Ages: An Essay in Social History.* New Haven: Yale University Press.

Monsma, Stephen V. 1996. *When Sacred and Secular Mix: Religious Nonprofit Organizations and Public Money.* Lanham, Md.: Rowman and Littlefield.

Monsma, Stephen V. and Christopher J. Soper. 1997. *The Challenge of Pluralism.* Lanham, Md.: Rowman and Littlefield.

Moore, Art. 1998. Can foster care be fixed? Churches partner with parents to care for at-risk children. *Christianity Today* 43 (August 10):54–57.

Moore, Thom. 1991. The African-American church: A source of empowerment, mutual help, and social change. *Prevention in Human Services* 10:147–67.

Morris, Aldon D. 1984. *The Origins of the Civil Rights Movement: Black Communities Organizing for Change.* New York: Free Press.

Morris, Robert. 1986. *Rethinking Social Welfare: Why Care for the Stranger?* New York: Longman.

Mukenge, Ida R. 1983. *The Black Church in Urban America: A Case Study in Political Economy.* Lanham, Md.: University Press of America.

Nakhaima, Jem M. and Barbara H. Dicks. 1995. Social work practice with religious families. *Families in Society* 76:360–68.

Nathan, Richard P., Frederick C. Doolittle, and Associates. 1987. *Reagan and the States.* Princeton: Princeton University Press.

National Alliance to End Homelessness. 1994. *Alliance: A Publication of the National Alliance to End Homelessness.* (July):1–3.

National Association of Social Workers. 1996. *Code of Ethics.* Washington, D.C.: National Association of Social Workers.

Negstad, Joanne and Roger Arnholt. 1986. Day centers for older adults: Parish and agency partnership. *Journal of Religion and Aging* 2 (4):25–31.

Netting, F. Ellen. 1982a. Church-related agencies and social welfare. *Social Service Review* 56:404–20.

———. 1982b. Secular and religious funding of church-related agencies. *Social Service Review* 56:586–604.

———. 1984. The changing environment: Its effects on church-related agencies. *Social Service Review* 60:16–30.

Netting, F. Ellen, Jane M. Thibault, and James W. Ellor. 1990. Integrating the content of organized religion into macropractice courses. *Journal of Social Work Education* 26:15–24.

Niebuhr, Gustav. 1997. Increasingly, men in midlife answer call for priesthood. *New York Times* (June 8):1, 32.

Niebuhr, Reinhold. 1932. *The Contribution of Religion to Social Work*. New York: Columbia University Press.

Nowak, Jeremy. 1989. *Religious Institutions and Community Renewal*. Philadelphia: Delaware Valley Community Reinvestment Fund and the Philadelphia Historic Preservation Corporation.

Oates, Mary J. 1995. *The Catholic Philanthropic Tradition in America*. Indianapolis: Indiana University Press.

O'Connell, Brian. 1983. *America's Voluntary Spirit*. New York: The Foundation Center.

O'Grady, John. 1937. Catholic social services. In Russell H. Kurtz, ed., *Social Work Year Book*, pp. 54–57. Fourth issue. New York: Russell Sage Foundation.

Olasky, Marvin M. 1992. *The Tragedy of American Compassion*. Washington, D.C.: Regnery Gateway.

———. 1996. *Renewing American Compassion*. New York: Free Press.

Olson, John Kevin. 1990. Crime and religion: A denominational and community analysis. *Journal for the Scientific Study of Religion* 29:395–403.

O'Neill, Michael. 1989. *The Third America: The Emergence of the Nonprofit Sector in the United States*. San Francisco: Jossey-Bass.

Orr, John B. 1998. *Los Angeles Religion: A Civic Profile*. Los Angeles: University of Southern California, Center for Religion and Civic Culture.

Orr, John B., Don E. Miller, D. C. Roof, and J. G. Melton. 1994. *Politics of the Spirit: Religion and Multiethnicity in Los Angeles*. Los Angeles: University of Southern California.

Orsi, Robert A. 1991. He keeps me going: Women's devotion to Saint Jude Thaddeus and the dialectics of gender in American Catholicism, 1925–1965. In Thomas Kselman, ed., *Brief in History: Innovative Approaches to European and American Religion*, pp. 137–69. Notre Dame, Ind.: University of Notre Dame Press.

Ortega, Suzanne T., Robert D. Crutchfield, and William A. Rushing. 1983. Race differences in elderly well-being: Friendship, family, and church. *Research on Aging* 5:101–18.

Osborne, David and Ted Gaebler. 1992. *Reinventing Government: How the Entrepreneurial Spirit is Transforming the Public Sector, from Schoolhouse to Statehouse, City Hall to the Pentagon*. Reading, Mass.: Addison-Wesley.

Ozorak, Elizabeth Weiss. 1996. The power, but not the glory: How women empower themselves through religion. *Journal of the Scientific Study of Religion* 35:17–29.

Paloutzian, Raymond F. and Lee A. Kirkpatrick. 1995. Introduction: The scope of religious influences on personal and societal well-being. *Journal of Social Issues* 51:1–11.

Parsloe, Phyllida. 1996. *Pathways to Empowerment*. Birmingham, Eng.: Venture Press.

Parson, Naida M. and James K. Mikawa. 1991. Incarceration and nonincarceration of African-American men raised in black Christian churches. *Journal of Psychology* 125:163–73.

Pateman, Carole. 1970. *Participation and Democratic Theory*. Cambridge: Cambridge University Press.

Payne, I. Reed, Allen E. Bergin, Kimberly A. Bielema, and Paul H. Jenkins. 1991. Review of religion and mental health: Prevention and the enhancement of psychosocial functioning. *Prevention in Human Services* 9 (2):11–40.

Pena, Milagros. 1994. Liberation theology in Peru: An analysis of the role of intellectuals in social movements. *Journal of the Scientific Study of Religion* 33:34–45.

Perry, Troy D. 1972. *The Lord Is My Shepherd and He Knows I'm Gay*. Los Angeles: Nash.

Perry, Troy D. and Thomas L. P. Swicegood. 1990. *Don't Be Afraid Anymore: The Story of Reverend Troy Perry and the Metropolitan Community Church*. New York: St. Martin's Press.

Personal Responsibility and Work Opportunity Reconciliation Act of 1996. P.L. 104–193. H.R. 3734. 104th Cong., 2d sess.

Pescosolido, Bernice A. 1990. The social context of religious integration and suicide: Pursuing the network explanation. *Sociological Quarterly* 31:337–57.

Pew Research Center for the People and the Press. 1996. *The Diminishing Divide . . . American Churches, American Politics*. Washington, D.C.: Pew Research Center for the People and the Press.

Polis Center. 1996. *The Indianapolis Economic Times: The Newspaper of Faith and Economic Struggle*. Indianapolis: Polis Center, Indiana University Purdue University Indianapolis.

Pollner, Melvin. 1989. Divine relations, social relations, and well-being. *Journal of Health and Social Behavior* 30:92–104.

Popple, Philip L. and Leslie Leighninger. 1996. *Social Work, Social Welfare, and American Society*. 3d ed. Boston: Allyn and Bacon.

Pottenger, John R. 1989. *The Political Theory of Liberation Theology: Toward a Reconvergence of Social Values and Social Science*. Albany: State University of New York Press.

Pratt, Renate. 1997. *In Good Faith: Canadian Churches Against Apartheid*. Waterloo, Can.: Wilfred Laurier University Press.

Printz, Tobi. 1997. Services and Capacity of Religious Congregations in the Washington, D.C., Metropolitan Area. Paper presented at the 26th annual meeting of the Association for Research on Nonprofit Organizations and Voluntary Action, Indianapolis, December.

Purvis, Sally B. 1995. *The Stained-Glass Ceiling: Churches and Their Women Pastors*. Louisville: Westminster/John Knox Press.

Putnam, Robert D. 1995. Bowling alone: America's declining social capital. *Journal of Democracy* 6:65–78.

Queen, Edward L. 1996.*The Religious Roots of Philanthropy in the West: Judaism, Christianity, and Islam*. Indiana University Center on Philanthropy, working paper #96–4.

Quinn, Sandra Cruise and Stephen B. Thomas. 1994. Results of a baseline assessment of AIDS knowledge among black church members. *National Journal of Sociology* 8:89–107.

Raboteau, Albert J. 1978. *Slave Religion: The Invisible Institution in the Antebellum South*. New York: Oxford University Press.

Raheja, Gloria Goodwin. 1988. *The Poison in the Gift: Ritual, Prostration, and Dominant Caste in a North Indian Village*. Chicago: University of Chicago Press.

Randall, Elizabeth L. and Bruce A. Thyer. 1994. A preliminary test for the validity of the LCSW examination. *Clinical Social Work Journal* 22:223–27.

Ransdell, Lynda B. and Sandra L. Rehling. 1996. Church-based health promotion: A review of the current literature. *American Journal of Health Behavior* 20:195–207.

Rappaport, Julian. 1987. Terms of empowerment—exemplars of prevention: Toward a theory for community psychology. *American Journal of Community Psychology* 15:121–45.

Rauschenbusch, Walter. 1907. *Christianity and the Social Order*. New York: Macmillan.

Reagan Home Page, The. 1997. Reagan's Speech to the Annual Prayer Breakfast (August version). [WWW document] *http://pages.prodigy.com/christianhmsc/speech1.html*.

Reese, Laura A. and Ronald E. Brown. 1995. The effects of religious messages on racial identity and system blame among African Americans. *Journal of Politics* 57:24–43.

Resnick, Michael D., et al. 1997. Protecting adolescents from harm: Findings from the national longitudinal study of adolescents health. *Journal of the American Medical Association* 278:823–32.

Riegel, Robert Edgar. 1980. *American Feminists*. Westford, Conn.: Greenwood.

Rogalski, Sharon and Timothy Paisey. 1987. Neuroticism versus demographic variables as correlates of self-reported life satisfaction in a sample of older adults. *Personality and Individual Differences* 8:397–401.

Roof, Wade Clark and William McKinney. 1987. *American Mainline Religion: Its Changing Shape and Future*. New Brunswick, N.J.: Rutgers University Press.

Roozen, David A., William McKinney, and Jackson W. Carroll. 1984. *Varieties of Religious Presence*. New York: Pilgrim Press.

Rose, Arnold M. 1956. Conscious reactions associated with neuropsychiatric breakdown to combat. *Psychiatry* 19:87–94.

Rosenberg, Charles E. 1987. *The Care of Strangers: The Rise of America's Hospital System*. New York: Basic Books.

Ross, Alfred and Lee Cokorinos. 1997. *Promise Keepers: The Third Wave of the American Religious Right*. New York: Center for Democracy Studies.

Rubin, Roger H., Andrew Billingsley, and Cleopatra Caldwell. 1994. The role of the black church in working with black adolescents. *Adolescence* 29:251–66.

Ruffing-Rahal, Mary Ann and Judy Anderson. 1994. Factors associated with qualitative well-being in older women. *Journal of Women and Aging* 6 (3):3–18.

Russ Reid Company. 1995. *The Heart of the Donor*. Pasadena, Calif.: Russ Reid Company.

Ryan, John A. 1983 (1920). A practical philosophy of social work. *Social Thought* 9 (4):4–9.

Ryle, Edward J. 1989. The developments in Catholic moral theology and their promise for social workers. *Social Thought* 15 (3–4):79–89.

Salamon, Lester M. 1992. Social services. In Charles T. Clotfelter, ed., *Who Benefits from the Nonprofit Sector?*, pp. 134–73. Chicago: University of Chicago Press.

——. 1995. *Partners in Public Service: Government-Nonprofit Relations in the Modern Welfare State*. Baltimore: Johns Hopkins University Press.

Salamon, Lester M., David M. Altschuler, and Carol J. De Vita. 1985. *Chicago Nonprofit Organizations: The Challenge of Retrenchment*. Washington, D.C.: Urban Institute.

Salamon, Lester M. and Fred Teitelbaum. 1984. Religious congregations as social service agencies: How extensive are they? *Foundation News* 5:B2–G4.

Salamon, Lester M. and Stephen Van Evera. 1973. Fear, apathy, and discrimination: A test of three explanations of political participation. *American Political Science Review* 6/:1288–1306.

Saleebey, Dennis. 1992. Introduction: Power in the people. In Dennis Saleebey, ed., *The Strength Perspective in Social Work Practice*, pp. 1–7. New York: Longman.

Salmons, Paula H. and Richard Harrington. 1984. Suicidal ideation in university students and other groups. *International Journal of Social Psychiatry* 30:201–5.

Samson, C. Mathews. 1991. Texts and context: Social context and the content of liturgical texts in Nicaragua and El Salvador. *Human Mosaic* 25 (1/2):25–35.

Sarfoh, Joseph A. 1986. The West African Zongo and the American ghetto: Some comparative aspects of the roles of religious institutions. *Journal of Black Studies* 17:71–84.

Scherer-Warren, Ilse. 1990. "Rediscovering our dignity": An appraisal of the utopia of liberation in Latin America. *International Sociology* 5:11–25.

Schnall, David J. 1995. Filial responsibility in Judaism. *Jewish Journal of Sociology* 37:112–18.

Schumm, Walter R., Stephen R. Bollman, and Anthony P. Jurich. 1982. The "marital conventionalization" argument: Implications for the study of religiosity and marital satisfaction. *Journal of Psychology and Theology* 10:236–41.

Schweinitz, Karl de. 1943. *England's Road to Social Security*. New York: A. S. Barnes.

Sengupta, S. 1995. Meshing the sacred and the secular: Floyd Flake offers community development via church and state. *New York Times* (November 23):B1, B12.

Shapiro, Joseph P. and Andrea R. Wright. 1996. Can churches save America? *U.S. News and World Report* 121 (10) (September 9):46–53.

Shaver, Phillip, Michael Lenauer, and Susan Sadd. 1980. Religiousness, conversion, and subjective well-being: The "healthy-minded" religion of modern American women. *American Journal of Psychiatry* 137: 1563–68.

Sheridan, Michael J. and Katherine Amato-von Hemert. 1999. The role of religion and spirituality in social work education and practice: A survey of student views and experiences. *Journal of Social Work Education* 35:125–41.

Sherman, Amy L. 1995. Cross purposes: Will conservative welfare reform corrupt religious charities? *Policy Review* 19 (Fall): 58–63.

———. 1996. STEP-ing out on faith—and off welfare. *Christianity Today* (June 17):35–36.

———. 1997a. *An Evaluation of Mississippi's Faith and Families Initiative.* Report prepared for the workshop "Implementing Government Cooperation with Religious Social Ministries." Washington, D.C. and Annandale, Va.: Center for Public Justice and Center for Law and Religious Freedom.

———. 1997b. *Fruitful Collaboration Between Religious Groups and Governmental Entities: Lessons from Virginia and Maryland.* Report prepared for the workshop "Implementing Government Cooperation with Religious Social Ministries." Washington, D.C. and Annandale, Va.: Center for Public Justice and Center for Law and Religious Freedom.

Sherwood, David A. 1997. The relationship between beliefs and values in social work practice: Worldviews make a difference. *Social Work and Christianity* 24:115–35.

Shokeid, Moshe. 1995. *A Gay Synagogue in New York.* New York: Columbia University Press.

Shuler, Pamela A., Lilian Gelberg, and Aries Brown. 1994. The effects of spirituality/religion practices on psychosocial well-being among inner city homeless women. *Nurse Practitioner Forum* 5 (2):106–13.

Simkhovich, Mary Kingsbury. 1907. The settlement relation to religion. *Annals of the American Academy of Political and Social Sciences* 30:490–95.

Simon, Arthur 1987. *Christian Faith and Public Policy: No Grounds for Divorce.* Grand Rapids, Mich.: Eerdmans.

Simon, Barbara. 1990. Rethinking empowerment. *Journal of Progressive Human Services* 1 (1):27–40.

Singh, Avtar. 1979. Note: Religious involvement and anti-social behavior. *Perceptual and Motor Skills* 48:1157–58.

Siporin, Max. 1985. Current social work perspectives on clinical practice. *Clinical Social Work Journal* 13:198–217.

———. 1986. Contribution of religious values to social work and the law. *Social Thought* 12 (4):35–50.

Slagle, A. Logan and Joan Weibel-Orlando. 1986. The Indian Shaker church and Alcoholics Anonymous: Revitalistic curing cults. *Human Organization* 45:310–19.

Sloane, Douglas M. and Raymond H. Potvin. 1986. Religion and delinquency: Cutting through the maze. *Social Forces* 65:87–105.

Smith, Christian. 1991. *The Emergence of Liberation Theology: Radical Religion and Social Movement Theory.* Chicago: University of Chicago Press.

Smith, Christopher E. 1993. Black Muslims and the development of prisoners' rights. *Journal of Black Studies* 24:131–46.

Smith, David Horton. 1983. Churches are generally ignored in contemporary voluntary action research: Causes and consequences. *Review of Religious Research* 24:295–302.

Smith, Huston. 1958. *The Religions of Man*. New York: Harper.

Smith, Steven Rathgab. 1996. New directions in nonprofit funding. In Dwight F. Burlingame and Warren F. Ilchman, eds., *Alternative Revenue Sources: Prospects, Requirements, and Concerns for Nonprofits*, pp. 5–28. San Francisco: Jossey Bass.

Smith-Rosenberg, Carroll. 1971. *Religion and the Rise of the American City*. Ithaca, N.Y.: Cornell University Press.

——. 1985. *Disorderly Conduct: Vision of Gender in Victorian America*. New York: Knopf.

Snelling, John. 1991. *The Buddhist Handbook: A Complete Guide to Buddhist Schools, Teaching, Practice, and History*. Rochester, Vt.: Inner Traditions.

Solomon, Barbara. 1976. *Black Empowerment*. New York: Columbia University Press.

Solow, Barbara. 1997. Churches wrestle with welfare reform. *Philanthropy Journal* 1 (May 12):3.

Sosin, Michael. 1985. Social problems covered by private agencies: An application of niche theory. *Social Service Review* 61:76–94.

Special Committee on Aging, United States Senate. 1984. *Section 202 Housing for the Elderly and Handicapped: A National Survey*. Washington, D.C.: U.S. Government Printing Office.

Speer, Paul W., Joseph Hughey, Leah K. Gensheimer, and Warren Adams-Leavitt. 1995. Organizing for power: A comparative case study. *Journal of Community Psychology* 23:57–73.

Spees, H. 1996. Fresno blessed with churches that care. *Fresno Bee* (October 23):B5.

Spencer, Sue W. 1957. Religious and spiritual values in social work. *Social Casework* 38:519–26.

——. 1961. What place has religion in social work education? *Social Service Review* 35:161–70.

Spilka, Bernard, Ralph W. Hood Jr., and Richard I. Gorsuch. 1985. *The Psychology of Religion: An Empirical Approach*. Englewood Cliffs, N.J.: Prentice Hall.

Spilka, Bernard, William J. Zwartjes, Georgia M. Zwartjes, D. Heideman, and K. A. Cilli. 1987. *The Role of Religion in Coping with Cancer*. University of Denver, unpublished paper.

Stack, Steven. 1983a. The effect of religious commitment on suicide: A cross-national analysis. *Journal of Health and Social Behavior* 24:362–74.

———. 1983b. The effect of the decline in institutionalized religion on suicide, 1954–1978. *Journal for the Scientific Study of Religion* 22:239–52.

Stack, Steven and Mary Jeanne Kanavy. 1983. The effect of religion on forcible rape. *Journal for the Scientific Study of Religion* 22:67–74.

Stack, Steven and Ira Wasserman. 1992. The effect of religion on suicide ideology: An analysis of the network perspective. *Journal for the Scientific Study of Religion* 31:457–66.

Stark, Rodney and William S. Bainbridge. 1980. Toward a theory of religious commitment. *Journal for the Scientific Study of Religion* 19:114–28.

Ste. Croix, Geoffrey Ernest Maurice De. 1982. *The Class Struggle in the Ancient Greek World: From the Archaic Age to the Arab Conquests.* Ithaca, N.Y.: Cornell University Press.

Steinberg, Richard. 1996. Can individual donations replace cutbacks in federal social-welfare spending? In Dwight Burlingame, William A. Diaz, Warren F. Ilchman, and Associates, eds., *Capacity or Change? The Nonprofit World in the Age of Devolution,* pp. 57–79. Indianapolis: Indiana University Center on Philanthropy.

Steinfels, P. 1995. As government aid evaporates, how will religious and charity organizations hold up as a safety net for the poor, the sick, and the elderly? *New York Times* (October 28):11.

Steinitz, Lucy Y. 1980. *The Church Within the Network of Social Services to the Elderly: Case Study of Laketown.* Ph.D. dissertation, University of Chicago.

Stern, Mark. 1984. The emergence of the homeless as a public problem. *Social Service Review* 59:291–301.

Stodghill II, Ron. 1996. Bringing hope back to the 'hood. *Business Week* (August 19):70–73.

———. 1997. God of our fathers: The Promise Keepers are bringing their manly crusade to Washington. *New York Times Magazine* (October 6):31–35.

Strader, Ted, David Collins, Tim Noe, and Knowlton Johnson. 1997. Mobilizing church communities for alcohol and other drug abuse prevention through the use of volunteer church advocate teams. *Journal of Volunteer Administration* 15 (2):16–29.

Suksamran, Somboon. 1977. *Political Buddhism in Southeast Asia: The Role of the Sangha in the Modernisation of Thailand.* London: Hurst.

Sweet, Dennis M. 1995. The church, the Stasi, and socialist integration: Three stages of lesbian and gay emancipation in the former East German Democratic Republic. *Journal of Homosexuality* 29:351–67.

Tapia, Andres. 1996. How is the black church responding to the urban crisis? *Christianity Today* 20 (March 4):26–30.

Tenenbaum, Shelly. 1993. *Credit to Their Community: Jewish Loan Societies in the United States*. Detroit: Wayne State University Press.

Thomas, Stephan B., Sandra Cruise Quinn, Andrew Billingsley, and Cleopatra Caldwell. 1994. The characteristics of northern black churches with community health outreach programs. *American Journal of Public Health* 84:575–79.

Thompson, William D. 1989. *Philadelphia's First Baptists*. Philadelphia: First Baptist Church of Philadelphia.

Thumma, Scott. 1991. Negotiating a religious identity: The case of the gay evangelical. *Sociological Analysis* 52:333–47.

Tice, Caroline. 1992. The battle for benevolence: Scientific disciplinary control vs. indiscriminate relief—A case study of the Lexington Associated Charities vs. the Salvation Army. *Journal of Sociology and Social Welfare* 21 (2):59–77.

Tippy, Worth M. 1937. Protestant social services. In Russell H. Kurtz, ed., *Social Work Year Book*. Fourth issue. New York: Russell Sage Foundation.

Tittle, Charles R. and Michael R. Welch. 1983. Religiosity and deviance: Toward a contingency theory of constraining effects. *Social Forces* 61:653–82.

Tocqueville, Alexis de. 1969 (1835). *Democracy in America*. New York: Vintage.

Toren, Nina. 1972. *Social Work: The Case of a Semi-profession*. Beverly Hills, Calif.: Sage.

Traer, Robert. 1988. Religious communities in the struggle for human rights. *Christian Century* 105:835–38.

Troeltsch, Ernst. 1992. *The Social Teaching of the Christian Churches*. Louisville: Westminster/John Knox Press.

Trolander, Judith Ann. 1997. Fighting racism and sexism: The Council on Social Work Education. *Social Service Review* 71:110–34.

Trost, C. 1988. Debate over day-care bill spurs odd alliances and raises issue of church-state separation. *Wall Street Journal* (August 29):32.

Trueheart, Charles. 1996. Welcome to the next church. *Atlantic Monthly* 278 (2) (August): 37–58.

Tucker, Sara Waitstill. 1983. The Canton Hospital and Medicine in Nineteenth-Century China, 1835–1900. Ph.D. dissertation, Indiana University, Bloomington.

Turner, Frank M. 1974. *Between Science and Religion: The Reaction to Scientific Naturalism in Late Victorian England*. New Haven: Yale University Press.

Turner, Richard. 1997. *Literary Criticism, the Public Sphere, and Voluntary Action for the Public Good*. Paper presented at the 26th annual meeting of the Association for Research on Nonprofit Organizations and Voluntary Action, Indianapolis, December.

Twyman, Anthony S. 1995. Once again the search for "una vida major." *Philadelphia Daily News* (April 17):21–22.

U.S. Bureau of the Census. 1981. Private philanthropy funds, by source and allocation 1960–1980. In R. Dolgoff and D. Feldstein, eds., *Understanding Social Welfare*. New York: Longman.

Van-Dartel, Geert. 1995. Towards a culture of peace: Remarks on the religious aspects of the war in Bosnia and Croatia. *Religion, State, and Society* 23:199–205.

Van Hook, Mary P. 1997. Incorporating religious issues in the assessment process with individuals and families. *Social Work and Christianity* 24:136–57.

Verba, Sidney, Kay Lehman Schlozman, and Henry E. Brady. 1995. *Voice and Equality: Civic Voluntarism in American Politics*. Cambridge: Harvard University Press.

Vitillo, Robert J. 1986. Parish-Based Social Ministry: From a Theological and Historic Perspective. *Social Thought* 12 (3):30–38.

Von Matt, Leonard and Louis Cognet. 1960. *St. Vincent de Paul*. Chicago: Regnery.

Vuyst, Alex. 1989. Self-Help for the Homeless. *Humanist* 49 (3):13, 49.

Wallace, Ruth A. 1992. *They Call Her Pastor: A New Role for Catholic Women*. Albany: State University of New York Press.

Wallis, Jim. 1997. Toward a new spiritual politics. Source: http://www.ari.net/calltorenewal/ctr0002.html.

Walsh, Anthony. 1980. The prophylactic effect of religion on blood pressure levels among a sample of immigrants. *Social Science and Medicine* 14:59–63.

Ward, Naomi, Andrew Billingsley, Alicia Simon, and Judith Crooker Burris. 1994. Black churches in Atlanta reach out to the community. *National Journal of Sociology* 8:50–74.

Waring, Anna L. and Susan M. Sanders. 1997. *African-American Churches: New Supporters of Community Policing*. Paper presented at the 26th annual meeting of the Association for Research on Nonprofit Organizations and Voluntary Action, Indianapolis, December.

Warner, Amos. 1908. *American Charities*. New York: Thomas Y. Crowell.

Warner, R. Stephen. 1989. *The Metropolitan Community Church as a Case Study of Religious Change in the USA*. Paper presented at the annual meeting of the Society for the Scientific Study of Religion, Salt Lake City, November.

———. 1993. Work in progress toward a new paradigm for the sociological study of religion in the United States. *American Journal of Sociology* 98:1044–93.

Warner, W. Lloyd and Paul S. Lunt. 1941. *The Social Life of a Modern Community*. New Haven: Yale University Press.

Watson, Frank Dekker. 1922. *The Charity Organization Movement in the United States*. New York: Macmillan.

Webber, George. 1964. *The Congregation in Mission*. New York: Abington.

Weisbrod, Burton A. 1993. *Does Institutional Form Affect Behavior? Comparing Private Firms, Religious Nonprofits, and Other Nonprofits*. Paper presented at "Private Action and the Public Good," a conference sponsored by the Center on Philanthropy, Indiana University, Indianapolis, November.

Wenocur, Stanley and Michael Reisch. 1989. *From Charity to Enterprise: The Development of American Social Work in a Market Economy*. Chicago: University of Illinois Press.

Werner, Emmy E. and Ruth S. Smith. 1982. *Vulnerable, But Invincible: A Longitudinal Study of Resilient Children and Youth*. New York: McGraw-Hill.

Wilcox, Clyde and Leopoldo Gomez. 1990. Religion, group identification, and politics among American Blacks. *Sociological Analysis* 51:271–85.

Wilensky, Harold L. and Charles N. Lebeaux. 1965. *Industrial Society and Social Welfare*. New York: Free Press.

Willis, Garry. 1990. *Under God: Religion and American Politics*. New York: Simon and Schuster.

Willitis, Fern K. and Donald M. Crider. 1988. Religion and well-being: Men and women in the middle years. *Review of Religious Research* 29:281–94.

Wilson, Bryan R. 1986. Religion, rational society, and the modern concept of peace. *International Journal of World Peace* 3 (2):67–82.

Wilson, James Q. 1974. *Political Organizations*. New York: Basic Books.

Wilson, John and Thomas Janoski. 1995. The contribution of religion to volunteer work. *Sociology of Religion* 56:137–52.

Wiltfang, Gregory L. and Doug McAdam. 1991. The costs and risks of social activism: A study of sanctuary movement activism. *Social Forces* 69:987–1010.

Wineburg, Catherine R. and Robert J. Wineburg. 1987. Local human service development: Institutional utilization of volunteers to solve community problems. *Journal of Volunteer Administration* 5 (4):9–14.

Wineburg, Robert J. 1990–1991. A community study on the ways religious congregations support individuals and human service network. *Journal of Applied Social Sciences* 15 (1):51–74.

———. 1993. Social policy, service development, and religious organizations. *Nonprofit Management and Leadership* 3:283–99.

——. 1994. A longitudinal case study of religious congregations in local human service delivery. *Nonprofit and Voluntary Sector Quarterly* 23:159–69.

——. 1996. An investigation of religious support of public and private agencies in one community in an era of retrenchment. *Journal of Community Practice* 3 (2):35–55.

Wineburg, Robert J., Fashi Ahmed, and Mark Sills. 1997. Local human service organizations and the local religious community during an era of change. *Journal of Applied Social Sciences* 21 (2):93–98.

Wineburg, Robert J. and Catherine R. Wineburg. 1986. Localization of human services: Using church volunteers to fight the feminization of poverty. *Journal of Volunteer Administration* 4 (3):1–6.

Winland, Daphne N. 1994. Christianity and community: Conversion and adaptation among Hmong refugee women. *Canadian Journal of Sociology* 19:21–45.

Wittberg, Patricia 1994. *The Rise and Fall of Catholic Religious Orders: A Social Movement Perspective*. Albany, N.Y.: SUNY Press.

Witter, Robert A., William A. Stock, Morris A. Okun, and Marilyn J. Haring. 1985. Religion and subjective well-being in adulthood: A quantitative synthesis. *Review of Religious Research* 26:332–42.

Wood, Richard L. 1994. Faith in action: Religious resources for political success in three congregations. *Sociology of Religion* 55:397–417.

——. 1997. Social capital and political culture: God meets politics in the inner city. *American Behavioral Scientist* 40:595–605.

Worthington, Everett L. 1989. Religious faith across the life span: Implications for counseling and research. *Counseling Psychologist* 17:555–612.

Wright, Conrad Edick. 1992. *The Transformation of Charity in Post-Revolutionary New England*. Boston: Northeastern University Press.

Wright, S. Lloyd, J. Christopher Frost, and Stephen J. Wisecarver. 1993. Church attendance, meaningfulness of religion, and depressive symptomatology among adolescents. *Journal of Youth and Adolescence* 22:559–68.

Wrigley, Michael and Mark LaGory. 1994. The role of religion and spirituality in rehabilitation: A sociological perspective. *Journal of Religion in Disability and Rehabilitation* 1 (3):27–40.

Wuthnow, Robert. 1988. *The Reconstructioning of American Religion: Society and Faith Since World War II*. Princeton: Princeton University Press.

——. 1991. *Acts of Compassion: Caring for Others and Helping Ourselves*. Princeton: Princeton University Press.

——. 1992. *Rediscovering the Sacred: Perspective on Religion in Contemporary Society*. Grand Rapids, Mich.: Eerdmans.

——. 1994. *God and Mammon in America*. New York: Free Press.

Wymer, Walter. 1997. Marketing management in nonprofit organizations: A customer analysis of church volunteers. *Journal of Nonprofit and Public Sector Marketing* 5 (4).

Xi, Lian. 1997. *The Conversion of Missionaries: Liberalism in American Protestant Missions in China, 1907–1932.* University Park: Pennsylvania State University Press.

Young, Marjorie Hope. 1980. Nonviolent action in Brazil. *Social Development Issues* 4 (2):71–93.

Young, Mark C., John Gartner, Thomas O'Connor, David Larson, and Kevin Wright. 1994. Long-term recidivism among federal inmates trained as volunteer prison ministers. *Journal of Offender Rehabilitation* 22 (1–2):97–118.

Zayas, F. G. De. 1960. *The Law and Philosophy of Zakat.* Damascus, Syria: Al-Jadiah Printing Press.

Zuckerman, Diane M., Stanislav V. Kasl, and Adrian M. Ostfeld. 1984. Psychosocial predictions of mortality among the elderly poor: The role of religion, well-being, and social contact. *American Journal of Epidemiology* 119:410–23.

CONTRIBUTORS

Robert J. (Bob) Wineburg, Ph.D., is a professor of social work at the University of North Carolina–Greensboro, where he teaches social welfare policy, agency program development, and grant writing. His research for the past fifteen years has concentrated on the ways in which federal and state budget and policy changes have stimulated the increasing involvement of the religious community in social services. He has published numerous scholarly articles on that subject. He has also served as a consultant for various national, state, and local secular and sectarian agencies and foundations, including the Urban Institute, Catholic Charities USA, the Salvation Army, and the Lilly Endowment. His current research centers on analyzing the role of the religious community in welfare reform.

Stephanie C. Boddie, M.S.W., is a doctoral candidate at the University of Pennsylvania School of Social Work. She received her master's of social work from the University of Pennsylvania and her bachelor's degree in natural science from Johns Hopkins University. She has more than twelve years of community experience with community agencies, local congregations, para-church organizations, and denominational groups. She was the coordinator for the Lutheran Mission Society of Maryland Compassion Center in Havre de Grace, Maryland. Her research interests focus on the topics of community service and religious organizations and natural support systems. She is particularly interested in the social and community involvement of local congregations, and she has been working with Dr. Cnaan on a study of congregations in seven cities. Other research experience includes collaboration with faculty of the Lincoln Urban Center on the Black Lawyers and Black Churches in Philadelphia project and participation in the multiracial communication project sponsored by the University of Pennsylvania Law School and the psychology department.

NAME INDEX

Hendrickson, S. L., 163, 326
Hessel, Dieter T., 67, 102, 326
Higgins, Lynn M., 192, 319
Hinson, E. G., 107, 326
Hirschi, Travis, 147, 327
Hochstein, Lorna M., 203, 320
Hodgkinson, Virginia A., 11, 12, 13, 16, 21,
 158, 159, 160, 180, 212, 237, 241, 327
Hodgson, Irene B., 209, 323
Hoelter, Jon W., 138, 327
Hoff, Marvin D., 52, 327
Holland, Thomas P., 50, 51, 57, 68, 329
Hood, Ralph W. Jr., 139, 340
Hopkins, Charles Howard, 117, 122, 327
Horwitt, Sanford D., 171, 327
Hovmand, Peter, 241, 306, 325
Howard, Johnette, 43, 327
Hu, Teh-wei H., 152, 332
Hughes, Robert H., 151, 331
Hughey, Joseph, 340
Humm-Delgado, Denise, 167, 322
Hunt, Governor Jim, 6, 286
Hunt, Richard A., 146, 327

Isaac, Rhys, 85, 327

Jackson, Reverend Jesse, 192
Jackson, Maxie C., 242, 327
James, William, 146, 327
Janoski, Thomas, 154, 159, 344
Janowitz, Morris, 166, 327
Jeager, A. Robert, xiii, 161, 320
Jeavons, Thomas H., 28, 216, 242,
 327, 328
Jefferson, President Thomas, 113
Jenkins, Paul H., 335
Jenkins, Richard A., 142, 328
John Paul II, Pope, 134, 206
Johns, Major Tom, 19
Johnson, Arthur, 153, 317
Johnson, Colleen L., 140, 328
Johnson, D. Paul, 32, 328

Johnson, F. Ernest, 60–62, 125–126, 128, 328
Johnson, Knowlton, 341
Johnson, Louise C., 54, 328
Jones, Joyce, 173, 192, 193, 322
Jones, M. G., 101, 328
Jordan, Clarence, 36
Joseph, M. Vincentia, 52, 55, 66, 135, 328
Joubert, Charles E., 136, 328
Jung, Carl, 141
Jurich, Anthony P., 146, 338

Kaczorowski, Jane M., 142, 328
Kammer, Fred, 17
Kanavy, Mary Jeanne, 72, 155, 341
Karraker, Bufe, 33
Kasl, Stanislav V., 142, 346
Katz, Michael B., 87, 328
Kegley, Charles W., 169, 328
Kehoe, Nancy C., 139, 328
Keith-Lucas, Alan, 91, 101, 328
Kerr, John, 129
Kilpatrick, Alice C., 50, 51, 57, 68, 329
Kim, Jung Ha, 198, 329
Kim, Kwang Chung, 169, 329
Kim, Shin, 169, 329
King, Martin Luther Jr., 103, 192
King, Morton B., 146, 327
Kirkpatrick, Lee A., 155, 335
Kirsch, Arthur D., 11, 12, 327
Klein, Helen E., 141, 319
Klein, Joe, 285, 329
Kluth, Brian, 101, 329
Knauft, E. B., 327
Koch Jerome R., 143, 324
Koeing, Harold G., 140, 329
Kramer, John W., 121, 329
Kramnick, Isaac, 285, 329
Kress, June B., 162, 329
Kriplin, Nancy, 174, 329
Kunzel, Regina G., 62, 63, 329
Kutter, Catherine J., 151, 329
Kvale, James N., 140, 329

SUBJECT INDEX

Young Men's Christian Association
(*cont.*)
Children, Youth, Family Services
Inc., Sarasota, FL, 40
Young Men's Christian Association
(YMCA) of Philadelphia and Vicini-
ty, 274–275; Active Older Adult

Program, 275; Black Achievers
program, 274; Child Readiness
Center Day Care, 275
Young Women's Christian Association
(YWCA), 36, 127

Zakat, 104, 303